THE RADICAL SPIRIT

Joel Kovel is nearly unique in North America and Britain in being, as he puts it in one of the essays in this collection, a Marxist psychoanalyst and a psychoanalytic Marxist. In his books he has looked deeply into social and political issues: *White Racism; A Complete Guide to Therapy; The Age of Desire; Against the State of Nuclear Terror; In Nicaragua.*

This volume brings together his reflective and speculative writings under the following headings: Personal; From Psycho-history to Critical Theory; The Politics of Psychological Practice; Marx and Freud; The Crisis of Materialism. Many are published here for the first time while others have appeared in specialist journals. His subjects range from Reich and Marcuse to Madame Bovary, William Blake and Erik Erikson. Cultural themes include the Greek state, the family, narcissism, metapsychology, liberation theology.

His is an exploratory style, always pondering the sorts of questions which many psychoanalysts have regrettably come to eschew.

Joel Kovel studied science, medicine and psychiatry before becoming a psychoanalyst in New York, where he taught for many years at Albert Einstein College of Medicine. He has also held posts at the New School for Social Research, New York, and at other universities in California and New York. He has held a Guggenheim Fellowship and has lectured widely in America, Nicaragua and Europe. His most recent work is concerned with the bearing of liberation theology on Marxism and on psychoanalysis.

THE RADICAL SPIRIT

Essays on Psychoanalysis
and Society

By JOEL KOVEL

'an association in which the free development of each
is the condition of the free development of all'

FREE ASSOCIATION BOOKS / LONDON / 1988

First published in Great Britain 1988 by
Free Association Books
26 Freegrove Road
London N7 9RQ

British Library Cataloguing in Publication Data

Kovel, Joel
  The Radical Spirit
  Essays on psychoanalysis and society.
  1. Psychoanalysis. Social aspects
  I. Title
  150.19'5

  ISBN 0–946960–57–7
  ISBN 0–946960–58–5 Pbk

Typeset by Input Typesetting Ltd, London

Printed and bound in Great Britain by
Bookcraft, Midsomer Norton, Avon

To the memory of Nora Astorga

CONTENTS

ACKNOWLEDGEMENTS

The articles in this collection first appeared as shown below and my thanks are due to copyright-holders for permission to publish them here:

1 'From Reich to Marcuse', in Sonya Sayres *et al.*, eds *The Sixties without Apology*, Minneapolis, MN: The University of Minnesota Press (Social Text), 1984, pp. 258–61.

2 'Between two schools: a discussion with Alan Sussman', *The Woodstock Times* (Woodstock, New York), 27 November 1985, pp. 14–15. Copyright © 1985 Alan Sussman.

3 'On reading *Madame Bovary* psychoanalytically', *Seminars in Psychiatry* 5: 331–45. © 1973 by Grune & Stratton, Inc.

4 'The psychohistorical value of built things', unpublished lecture given at the Columbia University School of Architecture and Urban Planning, 14 November 1973.

5 'Erik Erikson's psychohistory', *Social Policy* 4: 60–4, March–April 1974.

6 'Things and words: metapsychology and the historical point of view', *Psychoanalysis and Contemporary Thought* 1: 21–88, 1978.

7 'Therapy in late capitalism', *Telos* 30: 73–92, winter 1976–7.

8 'Values, interests and psychotherapy', *The American Journal of Psychoanalysis* 42, 2: 109–19, 1982. © 1982 Association for the Advancement of Psychoanalysis.

9 'The Marxist view of man and psychoanalysis', *Social Research* 2: 220–45, summer 1976.

10 'Narcissism and the family', *Telos* 44: 88–101, summer 1980.

11 'Mind and state in ancient Greece', *Dialectical Anthropology* 5: 305–16, 1981. © 1981 Elsevier Scientific Publishing Company.

12 'Marx on the Jewish question', *Dialectical Anthropology* 8: 31–46, 1983. © 1983 Elsevier Science Publishers B.V.

13 'Why Freud or Reich?', *Free Associations* 4: 80–99, January 1986.

14 'Some lines from Blake', unpublished manuscript, January 1977.

15 'Human nature, freedom and spirit', unpublished manuscript, November 1985.

16 'Marx, Freud and the problem of materialism', *Dialectical Anthropology* 10: 179–88, 1986. © 1986 Elsevier Science Publishers B.V.

17 'Cryptic notes on revolution and the spirit: times change', *Emergency* (London) 3: 34–9, 1985. *The Old Westbury Review* 1, 2: 23–34, autumn 1986.

INTRODUCTION

T HE ESSAYS gathered here comprise most of my shorter psychoanalytic writings for the period 1972–86. They cover a wide range of topics, from studies in literature, architecture, classical civilization and anti-Semitism, to a number of meditations on the politics of psychotherapy and contemporary subjectivity, and finally, to a series of reflections which reopen the question of spirituality in psychoanalytic discourse. What will not be found here, by contrast, is much concerning clinical psychoanalysis as generally conceptualized. There are a number of clinical observations and reflections to be found in these pages, to be sure, but always as part of a wider inquiry: an interrogation of the psychoanalytic project itself. And this is because I have never been able to take psychoanalysis for granted. From the first, I knew it moved me greatly. I knew, too, that it marked a profound breakthrough in human self-recognition. Yet I could never accept the limitation of psychoanalysis to the clinical realm, or its use as an ancilla to the social sciences, a way of getting at the 'unconscious factors' in the human situation. For the human situation itself had been called into question.

I first encountered Freud through *The Interpretation of Dreams* (1900), the summer before entering medical school. I had avoided reading him during college, from a vague distaste for 'soft' social science, which I mistakenly thought he represented. But the fact that Freud had been a doctor turned my attention in his direction as I commenced my own medical career. The results fairly took my breath away. This was not what I had expected, these flights of intellectual daring, this dismantling of the self, of the whole Cartesian certainty of a civilization.

And so I began to wonder about psychoanalysis, and have continued wondering to the present. I also was learning it, and learning to use it, first in medical school, then as a psychiatric resident, eventually (after a detour through

Reichian therapy, described sketchily in several of these essays) in formal analytic training. There was from the beginning a tension between what I felt Freud was saying to me and what my teachers were making of what he said. It was hostility at first sight: an intuitive aversion to the 'Americanization' of psychoanalysis – that castration of Freud into the progenitor of an adjustment psychology. For a long time I held on to the image of a Freud who spoke to me, who had articulated and placed into formal scientific discourse ideas about being which I had only recognized as the province of poet-visionaries like Blake or philosophers such as Nietzsche. It took me some time to broaden the question further yet, and wonder whether Freud himself had meant what I wanted him to say, or whether he was only a vehicle for something else, a protean figure on to whom I had projected my philosophical ambitions and radical doubt. But by then I had undergone my socialization into the discipline of psychoanalysis, had become a card-carrying member of the analytic elect, and had to deal with the contradictions of bourgeois practice.

These contradictions – which have shaped the entire development of my work – surfaced very sharply at the beginning of my analytic training. The year was 1967, the Vietnam war was raging, I had just finished two years of military service as a psychiatrist in the one-dimensional atmosphere of Seattle, Washington, and I had become a furious, if unfocused, anti-imperialist radical. I was also a trained psychiatrist with a defined position in society, unlike the student radicals who supplied the dynamism of the sixties. On the other hand, I was a greenhorn psychoanalyst, very much a student so far as the analytic institute was concerned, and deeply immersed in a process that provided no point of mediation for my political life. More, I had chosen for my training an institute known for its severe orthodoxy: that of the Downstate Medical Center in Brooklyn, New York.

The choice was in some measure deliberate, because I wanted the most rigorous and tough-minded Freudian training available. Some of these merits were indeed conveyed to me in the years of my training. But the price was considerable. I recall being appalled at my immersion into the utter conformism and arid, guild-like atmosphere of the analytic institute. What had happened to the excitement of ten years before? There seemed to be nothing

beyond a narrowing horizon. Psychoanalysis – that is, the
type taught at Downstate – was declared by ukase to be the
best psychotherapeutic modality, and nothing else. Any
larger concern could be checked at the door. Hartmannian
Ego Psychology was at the helm: that was all we needed to
know, all there was to be known. We were spared the trouble
of even having to read Melanie Klein in class (though were
filled with scare stories, at times covertly racist, about the
horrors and excesses of Kleinianism as practised in remote
and backward parts of the world such as Argentina). 'Miss
Freud' was spoken of in hushed tones as the 'true scion of
an immortal sire' (to advert to the words of Ernest Jones).
Reich was the fellow who made certain technical advances
with his *Character Analysis*, then went crazy. And as for Erik
Erikson, the only time my poor opinion of him (as described
herein) underwent an amelioration was when the instructor
of our senior theory class (our first occasion of being allowed
a glimpse at the heretic) attacked the author of *Identity and
the Life Cycle* (1959) as being outside the purview of 'our
science'.

Technocratic immersion in the arcana of training kept
the potential crisis submerged for some time, despite an
occasional rumble. But it could not be suppressed for ever.
Indeed, with each year the tension became more acute. For
I was, in a sense, living two sharply contradictory lives, both
of them public and avowed. On one level I was a rising
young professional and academic psychiatrist, committed
to mastering an esoteric doctrine the essence of which was
antipolitical and élitist. And on another, I was a political
intellectual and activist, committed to radical social transformation and forming a network of associations which had
nothing in common with my professional life.

For some years my energies were absorbed in the writing
of *White Racism* (1970), my first book. My training analyst
made no effort to interfere with the development of this
project, which must have run against most if not all of his
inclinations. This tolerance – and my eagerness to prove my
analytic bona fides – was reflected in the book itself, which
attempted to put together into one coherent work the two
strands of my activity: psychoanalytic and political. I tried,
more or less consciously, to write something which proved
that one could make a very radical statement about the
nature of Western civilization and contemporary society by
using the existing psychoanalytic discourse – that is, the one

I was being taught – as the leading theoretical term. I suppose
it was an honest conviction which led me to imagine I could
be at the same time a good, responsible and rising member
of the psychoanalytic establishment, and a principled and
deep critic of society.

For a while after the publication of *White Racism*, it seemed
as if the idea was feasible. It was the early seventies and
there was still a market for recycled sixties thinking. I was a
rising academic star, and it looked as if I would be able to fill
the niche within the liberal New York intellectual establishment for *Angst*-ridden psychoanalytic culture criticism. This
was especially likely in view of the fact that my psychoanalytic parlance – perhaps in mimicry of Freud – gravitated
toward the use of the high and dry term, 'culture', whenever
I wanted to describe the power structure of society. In any
case, I was sought after by the *New York Times Book Review*,
Partisan Review, several fashion magazines whose names I
no longer recollect, and a number of talk shows. The subtitle
of my book, *A Psychohistory*, seemed also to fall into place
in a growing field of endeavour which attempted to put
together the subjective and objective sides of social existence
within the framework of normal social science. There were
interdisciplinary colloquia at the New York Psychoanalytic
Institute, symposia at the annual conventions of the Psychoanalytic Association, and the emergence of a new academic
society of psychohistorians, complete with meetings and
journals, which I was invited to join. It very much seemed
as if the two-tier strategy was going to work.

And then a review of *White Racism* appeared in an obscure
radical philosophy journal called *Telos*. At least, I had never
heard of it before. It was a very favourable review, as well
as being quite the most thoughtful confrontation of my work
I had yet seen, and it made one critical point which stirred
me deeply. 'Kovel's work', said the reviewer (a man named
Chip Sills, who was only identified as someone who 'is in
his late twenties and teaches Karate in the San Francisco
area'), '*does* suffer throughout from the lack of an adequate
contact with the Marxist frame of reference.' He went on to
say that I had been using Marxist categories intuitively, but
that I would be better off if I explicitly appropriated the great
radical tradition into my thinking.

I cannot say that the scales fell from my eyes at that
moment, but I was set thinking. And what I concluded
altered the shape of my work. Sills was of course right: I had

been producing a crypto-Marxism as a kind of automatic writing. So much was clear. The real question was, what to do? The defect could not be filled by a few citations from the Marxist literature. In fact, one of the first things I realized upon considering Marxism in some depth was that it could not be tacked on to psychoanalysis at all. The discourses were not commensurate. Each had a terrible truth to it – and each negated the other. What I had to do therefore was systematically to rethink my theory – and inquire as well into the fact of my long ignorance of Marxism, and the social arrangements necessary for this to have taken place, including, most significantly, the nature of the psychoanalysis I had embraced.

The intellectual excitement at this discovery was quite comparable to that first experienced upon reading *The Interpretation of Dreams*. No, it was greater, because it included an opening – which I had never felt with any real conviction through all my psychoanalytic training – on to the possibility of really unifying my theoretical and practical interests. I was emboldened, too, by the discovery of the forgotten radical history of psychoanalysis itself. I learned with excitement that my old ideal, Reich, had been a leading Marxist, and that Otto Fenichel, whom I had always taken for a high priest of analytic orthodoxy, had been one, too. Why was this not taught at the Downstate Institute, or the Albert Einstein College of Medicine residency training programme, or Columbia's College of Physicians and Surgeons? Why were its implications not drawn – for if psychoanalysis had been this way once, and if its radical content had been repressed, then should there not be a recapture of that repressed truth, a kind of psychoanalysis of psychoanalysis . . . except that Marxism would have to be the means of analytic praxis?

But this also meant that the uneasy liberal synthesis was going to unravel. The decomposition can be traced in my writings across the years, as *Angst* yields to anger, 'culture' to class power, and the theory, then the practice, of my psychoanalysis becomes subjected to an increasingly pointed critique. Of course, this was not going to work as a means of unifying the strands of my work. To the contrary, I was inviting trouble and not unification. Psychoanalysis, though powerless in itself, is a link in the great chain of capitalist being. To submit its institutionalization to a Marxist critique is to question the structure of power in our society.

This is not a good way to get ahead in the Western world.
It may be added that I was also doing the obverse at the
same time – turning the critical power of psychoanalysis on
to the blind spots in Marxism, as Reich had pioneered in
doing. But there was no harm in this, since no powerful
interests are represented by Marxism in our society.

Because there is no way of synthesizing the opposing
world-views of Marx and Freud, there is the necessity of
taking one side or the other. I found myself choosing Marx,
because of his greater sense of justice, even as I continued
practising Freudian psychoanalysis. And so I became
assured of a persistent tension in my psychoanalytic
writings, and a trajectory whose path would be subjected to
a threefold influence: the internal logic of the dialectic
between Freud and Marx; my own development through
life; and thirdly, history, which continually gives us new
things to struggle with.

I have tried to represent something of this journey by the
arrangement of articles, which have been divided into four
parts, preceded by a set of brief personal pieces. Thus the
essays are roughly arranged by chronology, but more truly
by stage, since it is only to be expected that earlier work
might anticipate what is to come. To aid in the understanding
of the often complex interconnections between the pieces
and intercurrent events, I have continued this introduction
forward as a brief summary of the essays in each part,
relating them to each other and to what had been going on
in the world. In this way the reader may be able to keep
track of the continuing evolution of theme.

PART ONE

PERSONAL WRITINGS

THE MATERIAL in this Part consists of two short and informal pieces which highlight some of the themes of the Introduction. The first, 'From Reich to Marcuse', was my contribution to a volume, *The Sixties without Apology*, in which various individuals who had played some role in radical politics of the sixties gave an account of what had influenced them. The tale thus breaks off at the point, after the publication of *White Racism* in 1970, when I began a study of Marx. As I state in the essay, Marcuse has been a major influence on me. More than any other figure, he led me towards the Frankfurt School and critical theory. It is worth remarking that when I first saw *Eros and Civilization* in a bookstore in the late fifties, the only thing that impressed me about it was that the author combined the names of two of my friends, Herbert Schwartz and Donald Marcuse. For the rest it was meaningless, and would remain so until the agony of military service in Seattle during the Vietnam war forced my thinking in a radical direction.

The interview from the *Woodstock Times*, conducted by Alan Sussman in November 1985, gives a sense of the positions hewn out in my two books of the early eighties, *The Age of Desire* (1982) and *Against the State of Nuclear Terror* (1984a), after I had developed the Marxist position outlined in these essays. It contains an assessment of the therapeutic society, and a sense of my antinuclear politics.

1 FROM REICH TO MARCUSE

IN 1960 I was a medical student and ardent follower of the recently deceased Wilhelm Reich. In common with other Reichians, I regarded society as at most an impediment to the full expression of the life force, or orgone. Such had been the master's final opinion, forged by the unmerciful repression to which he had been subjected by the US government. In retrospect, Reich's martyrdom was an important element of his appeal. Anybody this far out had to be worth following. It did Reich's radical reputation no end of good, for instance, to have his books actually banned – not to mention burned – in this land of liberty; and I recall the outraged excitement when I had to get my copy of *The Function of the Orgasm* (1927) smuggled in by a friend returning from abroad.

However, unlike Reich himself, we who followed him did not have the benefit of a real engagement with society from which to retreat. Our radicalism, therefore, was shallow, romantic, and potentially reactionary. Indeed, Reich's Marxist period had not only been repudiated by him, but was repressed as well by his epigones, so much so that I did not take cognizance of it until 1972, when 'What is class-consciousness?' appeared in *Liberation* magazine. This revelation, along with Baxandall's edition of the *Sex-Pol Essays*, published a few years later, played a major role in the later direction of my work. But I, too, had changed by 1972; the same works presented to me a decade earlier now elicited only a mild curiosity. What lay between was the sixties and my own discovery of society – a process which placed the course of my own development in the reverse order from that of my youthful hero.

During the fifties my innate radicalism had been pretty well checked by the bourgeois, rabidly anti-Communist world that surrounded and nurtured me. As a result, I found myself pushing towards science and medicine (and eventually orgonomy, as the most radical scientific-medical

movement I could find). At least in nature things could be
made to make sense; there one might look and explore
without running into a sheer wall of mystification (a word I
did not of course know at the time). Another vicissitude was
social-democratic politics. At Yale, in the fifties, to be with
Norman Thomas and the League for Industrial Democracy
was as far left as could be seen: beyond, one fell off the end
of the world into the fathomless hell of Communism.

Medical training seemed to have taken me completely
outside the realm of sociological thought. Of course this
detour was a good thing, since it spared me exposure to
much nonsense and left me free to think for myself. But it
did delay my development and dictated, moreover, that the
pathway I would take towards social theory must pass
through the defiles of that portion of medical discourse
moulded to accommodate itself to the historical world,
namely, psychiatry and psychoanalysis.

Thus, when the sixties burst in upon me, which as I best
recall came with the murders of Chaney, Goodman and
Schwerner, and the Harlem riots, I met it with the eyes of
one trained to look at the mental depths. By 1963, I had
pretty much lost interest in orgonomy, which had fallen into
a mechanistic cultism, and had commenced a serious study
of Freud. For the first half of the decade, the psychoanalytic
classics were my intellectual staple, and my proudest
moment of possession came with the opening of the carton
containing the twenty-three beautifully bound volumes,
complete with pale-blue dust covers, of Freud's *Standard
Edition* (purchased cut-rate from Blackwell's of Oxford, the
only bookseller, or commercial establishment of any kind,
who ever sent me hand-written Christmas cards).

Psychoanalysis had done more than stir my intellect or
provide a framework for a life's work. It had also absorbed
into itself my radical energies, drawing them into the
comfortable illusion that by carefully tending the subjectivity
of a bourgeois individual one was fulfilling some measure
of the revolutionary project. The fact that such an individual
remained bourgeois for all that did not trouble me then, in
the golden age of one-dimensionality. After all, what else
was there to be but a bourgeois individual? In any event,
psychoanalysis was fast finishing what medical technocracy
had well begun, namely, depoliticization, manifested by the
near complete loss of any oppositional sense to democratic
fascism and imperialism. When the sixties struck me, I was

a Kennedy, and then a Johnson man. The idea that 'our'
motives were anything but well-intentioned in Vietnam
struck me as outrageous, for example, as did the insinuation
that the liberal state might be less than single-mindedly bent
on eliminating racial injustice.

But the negativity of the black experience in America
struck deep in my soul. And here a remnant of my discarded
Reichianism was stirred forth: an instinctive mistrust of the
state. I had become an anarchist despite myself, unconsciously, slowly but inevitably over the years. All that I
lacked was a vision of society to be set against the state
(Reich having lumped them uncritically together), and a
voice to articulate what was growing inside as the true
nature of the Indo-China war and the depths of American
racism dawned on me.

To be sure, this was not a light that came on of its own. It
had to be transmitted by others, through the murk eman-
ating from the ideological apparatus – a demon whose
existence I only began to suspect then, in the middle of the
decade, through the genius and courage of those who dared
pierce it. Two names stand forth in the memory of that
period: I. F. Stone and Noam Chomsky. To subscribe to
Stone's Weekly was exhilarating, like snapping an invisible
chain that had been binding me without my knowledge.
And when he exposed the lies about the Gulf of Tongking
resolution, I began to awaken to my rage and saw myself
outside this monster that was sowing death and lies, began,
too, to wonder at my previous complicity with it. This
continued when I read Chomsky, who was to prove an even
greater influence. Stone had been a professional journalist.
Here, however, was a man of science with whom I could
identify, who had changed his life in response to the war.
Chomsky's essay (1967), 'On the responsibility of intellectuals' (which appeared in a *New York Review of Books* that is
no more except in externals), became, therefore, a turning-
point for me. He made me realize that it was not enough to
oppose the war abstractly, or to receive criticism of the state
from others. One had to proceed from one's place of social
reproduction (another term I would not have recognized at
the time), taking it on, in other words, from where one had
been formed by it. My appetite for the negative had been
whetted. I began to read those works which would confirm
this negativity: Fanon; Genet's *The Blacks*; *The Autobiography
of Malcolm X* (this last especially powerful, in part because

of its insight into the Afro-American experience, but chiefly because I had been very much terrorized by the media's image of Malcolm).

A work was taking shape, moulded by practical circumstances no less than by intellectual concerns. We had moved to the west coast, to Seattle, where I was doing obligatory medical duty for the state in the Public Health Service. Scarcely a black face was to be seen. Only the facelessness of bureaucracy and shopping-mall America surrounded me; I, in uniform, spent the day consoling military wives and helping the services get rid of their undesirables through 'administrative' means, i.e. finding a mental illness to pin upon them. I decided to write.

After outlining the main argument of *White Racism*, I had to face the fact that I had nothing to put inside those outlines. Ostensibly for the book, but also for the moment of liberation this afforded from my stay in the belly of the beast, I discovered Weber, Karl Polanyi, Hannah Arendt, Sartre, Huizinga and Whitehead. I allowed myself to see literature – Faulkner, Conrad, above all, *Moby Dick* – as critique as well as case study. And I eventually let myself see psychoanalysis itself in the same way, first through Roheim, then Norman O. Brown, and finally, in the culmination of my studies, through the encounter with Marcuse.

One-Dimensional Man (1964) had become, then, the counter-revelation. At last, I could see the way between that desire which formed for me the Archimedean point of human experience and the domination whose racist forms I was chasing. More, I could now see how to trace this line 'laterally', away from the Father and into the colourless administration of everyday life. I still remember reading the line, 'administration is the pure form of domination', then placing exclamation points like flags all over the page. I had found the theoretical structure for my work.

That it was Marcuse rather than Brown who had the greater influence meant that I had better confront that tradition standing behind Marcusean thought, but which I, schooled in bourgeois post-war America, could only approach through intuition: Marxism. This, however, was a job for the next decade.

2 BETWEEN TWO SCHOOLS

A discussion with Alan Sussman

ALAN SUSSMAN: You're a psychoanalyst as well as a psychiatrist. Would it be unfair to say that you practise according to the precepts of one or another school of thought?

JOEL KOVEL: A little unfair. I was trained in a very particular Freudian school. I absorbed that. But on the other hand, my own work has evolved over the years, and I'm not at all sure that I belong to one school or another.

AS: In your book, *The Age of Desire*, you made a number of statements critical of the psychiatric establishment. You wrote, 'The mental health industry is no free-standing entity. It belongs to the totality of capitalist society and more particularly to that organ that stands over the rest of society and regulates it . . . the state.' Why do you refer to it as an industry?

JK: I call it an industry as a way of sharpening a point. I want to try to puncture the claims of its proponents that they are practising some kind of purified medical discourse that is above society, above economics. I don't think it's anything of the sort. I think that they're very hooked into society at every level.

AS: Who are 'they'?

JK: The 'psy' professions, psychology, psychoanalysis, psychiatry, psychiatric social workers, etc. It's an industry in the sense that it has a very definite institutional formation. It produces something – changed behaviour. It sells its product on the market. There are individual firms within the industry that compete to sell their products. It's deeply imbedded in the capitalist system. Although Freud and his colleagues studied elsewhere, they became important when they were drawn into industrial management, military medicine, and so forth. The fortunes of psychoanalysis and the professions have been dependent on the social demand and need for their services. It's a social practice, involved in the way *this* society of *this* time has to organize its behaviour.

AS: Are you saying it's more prone to attach itself as an adjunct of capitalist society than of any other economically organized society?

JK: It belongs to this type of society for a number of reasons. Ours is a society which has a peculiar form of self experience. The individual person conceives of him or herself as separate, cut off, and a problem; as a project to be fulfilled. In addition, there is a decline of all the traditional modes which make life intelligible. Particularly the church, but also the local community – organically related groups of people – and the family. We're the first society in the history of the world that has created a family system that is unstructured, problematic, and so . . . up for grabs. I'm not saying it's necessarily a bad thing, but if you ask any person to trace his or her family back two or three generations, you encounter a kind of firmly anchored, solid organic system, related to productive life. Skills and crafts were passed down . . .

AS: What you're saying is not too different from Marx's notion of alienation. He dealt with it economically and you are saying it's important to deal with it psychologically, is that right?

JK: Absolutely.

AS: Let me quote from your book. You were writing about what we discussed earlier, the institutionalization of psychology, and you stated: 'The administration of the mind goes far beyond the binding up of the mentally disturbed. Of greater importance is the prevention of social unrest among the normal.' Do you believe that?

JK: Oh, sure. I don't think that's the only way social unrest is prevented, and controlling social unrest is a very vague term. The important thing is that psychiatry provides legitimacy to the society and develops a productive and reasonably docile work-force.

AS: The police do that, too.

JK: Yes, but the police are there to deal with deviations after they have occurred. The point of these [psychological] institutions is to create a kind of social individual who accepts his or her place within the system and reproduces it faithfully, before getting into trouble.

AS: You don't mean 'institution' as a building – like Hudson River State Hospital – you mean the institution of . . .

JK: . . . actual mental health practices. If you study the

history of these things in the last century, the centre of
gravity of the professions gradually shifts from dealing
with the disturbed to dealing with the normal, ordinary
individual. I could be very blunt about it. In psychiatry,
every time there is a problem of federal funding, the 'lobbies'
– the psychiatric associations – go to Washington with
statistics proving that when insurance agencies pay for
mental health care, when there is good psychiatric coverage,
productivity rises and absenteeism declines. That's their ace
in the hole.

I once got a letter from a psychoanalytic association saying
that an insurance company was going to cut off psychiatric
benefits, which is always a nightmare. These guys hired a
management consultant – this is why you have to call it
an industry – which did studies that were shown to the
insurance companies which proved that when they funded
psychiatric therapy it was good for business. And the
insurance companies restored coverage.

AS: What about the rest of your statement, that mainstream psychiatry seeks to prevent social unrest?

JK: Well, I'm not interested in social unrest for its own
sake. But I am concerned about having a population that
loses its critical faculties.

AS: OK. Someone comes to you with a problem that
causes him or her great difficulty. You hear the patient and
conclude that a great portion of the problem is caused by
social realities rather than personal conflicts, or that the
personal conflicts are caused in turn by unhealthy social
contradictions. Is your job, as a professional, to make the
person more comfortable in accepting the social contradictions with which he or she must deal, or is your job to point
out the social realities and prepare the patient to struggle
against them?

JK: There is no prescribed job as a professional. The task
I assume is one of trying to promote the greatest degree of
inner freedom so a person can make choices and take
responsibility for his or her existence. That means putting a
person up against a world which may be very harsh, and it
means not offering any clean and easy answers. This is a
difficult point, because if people are unhappy and you
simply want to make them function and feel better, you can
do so by obliterating their consciousness. You can have the
depressed housewife go back and accept her oppression at
home. You can teach the worker to put up with his or her

oppression smoothly. Or you can just give drugs and make
the person not think or feel anything. The ultimate in
happiness can be minimum in consciousness. Consciousness is often associated with pain. A fully conscious person
could well go mad.

I'm not involved in making people go mad, or in telling
people to go out and smash the state, or telling them to leave
their husbands. What I am involved in is bringing them to
the point where they can begin taking responsibility for
those decisions. And that's a very subtle thing. It does not
lend itself to any kind of simple-minded view of human
beings or of change. And it's for that reason I don't believe
that any studies on therapy outcome are worth the paper
they are printed on. I'd rather they save the trees. Because
all these studies on therapy outcome beg the question:
'Outcome for what?' What's the purpose of therapy? Do you
make a person feel better by making him or her adjust
to atrocious conditions? There is no way to measure the
outcome of therapy in any objective manner.

AS: You have stated that part of the whole of capitalist
society is the neurosis of its members. 'Capitalism does not
create neurosis,' you wrote, 'but it does decree that neurosis
be a part of its totality.' Are you saying we have no choice?

JK: The word 'decree' should be taken figuratively, but
what I do mean to say is that personal life is absolutely
contradictory in this kind of society because it's based on
the maximization of self. But maximization of the individual
is inherently impossible, because it always involves maximization at the expense of *other* individuals, whether materially, or now in its new narcissistic phase, in the ability to
sell, have orgasms, or whatever; everything better, more
and more for the self. And the competition in the capitalist
market-place is reproduced in interpersonal relations.

Plus, the nature of the family in capitalism is inherently
contradictory. If you look at the size of the household in
capitalist societies, at the size of the child-rearing unit, it
constantly diminishes. It was about seven in the 1800s and
is down to 1.2 now. It's absolutely built into the nature of
the economy. At the same time, the base shrinks not only
in terms of numbers but in terms of its autonomy. The
family no longer has its own organic values. The values are
imported; they come through TV, through the psychiatrist,
through schools, etc. So the family loses its normative
functions.

There is also an absolute contradiction *between* the generations. In all pre-capitalist societies there is an identity of
interest between parents and children. That's why people
had so many children, because the children were producers.
In this society, children turn into pure consumers. They just
take. So there is an objective conflict of interest between
parent and child. How can you avoid neurotic development?
That's what I mean by neurosis being built-in.

AS: Traditional psychoanalysis takes less note of this than
you do.

JK: It doesn't take any interest in it at all.

AS: Your blend of Freudianism and Marxism is curious,
because the former school of thought suggests that certain
human characteristics are almost innate and the latter is
based on the belief that human nature is malleable; that we
can change human characteristics by changing the economic
structure of society. Can these be reconciled?

JK: That is the most difficult question I have to face. It's a
fascinating question and I don't have any ready answer. If
I had to choose, I would say that I'm more a Marxist than a
Freudian. By values. On the other hand, by training, and in
terms of my immediate 'take' on the world, I'm more of a
Freudian. I'm always back and forth on that question, which
I regard as a very fruitful, dialectical one.

One way I've dealt with it is to be very critical of what
Freud and the psychoanalytic establishment did with the
question of human nature, which was to mystify it, misun-
derstand its biological roots and assume that bourgeois
society offered a rational set of choices, which it doesn't. On
the other hand, I have a lot of difficulty with my Marxist
friends who refuse to think of human nature as involving
deep subjective factors.

AS: How does your synthesis of Marx and Freud differ
from Marcuse's or Reich's – in twenty-five words or less, of
course.

JK: Marcuse didn't think that the individual person
mattered very much. He had no interest in psychology. He
felt that history sort of circumvented the family. I'm more
inclined to show not that it circumvented the family but that
it made the family problematic and weak. But, you know,
he was a philosopher who was above the real world. . . .
Also, politically, that stuff went over more in the sixties and
I never swallowed it then and I certainly don't now. Having
said that, I still think he was a major thinker.

Reich was an early influence on me and a very profound one. I went through a Reichian phase and was in Reichian therapy in the early sixties. With Reich the problem was similar, but here there is a collapsing of mind into body. There was no recognition in Reich of the ontological problem of the self; [he had] the feeling that human beings could be completely assimilated back into nature. That became anti-subjective and anti-intellectual. I think he was a very great 'fallen angel' of a genius, but he really fell. And there was a kind of madness about his refusal to accept the realities.

AS: Let me rephrase a question I asked earlier. As a psychiatrist, how can you tell when something is a personal problem and when it is a social problem? I mean, paranoia is not an accurate label for someone who really has good reason to believe that someone is after him.

JK: This is one thing I feel very comfortable with. I am sufficiently tuned in to social problems, and willing to recognize them, that I can allow for them and still say, 'But that isn't all there is to it.' And it never is all there is to it. Never. If a person has been laid off from work, the important thing is to deal with that. But even there, how they respond to it (being out of work) is their own agency, their own humanity at work. Short of a situation of a complete lack of choice – someone who is about to be shot by a firing squad – you have to grant people their own subjectivity, which means their own distortions and their own ways of describing a situation. Individual A will become apathetic and depressed when laid off; individual B will organize; C will find work; D will take to drugs, and so on. Any external thing is going to be responded to in one way or another, and some people respond neurotically. By neurotic, I simply mean that there is a compulsive, self-destructive, self-alienating [way], in other words, an individual responds as if his or her life were being lived for him or her by another. And who of us is to say that we are above this kind of response? We always have some degree of it.

AS: What would you have said to Joan of Arc?

JK: Joan of Arc? That's real interesting. I would have listened very closely.

AS: In your book on nuclear terror you wrote about a topic most of us are afraid to confront, which is how we, who consider ourselves rational beings, come to grips with an enormously irrational nuclear arms race. To think about it

makes us aware of our acquiescence in the system and hence
we begin to think of ourselves as conspirators.

It's easy for us to point the finger at the Nazis, for example,
and accuse them of complicity in the massively inhuman
acts of their system, even though they may have been
underlings or just 'went along'. Yet, if we condemn them,
what do we do about ourselves?

JK: We don't condemn ourselves, but I think we should
draw that lesson, an excellent lesson to be drawn, which is
that this society in particular is filled with good Germans.
People who go along. It's a paradox, because this is a country
full of rugged individuals. But as de Tocqueville pointed out
in the 1830s, it's very hard to get American people to say
'no' to what is happening.

AS: Let me continue my analogy, if I may. Obviously, we
are not Nazis. But as others have pointed out, a missile with
nuclear warheads is like a hundred Auschwitzes, ready to
explode. Less systematic, less selective in its victims, but
equally destructive and senseless. Now, trains carrying
missiles to their launching pads cross America all the time.
And how many people – a dozen? two dozen? – have taken
courage to lie down in front of the trains? Germans didn't
lie down before trains carrying Jews to their death either.
Would it be a demonstration of mental health to block trains
carrying missiles to the Trident submarine?

JK: This is one example of why I don't use the term 'mental
health'. There is no way to say that that is a healthy thing to
do. You are outside the framework of mental health here.
To me, the nuclear age is so radical a challenge to previous
modes of thinking that it transcends issues of mental health.
It's a new ball game. You have to begin to find more
transcendent practices. This is why you get the spiritual
disciplines and non-violent movements having such an
important role. Not because non-violence is such a nifty
strategy, but because it expresses – in the way that Gandhi
did – a radical break with the system. You have to step
outside the system, and none of us can. I'm a fairly radical
person, yet I constantly slip back in; I don't make the
necessary leaps. I'm not, as it were, mad enough, or insane
or angry enough to do all that should be done. But I don't
think we should get hung up in scolding people for that.
The important point is that you have to begin thinking
of intermediary steps, of practices that place you in that
direction. There are a number of things to be done, the most

important being the creation of certain forms of anti-nuclear associations. The whole question of disarmament is terribly important. In my book, I discuss 'affinity groups' where people try to come to grips with the problem collectively. This is my suggestion: to discuss not only what happened in 1939 and 1945 and who has more missiles, but how this affects our daily lives, how it affects our community relations, work relations, and our family relations. We reproduce the nuclear state politically but we also reproduce it internally. It requires continual work. And I'm not particularly optimistic.

AS: Do you think there's a concerted effort on the part of the government to make the nuclear state, as you call it, rational?

JK: To make it rational, to make it virtuous, to wrap it all in the flag. It's all dressed up as perfectly sensible. But it's false to see this whole nuclear thing as a single issue. When you see it that way, you just get into 'nuke-ness'. Then you can't relate it to anything and you are only faced with that terrible fear of annihilation. It is a necessary thing to face: one must encounter one's fear of the horror of it all. But if you only encounter it as BOMB, which most people do, you're going to be so frightened and upset, so scrambled, that you become ready game for the government and its propaganda. Some people are so traumatized by that 'bombness' that they become sucked into the usual assurances of meeting the Soviet threat, etc. As crazy as that is, it seems rational because the government said it.

AS: Do you think the government and military know that the arms race is irrational, and simply succeed in fooling the people, or do you think that they believe what they are doing is rational?

JK: I think the members of government fool themselves as long as they are in government. When they retire, they suddenly wake up. The McNamaras, the McGeorge Bundys, the William Colbys. I bet if Casper Weinberger retires, he'll come back in a few months and say, 'We've got to stop this nuclear madness'. It happens. It's a testimony to the psychological effects that power has over people, and the group pressures to which they are subject. When on the inside, they believe that stuff. I'm convinced it's only when they retire, you know, like George Kennan, that they get a little wisdom.

AS: You concluded your book on the nuclear state with a chapter on hope.

JK: Hope is a non-rational feeling, and yet, of course, it is absolutely necessary. It is not irrational. You have to invoke it because it's so difficult; there seems to be no way out of this trap. The only thing that will turn it around is, 'don't give up, keep struggling'. I frankly don't have faith and confidence in the capacity of the security apparatus to save itself. Speaking of hope, I can say I hope I'm wrong. I hope they pull back and say, 'This is crazy. We have to reorganize relations among states.' On the other hand, if I am not wrong, then the only thing we have to invoke is the will to survive and the hope of masses of people not to give up.

AS: And if you give up that non-rational feeling?

JK: Then you've given up on your humanity.

PART TWO

PSYCHOHISTORY

T HE ESSAYS of this Part belong to a period when my
psychoanalytic career was in full swing. They are diverse
in subject-matter, but united by a conviction about the
primacy of the psychoanalytic. By the end of this period I
had discovered Marxism and was consciously attempting to
bring Freud and Marx together along the model developed
by the Frankfurt School of critical theory. Beforehand,
however, I thought first and foremost in psychoanalytic
categories; and when I wanted to speak in a radical way
about the human world, imported psychoanalysis for the
purpose, often calling the product *psychohistory*, after the
subtitle of *White Racism*. On the other hand, each of these
pieces strains in its own way against the limits of psychoanalytic subjectivism.

The first essay, 'On reading *Madame Bovary* psychoanalytically', belongs to a genre which to my great regret I
have scarcely touched. For a number of years I conducted
seminars for psychiatric residents on the psychoanalytic
study of literature. It was a labour of love, and yielded a
whole file drawer full of notes and drafts. When Dr Paul
Meyerson, the editor of a special issue of the journal,
Seminars in Psychiatry, devoted to the use of literature in
psychiatric training, invited me to compose a piece, I riffled
through the file and chose Flaubert's master-work as my
subject. I had been first introduced to this approach by a
charismatic teacher during my days as a psychiatric resident,
Dr Jose Barchilon. It was with Barchilon that I wrote my first
published essay, 'A psychoanalytic study of *Huckleberry
Finn*'. Barchilon was a brilliant exponent of the Freudian
approach to literature whose approach was to treat the work
as though it were a case study. He produced dazzling results
this way, but it seemed to be in spite of rather than because
of his theoretical model. After all, there is no obligation
upon an author to reproduce whole-person psychological
relations. In any case, I wrote my *Madame Bovary* with an

eye towards using psychoanalysis without being submerged in it . . . and, what came to the same thing, with an insistence upon seeing the novel as a critique of society as well as the psyche.

'The psychohistorical value of built things' is a hitherto unpublished piece delivered as a lecture at Columbia University's School of Architecture in 1973. Aside from its odd subject-matter – odd, that is, for a psychological treatment – the chief interest of the essay lies in its effort to develop the 'psychohistorical' explanatory structure of *White Racism*. I think it is evident that, whatever the insights of the essay, this effort fails. That is, the attempt to use a theory of 'primary' and 'secondary' symbols (with obvious reference to Freud's primary and secondary process) fails to engage the basic fact of any 'psychohistorical' process – that mind and society move in different orbits and require some theoretical distanciation, in other words, some principle of what Adorno called 'non-identity'. In the model employed here, I strive for the distance at one level, then negate it at another: in the use of 'symbols', which collapses everything into subjectivity. The essay also reflects, somewhat pretentiously, the influence of Freud's *Civilization and its Discontents* (1930): 'Man' is overcome by the internalized products of his own aggression. Such a conception remains the core, it seems to me, of any strictly psychoanalytical approach to 'culture'. Its immanent one-dimensionality and unrelieved gloom can only be overcome by a philosophy of praxis, that is, historical materialism.

'Erik Erikson's psychohistory' sharply reflects my discontent with a facile identity theory and my conviction that this kind of thinking had bad political implications. I had been wrestling since the early years of my training with why I felt so suffocated when reading Erikson, who was being lionized at the time as the genius who had successfully integrated psychoanalytic and social theories. Was this my hostility to authority figures in analysis, or a genuine intuition? Or both? It was ironically fortunate that Erikson was also under attack by the authorities of my institute. Still, I remember the writing of this essay as a slow and painful process . . . and remember, too, the initial rejection of the piece by *Partisan Review*, which had commissioned it, for 'lacking critical density and having Stalinist overtones'. I was learning the hard way of the long arm of anti-Communism which had overtaken the liberal intellectual – and liberal psychoanalytic – establishments. I am grateful to Colin Greer, who accepted the piece speedily for *Social Policy*. In addition to its all but explicit consciousness of critical theory, the essay is notable for raising for the first time in my work the question of religion and politics. If I have come around in later years to a much more sympathetic view of Gandhian non-violence, I hope it has not been through the mystifications chosen by Erikson.

'Things and words' differs from the other essays in this section by explicitly raising the issue of Marxism within psychoanalysis. It is also the most 'psychoanalytic' of all the pieces in this volume. Indeed it was written to provide a line of connection, an umbilicus, if you like, between the mainstream psychoanalysis in which I had trained, and a project which I could sense was going off in another direction altogether. The essay dates from 1977, several years later than the others in this section, and after I had, so to speak, entered a different phase. However, its frame of reference and mode of address remain within the scope of contemporary psychoanalysis. Note again the insistence on a notion of non-identity (between 'thing-representation' and 'word-representation') as the pre-condition for a valid psychoanalytic discourse, as well as the appropriation of Marxism by that discourse. In this sense, an adequate psychoanalysis is one open to Marxism. I am grateful to Leo Goldberger for assistance with the essay. It appears abridged, without a long clinical excursion which occupied roughly the last third of the piece.

3 ON READING
MADAME BOVARY
PSYCHOANALYTICALLY

As Emma Bovary, poisoned, writhes in agony, her husband Charles and the apothecary Homais frantically attend her. The former seizes her suicide note: ' "No one is guilty" ', it begins, then goes on to reveal the toxin as arsenic.

' "Well then," ' said Homais, ' "we'll have to make an analysis." '

He knew that analyses were always necessary in cases of poisoning; and Charles, who did not understand, answered: ' "Do it, do it. Save her" ' (Flaubert, 1857, p. 295).

Charles never understood anything. Nothing could save Emma. Flaubert made her to die, consumed by passion. But he was more concerned to mock the redoubtable Homais, eventual inheritor of the earth, than obtuse, but loving Charles Bovary. The pharmacist may ride his ascendant materialism to worldly success, but the author has revenge on him. When I reread the book prior to writing this essay, I found myself involuntarily gasping in outrage at the final triumph of this horrible man. Gasping, then recovering by means of a fresh access of contempt, prepared just by passages such as the above.

I was responding according to the author's plan. Flaubert – any novelist – conveys certain ideas by cloaking them in words that in literal usage may also describe real people and events. The reader absorbs those ideas through the medium of dramatic prose, and so finds himself imaginatively in the room with these synthetic beings, watching them, but also sharing their turmoil, and indeed their individual existence. We become in that moment of terror the dying woman, the anguished husband, the fatuous apothecary, and the observer of all three; and we feel their situation so vividly as to lose sight quite easily of the fact that these 'people' do not exist at all, never existed save as models from whom the author extracted his ideas, that they are only squibbles on a page and that we know nothing about them, if knowledge be defined as something built from objective fact.

Our knowing of the novel arises ultimately from fact, of course – from the material facts of our own individual and historical existence. In a proximate, immediate sense, however, the only facts are those squibbles, symbols capable of calling forth the numberless facets of our existence and reorganizing them under the terms of our multiple identifications with the personages of the novel. The special form of reorganization thus engendered is the artistic experience, which is not simply an emotional event but a very special new form of knowledge, a recognition and illumination of what our life is about. Now, while the artistic experience in literature must be approached on its own terms – else it would be reduced to what it is not – we must recognize that those terms proceed through the evocation of psychological qualities. Indeed, on its face, a novel seems to be 'about' real, whole people, people with families and memories, bodily desires, and social relationships; people, that is, with completely worked out personalities.

Although this existence is of course illusory, and while these 'people' stand for much more than themselves, the fact remains that we largely get to the artistic experience by reproducing psychological relationships according to our identifications with the book's characters. And so it is that a system of psychological explanation may prove a powerful tool in the understanding of literature.

It should be clear from the above, however, that such a tool should remain the servant of its user, and that it needs to be subordinated to his overall conception of the literary work of art. The more powerful the tool, the more necessary would be this restraint. Sophisticated mining equipment can tear up the landscape as well as it can strike valuable ore; and the most expert use of psychoanalytic insight can leave a work in tatters no less than it can gain a deep vision of its inner unity.

This would be no less so, I should think, in those instances where the insights of great authors are used ancillary to the teaching of psychology. For the work of art is so intrinsically suggestive and ambiguous as to afford the unwary clinician chances for an interpretative free-for-all. Relaxing in the knowledge that there are no clinical consequences to worry about, and freed from the exigencies of future data that might disprove his hypotheses, such an interpreter can all

too easily arrive at something that does as little credit   33
to psychoanalysis as to literature (Kovel, 1971, pp. 20–7).
Psychoanalysis is, after all, essentially a calculus of meanings, which has to be applied anew in each situation
according to its given nature. The alternative is to do a
Homaisian analysis – which brings us back to the work at
hand.

What was wrong with Emma Bovary? 'None the less she
was not happy, had never been happy. Why then was life
so inadequate? Why did she feel this instantaneous decay
of the things she relied upon?' (p. 267). Flaubert is posing
the central problem of his work. No one can sensitively read
Madame Bovary and not feel Emma's despair as her youthful
illusions rot away. Nor does the author spare any of his
genius in representing this decay in the most exquisite and
loathsome terms. The black liquid pouring out of the mouth
of Emma's corpse is only the culmination of a host of sharply
drawn images of disintegration. It is necessary to recognize,
however, that decay is not shown simply in itself, but
linked with, indeed issuing from beauty and purity. At the
beginning of the main action the theme appears subtly when
Charles first comes to the prosperous Rouault farm and
sees liquid manure oozing from beneath a dunghill; and it
reappears immediately after we are shown that Emma had
given her father an inscribed portrait of Minerva, which
was, however, hanging in the midst of a wall whose paint
was 'scaling off from the effects of saltpetre'.

A key to appreciating the work of literature is the choice
of significant detail. Here the playing off against each other
of sensuously described, physical antinomies becomes a
means through which the main direction of the novel is
conveyed. The pure 'goddess of knowledge' surrounded by
paint decaying under the influence of a chemical is of course
a premonition of Emma's own chemically induced decay.
But it brings to mind as well the ascendant chemical ideology
of Homais, from whose inner sanctum, or *Capharnaum*,
Emma is to obtain the poison. Again, the island of sublimated
purity represented by the painting is to become eroded,
dissolved in the oceanic expanse of the surrounding wall. So
too will Emma's adolescent garlanding of idealized romantic
fantasies ('the sweet friendship of some dear little brother
who gathers ripe fruit for you in huge trees taller than
steeples or who runs barefoot over the sand, bringing you
a bird's nest' (p. 51)) decay, disintegrate, desublimate, under

the pressure of experience into increasingly erotic, then
destructive versions, until she is ready at the end, in her
desperation, to lie, steal and prostitute herself. Indeed the
suicidal act, coming at the precise nadir of this series,
logically completes it, signalling the final substitution of raw
destruction for sublimated Eros. We can closely map the
gradually developing ascendance of the death force in
Madame Bovary, which appears as a kind of gathering spell,
seeping into the narrative despite – rather, in the midst of –
Emma's erotic protest. Here it is at the midpoint (which
occurs with Flaubert's unfailing precision – how he must
have mocked this part of himself in the rapt, pseudo-
scientific Homais! – just midway through the narrative) of
its development: 'So the great love affair in which she had
plunged seemed to diminish under her, like the water of a
river being absorbed into its own bed, and she began to see
slime at the bottom' (p. 170).

More of this central motif below. For the present, let us
consider its formal quality. What stands out, quite apart
from any particular content, is the representation of radically
opposed entities: hope–despair, purity–decay, absorption
into the social order–alienation from it. Moreover, and this
gets us closer to what is specific about art, the opposition is
set up in a multivalent way, across many planes that may
have no given relationship in the world of objects and
phenomena, but are instead given life through the fertility
of the symbolic process.

Observe that each of these images is what might be called
'highly charged'. Whether or not it plays a prominent part
of the main narrative (the image of the picture of Minerva,
for example, can easily be eliminated with no loss to the
plot), each such motif focuses, fully consciously or not, the
attention of the reader by representing qualities in a state of
opposition. The ego of the reader attempts, as ever, to
synthesize and bring together what it takes in. But the image
that the author presents is of entities that belong together in
one sense – a picture and the wall on which it is hung, or a
river and its bed – while flying apart in another – the
sublimated goddess of knowledge and peeling paint, or fire,
rushing water and stagnant slime. Each such conflict or
antinomy creates a point of intensity in the reader's experience, from which it draws to itself other psychic material.
Since the conflict may be manifestly minor, it may not even
be perceived as such, yet it is there; and since the points of

intensified experience are related one to another (here, in these two minor examples, around the abstract theme of the purity of illusion versus the decay of disillusioning experience), and to many other similar foci of symbolic interchange, including the most important one of the main narrative line itself, we have an accumulating series of symbolic events, all remaining to some extent open (that is, we can never exhaust the meaningfulness of literary representation by statements of the form A means B and not C, D, or . . .), and building upon each other until the novel comes to occupy the whole experience of its reader.

I mean here to include the greatest possible range of meaningful symbolic relationships, not just those that could arise as a result of literal reading of the text. However, a literal reading remains vital to any consideration of the work of literature, since we first approach the author's artistic intention by regarding what he says as though it pertained to whole, real people and concrete events. Thus, we take it for granted that the properties ascribed to Emma Bovary are those of a real flesh-and-blood woman. And what strikes us first of all about this illusory female is a beauty and passion marred by a deep-seated, pervading, ultimately fatal banality and greediness. We note in her many attributes a pathologic narcissism. Put more formally in psychological terms, it may be held that this illusory Emma is one who was indifferent to the qualities of the object except in so far as it enhanced the self or supplied it with gratification. These qualities are, to be sure, brilliantly portrayed and can well serve as examples to teach students something of the psychology of narcissism. Consider only Emma's response to the sexual consummation with Rodolphe, her looking in the mirror and seeing herself 'transfigured by some subtle change permeating her entire being', then telling herself, ' "I have a lover! A lover!" ' Here is a woman concerned primarily with ownership, 'to possess those joys of love, that fever of happiness, of which she had so long despaired'. The other person for Emma is no more than a conveyer of narcissistic supplies; he has no independent value, and when she is let down, as by Charles when he botched the club-foot operation on the stable boy Hippolyte, she loses all concern for him: 'Emma sat opposite, looking at him. She was not sharing his humiliation but enduring a private one, that of having imagined that such a man could be worth something' (p. 182).

There is no doubt, then, that if this were a real woman
she would be a mightily narcissistic and indeed unpleasant
one, nothing but a greedy, frantic bitch. But the use of the
term narcissism is certainly no talisman here. After all, if
Emma is so obnoxious, so selfish, and banal why should her
fate move us? Why does not even the disgusting portrayal
of her end turn us away? And why should the work have
had such revolutionary implications as to virtually bring on
itself banning if it is only an account of the retribution
meted out to one wretched woman as punishment for
her selfishness and transgressions? And while it might be
claimed that she is redeemed for us by her beauty, and by
the beauty of Flaubert's description, this to me is only a
preliminary, even evasive, answer that leads to the more
fundamental questions: What is beauty? And why should it
appear in such an unlikely setting? How, to use a widely
accepted critical evaluation, does Flaubert turn banality into
poetic beauty?

The clinical term, and the whole-person model, leaves no
room for subversive implication, nor for the power of art.
Interestingly enough, at the trial, the defence attorney for
Flaubert won his case against banning the book by appealing
to just such a model (Flaubert, n.d.). In his hands, the novel
became a cautionary tale and much clinical-type description
(such as would have been employed in 1857) was used to
develop this theme. But in that instance, a defensively
distorted reading was justified, and while we may screen
out some portions of the book's artistic impact for one
purpose or another, our overall grasp will be greatly weakened unless we consider what the author tells us beyond
literal representation, that is, at the level of artistic
transformation.

Here is where the true affinity between literature and
psychoanalysis resides. As emphasized above, this consists
not in the tacking on of labels to gross phenomena, but in
discovering, through attention to unconscious patterns of
meaning, an inner richness and unity. Art, like good clinical
work (which is in this sense an art form), removes us from
labels and slogans to bring about a deeper unity with that
from which we might ordinarily turn away. Put another
way, paying attention to narcissism will help us less in
grasping the book than will paying attention to the book,
and its specific artistic realization, help us in grasping the
essence of narcissism.

The psychoanalytic approach to literature shares with clinical work a common methodological ground: attention to conflict and antinomy. Conflict and the ceaseless effort at resolution is the very stuff out of which human reality is constituted. Art may be understood as an intensified struggle for resolution under the terms of the imagination. We attend most to representations of contrast and tension, towards which the unconscious mind surges in its unending quest to resolve contradictions. The art work begins where common sense can no longer answer the question: if Emma Bovary is to be seen as someone who can only live narcissistically, why is it that we feel for her so? And our answer to such a question must derive not from some hypothetically analogous clinical setting but from the symbolic transformation of the reality that is the work itself.

Thus, we may be concerned less with what is directly indicated than with formal devices, such as style, that work pervasively to bend surface content towards deeper levels. The antinomy generated here is all the more powerful for arising directly from the art work itself, without mediation by anything to which it refers.

We are struck in this regard by a peculiar quality of Emma Bovary – her indifference to the individual qualities of objects. 'She sought emotions and not landscapes', claims her creator; and later, when Emma lushly fancies her escape with Rodolphe, he adds, 'Nevertheless, in the vastness of this future she was creating for herself, nothing in particular stood out.' But what stands out so for us in reading about Emma's indifference is the contrast with her creator, Flaubert's extraordinary fascination with physical detail. This exceptional quality in his prose style is often cited as evidence for Flaubert's 'realism' – a term that makes a limited sense when contrasted to the sloppy romanticism that he so disdained, but it should not be construed to mean that Flaubert was simply trying to be candidly – and coldly – objective. There is no coldness for me in Flaubert, only a passion made more intense by restraint. He chose a detached physical objectivity as his particular way of representing human reality with its primacy of its subjectivity. Those lovingly exact, at times gorgeous, at times nauseating details are objectifications of subjective qualities. Flaubert's physical universe is saturated with subjectivity; and since he writes of a woman who cannot perceive details, we, the readers, join with the author in watching her surrounded

with split-off things that are neither in her nor perceived by
her, yet part of her (since she *is* the novel, its entire being),
and, as the paint on the wall did to the portrait of Minerva,
menace her with engulfment and penetration. Thus her
entrance into Yonville:

*Madame Bovary entered the kitchen and walked over to the fireplace.
She took hold of her dress at the knees with the tips of two fingers,
and having lifted it in this fashion to the ankles, held out to the
flame a foot encased in a black boot, above the leg of lamb turning
on a spit. The fire cast a glow over her entire body, its harsh glare
penetrating the cloth of her dress, the even pores of her white skin,
and the eyelids that she blinked from time to time. The wind coming
in through the half-open door intensified the reflection.* (p. 93)

Although the image of penetration is used explicitly here, it
is plain through the exquisite choice of sensuous detail – tips
of two fingers, even pores in the skin, transilluminated
eyelids – that the very instrument of description serves to
penetrate physical substance, to get inside the body. The
erotic and narcissistic change of Emma's being exists in the
details of her bodily substance. She, the most indifferent of
women to physical details, moves in a universe of transfigured matter. And in the association of her beautiful living
leg with the roasting dead leg of lamb, we see prefigured
the consuming transformation of her body by the passion
that is to ravage it – richly condensed by the image of fire
and presented in alimentary terms of things fed, or inside
the body. Only a few pages before, in Tostes, the town from
which she had just fled in depressed despair, her misery
had been represented as it appeared at mealtime – 'all the
bitterness of her existence seemed to be served up to her on
her plate, and the steam from the boiled beef brought up
waves of nausea from the depths of her soul' (p. 81) – while
flames had been the fate of her faded, decaying wedding
bouquet that pricked her as she uncovered it in the process
of moving. Does not her burning of the bouquet accelerate
greatly the rate of its decay? And does it not also call to mind
her sexual passion itself? Does Eros serve here to gain new
objects, or to use up, consume old ones – or does it somehow
combine both terms of the antinomy?

Thus, choice of image and style generates meaning. There
is no end to the interconnectedness of these symbolic forms;
the only bound to the meaning we can extract from them is
the degree of attention we pay to what is presented. The

art work itself is like an open matrix. Through its lucid ambiguity, it keeps the possibility of new meaning continually before us. But unlike the Rorschach blot, which generates infinite meaning from a vacuum of intentionality, the work of literature opens up new pathways of meaning from the representation of something exact and highly intentional.

No choice of psychoanalytic framework would be necessary to obtain meaning from literature. The work is so inherently fecund of symbolic forms as to accommodate virtually any frame of reference that deals with human reality. But our considerations so far give reason why the psychoanalytic frame of reference should be particularly important. For the kind of concern psychoanalysis gives to human reality is that which parallels the artistic pattern: to derive a myriad of interconnected meanings and to work towards their resolution into a more fundamental, unifying idea. It is the moving *towards* this idea – for knowledge of a human being can no more be closed than an art work – that gives psychoanalysis its value.

The key to the art work lies less in its particular discursive meaning, which, after all, can be substituted for by any number of frameworks, than in the very openness of symbolic connectedness added to that meaning, the sense of freedom from the constraints of given knowledge, the sense that a 'new world' has indeed been brought into existence. This adds, to be sure, richness and depth to the particular discursive meaning of the art work, but it also adds a different kind of experience – the aesthetic – that goes beyond any discursive account.

It is in the description of such a state of affairs that psychoanalysis, with its concept of the primary process, can be of great value. If we are taught well to think in the psychoanalytic form then the final shifting back and forth between levels of meaning, the sudden sense of illumination and unification, the acceptance of antinomy and surprises – all that comprises the workings of the artistic process should prove congenial.

We must, however, learn to apply psychoanalytic canons to a range of broader scope than the depiction of evident psychological matters. Something of this has been done above where we saw how Emma's narcissism was represented in terms more general than psychological description. It remains, however, to extend this approach if we are to go beyond the descriptive.

The psychoanalytic reader of *Madame Bovary* will recognize that Flaubert's transfiguration of the material world bears comparison with a universal, basic, and very primitive mental operation, namely, the development of transitional objects (in Winnicott's (1953) sense) in the course of separation and individuation. It is as though the artist were a toddler–genius describing the crystallization of a material universe out of the primary matrix of the mother–infant bond. Our language recognizes the fundamental nature of this process with the etymological correspondence, material–matrix–mother; but what appears only in the form of abstraction in psychoanalytic or linguistic science is evoked into full life by the artist's style.

In the first experiences of separateness, all humans invest the physical world with libidinal and aggressive wishes originating from the primarily narcissistic relationship to the mother. Emerging self and object representations overlap in these first organizations of the physical universe; and the development of both self and object worlds are, so to speak, cast in symbolic moulds of physical substance, including the most important organization of such substances, the body itself. What we will come to call, in our psychoanalytic metaphor, the good or bad introjected object, is from the first part of life also invested in actual physical things. Accordingly, thinking must pass through an *animistic* phase. As we know, this stage never dies out, but only becomes adulterated, mixed in with subsequent conceptualizations or split off from the main body of consciousness, alongside of which it persists. And, such being the gravitational pull of archaic modes of thinking, animism remains potentially available for a full-blown reawakening.

Artistic representation energizes animistic thought through its provision, noted above, of an open matrix of symbolic forms, in which all things can once more be each other. This much is generally true despite individual style. But, when a writer such as Flaubert is able to so intensively invest physical substances with psychological qualities, and to recapitulate, as in the image of burning, the entire direction of the novel's action in the consumption of physical substance, we, the readers, become even more powerfully drawn towards the re-experiencing of our infantile animism.

This subtle yet pervasive highlighting affords illumination

to congruent areas of psychologic description. Given Flaubert's style, it has to concern us deeply that Emma Bovary is described as having had a dead mother. The reason this takes on such significance is, of course, psychological, but we will be led astray if we regard the matter too literally. Thus, the point is not whether having had a mother who dies, as did Emma's, in one's mid-adolescence confers such wretched traits of mind as Madame Bovary suffered from. It need not, for one thing, and even if it did, would prove absolutely nothing so far as the novel were concerned.

No, the fact that Emma is given such wretched traits would indicate only that bad mothering was received, perhaps, let us guess, in the form of a great deal of attention to physical appearance without any real availability. Yet, even this adds little or nothing. But what does add to understanding is the realization derived from the whole content and style of this work, that a bad, dead, hated, yet longed-for mother lies behind the screen of events. Emma's character suggests this, with its orality, impulsivity, narcissism and depression; and so does her ultimately addictive search for less and less differentiated, and more and more toxic substances; but it is co-ordinatively suggested, and so drawn into deeper layers of meaning for us, by every element of Flaubert's sensuously exact style. The manifest flow of things becomes thus organized about a central hidden idea, an idea of the profoundest import to any reader, from whatever age or culture. The book then is 'about' the effects of maternal absence upon the world while Emma Bovary becomes a specially contrived concentration of this principle in the shape of a whole person, a form that allows us to penetrate into Flaubert's conception via the process of identification.

We note now with renewed interest that upon learning of her mother's death Emma cried a lot, and re-created momentarily the transitional object by having a portrait made from the lost woman's hair. This prepares the way for Charles's agonized clinging to his dead wife's hair at the end. But while the dumb, dogged husband, all object love, lets himself sink into death holding the material token of his lost beloved, Emma, wholly self-absorbed, gave up direct material contact and succeeded, not so much in forgetting her dead mother as in evading the experience through a decisive narcissistic turn. By mimicry of mourning, she managed to control feeling through its theatrical intensification. The excessive volume of feeling worked to cancel out her diminished sincerity; meanwhile, she gained an audience: father, nuns (she was at a convent at the time), but mainly herself, now identified with the lost mother watching and admiring her grieving daughter. In this way, with its eventual toll, were the effects of object loss warded off:

> . . . in a letter that she sent to Les Bertaux, all filled with sad reflections about life, she asked to be buried in the same tomb when she died. Her father thought she must be ill and came to see her. Emma was inwardly pleased to feel that she had achieved at her first attempt this rare ideal of pallid existences that mediocre hearts never achieve. She let herself glide into Lamartinian meanderings, listened to all the harps on the lake, to the songs of the dying swans, to all the falling leaves, the pure virgins rising to heaven, and the voice of the Eternal reverberating in the valleys. She tired of this, didn't want to admit it, continued first out of habit, then out of vanity, and was finally surprised to find herself soothed and with as little sadness in her heart as wrinkles on her forehead. (p. 58)

Compare her response to her father's account of his reaction to the same event:

> When I lost my poor wife, I would go into the woods to be all alone. I would sink down at the foot of a tree and cry or call out to God to tell him all sorts of foolish things. I wanted to be like the moles I saw in the branches, with worms crawling in their bellies. In a word, dead. And when I remembered that others at the very moment were holding their beloved wives in their arms, I would beat my stick into the ground with fury. I was half crazy. I stopped eating. The mere idea of going to the café repelled me. You wouldn't believe it. And then, slowly, as one day followed another, springtime replaced winter, and autumn summer, it dwindled away bit by bit, crumb by crumb. It went away, and disappeared. It went inside, I mean, because you always retain something deep down, a sort of heaviness here, in the chest. But since we all share that fate, we mustn't let ourselves waste away hoping to die because others are dead. (p. 42)

In contrast to his daughter, the old man retains a hold on the real, concrete physical world. Note the distinctness of his identification of the lost object with specific images of animal life – a trend that receives an important reinforcement, in a way that we shall discuss below, from his successful pursuit of agriculture. Note further his solid resolution of the loss, presented with such acumen by

Flaubert as virtually to describe the internalizing process in 43
clinical terms. And note how this had to be accomplished
by the *externalization* of rage, a hostility directed towards
the lost object (as with the earth-mother imagery at the
agricultural fair; or in the way Rodolphe grinds his walking-
stick into the ground upon resolving to 'have her'), yet
without devastating, and hence, inhibiting effects.

Emma, however, turns away from outward aggression.
In her instance we must regard it as devastating in the
immediate sense. At any particular point where aggression
could be expected to become directed outward, it fails to
appear, and as it does appear, it is seen heading towards
Emma herself. As an example, consider the way, when
criticized by the father for slowness in the very first page of
her appearance, Emma 'made no comment. But as she
sewed she pricked her fingers and then put them into her
mouth to suck them' (p. 38).

This brilliant detail sums up once more Emma's entire
narcissistic and masochistic response to object-loss and
hostility. Again, it is of no particular interest in itself, but
only as it works toward the unification of underlying trends.

The devastation that eventually overtakes Emma is the
correlate of the hypothetical immediate mental state in
which she could not express aggression. What her father
can permit himself to imagine and is able to work through
by engaging the world of reality she loses sight of in the
haze of fantasies with which she surrounds herself and in
her yearning to be comforted and admired. Eventually
though, she brings destruction to bear through the agency
of her frantic, unfaithful search – through, that is, the
activity of the book itself, which is thus the chronicle of her
efforts to objectify an already ruined subjective state.

The devastation that accrues to Emma at the end of the
novel is thus seen to be a projecting forward of the terror,
rage and complete helplessness of the state of infantile
separation. Here again our clinical model is of help. For a
woman so described is felt to be (whether one has clinical
terminology with which to describe the feeling or not) one
who has been emotionally abandoned at a very early age,
and for whom synthetic external admiration came early to
replace a lost or non-existent love.

Madame Bovary awakes in us an inchoate terror of separation. We share, then, the deeper truth that Emma's
narcissistic defence signals the loss for her of an object

world. Behind the haze and indistinctness of her fantasies is
emptiness itself, nothing but amorphous feeling. In her
groping for objects, only this feeling itself can be mobilized:
'. . . her desires, heightened by regret, became even more
ardent' (p. 131). Thus, 'hers was a burning desire, inflamed
by all her memories' – but as none of these memories can
find their way to any concrete, actual present object, it
must become the case that 'nothing was worth looking for;
everything was a lie. Each smile hid a yawn of boredom,
each joy a curse, each pleasure its aftermath of disgust, and
the best of kisses left on your lips only the unattainable
desire for a higher delight' (p. 267).

As pleasures and sensations became the only locus of
psychic reality, the quality of the object recedes, as 'gilt rubs
off on one's hands' (p. 265), leaving behind the spectre of
addiction. Sensations and desires themselves are defensively intensified to ward off the pain of an inner loneliness
that can no longer be assuaged by anything both real and
loving; and without erotic attachment to the object world
increasingly unadulterated destructive elements rise to the
surface. These then become the means of holding on to
objects, as the infant comes to realize that he can only cathect
the image of the mother so long as the rage associated with
it is experienced as well. But where there is no libidinal
admixture, we become, in the words of Père Rouault's
fantasy, one with the 'moles . . . in the branches, with
worms crawling in their bellies. In a word, dead.' Thus the
theme of *intoxication*, which occurs in countless allusions
and gathers about Emma throughout the book until it at last
overcomes her.

The world-view of this state of mind exists latently in all.
We allow it to be conjured up by Flaubert because the elegant
purity of his art fixes objects with such precision as to
reassure us against the very decay of the object world he is
representing. And yet the terror of that decay is matched
only by its fascination. This fascination arises from the
universal urge to merge with an object that is undifferentiated from the self. Held in check by the ordinary reins of
life, it is allowed expression under the special terms of art.
The wish for fusion underlies all the particular fantasy
derivatives also represented in the work of art; indeed it is,
I believe, the specific quality of the artistic experience to
allow us to experience the state of fusion between self
and object without irreversibly dissolving the self. For this

purpose, it is necessary that the artist objectify subjective qualities by linking the inner psychic world with the outer one of culture. And these links must therefore be given full due, else we will lose track of a main current of representation in *Madame Bovary*, which is not intrinsically psychological yet intersects with the psychically determined qualities at the point of material transformation. And it is through his mastery of this point of crossing that Flaubert succeeds in meeting the standards of great art.

Recall that old Rouault's conquest of object loss is associated with his success as a farmer. He is able, in other words, to find the active exteriorization denied to his daughter. But how is this exteriorization made available, and, if it is not to be Emma's, how is it denied to her? It is not something that can be described in purely psychological terms, and certainly not just the consequence of a flawed childhood. Were that so, then the element that moves us the most – the decay of Emma's dreams – would be without connection to the actual content of Flaubert's creation, which is, like that of any novelist, an entire world, complete with institutions and a physical environment in which its inhabitants exist. The nuclear themes of the novel – including that of the absent mother – animate this world in its entirety.

Just as the symbolic value of literary representation allows us to see Emma's narcissistic disorder as part of a larger whole – and thereby teaches us something about narcissism – so does it ask us to see farming, and the pharmacy of Homais, the money-lending of Lheureux, the whole culture presented by Flaubert, also as part of this whole – and gives us insight into this culture as well. The new whole is the imaginary universe of relationships conjured up by the symbolic process out of the author's offerings. It encompasses the entire symbolic universe of the reader, arranged like a Ptolemaic solar system about the symbolic centre of the novel.

It is not difficult, for example, for the contemporary reader to sense in *Madame Bovary* an ecological interpretation that could not have been conscious to Flaubert for the simple reason that history had not yet made the issue manifest. And yet we are distinctly led to see in Emma's gathering intoxication a metaphor of the eventual pollution of the natural order. To do so is not idly to collect meanings, for this novel moves us not simply by presenting the failure of object love in an isolated spirit but by uniting us with the concrete, sensuous, socially embedded woman in whom that spirit dwells. But to say thus that we share a 'common humanity' with Emma Bovary means also that she is a member of our civilization, she shares with us a common historical process, separated only by phase and relatively minor local distinctions. The same process underlies the defilement both of the natural world and of Emma Bovary. When I call it *capitalism*, the reader will understand that I am referring to an extremely broad and complex historical trend with particular political/economic details of no present concern, and a basic, underlying attitude towards the human and material universe of deep, present concern, because it is consummately portrayed by Flaubert, and we can see it destroy Emma Bovary then no less than it attacks nature today.

Note that Emma is estranged, not only from herself, but to a remarkable degree from the times in which she lives. Now to see this as simply Emma's doing is to ignore the enormous effort made by Flaubert to show us just how actively alienating her society was. Mary McCarthy (1964, pp. vii–xxiii) makes the important point in her essay on *Madame Bovary* that it 'is the first novel to deal with what is now called mass culture', banal and alienating: '. . . ideas and sentiments, like wallpaper have become a kind of money too and they share with money the quality of abstractness, which allows them to be exchanged.' It is the function of mass culture to offer a pseudo-compensation to people for their alienation, to make them better consumers and to prepare them to accept the established order of things.

Emma Bovary, for all her pursuit of fashion and borrowed ideas, was deeply cut off from this order. This is manifest in the fact that there is never any work for her to do once she leaves her father's farm. One cannot simply say, therefore, that Emma has, on a purely psychological basis, an incapacity for active, aggressive response. We must also consider the deep implication of the fact that society complements her deficits by offering her no useful role in its activities.

Indeed, we are led to feel that Emma is justified in breaking the codes of the social order despite her evident lack of heroic stature and her purely selfish goals. However deficient in inner substance, Emma's protest makes sense when seen against the stifling and alienating world she inhabits. This poses for us a problem similar in some respects to the dilemma we face as clinicians when we have to deal with an obviously inwardly troubled youth who rebels against a grossly warped environment.

But where in the clinical setting our primary attention must be focused on the psychological (just as, were we to deal in political or legal terms, we would be concentrating on the social aspect), with literature we are in a symbolic universe of fused qualities. Emma is then more than an individual; she becomes an element of the social order, while society also no longer exists only in itself, becoming as well an exteriorization of Emma's self.

Ranged on one side of the divide is society itself, while on the other side is nature, to which Flaubert gives the quality of taking no active role in social process, but only being consumed by it, as the wedding bouquet was burned. And although Flaubert spent his life as an artist in resisting the romantic self-indulgence of a Rousseau, there is no doubt – indeed his work gains a kind of ascetic power from its denial – of his essential yearning for the breast, his equation of natural substance with the good. And, like Rousseau, he too saw natural goodness destroyed through the activity of civilization; hence, the loving transfiguration of physical substance. Translated into these terms, Emma's beauty becomes her own reflected imprint of maternal substance: Narcissus's reflection in the water, to be slimed over.

In other works Flaubert was directly to portray the patient, awaiting, selflessly giving maternal pressure. One thinks of Mme Arnoux in *Sentimental Education* and Felicité of *A Simple Heart*. Here in *Madame Bovary* the good mother is directly absent or represented almost as a grace note, as in the little gnarled figure of Cathérine Leroux 'more wrinkled than a shrivelled apple', who wins a silver medal, valued at twenty-five francs, at the agricultural fair for fifty-four years of service in the same farm, service that has reduced her to the level of a barnyard animal. The maternal presence, if not actually expunged, exists only in degraded form.

Charles himself is its most important representative. Mirrored in his infinitely benignant eyes, Emma becomes resplendent as only a narcissistically complete infant can be. It is the image shared by Flaubert who invests her with the same love through his sensuous mastery of detail; and we, the readers, share in it too, quite ready to love Emma and forget her real limits even as we are continually brought up against them. And, of course, it is this actual crippled Emma who, although she may have been attracted to Charles at

first in hopes of becoming what he saw in her, soon loses
her way with him because her guilt will not allow her to
accept his ox-like love, even as his actual limitations preclude
anything more mature. For all his redeeming love, Charles
remains a very stupid, inept person, good only for standing
and waiting, and in real terms he has nothing to offer Emma,
nor any genuine sense of what she is about.

And everywhere else the field is held by those who
would actively destroy the breast. Old Rouault's farm, the
actualization of his capacity to hold on to objects, is to
fail; the farmers and townspeople themselves are puppets
governed by a fatuous authority who turns the agricultural
fair into a travesty on nature and renders a philippic against
revolution, and Charles's very inadequacies as a husband –
his passivity and lack of penetration – also signify his social
failure.

The world is instead ruled by a falsely penetrating, phallic
principle. False because, like Emma's own hazy distortion, it
translates destructivity against natural forms into possession
and power over them. Unlike Emma, however, it wins –
gaining a material world at any rate; holding on to objects,
it avoids the narcissistic trap, and so prosperously stabilizes
itself while Emma is to rot. This is the world of Rodolphe,
who idly lives off the land and grinds his stick into it; it is
the world of 'slack-mouthed' old aristocrats who 'had lived
at Court and slept in the bed of queens'; it is the world of all
these artificial things Emma must crave, since she recognizes
in them her own hopeless striving made powerful and
secure. Hence her phallic yearnings, her dressing up in
men's clothes, her wish for a male child as 'anticipatory
revenge for all her earlier helplessness'; hence even the
pricking of her fingers, at the beginning of the book, when
self-directed aggression can be aimed along more 'advanced'
lines.

The power that these images hold over our mind must be
drawn from their unending roots in infantile, bodily striving.
Yet the artistic unity of the work derives from the representation of bodily conflict in the world at large; literature shows
us, with a clarity that ordinary life never can, how culture
itself is a fabric of infantile symbolism. We thus live in a
network of exteriorizations of our unconscious, no less than
we internalize history into the psyche. Such is the unity of
mankind, which it is literature's function to criticize in depth
from an erotic standpoint.

Emma's doom is to pursue erotic attachment against the twofold odds of her personal weakness and the ungiving external world. The depth to which Flaubert plunges in delineating her struggles gives her a tragic, a heroic cast for all her banality. But tragic or trivial, Emma is bound to lose; and the unity of Flaubert's conception is not fully grasped until we come to terms with the book's winners, Lheureux and, especially, Homais.

These two, unrelated to each other, are related to Emma as a couple of bad, greedy brothers. Unable to love at all, forsaking the risks of Eros, they come to full terms with the emerging capitalist culture. Their success is Emma's disaster; indeed they virtually feed on her, the dry-goods merchant cum money-lender consuming her substance, while the apothecary plucks her narcissistic dreams.

Lheureux is an externalized conscience to Emma. He is the first to spot her transgression and the first to bring it to her attention. And he treats her sequentially the way her super-ego would treat her topographically; starting with a good bit of flattery and cajolery, then gradually hardening his position and deepening the toll he exacts until, at the end, his demand for payment becomes the precise equivalent of her death wish.

It is important to recognize the power money and commerce holds over this narrative. Emma does not die from love itself but from love rendered into money through the influence of civilization. And money here is no rational medium of exchange, but desire transformed by guilt to be affixed as value to material power. Attached at one end of the symbolic chain to narcissistic supply, and hence lost object love, at the other it becomes bad bodily contents, the bad objects turned outward: ultimately equated with the poison itself and the rotting black stuff pouring out of Emma's dead mouth. And so Lheureux becomes not just a premonitory ad-man, promoter of the mystique of production and consumption, but an executioner as well, direct agent of the polluting process through his control of the dynamic of guilt. It is thus that we can see in *Madame Bovary* a critique and illumination of the ecological crisis wrought by capitalism.

And Homais? If there is a historical creature whom he harbingers, it is Dr Strangelove, the mad scientist so bemused by his dream of power over the physical universe that to destroy the world becomes an incidental. Of course this is no new dream; men have held it since Icarus, and Homais himself, for all the caricature, is presented as the inheritor of an ancient role; by the end, swathed in his alluring 'Pulvermacher hydroelectric belt' (which gives him sexual potency), he is revealed in his inner self 'as splendid as a Magian priest'. And we cannot overlook the significance of the *Capharnaum*, his inner laboratory, guarded as jealously by its proprietor as if it were a body cavity containing secret substances, among which is the arsenic itself.

Here psychoanalytic understanding can provide critical symbolic linkage. For the power of the narrative culminates in Emma's frantic gobbling of the arsenic. With an almost orgiastic sense of discharge she sweeps aside the façade of sexual pleasure and material baubles to reveal the accumulated guilt within. And as the poisonous materialization of this guilt is taken from something regarded as a bodily cavity, we have in the *Capharnaum* a key symbolic exchange between the psychological and historical dimensions, one that organizes Flaubert's entire conception of material substance at the deepest level. The novelist thus enriches his tale by drawing upon the universal symbolism of material substance, according to which it is thought of as primarily contained within or issuing from the body. Thus the value we place on matter, whether it is good or bad, milk or poison, gold or excrement, corresponds to the play of ambivalent feelings towards the bodies of those we care about.

In killing herself Emma reveals – and finally pays for – her deepest libidinal wish, fusion with the bad mother. But she also certifies the bad brother's hold over this mother through his sorcery, or, rather, technology. Further, the *Capharnaum* conjures up not just the control of technics, looking backward to magic and alchemy and forward to modern chemistry. It is also a reference, as the name indicates, to the entire religious controversy over *transubstantiation* – can the aliment of the Eucharist become the bodily substance of God? *Capharnaum* was, the Bible tells us (John 6), the place where Jesus proclaimed the Eucharist. 'I am the living bread which came down from heaven; if any man eat of this bread, he shall live for ever: and the bread that I will give is my flesh, which I will give for the life of the world.' To this, the 'Jews therefore strove among themselves, saying, How can this man give us *his* flesh to eat?' and Jesus responded: '. . . Except ye eat the flesh of the Son of Man, and drink his blood, ye have no life in you' (6:51–3).

Well might the Jews have wondered, since Jesus was here proposing to return religion to a more directly cannibalistic course, stripping away Hebraic reaction formations against such impulses, even returning matters to the stage of the totem feast, as Freud indicated in *Totem and Taboo* (1913, pp. 154–5). Now this was indeed a critical development, as evidenced by the walking away of many of Jesus's disciples upon his proclamation. Those who remained were to do so through adopting a different stance towards bodily substance, replacing the reaction formation of dietary ritual with sublimation and mystification of the flesh: 'It is the spirit that quickeneth, the flesh profiteth nothing' (6:63). And those changes were mandated by the culture of the time. Now, what *Madame Bovary* suggests to us is that a new form of solution arises in the modern age: the body mechanized, split up and drained of value, subject to the manipulations of sensation and science, while the cannibalistic urge, which is at heart a response to object loss, can be satisfied through mastery of nature.

The religious scenes in *Madame Bovary* develop the theme powerfully by revealing the psychic core of religion, then mocking it in proof of Emma's hopeless position. For here Emma seeks and, for a moment at least, attains the sense of fusion with godhead: once during her Communion after Rodolphe abandons her ('she nearly fainted with a celestial joy as she offered her lips to receive the body of the Saviour' (p. 207)), and again at extreme unction just before her death, when, given the crucifix, 'she stretched out her neck like one who is thirsty and, pressing her lips to the body of the Man-God, she placed on it the most passionate kiss of love she had ever given' (p. 301). After this the removal of her carnal sins is, psychologically speaking, incidental, her sexual need for living persons having been superseded by a deeper desire – realized, to be sure, at the cost of her dissolution.

Even here Flaubert takes the trouble to note that the priest, after wiping his fingers, 'threw the oil-soaked bits of cotton into the fire'. Whatever touches upon life will surely be consumed. The grim choice posed by Flaubert is between holding futilely to real people, as did Charles, striving like Emma for reunion in fantasy with lost objects, or taking the course of a Homais, who survives and prevails by joining a cultural effort that constructs a civilization out of a false science based upon the pulverization of nature.

' "But what's your connection with farming?" ' asks the widow Lefrançois. ' "Do you know anything about it?" ' And Homais replies: ' "Of course I do, since I'm a pharmacist, that is to say, a chemist. And chemistry, Madame Lefrançois, having as its goal the knowledge of the reciprocal and molecular action of nature's bodies, it follows that agriculture is included in its domain. After all, the composition of manure, fermentation of liquids, analyses of gas, and the influence of miasmas – what is all that, I ask you, if not chemistry pure and simple?" ' (p. 139).

We have grown accustomed by now to the observation that science has been a tool much abused by the hands of modern man. The brilliant synthesis of, say, the atomic theory can be, we know too well, employed for the development of Agent Orange no less than a better antibiotic. *Madame Bovary*, by exposing some continuities of the scientific attitude with the history of our race and the most archaic, cannibalistic stratum of the mind, gives a perpetually fresh insight into this trend. And this does not take away from the tragedy of love that Flaubert also presents, but rather adds to it, confirming the essential unity of all things human.

4 THE PSYCHOHISTORICAL VALUE OF BUILT THINGS

IN HIS bitter-sweet parable of alienation, 'Bartleby' (1952), Herman Melville situates his characters somewhere on Wall Street in a law office. High walls are described framing this construction, a white one at one end, forming the 'interior of a spacious skylight shaft' while at the other the window gave 'view of a lofty brick wall, black by age and everlasting shade'. This structure was only ten feet from the window. However when the pallid, motionless Bartleby appeared and was put to work copying legal documents, he was placed closer still to an enclosure even gloomier, a small side window 'which originally had afforded a lateral view of certain grimy backyards and bricks, but which, owing to subsequent erections, commanded at present no view at all, though it gave some light. Within three feet of the panes was a wall, and the light came down from far above, between two lofty buildings, as from a very small opening in a dome. Still further to a satisfactory arrangement,' the narrator-lawyer continues, 'I procured a high green folding screen, which might entirely isolate Bartleby from my sight, though not remove him from my voice. And thus, in a manner, privacy and society were conjoined.'

And in this manner the scrivener's refusal – 'I would prefer not to' – proceeds. Here he will not copy, first the legal documents of his master, then the ways of others and finally their very life, first speech and movement, then eating. 'Like the last column of some ruined temple he remained standing mute and solitary,' comments the narrator, who soon comes to realize that he might have to let Bartleby 'live and die here, and then mason up his remains in the wall'. Instead *he* does the moving, leaving the scrivener behind; but the same result obtains: Bartleby is transferred as a vagrant to prison, the Tombs, where he is last seen facing a high wall, one, moreover, of 'amazing thickness' and 'Egyptian character'. The gloom was only relieved by a soft imprisoned turf underfoot. And here, 'strangely huddled at the base of the wall, his knees drawn up and lying on his side, his head touching the cold stones,' Bartleby chose to die.

Now, it is the function of art to generate symbolic form to at once instruct and free us. Bartleby is offered as an enigma; and his blankness touches something far wider than a personal dilemma. We recognize in him the dissolving of a personality and its flow towards the inanimate. The path leads through infancy – with his passive attachment to his master – then back, by his process of refusal, to the assumption of foetal form and finally into the non-living itself. The built things around him are stripped meanwhile by Melville down to their essentials – plane surfaces: enclosing volumes, admitting slabs of light. Their very abstraction permits greater symbolic play. The office, and what goes on in it, becomes equated then with the prison, and both with the antiquity of mausoleum and sarcophagus, the 'flesh-eating' stone. At another level we may conceive of these built things as the womb, and Bartleby's passage, which moves us by its non-violent protest, as both a return to a bad mother and the progressive entrapment of man by built things in the modern world, his identification with them, becoming one with the engulfing stones of the modern city. These things, also the offspring of men, grow into mothers themselves, and, like the final image of *Moby Dick*, claim their lost children.

A brief historical note. 'Bartleby' was written in 1853, a time of restless acceleration. During the five-year stretch between 1850 and 1855 the population of New York City was increasing by 20 percent from 515,000 to 630,000. In Europe, though the spectre of Communism had already begun to haunt it, the bourgeoisie had solidified its hold on society after the upheavals of 1848; while here too the great age of capitalism was fast under way. It was indeed the day of the Crystal Palace, built in 1851 to launch the modern technocratic era of capitalism. Meanwhile, New York, the city which was to become the cockpit for the capitalist world order, bore, for all its ferment, little resemblance to what we live in today. Illustrations of the time show the Wall Street area to be what one would expect of a mid-nineteenth-century town: scattered low buildings with ornate façades, gentlemen strolling about at leisure (see, for example, *Valentine's Manual of the Corporation of the City of New York*, 1856). Yet Melville places his story in a setting that evokes the

glassy forest of today. A few years ago, when a film of
'Bartleby' was made in England, it was shot, quite properly
I thought, in contemporary London, not the London of
Parliament and Palace, but a world of smooth, blank
surfaces, a London that could have been sections of New
York, Moscow, or São Paulo. In other words, Melville's
choice of key symbolic form became materialized reality. He
draws upon a received image, for the representation of a
wall is as old as walls themselves; but he sensed what was
to come, and presented it, as here, by the blanking out of
the surface and its transformation into the mirror absorbing
the abstracted humans who become rooted to its side.

The wall of Wall Street, we know, had been built of wood
200 years before by the Dutch to keep out marauding
Indians and Englishmen. A hallowed tradition. For the
first, Mesopotamian, walls, we know too, were defensive
ramparts to keep the enemy out. Of course this gave security,
but it also meant, needless to add, that there was an enemy
who had to be withstood. In other words, the nerve centre
and symbol of capitalism arose at the site of an early
imperialist struggle.

Thus the wall signifies conflict and the need to segregate
space into safe and unsafe territory. More generally, it
defined the space created by human activity. The natural
volume of the universe became hewn into segments of
different order – and value.

Nature is inherently indifferent. We know this, and cannot
tolerate it. Better to be hated than ignored, to face what
Melville called the 'heartless voids and immensities of the
universe'. Value must be placed on things; if the world were
to have no valence of desire, no welcoming arms, even no
ferocity, if it were scurrying matter alone . . . this realization
annihilates the frail ego.

But we are given the opportunity to decide how it shall
be carved up. What walls and the spaces defined by them
are to mean is a historical decision. Those lands which were
eventually to be subsumed into the civilization of the West
early chose to see goodness in such bits of matter as had
been altered by human activity and to impose badness on
the rest. By contrast, oriental cultures were less inclined
towards such a sharp differentiation between natural and
built forms. Goodness and deity resided in nature itself,
union with which would bring a man to completion. But in
the West from earliest times, untouched nature was bad:

wilderness, full of split-off destructive urges, hence the etymological connection: 'willed' – wilderness (Nash, 1967, p. 1). Opposed to wilderness in early belief was *paradise*, which is not at first a garden but an enclosure, or as the ancient Zoroastrian text would have it, a *pairi-daēza*, or 'walled-around' place (Thass-Thienemann, 1973, p. 176).

If the walled city signified, as Lewis Mumford observed (Mumford, 1961), the coming of anxiety and warfare into human life, it also was the sign of an advancing differentiation, separating regions of greater value from those of lesser. Good volumes bear the imprint of valued activity; they are concretions of the bodily effort that went into them and they bear from the beginning the symbolic impression of the body-self that made them. They are given the gift of our narcissism.

From earliest times value accrued to these containers that kept bad nature and the human enemy out while creating a new, managed nature certifying human control. The historian and critic of architecture, Siegfried Giedion, has described this as the phase of the first space conception (Giedion, 1962, 1964, 1971). The new man-made volume in space becomes valued in itself, with no coherent notion of perspective or interior space. Going through the wall was considered of great significance, hence the elaborate differentiation of the gateway and the ceremonial arch, passage through which was to cleanse the victorious general of guilt.

Thus from the beginning a positive attitude was taken towards built things. Building was a sacred activity, protected by ritual in Egyptian times; while the old German root of our word 'to build' refers both to the process of making, and of dwelling within. This was developed by Martin Heidegger (cited in Norberg-Shulz, 1971) into an association between the German root, *buan*, and the cognate, *bin*, to *be*.

I build, therefore I am, could be the motto of Western man, who lives within what he constructs: hence the universal feminine designation of built things, extending all the way to that aggregate called the city and beyond to the nation itself. The Egyptian hieroglyph for city was the same as that for mother (Norberg-Shulz, 1971) – the good mother, whose boundaries are not to be violated by strangers, who cleanses the children who pass back through her orifices. And by the dialectic that governs us, the creatures who achieve being through building are defined as male, *man*kind who builds

the female structure, Adam's rib, outside of himself, thus
denying through reversal their making inside a woman.

There is a reassurance here, an anchoring of narcissism in stone that will not move or fade, a hedge against death, for passive absorption into the bad, wild mother of nature. To this day we see – have seen enough of no doubt – ruling élites who reassure themselves with Albany Malls or World Trade Centers. But we are set up so that one element of value cannot remain free of its opposite.

We have to consider therefore a repressed, negative value to the building as wall, derived from the ancient fear that went into its making. The guilt which had to be cleansed from the conquering general was a real one, earned by real destruction – and some of it could not help but wipe off on to the structure through which he passed. Alongside this were to be added the real dangers posed by the enemy. The more he was attacked, the more he would wish to retaliate and the thicker would become the wall – built, no doubt, by slaves captured in warfare, slaves who were drawn into the mother-city to do the dominated labour, to toil and die building for masters whose tombs grew thicker, walled for protection against time and retaliation. The sacredness of ancient temple-building cannot be dissociated from the fact that this form of work would use up men the way syringes are used up in the modern hospital. Nothing, I think, becomes sacred unless it has also been quite cruel. Later, when slavery ceased to be the mode of labour, wages were developed as the means of ensuring work. Yet the basic mode of domination persisted and the meanings of the wall were swept along.

A wall, remember, has two surfaces. It can take the imprint of that which has been expelled to the outside no less than that of the valued space within. And the meaning left out is that of a hidden, destructive factor behind building-*buan*-being: that which has had to be destroyed, and relegated to non-being.

We do not like to give up on anything once invested with desire, even when desire turns to split-off, unconscious hatred. This may have something to do with the ambivalence towards garbage, which is destroyed, consumed matter, of opposite value to the built thing that was meant to endure, to be used and admired. Garbage should be hated and removed; yet as Mumford (1961, p. 75) notes, 'For thousands of years city dwellers put up with defective, often quite vile

sanitary arrangements, wallowing in rubbish and filth they
certainly had the power to remove.' The implication is clear:
men unconsciously want their garbage, they need to have
matter around that has been ruined, if only to secure
the precious sense of constructiveness revealed in their
surrounding proud walls and towers.

Garbage is but the visible sign of hated substance. Unconsciously meanwhile, that which is built, the wall itself, can
be invested with malevolence; and wilderness can return,
strike in the heart of a built-up place. This moment occurs
when the sense of alienation, the fission between maker and
made thing grows to the point when narcissistic identification is no longer possible, when the builder no longer feels
one with that which has been built, when the inanimate
form ceases to embrace as a good mother and turns into a
prison instead. Then, as Melville has Ahab exclaim in *Moby
Dick*, 'How can the prisoner reach outside except by striking
through the wall? To me the white whale is that wall shoved
near to me.'

From a psychohistorical perspective, this begins to
happen in the mid nineteenth century, a time when architecture remains in the grip of old assumptions while germi-
nating the transformation Giedion called the third-space
conception: the interpenetration of inner and outer space,
co-ordinated with the loss of a single viewpoint of perspective. This revolution entailed a deep dislocation in the
experience of space and time, and in the self's relation to
the material world. For, with the loss of a clear distinction
between inside and out, the inside must in a sense turn out,
and the outside in. In another metaphor, the repressed
returns; and since what has been held back in an earlier
cultural formula includes destructivity, so must destructivity
be manifest when the old order becomes obsolete.

Again, literature gives a clue to psychohistorical symbolism. The ominous, man-swallowing surface of Melville's wall is prefigured in more direct, vivid form in the
works of Edgar Allan Poe. When Poe chooses to display his
macabre insight in *The Fall of the House of Usher*, *The Black Cat*,
and *The Cask of Amontillado*, by portraying the very walls as
sarcophagi, tombs, places where the dead and murdered
are secreted, he offers an insight into the suffocation of man
by the structure he has built, the weight of the destruction
dealt out by history and – quite literally – *incorporated* into
built things. It is not that the dead are placed inside the wall,

but that they come back to life once there; they become demons, lending the stone itself a murderousness. It is the *Frankenstein* story again, but deeper, really, than that premonition of a technology run wild. For in Poe's demonic walls we see represented the eventual autonomy of the built structure. The monster now is no longer in human form, but the thing itself, ready to destroy its master with his accumulated murderousness.

This sinister current runs alongside the still-dominant positive concept of the built thing, though split off and overshadowed for purposes of consciousness by the proud achievements of contemporary technology. The wall once securely surrounded the city, defining it, protecting it and giving it pride. As in Franz Kafka's *The Great Wall of China* (1946), a parable which sums up the modern predicament, 'the art of architecture, and especially that of masonry, had been proclaimed as the most important branch of knowledge throughout the whole area of a China that was to be walled around . . .' (pp. 150–1). So much is the legend: the protective wall becomes the integument of the social body. When the people saw the great wall, a surge of pride swept through them.

Every fellow countryman was a brother for whom one was building a wall of protection and who would return lifelong thanks for it with all he had and did. Unity! Unity! Shoulder to shoulder, a ring of brothers, a current of blood no longer confined within the narrow circulation of one body, but sweetly rolling and yet ever returning throughout the endless leagues of China. (p. 154)

Yet the truth is darker. The wall, built in fragments, dwarfs the men who build it. Contact is lost with those from whose attacks it is to protect China, the northern barbarians, with their 'half-shut eyes that already seem to be seeking out the victim which their jaws will rend and devour' (p. 160); they persist inwardly only as bogy-men to scare the children. Meanwhile the wall becomes unfathomable and unreachable, like the High Command and the Emperor himself, who may not even exist. The villagers live in safety, but there is a pervasive subtle terror, a loss of contact with the very processes of civilization.

Kafka provides a screen upon which is reflected both past and future. Today the sense of fragmentation he described is with us in more extreme, yet continuous form. The protective wall is down, the brotherhood it promised a mere slogan, while barbarity reigns within the city. The one urban image which prevails today is that of a prison without walls. Vitality continues within the urban mass – indeed, this is our main hope – but no one would disagree that the struggle to be waged is confused and at best uphill, against the mound of constructed-destructed stone we have heaped up all around us, a pile without religious signification, without protectiveness, with only occasional flashes of beauty, reflection only, it seems, of a purified commercial process that has crystallized out of historical flux and run wild.

The psychohistorical task is to make sense out of the symbolic shifts that have entered into this process. As with psychoanalytic study of the individual, it is an effort to comprehend the irrational within a rational frame of thought. Here, however, the object of our calculation is not an individual mind but the meaningfulness in historical activity. And such activity, though it must resonate with psychology, is not inherently psychological, nor does it lend itself to direct interpretation. Thus psychoanalytic writings are virtually barren of reference to architecture and urban planning. Contrast this with the great wealth of commentary on literature and the plastic arts, forms where the imagination is given free sway, which are, so to speak, screens for a more direct transposition of the inner fantasy world on to some malleable medium.

But buildings are to be lived and worked in. They struggle against the laws of gravity and mechanics, the properties of materials, and the exigencies of political economy. In so far as our mind is drawn into the struggle, it is mainly by the cultivation of objective, scientific, technical thought. Hence the striving for order and proportion in the aesthetic of architecture. At another, connected level we have the domination of urban study by the 'planning' approach, with its supposedly 'pure' application of technical thought (see Bookchin, 1973).

The trouble with these modes of thinking lies not in their applicability – which is beyond question – but in the way they can serve to obliterate the basic truth that buildings and cities are of, for and by people. Thus we need a social calculus that includes the human factor in its political and psychological dimension. Here psychoanalysis can play a role – if only we can devise a means for its application. This is, however, no easy matter.

At the core of a psychoanalytic critique is the rediscovery

of the repressed infantile body in the world of events. But   61
in architecture the flow of events does not lend immediate
support to a psychoanalytic interpretation. Figural symbolism plays a role no doubt in ancient and primitive
architecture, but the entire thrust of building since then has
been towards its minimization. True, Vitruvius, in laying
down the rules of the classical idiom which was to dominate
Western architecture for a millennium and more, specified
that the different classes of column were to convey sexual
qualities, maleness for the Doric, a feminine slenderness for
the Ionic, while the Corinthian was to represent the slight
figure of a girl (see Summerson, 1963). However, the significance here is not that bodily qualities were being represented
but that they were in process of being sublimated, eventually
to be lost in the rationalized form of the building. Further,
what was once the formal, symbolic intention of an element
of a built thing can, and most likely will, change its signification with time. Beware of the genetic fallacy: what began
in conflict, or with the representation of a bodily based
concern, need no longer stay that way; independent determination can set in, and control the course of meaning. Thus
to trace the sexual symbolism in architecture as though it had
persistent active meaning – to see, for instance, phalluses in
skyscrapers, or bowels in subways – would be simply an
exercise in fanciful thinking. A person may dream of a house
and it may, that night, represent his mother, but the house
he lives in was not so easily conjured up, and will represent
ever so much more than maternal form.

I say this, you may be sure, not to vitiate the interpretations
given above but to put them on a more secure footing. The
key is to become clearer about the nature of meaning,
whether in history, architecture or the interior of the psyche.

Meaning, or symbolic form, is at the centre of any human
phenomenon. What something is taken to mean determines
in a real sense its structure, its relationship to other entities
and the activities associated with it. I do not, of course, intend
'meaning' here to signify anything static, independent of
material givens or purely conscious. The utility of psychoanalysis for any general human science lies precisely in its
openness to dynamic, material and unconscious layers of
meaning. Thus we say that the meaning of a person's life
will not be adequately grasped unless we appreciate the
contributions of a non-conscious, material biological factor
such as sexuality. Similarly we would not regard this one

level of meaning as exclusive of others; rather would we search for some organism of meaning out of the many partial layers of meaningfulness that enter into somebody's life. And by giving symbolic form to this unified organism of meaning – and bringing such form within a person's awareness, we will, we know, bring about real changes: such, in any event, is the programme of psychoanalytic therapy.

Similarly, with the subject at hand, built things, numerous partial layers of determination enter into the organic pattern of meaningfulness: you are familiar with them as the categories of use, materials, economics, style and so forth. But part of the meaningfulness of a building would also be its historical situation. This might be read in the fantasy value placed on it, since the built thing was made by those fanciful creatures, men. I mean here a public dimension of fantasy, since building is public both in its drawing on social resources and, more fundamentally, its definition of social space. The mass psychology we are after, moreover, is not some simple aggregate of disembodied thought, but rather a sensuously derived, materially based, politically active organism of idea interlocked with the shifting institutional forces of society. In other words, a psychohistory needs to be true to the play of meanings developing out of the conjuncture of inner human strivings and outer created form – a play that contains within itself the principle of movement, historical time. What counts then is not the particular representational value of any given structure – though that is not without interest – but rather the meaningfulness of the total historical flow in which that structure is contained. Included here would be the activity of building as well as the content of what is being built.

Hence the aptness of literature, which is a natural medium for the cultivation of psychohistorical symbolism. But to unfold these meanings in objective form we need workable concepts. I should like to draw your attention therefore to an idea introduced in my psychohistorical study of racism (Kovel, 1970), and which I would like to expand upon now. This is the notion of primary and secondary symbolism.

The concept is a relative one, and refers to two ends of a continuous spectrum of symbolic form. At the near, primary end, meanings develop out of subjectivity; while at the far, secondary end, meaningfulness inheres in the objective. Near and far, primary and secondary here refer to distance

from the locus of subjectivity, the self. Primary symbolism 63
would therefore pertain to the experienced subjective state,
and this would build itself in substantial measure out of
memory and current bodily experience; hence the primary
reference of meaning would be to some extent turned away
from the public, historical arena. Similarly the secondary
system of reference would pertain mainly to what is in the
public, historically contingent arena. A phenomenological
account of a subject's life would be conducted largely with
primary symbolic elements; at least it would commence with
them. Contrariwise, a description of an objective entity
would begin with secondary symbolism – in the case of
buildings, the familiar vocabulary of architecture.

But the important part of this conception of symbolism
lies not in the segregation of subjectivity and objectivity, but
in their interpenetration. It consists of eliminating the logical
operator 'contrariwise' (which was, you may recall, part of
the lingo of Tweedledum and Tweedledee) from the above
definition, thereby seeing the individual life saturated with
history, and the so-called 'objective' form irradiated with
projected wishes and parts of the self. Thus primary and
secondary do not refer to any absolute sense of priority. Any
human phenomenon is necessarily imbued with meaning
from both ends of the spectrum, even though we are forced
to focus on one side or the other in the apprehension of that
phenomenon. The study of either mode of interpenetration
would be psychohistorical, the first being the more widely
practised type in which psychological study, for example of
leaders or national character, is historically informed; whilst
the second puts a psychological perspective to man-made
institutions, such as racism or things, such as buildings.

These considerations tell us why simply laying on the
unconscious meaning of 'mother' to a house gets us
nowhere. For it presents only the ends of the spectrum
and leaves out the psychohistorical context. We need the
symbolic passage in between, the critical mediation by which
the repressed finds its way to the surface of activity and gets
swept along in history.

I would venture to speculate that the linchpin here,
the mediation that permits symbolic exchange to be made
between the primary and secondary ends of the spectrum
of built things, lies not in any particular other person or
part of the self, but in ways of thinking that arise in the
experiences of infantile separation. Now this is clearly a

universal function, in that all humans, everywhere, have been born with no distinct self, but are rather profoundly, utterly attached to a being who gave them life. And we know that the formation of a discrete sense of 'I', a self with secure psychic boundaries, is no automatic matter, that it is fraught with passion and set about with danger. And we have no reason to doubt it should ever have been otherwise in form, although the context of the separation phase and the ideas of self which arise out of it would be given by the specific setting in which it occurs.

Out of the work of separation come certain fundamental ideas about the world as it peels away from the self. And these include notions about built things. Consider the nursery rhyme, 'Humpty-Dumpty sat on a wall/Humpty-Dumpty had a great fall/All the King's horses and all the King's men,/Couldn't put Humpty-Dumpty together again.' Here is a wall indeed, the very original one. As the British analyst, Ella Freeman Sharpe, once pointed out, the wall in this case stood for the mother's body, against which the infant, or lap-child, sits. The fall is the child's venture on to the floor and all that lies beyond. But all the achievement in the world cannot erase loss; and the Kings and their horses are, the child well knows, substitutes for the unity left behind.

Here the shattering is the product of the baby's rage at being untimely yanked from the wall, a rage familiar to observers of small children. The 'good' child, of course, forgets these tantrums by the simple expedient of taking the positive, active faculties that are also our legacy and applying them to the blocks provided by culture: indeed little children build their own wall, put it up, knock it down and put it up again. Thus the embryonic architect gets hatched. More, the first spirit of co-operation figured in Kafka's image of the brotherhood jointly building their wall, is formed in these nursery settings, dear to parental hearts.

The edifices so constructed become models of the lost unity, suitably abstracted (though often enough little people are juxtaposed to the walls, in concrete reminder) and greatly valued. It would seem to me that here we have the kind of primitive magical reassurance that must form a fairly universal element in human psychology, thus a continual source of primary symbolism. Note that language is developing at the same time as primitive building skills. Thus words, the products of the mind, and the products of

one's physical effort come to stand for each other. This
correspondence persists in the 'meaning of meaning', for
we say that to represent is to 'stand for', as the early wall of
blocks stood in place of the lost object.

At bottom, then, buildings are what Winnicott (1953)
called 'transitional phenomena', a fusion of subjective and
objective qualities, created in the process of individuation.
We do indeed come to be by building, just as we once were
by dwelling within. And archaeology reveals the same
dialectic in the ceremonial construction of early men. Thus
the first dimension to be differentiated out of dimensionless
space was the vertical, in celebration of the standing person,
while the first form was the smooth unbroken plane, sign
of unity. Humpty-Dumpty had survived his fall.

We see here that, as one might expect, primary and
secondary symbolism matches up rather well in the early
stages of civilization. It remains, however, to add a dynamic
dimension, else the principle of historical movement gets
lost. This too is possible, since the wall as built long ago had
the same objective function for the infant-mind as it has had
ages – namely, the denial of separation and a protection
against hostility. For built things demand co-operation in
the making and, once made, are reassurances against both
actual aggression from outside and one's own aggression.
The banal fact that real stone structures do not move is
actually of deep importance here, for it assures us of their
reality. What better proof for the magical mind seeking to
reassure itself against its own destructivity than to be able
to build something up that is bigger than one's self and that
will neither decay, run away nor strike back?

When symbolic structures from the primary end display
congruence with those at the secondary one, a psychohistorical circle is closed. The superimposition of subjective
and objective symbol creates a nuclear psychohistorical
structure, the symbolic matrix, which shapes the course of
both psychology and history, though it may eventually
become unrecognizable in its original form. The activity of
the matrix derives from inner contradictions at both ends of
the symbolic spectrum. From the primary side we have the
denial of rage and object-loss concealed within the act of
building; while at the secondary end arises the use of
dominated labour for building protective and fraternal structures. In each case the negated element remains despite the
act of denial: the need for retribution, revenge and reunion

with the lost object persists, as psychoanalysis of the individual regularly shows; while a dialectical history reveals
that the domination of labour creates class antagonism and
the need for more protection, hence more domination, and
so forth, from the days of Nebuchadnezzar to those of ITT.

The symbolic matrix gives meaning to the material products of human activity even as it grounds psychology in
what is externally real. We observe in this regard that the
unfulfilled business of each end of the symbolic spectrum
is transferred through the psychohistorical matrix to the
resolution offered at the other. Thus we have the overestim-
ation of the built thing as a denial of narcissistic loss, along
with the dehumanization of the individual and his eventual
identification with the dead stone product of dominated
labour. Hence the genius of a Poe who could see the horror
immured within stone walls, and of a Melville who could
prefigure with his Bartleby the eventual petrification of the
self.

And all this while the Crystal Palace was being built and
the age of positive technology was being launched. Melville
said indirectly in 'Bartleby', then, what Dostoevsky may
state more explicitly in *Notes from the Underground*, a work
that directly criticized the Crystal Palace and, by choosing
to locate itself in a cellar, contradicted the forthcoming
assertion of the antihuman megatechnology whose symbol
is the skyscraper.

But to take these contradictions seriously we have to
recognize the positive side. Otherwise we flirt with breast-
beating, and, more important, lose grip of dialectical reality.
Thus it is far from my intent to disparage the achievements,
the built things, of modern technological society. To the
contrary, I regard them highly – as of the same order of
magnitude as the barbarity and dehumanization which have
developed in their wake. Given the extent of the chaos it has
sown, a system such as capitalism would not have survived
so long without real grounds for pride. This is not the same,
of course, as saying that it has grounds for survival, but that
is another matter.

My purpose, however, has been neither to view with
pride nor to point with alarm, but only to stress the immense
contradictoriness that underlies our material achievement.
These contradictions generate the passage of historical time,
for each extrinsic act fails to heal the inner split against which
it was intended; rather does the inner dissociation grow in

complexity, manifest itself as a sense of dissatisfaction and
incompleteness, and force new – and necessarily partial –
attempts to transform the outer world. In such a way is time
portioned out, its passage measured by the accumulation of
symbolic precipitate that collects like sediment obscuring
the oceanic floor. Thus, to resume with our psychohistorical
metaphor, the spectral distance between primary and
secondary symbolism increases, causing us to forget the
original nature of things.

The value of such a critique as I am offering lies in whatever
insight it affords into our alienation. The forms of alienation
discussed here are indicated in terms such as commodity
fetishism or the replacement of human relations with thing
relations. I might add the sense of *enthralment*, referring now
to the way we get bemused by what we have made, and
shift human considerations – love, hate, longing and guilt –
to the built thing.

The very loss of sight is the measure of alienation, of
a split between the self and the world it has made. It is this
split which allows the destruction worked by society to
proceed unchecked. With the consequences of our acts
disjointed from our inner being we are unable to check a
process that continues to degrade the labour of men and to
overvalue and worship the things they make. It is a situation
reminiscent of earliest times, including even the preponderance of blank abstract structures – as in our superhighways
– except that the blankness now represents not only a lost
unity with nature but a lost self as well.

As we enter the age of scarcity and the limits of the
inner assumptions of our capitalist order are ever more
prominently displayed before our eyes, we can none of us
afford to ignore our relationship to history or to pass it off
in a superficially positivistic way. As an ironic reminder of
this let me cite the words of one would-be architect to
another, successful, one, to the effect that 'the purpose of
. . . building was to transmit [one's] time and its spirit to
posterity, [for] all that remained to remind men of the great
epochs of history was their monumental architecture.' You
may recognize here the thought of Adolf Hitler as expressed
to Albert Speer (1970); perhaps we can also begin to
appreciate the obscure logic linking it with the abominations
that ensued – and, before the walls come tumbling down,
with our own distress as well.

5 ERIK ERIKSON'S PSYCHOHISTORY

FOR MANY, Erik Erikson stands as the most influential contemporary interpreter of Freud, the one who has done the most to bridge psychoanalysis and the rest of human science. It is not hard to see why. The body of his work itself represents more than three decades of effort touching all the major bases: studies of youth, religion, dislocation and upheaval, of the saintly and the wicked – the spectrum of historical flux is all there on his palette. And with Erikson there is no holding back from taking a stand, none of the hothouse aura that has come to surround psychoanalysis. On the contrary, for Erikson the question of value has always been uppermost. He has seen himself as having a mission to bring the truth-telling discipline of psychoanalysis directly into grips with the reality of events, which he calls 'actuality'. And he has done this, on the whole, with great subtlety and breadth of mind, achieving in the course of his career the first really systematic elaboration of a developmental point of view about human phenomena.

Virtually single-handedly, Erikson has launched the problematic and promising field of psychohistory. His sophisticated, humane approach, so free of psychoanalytic reductionism yet so demonstrably enmeshed with Freudian thought, has made his work – notably *Young Man Luther* (1958) and *Gandhi's Truth* (1969), along with a number of short essays – the touchstone of effort in the fledgeling discipline.

Yet it is a touchstone that is rarely subjected to critical investigation. Erikson has become something of a sacred cow surrounded by epigones who keep his own work above serious examination by comparing it to other, manifestly lesser psychohistorical ventures. But to be better than third-rate it is only necessary to be second-rate. And without any genuinely critical standard of psychohistory there is no way of taking the inquiry further. It is towards the development

of such a standard that this article is directed, spurred by
the intimation that for all its obvious merit there is something
deeply wrong with Erikson's psychohistory.

One picks it up in the reading. Not right away; look at
any page and at first all seems well: insightful, judicious,
balanced, an exemplary instance of humanism. But read on
and a strained quality sets in. Try to remember what he has
said and a cloud tends to form. After a while it begins to
oppress. The prose now appears glossy, pompous, senten-
tious, moralizing. We are being harangued, albeit with style.
The ultimate effect is obscurantist, repressive, politically
stagnant.

The problem cuts to the heart of the concepts with which
Erikson tries to explain things. And it is a problem in values
no less than in logic – more exactly, in the way values affect
explanation.

On the face of it Erikson set out to do something long
needed: to use psychoanalysis as a foundation for a general
theory of man, and at the same time to correct whatever static
or mechanistic qualities have dogged Freudian thought.
Freud's dilemma from the start was how to get from inside
to outside. That is, how is one to assess the impact of
unconscious mental life on external events; and conversely,
how does one work backwards to determine how events
affect the unconscious? Unless this can be done, we are left
with two parallel and separate explanations for any human
situation: one that posits subjective mental states as prime
determinants, another that rests on external, material
causes. This is as ancient a problem as can be found.
Psychoanalysis, however, added a new dimension whereby
inner mental states were seen to be determined at a level
that had no immediate input from the external world. For
example, if an individual is looking for a father that he or
she had to give up in childhood because of an impossible
ambivalence, then the repressed striving perpetually forces
him or her to find new objects in the outer world. Each
representative of the lost parent would be approached with
the same love and rejected with the same hate. Never
truly knowing the repressed wish, the individual would be
doomed to repeat this behaviour. And if this wish complex
were the prime determinant, then the quality of the object
would take on a certain indifference.

Powerful as such a conceptualization was, there is no
doubt of its incompleteness. It does not account for growth

or any kind of real change; and it fails to consider the whole
set of political and economic causes which shape the quality
of father figures in the actual world. Not the least of the
dilemma is the problem of formulating psychology in a truly
societal way – not simply a group psychology written large,
but a mass psychology that would define the psychological
properties of historically critical groups including classes,
races, nations, professions, institutions, and so on. While
Freud himself can be excused for resting with the intellectual
wealth he managed to extract, those who follow him have no
such exoneration. The task of synthesizing psychoanalytic
psychology with the study of society, that is, the business of
deriving a true psychohistory, remains a critical, unfulfilled
legacy.

Here is where Erikson has staked his claim. His major
developmental propositions and the identity concept with
which he ties things together are derived with the legacy in
mind. For Erikson, *epigenesis*, meaning a phasic, continually
developing series of new syntheses, replaces Freud's *originology*, or insistence upon the primacy of early childhood.
In Erikson's view the outside environment is in constant
interchange with the emerging self. People pass through a
series of developments, in each of which the environment
(mainly the social one) provides new material for synthesis.
Similarly, at each point the individual can use the tension
between the past, with its internalized givens, and the
present, with its cultural situation and its contingencies, as
a basis for new synthesis. To Erikson the human agent is
thus active, especially in his heroic form, as in the case of
Luther and Gandhi. Everyone, however, has the capacity
to make his or her world – even as he or she is made by
it. But Erikson is not satisfied with a purely intellectual
correction of Freud. He finds that he cannot simply amplify
the theory without at the same time correcting the deep
attitude of pessimism pervading Freud's work.

There is a certain logic to this. If we are determined mainly
by the most intractable dilemmas of our past, then hope,
which is the nucleus of optimism, is no more than an illusion.
But if, as Erikson holds, we are always renewing ourselves,
if we are not trapped in origins but remake the world, and
make a community in so doing, then hope is not only a
legitimate aspiration, but becomes, along with trust,
initiative, fidelity, and the other virtues postulated by
Erikson, part of the determining matrix of human life.

Thus it is that Erikson can introduce his cardinal concept of identity as an active synthesis of all that designates the essence of a person as he shares his life in a community. It is the configuration of past and present, inside and outside, into a new whole: what I am, what I am never not, who we are together. Identity, then, is not merely an idle naming but a

process 'located' in the core of the individual and yet also in the core of his communal culture, a process which establishes, in fact, the identity of those two identities . . . At its best identity is a process of increasing differentiation, and it becomes even more inclusive as the individual grows aware of a widening circle of others significant to him, from the maternal person to 'mankind'. (Erikson, 1968, pp. 22–3)

Erikson's optimism is thus linked with a basically monistic attitude. Goodness resides in drawing together, in the wholeness of a situation rather than in any particular part; mankind strives for a 'more inclusive identity'. Badness lies in moralistic exclusion, in splitting, condemnation of the other as a 'dirty speck in our moral vision'. Fortunately, development tends towards wholeness, greater inclusivity. What is and what ought to be converge, aided by truth-telling, as in psychoanalysis, or the great religious insights that succeed in re-establishing links between the adult, reasoning mind, and the well-spring of infantile trust as well as the ineffable mysteries of life.

What could be amiss with such a virtuous, noble-minded approach to life? How can it yield the fulsomeness observed above?

There is nothing wrong, of course, with having lofty, optimistic, or even Utopian aspirations for mankind. Some of the very greatest thinkers – for example, Karl Marx – have entertained such aspirations. And it is a moot point whether such goals are based upon illusions, as Marxism may be grounded in what Freud once called a 'fresh idealistic misconception of human nature'. All our values, after all, are based on illusion, or some infantile promise kept or broken. But, as Erikson rightly points out, the basis for something does not exhaust or limit its possibilities; and so it is with those values which guide investigation. The important issue is whether one sees enough of reality to count, and whether one sees what one looks at with fidelity and penetration. Sir Isaiah Berlin wrote movingly in the

Hedgehog and the Fox (1953) of Tolstoy's agony at the irrecon- cilability of his grand, holistic, religious views of human nature with the dazzling clarity of his particular vision of the world of men. Freud's pessimism and Marx's optimism are in the same category of necessary orientations based, like all our values, on a set of illusions but framing an extraordinary vision into an actual portion of human reality.

In Erikson's case, however, the frame becomes the picture, and his major conceptual and clinical talents get obscured. We are shown the world of men not simply as it is, and not simply as he wants it to be (which would make a nice fantasy like Dostoevsky's vision of the earthly paradise), but as a hodgepodge between the way it is and the way it ought to be. The effort to put together these irreconcilables creates the fulsomeness; and the villain of the piece is the identity concept, or, rather, Erikson's use of it, since taken by itself identity is a useful way of designating stability and organization of the self-image, and a necessary construct in any adequate social psychology. But Erikson doesn't take it by itself; he compulsively makes identity both a manifestation of the *summum bonum* and an active force, and so throws in a factor which can be used to cancel out anything penetrating in a psychoanalytical proposition.

What is characteristic in the most fundamental way about Freudian thought is not its 'originology' or even its insistence on instinctual drives. Both of these attributes are in any Freudian proposition. But a more primitive and elementary conception is that of *negation*; that is, to Freud human reality was a field of forces in conflict within which a trend, repression, exists to split off negated qualities from the main, official body of consciousness. Further, these split-off qualities continue to exert a major effect behind the screen of consciousness. This is the elementary, explanatory logic of psychoanalysis. The theory of infantile sexuality plays such an important role in Freudian thought precisely because of its essential negativity. To comprehend that the deepest wish, the most profound or ecstatic joy was also the source of greatest danger, despair and loss, to recognize the ambivalence in the midst of our nature – this was Freud's paramount achievement and the heart of his contribution. No doubt the whole business was cast in too physicalist a mode; no doubt also that conceptual room has to be made for the effect of more neutral and integrative psychic forces. But a theory remains coherent only if it sticks to a certain

cardinal form of explanation and organizes updated knowledge under its aegis. Thus when psychoanalysis loses its
explanatory principle of negation, it loses its critical and
penetrating power as well.

And this is just what Erikson's use of identity accom-
plishes. For he is basically a positive thinker. When it counts,
when it comes time to say, in effect, this is what is really
going on here, Erikson puts his conceptual money on
affirmative identity. But he also holds on to a simulacrum of
Freud. While positive theories yield grand designs of the
universe, they can also all too easily slide into banality.
Negativity can be a hedge against this, but, as negative and
positive tend to add up to zero, it can also be a source of
confusion. And so Erikson's work wanders back and forth
between these poles, only occasionally (as in some portions
of *Young Man Luther*) steering a course that really adds to
our grasp.

Meanwhile we get too much regaled with the cheap
perfume of identity, as handy an all-purpose concept as ever
existed for covering up a lack of critical conception. Now we
see identity linked to parallel developments in culture ('an
all-inclusive human identity must be part of the anticipation
of a universal technology'(1968, p. 42)); now we learn of it
apodictically ('For in all parts of the world, the struggle now
is for the *anticipatory development of more inclusive identities'*
(1969, p. 433) – note Erikson's emphasis, a much used way
to inflate a sagging idea); indeed, whenever we come across
some element of history with psychological qualities,
Erikson reaches into his satchel, hauls out an identity term,
and pins it on. Thus great leaders 'experience the identity
struggle of their people'; colonialism does 'nearly irrevers-
ible damage to a people's identity'; 'America neglected' to
cultivate for the Negro 'these components of identity which
neither a defined group nor an individual can do without'
(1969, p. 267). We hear of the 'identity-eroding aspects of
economic ruin' and of the 'concepts of law and legal truth –
always key elements in any national identity and a necessary
framework for individual identity' (1969, p. 274); we hear
of identity-this and identity-that until the word seems to run
off the page to cover all reality with a universal glaze.

Note the optative mood that steals into Erikson's propositions and his generally preachy tone. Squeezed by a
negative theory he espouses but cannot quite accept, there
is no way to look but up. Erikson's rhapsodies about identity

seem to me to be a rising away from something seen but unbearable. Sometimes the result is a straightforward Panglossism, for example:

From a psychosocial point of view at any rate, basic social and cultural processes can only *[there go those emphases again] be viewed as the joint endeavour of adult egos to develop and maintain, through joint organization, a maximum of conflict-free energy in a mutually supportive psychosocial equilibrium.* (1968, p. 223)

Although this formulation in itself leaves us a little high and dry in so far as any serious social criticism is concerned, it is only the beginning of Erikson's ascension, for his real passion lies with the spiritual. When, during his study of Gandhi, he has to deal with certain contradictions in the Mahatma's influence, Erikson spares himself critical reflection by keeping his eye on the heavens. Gandhi was, claims Erikson, 'on the side of a truth which transcends all facts'. And what is this truth? It is ingrained in the

all-embracing circumstance that each of us exists with a unique consciousness and a responsibility of his own which makes him at the same time zero and everything, a centre of absolute silence, and the vortex of apocalyptic participation. A man who looks through the historical parade of culture and civilizations, styles and isms which provide most of us with a glorious and yet miserably fragile sense of immortal identity, defined status and collective grandeur faces the central truth of our nothingness – and mirabile dictu, *gains power from it.* (1969, pp. 396–7)

The passage above positively preens itself on its wisdom – the happy fusion of mystical vision with mundane intelligence. But does true mystical or monistic spirit promise power from its exercise or inflate itself so pompously? It is mystical to look through things, and no doubt such vision is rare and beautiful in its way. But to pretend to look *at* the 'historical parade' and then look *through* it when one sees something obnoxious is not mysticism but mystification.

And what is it that Erikson doesn't like to explore? The same old things that have always stimulated the mystifying intelligence: sex and power – real power, the economic and political kind. It is scarcely necessary to add that Erikson, the apostle of inclusiveness, doesn't exactly parade his distaste for exploring these matters. He needn't, after all, thanks to his identity salad, within which any ingredient can be made to blend with the taste of the whole.

So it will all be there, comprehensive and subtly put. But
just read more closely and you will see where Erikson stands.
Consider the following passages from *Gandhi's Truth*,
presented in the course of a lengthy discussion of Gandhi's
youthful development, a process that eventuated in fanatical
vegetarianism, a horror of sexuality, and numerous remarkable qualities of leadership and political skill.

*When this boy appointed himself his father's nurse, there was a
drive in it which later would suffice for the care of all India as well
as Untouchables and lepers, of mankind as well as of an ashram . . .*
(p. 111)

*But even the most glaringly neurotic aspects of all this [absorption
of maternal religious influence] must not blind us to his often
successful attempts, born of his relation to his mother, to unite the
feminine and masculine aspects of religiosity – and to convey this
unification to the masses . . .* (p. 112)

*Here an overweening conscience can find peace only by always
believing that the budding 'I' harbours a truthfulness superior to
that of all authorities because this truth is the covenant of the 'I'
with God, the 'I' being even more central and more pervasive than
all parent images and moralities . . .* (p. 118)

*His wife . . . came to personify a threat to higher loyalties . . . At
the end only total abstinence would give back to him – and to his
wife – the sense of humour which can mark the triumph of self-
mastery . . .* (pp. 120–1)

In each passage explanatory power is given to something
ideal, even mysterious, while the sensuous, material facts
get brushed aside. This is characteristic of Erikson's work.
Whenever he deals with sexuality, one has the sense that a
faint cloud of moralizing hangs over the page but none of
Freud's remorseless vision.

Indeed, Freud had what Erikson, in the last analysis,
lacks: a sense of evil – the conviction that there is real
destructiveness in the world, that one should neither flinch
from this nor succumb to Manichaeanism, but rather give it
its due, then defy it with the critical truth. This truth saw
history as the struggle between sharply opposed forces, not
the search for a 'more inclusive identity'. Freud turned
perhaps too far away from recognition of hopefulness within
social systems (but then he was old and sick and had lived
through the First World War when he wrote his major

sociological works). Yet until the end he retained the central
insight without which any social critique becomes banal, if
not reactionary: that there is an established order of things
which keeps itself in power by falsifying the truth and
causing it to be repressed.

Power includes the capacity to make lies official. Any
identity concept is necessarily ambiguous when used to
account for history, for it can designate both the falsified
dominant image and the forces – erotic and destructive – in
contradiction to it. Despite Erikson's pieties, society does
not exist to form a 'mutually supportive psychosocial equilibrium'; its main forces are locked in conflict. By ignoring this
one falls in with the forces of 'order' and has no choice
but to go along with the ideology of, say, multinational
corporations which would like nothing better than for us to
see ourselves as inclusively under their umbrella – as, for
example, Coca-Cola some time ago flew youths from all over
the world to a hilltop in Italy to sing its praises.

Erikson's effort to bring in contradiction, his idea of the
'negative identity', gets nowhere at all, for it is nothing other
than what has been officially repudiated – 'all self-images
which are diametrically opposed to the dominant values of
an individual's upbringing' (1958, p. 102). We are still left
with the terms of the established order and without any
means of looking within these terms. Thus Erikson gives
up on what has to be the central problem of a critical
psychohistory: negation within the established order. For
example, he approaches the race problem from the obvious
vantage point of the negative identities dumped on Black
people by White culture but is unable to deal with the
historically central issue – the negation that is within the
positive identity of Whiteness itself. To do this we have to
begin to think negatively, which means to take seriously
what Freud taught. And for all of its absorption into a
behavioural 'revolution', repressed sexuality remains one
of the constituents at the core of the psychohistorical process.

Freud developed the insight that sexual repression creates
the nucleus of political oppression (however, he did not
pursue it, that task befalling Wilhelm Reich). The internalization of Oedipal strictness becomes the template upon which
future dominant and submissive patterns and the whole
sexualized core of the political process are constructed.

It seems to me, then, that whatever the autonomous
sources of religion in the appreciation of what cannot be

known empirically, it is its instinctualized and material 77
component that becomes important in any historical assessment. New religious insights may be made possible by the
breakup of an existing order, but if they are to survive
institutionally they soon enough become aligned with viable
sources of power for which they eventually serve as rationalizations. Thus the psychohistorical assessment of a religious
leader is subject to the same conditions that should
accompany any psychohistorical venture: to derive the
particular mass-psychological and political-economic situation in such a way that the nuclear conflicts in the one can
be related to the contradictions in the other; and then to
correlate this scheme with what can be legitimately inferred
about the psychology of individuals involved. This may be
an immensely difficult endeavour, yet I fail to see why it
cannot be done without reference to any transcendent or
mystifying factors.

What is at stake is more than conceptual clarity. Erikson
may see himself on the side of the angels, but his analysis,
at least of the Indian situation (with Luther he was on safer,
more remote ground), settles back to earth pretty much in
the camp of the masters. Given his dependence upon
explanations which remain fixed – for all the transcendent
rhetoric – to the values of the established order, there is
really little choice to do otherwise.

Gandhi's Truth culminates in an intensive study of the
Mahatma's discovery of *Satyagraha*, or militant non-
violence, during the Ahmedabad mill workers' strike of
1918, an event wherein certain contradictory tendencies
were bound to emerge. Erikson's effort to leapfrog over
these contradictions results in a prodigious mystification.

I am no judge of the modern Indian scene, yet, it would
seem that any student of it bears the burden of proving that
Gandhi's loyalty to India's propertied classes did not gravely
compromise any libertarian influence he may also have
had. Barrington Moore, Jr has written in *Social Origins of
Dictatorship and Democracy*:

*Thus Gandhi's doctrines, despite some characteristic traces of
peasant radicalism, brought water to the mills of the wealthy urban
classes. His ideas competed effectively with Western radical notions
(that were mainly limited to a few intellectuals) and in this way
helped to bring the masses into the movement for independence,
giving it power and effectiveness, while at the same time they*

helped to keep the movement safe for those with property. (1966,
pp. 377–8)

Erikson gets a little peevish in dealing with this point:

Those who would ride roughshod over such 'feudalism' should remember that Gandhi was an excellent judge of what values had retained their actuality, and what kind of actuality was apt to confirm an existing sense of identity – on both sides. (1969, p. 341)

His defensiveness makes sense when one realizes that no amount of identity or higher unity can evade the need to take sides down on earth. At this point, to go along with identity as the focus of value is to go along with the powers that be, even as those powers, the mill owners – and especially their prime representative, one Ambalal Sarabhai (a man who befriended both Gandhi and later Erikson himself) – went along with Gandhi, who they knew 'would keep violence to a minimum' (p. 328). Indeed some 'mill owners used Gandhi for their own purposes at the time and have used his memory ever since' (p. 421).

Erikson chooses, as he must, the side of property. Of course, he has to dress up his choice with a new law of history, which puts Marx on his back even as Marx stood Hegel on his feet. According to Erikson, Gandhi

saw to it that the issue was joined as one among equals. *He explained that the mill owners' assets (money and equipment) and the worker's assets (capacity to work) depended on each other, and, therefore, were equivalent in economic power and dignity. In other words, they shared an inclusive identity, they were – so to say – of one species.* (1969, p. 434)

No amount of pontification about ethics can conceal the moral confusion and political backwardness imposed here by the identity concept. Even as Erikson extols Gandhi's transcendence of mankind's pseudospeciation, he claims that *Satyagraha* 'conceded to the mill owners that their errors were based *only* [my italics] on a misunderstanding of their and their workers' obligations and functions, and he appealed to their "better selves" ' (p. 434). This constituted

an expression of faith in the opponent's inability to persist in harming others beyond a certain point, provided, of course, that the opponent is convinced that he is not only not in mortal danger of losing either identity or rightful power, but may, in fact, acquire

a more inclusive identity and a more permanent share of power. 79
(p. 435)

It is odd for a psychoanalyst to rest with the assertion that someone's 'errors were based only on a misunderstanding' unless he wants to defend him; and it is less than rigorous to write about 'a certain point' without specifying it, unless the intent is to blur things. But the real problem with this passage, the one that helps account for the defensive blurring, lies in the phrase 'rightful power'. Rightful by what standard? To turn mistily to God, as Erikson does, without criticizing what society has established in the way of morality and law is, in effect, to go along with the established order. With the numbing notion that 'law and legal truth' are 'key elements in any national identity', we are left to moralize within the terms of the status quo and to lose grip of the real role played by the moral factor in history. The only recourse is to admonish policemen, factory owners and statesmen for 'brutal righteousness' while losing sight of the material power for which they stand. It is to become blind to the actual content of history, to its outrages and tragedy no less than its hope, and thus to invite not transcendence but repetition.

6 THINGS AND WORDS

*Metapsychology and the
historical point of view*

THE HISTORY of psychoanalysis has been dogged by the
need to find a conceptual location for its theory. Is
psychoanalysis, as Freud hoped it would be, a new science,
or is it a special branch of psychology? Does it or should it
conform to the model of natural science or of social science?
Or is it not a science at all, but rather a canon for the
interpretation of hidden meaning, a hermeneutic? These
questions have been endlessly thrashed out, and without
resolution. Some have taken the lack of theoretical closure
as evidence for a basic defect in psychoanalytic theory.
Another alternative, however, is possible, for new ideas as
well as important lines of clarification of existing ones
generally emerge from the most obdurate theoretical
tangles. What seems nigh insoluble is where theoretical
opportunity lies. The present essay is written out of this
persuasion.

THE DUALISM WITHIN METAPSYCHOLOGY

The debate about the conceptual centre of psychoanalysis
begins, of course, with Freud. We see it surface sharply in
the Fliess letters, then take successive forms in the 'Project
for a scientific psychology', Chapter 7 of *The Interpretation of
Dreams* (1900), the metapsychological papers themselves,
and the great theoretical writings of the later phase. Indeed,
it is not possible to read any of Freud's psychological writings
without being struck by a sense of an underlying tension as
to the theoretical ground of psychoanalytic discourse. As I
shall argue below, Freud's genius lay in holding that tension
in a delicate state of equilibrium, one which permitted
empirical investigation to continue without forcing theoretical closure. By remaining faithful to a certain level of
theoretical contradiction Freud achieved both profundity
and fecundity. He also, however, left a legacy of doubt, some
dead ends, and in some places a sense that contradiction
can lead to confusion. Much of the subsequent history of

psychoanalysis, both here and in Europe, can be regarded
as the working out of that doubt and confusion.

The problematic of the conceptual centre of psychoanalysis may be regarded as contained in a series of linked
antinomies. The most general form taken by these
antinomies is, as pointed out by Paul Ricoeur in his illuminating study, *Freud and Philosophy* (1970), that between *force*
and *meaning*, where force refers to energic dispositions of
objects in the real, measurable world, and meaning to
subjective dispositions of symbolic value, communicable in
language but not otherwise measurable. Within this schema
the force term would then be something objective, or at least
objectifiable, and thus comprehensible within the terms of
natural science, whereas the meaning term would remain
outside the net of natural science, being determinable only
by symbolic means of one kind or another. The two forms
of discourse meet on countless occasions in the development
of Freud's thought. Sometimes the antinomy is implied, as
in the attempt to define 'quality' in purely neurological terms
in the 'Project' (1895), or the attempt to render the mind as
a 'mental apparatus' in *The Interpretation of Dreams*, or in the
first anxiety theory. Sometimes it appears directly but in
subtle form, as when Freud conceptualizes the dream work
as a 'psychical force' that disposes of meaningful dream
thoughts. And sometimes it appears grandly drawn, as in
the formulation of instinct as a borderline concept between
mind and body (1915a). The antinomy continues into clinical
theory in the tension between fantasy and reality and the
problematic of the reconstruction of infantile memories; and
it emerges – in a significantly wrong-headed way – in the
sphere of historical speculation when Freud insists on the
reality of the primal crime as the source of the Oedipus
complex, or on the actual existence of the mythological
figure Moses. Thus from the beginning to the end of his
psychoanalytic writings, in ways that are enormously vari-
egated yet unmistakably consistent, Freud insists on giving
what might be called a *heteronomous* or double registration
to basic psychoanalytic concepts: the objective discourse of
force uneasily combined with the subjective discourse of
meaning.

Although it is something of an oversimplification, it is
useful to recall that Freud inherited, from Helmholtz via
Brücke, a tendency to regard mental events as mechanist-
ically reducible to physical processes, and that the develop-

ment of psychoanalysis consisted of a more or less radical break with this tradition through the discovery of the technique of free association, the mode of interpretation, the replacement of the seduction theory by one of erotic fantasy, and so on (see Stewart, 1967). In any event, the question of the extent to which Freud's break was either less or more radical is often considered a measure of the degree to which he retained 'force' conceptions, borrowed from Brücke and tradition, as against the introduction of 'meaning' conceptions, which are more directly recognizable in terms drawn from clinical practice, with its verbalized dialogue. Since the latter was Freud's one unmistakable innovation, more, since it provides the empirical base without which psychoanalysis could not attain any scientific status, whether natural or social, and since the clinical theory has generated so many rich insights into the real activities of human beings (in contrast to the mechanistic psychiatry it superseded), the tendency to regard the meaning dimension in psychoanalysis as the more progressive one is understandable. A moment's reflection reveals, however, that what is at issue is not whether the meaning dimension is more progressive than the force dimension, but whether the two dimensions can or should be combined in the structure of psychoanalytic theory. In other words, is the force dimension a clumsily designed and antiquated heirloom from nineteenth-century biology, the sentimental attachment to which clutters up the functioning space of contemporary psychoanalysis, or does it rather reflect a level of truth which has to be included in psychoanalytic propositions, even at the cost of some tension with the rest of science?

Surely this will not be an easy matter to decide. A glance at the incomplete record of Freudian antinomies mentioned above reveals them to be at different levels of abstraction and of different logical structure. Recent psychoanalytic thinkers who have attempted to come to grips with this problem have sought a kind of theoretical razor with which to slice away backward features of psychoanalytic theory, while leaving intact its vital fabric. Of late a distinct trend of this kind has emerged, which might serve as a useful launching-point for further inquiry. The line drawn by this trend is suggested by the title of a recent collection of essays in which its point of view is developed: *Psychology versus Metapsychology: Psychoanalytic Essays in Memory of George S. Klein* (Gill and Holzman, eds, 1976). As the editors, Merton

Gill and Philip Holzman, point out, although the essays in
the volume by no means speak in one voice, they bear on
George Klein's 'central preoccupation at the time of his death
– the disentangling of the two theories of psychoanalysis,
the metapsychological, or mechanistic, and the psychological, or one of meaning' (p. 1). It goes without saying
that, of the two theories, it is the metapsychological that is
to be jettisoned, and the psychological retained.

Before analysing the propositions of the antimetapsychological school further, a preliminary source of confusion has
to be at least indicated. The term metapsychology, like all
definitions, expresses a convention of meaning in a state of
historical development. It would be interesting, but beyond
the scope of this paper, to trace fully the various meanings
of the term, both within and outside of Freud's thought. For
our purposes it is sufficient to realize that metapsychology
has generally referred to those parts of psychoanalytic
theory that are not immediately referable to the evidence of
conscious behaviour but that employ instead mediating
concepts such as 'structure', 'drive', 'libido', and so forth.
There are a number of phases in Freud's use of the term,
ably summarized by Gill (1976) in his contribution to this
collection, 'Metapsychology is not psychology'. Freud's
most explicit definition of metapsychology appeared in
his essay, 'The unconscious' (1915b), in the well-known
formulation 'that when we have succeeded in describing a
psychical process in its dynamic, topographical and economic aspects, we should speak of it as a *metapsychological*
presentation' (p. 181). Metapsychology can be regarded as a
set of theoretical propositions at a certain level of abstraction
concerning psychical processes. And as we know, the size
of this set – that is, the number of fundamental metapsychological aspects, or points of view – has undergone changes of
its own. The fact that metapsychology is a set of propositions
rather than a unifying and overarching system is itself an
indication of the theoretical tension within psychoanalysis.
The antimetapsychological school asserts that it can resolve
the tension through its critique of metapsychology. Its
conviction is that metapsychology has been a bad theory
through its retention of physicalistic assumptions. Since
metapsychology has become so identified with these
assumptions, it would be better to regard it as a hopelessly
burdened term that should be abandoned, not in the interests of eliminating theory as such, but in the hope of restoring

a cleaner slate for the reconstruction of a more adequate
theory.

The identification of metapsychology with physicalism is much more than a semantic problem, however. Gill (1976) argues persuasively that Freud's use of the term is ineradicably saturated with natural-science assumptions. The question we posed above is still before us: does this reflect the existence of two theories, one of which can be lopped off to the benefit of psychoanalysis; or does it reflect a double registration, involving both force and meaning, which itself is part of human truth and hence needs to be theoretically represented, albeit in a more adequate way than classical metapsychology was able to accomplish?

The antimetapsychological position generally holds for the two-theory concept. Let us consider a few concrete points of attack. For George Klein, Freud's conception of sexuality 'exists in two versions', the clinical theory having to do with 'values and meanings associated with sensual experiences in the motivational history of a person from birth to adulthood', and the 'drive-discharge theory, [which] *translates* this psychological conception into the *quasi*-physiological terms of a model of energic force that "seeks" discharge' (1969, p. 15; my italics). The latter theory is derived from Freud's fundamental belief upon which his entire metapsychology was constructed: '. . . its tendency to deal with the energic influxes of "stimuli", to discharge them, to reduce the tensions produced by their energic quantity' (pp. 15–16). The two versions are logically distinct, according to Klein, as well as inconsistent; and it is the drive-discharge theory that, though it occupies strategic territory on the heights of metapsychology, fails to account for the data of clinical psychoanalysis. More, the clinical theory has not been given due theoretical status; it is loosely regarded as raw fact, without regard for the subtlety and range of purely psychological mediations that have to be developed. These mediations, however, have to be put in the proper frame of discourse:

. . . whereas the drive-discharge model invites Newtonian metaphors of the motion of particles, the clinical theory implies a system lending itself to description in value terms, for example, actions that are permissible or not in relation to self, that have meanings of must, must not, ought not, and the like . . . Sensual experience always involves such value meaning to self. Thus, in the terms of

THINGS
AND WORDS *the clinical theory, the language of force is replaced by the language* 85
of activity and relationships. (pp. 41–2)

The most thoroughgoing attempt to eliminate energy and
drive from psychoanalytic discourse is that of Roy Schafer
(1976a; see also 1976b). Finding that natural-science terms
have infiltrated even clinical theory, Schafer has attempted
to give Klein's 'language of activity' real flesh. In the conviction that language and thought are mutually generative,
Schafer is currently attempting an ambitious overhauling of
psychoanalytic discourse into the framework of an 'action
language'. In his new mode of discourse, the only substantive is the person and all psychological processes are given
as verbs and adverbs. This reflects Schafer's view that the
distinctive feature of being human is action, and that a
science of the human, psychoanalysis, should express this
feature and not conceal it under terms drawn from the
description of natural phenomena. In the words of the
summary of his remarks made at the Panel on Metapsychology held at the 1975 spring meeting of the American
Psychoanalytic Association:

*Action is human activity of every sort. Defence is action in the
sense that it is an unconsciously performed action that insures one's
refraining from engaging in other actions that one views as somehow
dangerous. Fantasying, rather than being a substitute for action,
is an action of a certain sort, which is initially unconscious and
may not become conscious until interpretation makes that possible.
In contrast, biological and physiological processes may be regarded
as 'happenings', that is, non-symbolic events, definitely not to be
classed with the intrinsically meaningful or goal-directed perform-
ances that characterize specifically human activity. Similarly,
independently occurring events in the environment are also happenings, and it is only the subject's specific action of giving meaning
to these environmental happenings that is of particularly psychoanalytic interest.* (Meissner, 1976, pp. 174–5)

We shall return to some of these propositions below. Beforehand it should be noted that not all those who would
overhaul metapsychology feel the need for an absolute two-
theory model with the excision of natural-science concepts.
Benjamin Rubinstein, for example, is of the opinion that it
is necessary to keep the expanded theory open to neurophysiology mediation, even if energy terms need not appear
directly in psychoanalytic theory. For Rubinstein, we begin

with the person, 'an entity that is exhaustively defined by a particular, normally indissoluble combination of bodily and mental attributes' (1976, p. 239). When however, we begin to abstract anything from that person – for example, a wish – we have taken the first step towards seeing that person as an 'organism', which is an entity describable in the terms of natural science. This first step is unavoidable if we are to understand behaviour, and while it definitely does not commit psychoanalysis to a full-scale depersonalized meta-psychology, it does imply that in an 'expanded clinical theory' psychoanalysis would have to construct models that are compatible with the current state of neurophysiology. One type of such model is that based on information theory (for example, Peterfreund, 1971; Basch, 1976), of which more below.

This train of thought is also that of Robert Holt, one of the most consistent critics of the drive-discharge model. In his important contribution to *Psychology versus Metapsychology*, 'Drive or wish? A reconsideration of the psychoanalytic theory of motivation', Holt (1976) argues vigorously for the replacement by a cognitive-affective theory of wish as the main causal concept of psychoanalysis. Holt convincingly demonstrates the inadequacy, on physiological as well as psychological grounds, of a model of mind as a passive recipient of stimuli that it strives to keep at a minimum, in the manner of a reflex arc. And he is highly critical of Freud's classical conception of instinct as being 'on the frontier between the mental and the somatic', calling it 'one of Freud's baldest commitments to a dualistic interactionism, a solution to the mind–body problem that holds little favour among contemporary philosophers' (pp. 166–7) and Freud's taking 'refuge in a metaphor – here, that of a frontier between territories – instead of committing himself to a conceptual analysis' (p. 167). He none the less insists on developing a substitute theory that is true not only to the facts of human conflict and passion, but is also, in Rubinstein's sense, 'protoneurophysiological', as well as being conceptualized in 'a way that takes serious account of the person's environment, especially the threats and opportunities it presents' (p. 191). Reviving Henry Murray's (1938) concept of 'environmental press' for this latter goal, and pressing beyond Klein's (1967) reformulation of Freud's original concept of wish, Holt goes on to postulate a 'valued mismatch between a perceived and an imagined world'

(p. 191) as the fundamental unit of psychoanalytic
discourse. The 'mismatch' here 'implies a process (which
may be conscious, preconscious, or unconscious) of
comparing *both* a perceptual (input) and a centrally generated pattern (mainly from memory), *and* value judgements
attached to each pattern. In more phenomenological terms,
that means testing an existing and a potential state of affairs
for the degree to which they coincide, as well as for any
significant discrepancy in value' (p. 182; Holt's italics). A
wish would be the state in which we value what might be
more than what is; a fear, conversely, when we value what
is more than what might be.

IS METAPSYCHOLOGY PART OF PSYCHOLOGY?

I shall return to many of these propositions below. Enough
has been presented already, however, to indicate the degree
of theoretical ferment. It is striking to compare the current
state of affairs with that of, say, fifteen years ago. Then
metapsychology appeared to be – at least within the American psychoanalytic community – a seamless web of theory.
This was in good measure due to the theoretical hegemony
of Heinz Hartmann. Through his development of ego
psychology, Hartmann had made a real theoretical advance.
By establishing the contours of a realm of the mind that
stood for reality, ego psychology provided a bulwark against
a kind of depth-psychology reductionism that had plagued
psychoanalysis. Moreover, it provided a set of bridging
concepts to the rest of social and biological science. Hartmann, however, also held that the two territories bridged
by his ego constructs should eventually come under the
same administration. Psychoanalysis was a kind of outpost
of 'normal' science, one that would eventually develop
according to the plan of the original. Thus:

*Progress in physics, or in biology, has repeatedly led to demands
on psychoanalysis for reformulation of its theories in accordance
with these developments in other sciences. In principle there is no
reason why such borrowings could not enrich the tools or the clarity
of analytic thinking, as has happened with other models. But this
question is less one of the theory of science than of the, we could
say, 'practical' needs of a specific science – the empirical question
of the fitness of certain elements of logically well-structured sciences
for other less developed fields.* (Hartmann, 1959, pp. 334–5)

In this he was, to be sure, no more than the heir to Freud's

lifelong conviction that a point-by-point physiological basis
would one day arise alongside of, or even instead of,
psychoanalytic propositions. But while Freud's elaboration
of this idea was fragmentary and episodic, Hartmann
embedded it in ego psychology in a number of sophisticated
and closely reasoned hypotheses, such as that of ego apparatuses and drive neutralization. Moreover, the development
of ego psychology was carried out in an American milieu
both more receptive to psychoanalysis and more concerned
that it be assimilated into the prevailing modes of scientific
activity than had occurred in Freud's experience. In this
regard it should be recalled that the article from which the
above quotation is taken, 'Psychoanalysis as a scientific
theory', was Hartmann's contribution to a symposium,
Psychoanalysis, Scientific Method, and Philosophy (Hook, 1959),
in which the discipline was coming under sharp scrutiny
from philosophers of science.

The details of this critique would take us somewhat far
afield. What deserves emphasis, however, is the influence
that the cultural climate of American science has had on
psychoanalytic thinking. It is strongly likely that the metapsychological systematization from which current psychoanalytic thinkers are trying to extricate themselves is not
merely a residuum of Freud's so-called mechanistic tendencies, but also a product of the need to develop psychoanalytic theory in this country with a view to its integration with
prevailing normal-science practice. Not just Hartmann, but
David Rapaport as well, stands in this tradition. Rapaport,
whose thought decisively influenced many of the thinkers
in the antimetapsychology movement (indeed what Gill is
repudiating includes his own classic paper, co-authored
with Rapaport (1959), 'The points of view and assumptions
of metapsychology'), was above all concerned to bring
scientific rigour to psychoanalytic propositions. And the
crowning achievement of his career, *The Structure of Psychoanalytic Theory: A Systematizing Attempt* (Rapaport, 1959),
succeeded as has no other psychoanalytic work in drawing
basic psychoanalytic propositions together within the net of
normal science: the science of quantification, reproducibility
of results, a carefully designed hierarchy of models, a
specification of 'independent, intervening, and dependent
variables', and so forth. This work became a sort of *summa
psychoanalytica* (and was indeed the conceptual centre-piece
of my own psychiatric training – conducted in the days

when psychoanalysis could claim hegemony in the training of psychiatric residents!). That the period of its ascendancy was a brief one is shown by the antimetapsychological movement itself. Rapaport's work none the less casts doubt on the efforts of this school to locate the problem of psycho-analytic theory in Freud's residual biologism. For the full development of metapsychology was not undertaken by Freud in the name of physics and biology but by Rapaport in the name of 'psychology'. If there is a theoretical stumbling-block in metapsychology, (as I too believe to be the case) then it may not be the best strategy to turn to psychology (as in the title *Psychology versus Metapsychology*) for a way out.

In a time of uncertainty it is understandable to turn towards some source of stability for recourse. But why should the term 'psychology' indicate more for us here than a recently developed and theoretically incomplete practice, replete with fundamental problems of its own? No doubt, in an ideal and logical sense, psychoanalysis should belong with psychology, since its domain is mental life. But in actual practice there is no reason to assume that psychology, as a scientific institution within society, should be prepared to deal with the questions raised by psychoanalysis. If, as Klein and others have held, the problem of *meaning* is the central disclosure of psychoanalysis, and if meaning is imperfectly grasped by Freud's metapsychology, does that make 'mean-ing' into a psychological problem? Why should psychology be equipped to dispose of the problem of meaning, since the principal domain to which it has addressed itself and from which its concepts have arisen has been not meaning but *behaviour*?

Behaviour encompasses an empirical realm of facts about what someone does, feels, or thinks, and each fact has to be defined in a discrete and univocal sense – i.e., as 'this behaviour and not that' – for it to attain empirical status within recognized modes of scientific discourse. Meaning, on the other hand, refers to multivocal relations within a symbolic sphere. And in the sense of the concept unveiled by psychoanalysis, meanings exist in relation to two systems – say, the primary and secondary processes – in such a way that they can never be translatable in any discrete, countable operation. Within psychoanalysis the existence of the notion of meaning is given by a state of tension with the empirical: not a complete rejection of the empirical behaviour (so that,

whatever psychoanalysis will be, it will have to establish
contiguity with psychology), but never a complete yielding
to the status of a discrete fact either. As a result of this
latter property, all attempts to retain what is essential in
psychoanalysis while polishing it up to meet with the
approval of 'normal' scientists have met with rejection by
the latter, who, to the extent that they remain consistent,
ultimately have to throw their lot in with B. F. Skinner and
behaviourism.

It should be emphasized here that I am referring to
psychology as an institutional trend and not to the work
of any particular psychologist. By the former I mean an
organized practice with a definite social structure, a corresponding ideology, and a specific set of paradigms – in Kuhn's
(1962) sense – around which its concepts are organized. A
given psychologist, or group of psychologists, may move
away from these central paradigms. Indeed, under the
influence of a diverse group of factors, including psychoanalysis itself, a sizeable body of psychological work has broken
with the older paradigms of behaviourism. However, to
the extent that this represents a progressive development
within psychology, it provides all the more reason not to
hold out the present discipline as a suitable model under
which psychoanalysis is to be subsumed.

Thus psychoanalysis breaks with 'normal' psychology as
much as it does with biology and physics by introducing the
problem of meaning into its discourse. For this reason, it
might just as well be encompassed within philosophy,
linguistics, history, or even religion, as within psychology.
Since, however, we would have no difficulty in showing
that each of these modes of inquiry is as limited as, or
even more limited than, psychology as a proper home for
psychoanalysis, it may be concluded that they are best left
for now as contiguous territories rather than metropolitan
regions for the psychoanalytic hinterland.

In short, we are back at the starting-point: psychoanalysis
must develop a theoretical centre adequate for its own
domain of discovery, the repressed unconscious. This is
essentially what the antimetapsychological school has in
mind when they write of building on the clinical theory of
psychoanalysis. Here I would agree. So long as clinical
theory is regarded not as a special case of academic
psychology, biology, information theory, or what have you,
but as a disclosure that requires development on its own

terms, we may regard it as a valid starting-point for reconstructing the psychoanalytic model.

Yet the problem remains: in which direction? Let us return
to the attempt to replace metapsychology with psychology.
This attempt founders, I proposed, because the notion of
meaning introduced by psychoanalysis resists description
in empirical terms, while the disclosures of psychology, in
so far as it is constituted as normal science, refer to the
discrete behaviour of an individual person, behaviour that
can be observed, enumerated, and placed in the conceptual
schemata of the scientific model. There is, however, an
alternate way of stating the same proposition: that the non-
reducibility of psychoanalysis to psychology results from
the latter's taking for granted what the former regards as a
problem to be explained, namely, the *person* as an entity.
Normal-science psychology assumes that the *person* exists,
that he (or she) behaves in a demonstrable way, and that he
has a *personality* that can be appreciated as a kind of organism
abstractable from his personhood. It is on this basis, as
Rubinstein points out, that normal-science operations can be
conducted, whether these concern the neurophysiological
substructures of drives or the substructures of ego
psychology. In this sense, of course, metapsychology is
already psychology, although it may well be, as Klein *et al.*
point out, an inadequate, biologistic psychology.

But Freud discovered that one could not take the self-
experience of the person for granted. No doubt there is a
juridical or material basis for forming a provisional working
construct of a person, and no doubt immediate conscious
introspection tends to confirm such a construct. The instrument of psychoanalysis, however, in disclosing the unconscious, revealed a sphere of existence more fundamental
than the conscious, in which the construct of a person could
never be regarded as pre-given. It seems to me that one
cannot take the idea of the unconscious in a real sense by
regarding it as composed of contents that are translatable in
a linear way to the constructions of conscious thought,
including but not limited to those that describe the person,
or self. The attempt to return psychoanalysis to psychology
– including, to a substantial extent, the writings of the
antimetapsychological school – runs into the gravest difficulties when it tries, as it so often does, to map the unconscious into consciously apprehensible terms. Any infor-
mation-system approach, for example, must begin with

this hypothesis, since the concept of information is based on the assumption of countable bits of behaviour. To be consistent with this hypothesis it must hold that the work of interpretation can, at least in principle, completely render the unconscious into awareness. But this short-circuits everything that is fundamental in the problem of repression. It specifically contradicts Freud's observation that 'The dream-thoughts to which we are led by interpretation cannot, from the nature of things, have any definite endings . . .' (Freud, 1900, p. 525) – a statement grounded in practice and referring not even to the unconscious but to pre-conscious, logical derivatives of it. The fact that, as Freud held, there is a 'navel' in 'even the most thoroughly inter-preted dream', 'the spot where it reaches down into the unknown' (p. 525), is to be taken as one of the operational lines of evidence for his eventual conclusion that the uncon-scious *in its innermost nature is as much unknown to us as the reality of the external world, and it is as incompletely presented by the data of consciousness as is the external world by the communications of our sense organs*' (p. 613; Freud's italics).

Now this reflection of Freud's is neither mystical nor yoked to nineteenth-century 'Newtonian' biologistics. Indeed in a very deep sense any psychoanalytic theoretical reconstruc-tion that does not begin with it is being 'Newtonian' with respect to Freud in the same way that physical mechanics is Newtonian with respect to quantum physics: an indetermin-acy that calls into question our very construction of reality gets set aside in the interests of dealing with phenomena at the level of ordinary practice.

I shall return to this theme below. For now we may simply remind ourselves that clinical experience discloses that no interpretation is ever complete and that what is interpreted perpetually slips through the net of designations with which our work attempts to trap it. Moreover, this is no mere technical limitation. One need not be arbitrary or mystical here. There is a convergence of meaning, a certain recurrent specificity that gives us a reliable sense that, for a particular subject, the unconscious contains this set of meanings and not that set. Furthermore, the interpretation and recon-struction of the set of meanings has a real effect, so that analysis need not be, practically speaking, interminable. But just so it need not be terminable, and in general, only the pressure of the objective-fact world of practicality deter-mines the actual end point. Although the set of meanings disclosed by analytic practice has describable characteristics, it cannot be said to be either countable or reducible to conscious categories. Moreover, the 'identity' of the ego, that construction of the self-representations which enables one to say 'I am a person (of this kind)', is a process that occurs decisively with the aid of repression. In other words, unconscious disclosure tends to dissolve a sense of identity. Personhood is constructed in a state of resistance to the unconscious, a resistance critically abetted, as I shall discuss later, by social factors.

Thus the unconscious makes the idea of person problematic. Put slightly differently, it is not the unconscious so much as the admission of a depth dimension to subjectivity – 'psychic reality' – that tends to dissolve the sense of personhood. That is to say, thinking psychoanalytically, one comes upon self-experience in which the categories of a coherent personality are no longer given, but from which they have to be achieved.

The above proposition has been couched, so to speak, in Schaferian language. It is not the 'unconscious' as a mysterious substantive, but we in our psychoanalytic activity who disclose the problematicity of the idea of a person. This proposition is on the level of a first-order clinical generalization. Here 'action language' holds because the proposition encompasses the behaviour of people who identify themselves as psychoanalysts – or analysands. At this level – which is of conscious praxis – the person is indeed the only valid substantive, and activity – that is, real behaviour – forms the valid predicate of the clinical statement.

However, Schafer's attempt to generalize this form of proposition into theoretical statements about the kind of unconscious mind disclosed by the psychoanalytic method immediately runs into difficulty. Put succinctly, his choice of action language, once it moves away from the immediately observable, is forced to assume what it has to explain, namely, the person. The use of propositions in which the subject as person and the subject of the sentence are one and the same – as it has to be if all elements of behaviour are verbs or adverbs – makes it impossibly cumbersome to describe any problematicity of the self. Schafer says as much when he writes 'I think it permissible to set "the person" as one of the unquestioned starting-points of my discussion' (Schafer, 1973, p. 262). This is indeed essential if he is to

use ordinary grammar and language to describe depth-
psychological relata. But what if ordinary language is a form
of discourse that has evolved precisely in order to *avoid*
describing the unconscious end of experience? Thus in
excising heteronomous terms – in this case, natural-science
ones – from metapsychology Schafer may have forfeited a
main opportunity to register unconscious mental life in
theoretical terms. If we cannot know the unconscious
directly, we can at least surround it with modes of registration that give its forms some apprehensible quality. These
modes must be heteronomous with respect to ordinary
conscious experience, else the unconscious collapses into
conscious categories. If natural-science terms fail on a
number of counts, they at least meet the test of heteronomy:
indeed, by suggesting the realm of nature from which we
stem, scientistic discourse stakes out a meritable claim
for itself. Action language, on the other hand, betrays a
fundamental propensity to dedifferentiate the problem of
the unconscious and repression into something trivial.
Action, to be sure, does not lack a role in the description
of basic mental functions. Freud used the concept of action
widely. But it is essential to recognize that for Freud, action
was an element in a dialectical antithesis, not a generic
term for all forms of mentality and behaviour. Action was
construed as the basic mode of the *secondary* system as it
sought to replace the perceptual identity of the primary
system with a thought identity (1900, p. 600). Activity
necessarily involved alteration of the external, objective
world, an alteration by means of which the experiences of
both satisfaction and fright could be mastered. It was
through action, then, that the subject both created itself and
falsified itself at the moment of its creation. A necessary
construction, action, but not to be construed as the domain
of the entirety of mental life without collapsing subjectivity
into immediate consciousness. Indeed, it is with good reason
that analytic practice works in its most fundamental way by
stilling active manipulation of the objective world so as to
turn inward towards deeper levels of the subjective world,
in order, so to speak, to draw the unconscious closer and to
surround it with interpretative work. Schafer's use of action
language, therefore, is not simply a confusing extension of
a hitherto sharply delimited concept: it becomes rather a
kind of corrosive that dissolves the very distinction that

enables us to bring the unconscious into view and think
about it.

To return to the main thread of our inquiry, I observed above that the notion of an unconscious tended to make the idea of a person problematic and that psychoanalysis was in good measure concerned to account for this problematicity. It may be useful now to inquire into another sense in which the idea of a person becomes problematic. At first glance this second sense seems to stand in only the loosest kind of relation to the first. This very ambiguity, however, might prove a useful source of theoretical insight.

Rubinstein (1976) makes the point that scientific propositions about human beings begin with the idea of a person and then proceed to make various operations on that notion so as to bring some deeper aspect of its reality into view. In the sense we have been employing, psychoanalysis may be regarded as that endeavour which reveals that the idea a person forms of himself is not what he takes it to be. In order to admit genuine scientific explanation, however, the idea of person has to be converted to that of organism. For Rubinstein a person is 'an entity that is exhaustively defined by a particular, normally indissoluble combination of bodily and mental attributes' (p. 239). When we 'speak instead about the wishes, feelings, thoughts, etc., that have been abstracted from the person whose wishes, feelings, thoughts, etc., they are supposed to be, we have taken a first step toward description in the mode of natural science, i.e., toward seeing a person as an organism' (p. 239).

With this schema we can take no exception – beyond a certain point. For knowledge in the mode of science, an organismic abstraction of the 'common-sense conceptual scheme' of a person is necessary. The question we put, however, arises before that point. What if the notion of a person contains a hidden dimension that is blurred by the common-sense scheme but is not abstractable into organismic terms? In other words, is Rubinstein, like Schafer, assuming too much when he begins with the idea of a person, even if, unlike Schafer, his propositions move away from a personological action language?

I would hold that there is such a dimension to the idea of a person, one that natural-science discourse side-steps and psychoanalytic discourse discloses, although its existence can be demonstrated without the aid of psychoanalysis. And this is that the idea of a person is always and necessarily

constituted within a social field. More exactly, it occurs
intersubjectively – that is, through the agency of another
who also considers himself a person. Rubinstein himself
recognizes this essential aspect of personhood when he
writes that 'at least to its owner, a dog, too, is a person of
sorts. To most people, however, a jellyfish is not' (p. 239).
The dog and the jellyfish are each organisms that manifest
behaviour. Hence they each have a psychology. But one is
a person because another person cares about him and is
related to him, whereas the other, being outside the web of
care, is denied personhood, becoming neither him nor her,
but remaining 'it'. An organism – 'it' – is no-name; one can
be exchanged for another. A person, however, is named
and recognized by another. He or she thereby acquires an
individuality which only exists in so far as it is enmeshed
with that of others. Here the other can *represent* a person but
cannot be exchanged for him without violating his particular
being. This dual constitution of an individual person –
within one's self and between one's self and others – offers
a theoretical homology to the psychoanalytic finding that
our self-experience and identity are essentially problematic.
But this problematicity dissolves in the abstraction of person
into organism, an abstraction necessary for normal-science
activity.

The natural-science, organismic point of view cannot
encompass the reality of personhood. Something essential
is lost in the translation from intersubjective recognition to
intrasubjective structuralization. Moreover, this something
resides at the heart of psychoanalytic knowledge, and
becomes itself the essence of Freud's contribution, in all its
ambiguity. It is not far-fetched, therefore, to inquire whether
the 'mental life' that is the object of psychoanalysis exists
not so much within the organism as, so to speak, between
the individual as organismic monad and the individual as
constituted intersubjectively. In this sense we would not
regard the unconscious as some set of memories, fantasies,
and so on, a person 'has' within him. Rather might it be
considered as something that is evoked by and occurs within
an intersubjective field. It is important to note that this would
be faithful to the mode of knowledge of the psychoanalytic
situation, which is fundamentally an intersubjective field
rendered accessible to scientific method through the use of
the tool of interpretation. Because unconscious mental life
can only be registered at the conscious ends of this field (the

way light waves are registered by photographic plates that
interrupt them), where it gets translated into the categories
of language and experience, we tend to locate the unconscious within a person. But this may be only a matter of
convenience and might ultimately lead to dead ends if the
intersubjective element is disregarded.

Such a point of view should not be confused with an
'interpersonal' approach, which takes the person for granted
and loses the thread of the unconscious in any radical sense.
Nor should it be regarded as an opening for a Jungian
'collective unconscious', which is a mystical notion lacking
real mediation with everyday life. It is meant, rather, to
pose the question of theoretical heteronomy with Freudian
discourse, that is, thought that holds to a radical view of the
unconscious yet mediates it with the realities of everyday
life – a life of the family, the work-place, and so forth.
In short, it is concerned to further the development of
psychoanalysis as a dialectical psychology.

Freud's genius was to locate a space within which the
human subject constituted itself but was not yet itself. A
locus of radical becoming, the terms of this 'space' were
neither those of the space of the physical world (in the terms
of which he would try, despite all his caveats, to diagram
the 'mental apparatus' or the ego with its 'auditory cap' and
so on), nor of the world of meaning so far as this could be
deduced from what we know of language or indeed of
scientific psychology. Rather, Freud gave us something that
yielded to neither materialism nor idealism but showed us
instead how the elements of the human situation developed
out of negation and contradiction. In short, he provided us
with a dialectic of the person. And accordingly he had
to retain an energic, natural-science term along with a
symbolic, meaning term in his central theoretical propositions. As Ricoeur, himself a phenomenologist, has put it,

the notion of cathexis expresses a type of adhesion and cohesion that
no phenomenology of intentionality can possibly reconstruct [as
Schafer has tried to do with action language]. At this point the
energy metaphors replace the inadequate language of intention and
meaning. Conflicts, formations of compromise, facts of distortion
– none of these can be stated in a reference system restricted to
relations of meaning to meaning . . . the function of the energy
metaphors is to account for the disjunction between meaning and
meaning. (1970, p. 394)

To be sure, this only stakes out the boundaries of the problem. Critical work remains to be done; for if Freud's choice of energy terms leaves open the path towards a radical depth psychology, it still mainly works from a position of weakness. As Ricoeur puts it, it is, after all, an 'energy metaphor'. Taken too literally, the terms collapse psychoanalysis into a vulgar materialism, as the antimetapsychological school fears it may become. But since Freud seems to have all too often wished his energy terms to be taken literally, we are left in the unsatisfactory position of relying on defects in Freud's theorizing to maintain the dialectical structure of psychoanalytic theory! To return to Ricoeur's important presentation:

Freud developed the notion of an energy specific to each system and capable of cathecting representations. There is no denying that the difficulties surrounding this notion are numerous and perhaps insurmountable. The roles assigned to this cohesive force are not easy to co-ordinate; in one role, it is an energy that holds isolated elements together within the whole of a given system; in another, it collaborates in the repression of higher systems through the force of attraction exercised by the previously constituted unconscious system; in a third, it works to promote the process of becoming conscious in opposition to the vigilance of censorship. Nor is it easy to conceive just what relations this cathectic energy proper to each system has with the libido, for the latter, by reason of its organic origin, is neutral with respect to the systems and becomes localized in a given system according to the locus of the representations to which it attaches itself. The most difficult notion of all is the idea of an 'energy that is transformed into meaning'. Nothing, consequently, is firmly settled in this area; indeed, it may be that the entire matter must be redone, possibly with the help of energy schemata quite different from Freud's . . . *the co-ordination of the economic language and the intentional language is the main question of this epistemology and one that cannot be avoided by reducing either language to the other.* (pp. 394–5; my emphasis)

THING PRESENTATIONS
AND *WORD* PRESENTATIONS

There is one point about which all agree: if psychoanalysis is to develop as a science, then its theory must be put in a proper relationship to the evidence obtained by its method. There is, so to speak, a primary zone of reliable clinical knowledge corresponding to those facts disclosed within

the psychoanalytic situation; and there are then, around this 99
zone, other concepts that may be advanced in order to render
the primary knowledge more coherent. In this respect,
'metapsychology' is simply to be regarded as such a
secondary zone of theory – that is, a metatheory. It should
not be conceived as a substitute for clinical theory. Those
who would dispense entirely with metatheory have therefore the twofold task of demonstrating both the inadequacy
of the existing natural-science metapsychology and the self-
sufficiency of clinical theory. We have already found that
the first of these propositions was dealt with considerably
more successfully than the second. Indeed it seems that to
allow theory to proceed at a purely clinical level – that is,
without referring it to any other realm, even the inadequate
one of biology – is to allow psychoanalytic thought to
collapse into a common-sense psychology without depth or
penetration. Put another way, what clinical practice and
theory disclose as the primary discovery of psychoanalysis
is the repressed unconscious mind. Without this entity,
psychoanalysis literally ceases to be. And yet the repressed
unconscious cannot be adequately comprehended theoretically within the terms of clinical theory because the unconscious is heteronomous with respect to ordinary language
and psychological categories in general. But if a natural-
science model will not serve to explain the heteronomous
nature of the unconscious, what will?

In order to make headway into the problem it will be
necessary to have some properties of the unconscious in
mind.

My plan is to proceed phenomenologically, through a
precise delineation of the structure of consciousness as
revealed in the psychoanalytic situation. Our knowledge
begins with and returns to consciousness as revealed by
speech; and we assume, as Freud did throughout, that
consciousness acts as a kind of sensory screen registering
simultaneously the input from the objective world and the
deeper structures of subjectivity, including the unconscious.
In order to account for this dependence of consciousness on
verbalizable thought, as well as for the presence of deeper
structures of subjectivity that could not be given in verbal
terms, Freud, after much reflection, finally hit on a mode
of registration that seemed most adequate to reality. As
presented in 'The unconscious', it made use of two concepts,
the *word* presentation and the *thing* presentation, to account

for the distinction between conscious thought and the unconscious. As these terms will also be leading ones in this essay, I quote the relevant passage in full:

> *What we have permissibly called the conscious presentation of the object can now be split up into the presentation of the* word *and the presentation of the* thing; *the latter consists in the cathexis, if not of the direct memory-images of the thing, at least of remoter memory-traces derived from these. We now seem to know all at once what the difference is between a conscious and an unconscious presentation. The two are not, as we supposed, different registrations of the same content in different psychical localities, nor yet different functional states of cathexis in the same locality; but the conscious presentation comprises the presentation of the thing plus the presentation of the word belonging to it, while the unconscious presentation is the presentation of the thing [Sachvorstellung] alone. The system Ucs. contains the thing-cathexes [Sachbesetzungen] of the objects, the first and true object-cathexes [Objektbesetzungen]; the system Pcs. comes about by this thing-presentation being hyper-cathected through being linked with the word-presentations corresponding to it. It is these hypercathexes, we may suppose, that bring about a higher psychical organization and make it possible for the primary process to be succeeded by the secondary process which is dominant in the Pcs. Now, too, we are in a position to state precisely what it is that repression denies to the rejected presentation in the transference neuroses: what it denies to the presentation is translation into words which shall remain attached to the object. A presentation which is not put into words, or a psychical act which is not hypercathected, remains thereafter in the Ucs. in a state of repression.* (1915b, pp. 201–2; Freud's emphasis)

I have quoted this passage at length because it seems to me to contain the foundation-stone of psychoanalytic theory. If Freud's central discovery was of repression and the unconscious, then we have come upon the nuclear formulation of the theoretical meaning of that discovery. And it is 'metapsychological' without being biologistic or lapsing into personological idealism. Freud's proposition was, rather, a radical statement of the actual schism in the human subject, and its basis in the real, material world. This latter point awaits demonstration. For now, however, we can see that it is a proposition built of heteronomous elements: *words* and *things*. We may therefore conclude that the essential dialectic to be preserved in psychoanalytic theory is one that

encompasses a *word* term along with a *thing* term. We thus
postulate these as fundamental aspects of any genuinely
psychoanalytic proposition, and further claim that the goal
of such propositions is to explicate the various relations that
arise between *words* and *things* in the life of the human
subject – that is, in so far as *words* and *things* become
presentations, the content of thought.

The problem, of course, will be to make a little clearer just
what is meant by these mysterious concepts, in particular
that of the '*thing*'. The term itself connotes the maximum of
indefiniteness, which property is in line with Freud's notion
that the *thing* is a mental element that resists verbal translation. At the same time, everything we know about the
power and primacy of unconscious mental life argues
strongly against regarding its contents as vague or indefinite.
Moreover, there is little more that Freud had to say about
this, the most central of his concepts – and that little
came before the quotation just cited,[1] and is relatively
fragmentary. Faced with ineffability of this kind, the tendency is to fall back into tautology: the *thing* presentation
is the content of the unconscious; ergo, the unconscious
contains *thing* presentations. Our job is to go further than
that and to introduce some explanatory order into these
puzzling matters. To do so, however, will require a
digression into some of the philosophical pre-conditions
underlying psychoanalytic knowledge.

THE HUMAN AND NATURAL WORLDS

What we are asking is this: what must the world be like in
order that humans may arise within it having an unconscious
mind with *thing* experience? The flaw of traditional metapsychology was in the assumption that this question could be
answered within natural-science discourse, whereas the
flaw of the revisionists lies in the assumption that it can be
answered within psychology. Both of these viewpoints
overlook something decisive: that to comprehend the unconscious we must take the *relation* between the self and the
world into account; and to do this, the actual structure of
the world must be given conceptual weight. The original
metapsychology went half-way towards this goal by using
natural-science thinking to comprehend that part of the
world comprising the brain and other biological structures.
But this is only *part* of the world we are concerned with. The

remainder of the world is the *human world* itself: the world of social institutions and culture.

The point may seem rather trivial and self-evident. Psychoanalysis does not have to be reminded of its deep interest in culture, and psychoanalytic theory, whether through Hartmann's (1939) notion of adaptation or Erikson's (1959) psychosocial point of view, has long allowed for the influence of the social world in the formation of the psyche. None the less, it is my contention that the relationship has not yet been appreciated in a deep enough way, and indeed that it must be thoroughly rethought.

One might go so far as to say that the key to the theoretical problem I have been posing lies in a deep enough appreciation of the human world. We may put the matter as follows: if the task is to understand the heteronomy of the unconscious, then the solution must lie in grasping a split within the world as radical as the one psychoanalysis discovers within the psyche. If the problem of the unconscious lies in the relation between the self and the world, then the world's disjunctions must be adequate to explain those within the self (as the self's must be adequate to explain those within the world). The fact that it is possible to describe the world as composed of a 'natural' part describable by natural science and a 'human' part describable by social science indicates that the central problem of metapsychology lies neither in the natural science of organisms nor in the social science of culture, but in the *interface between nature and culture*. If the existence of two tiers of science indicates that man lives in an uneasy relation with nature, then the unconscious must be primarily grasped as the indwelling, subjective record of that uneasy relationship. To study it, then, basic metapsychological science must be the science of the exchanges between the human and the natural worlds. Just what form such a science may take will be discussed presently. Whatever it is, however, it will have to draw on but not be the same as natural and social sciences. That is, an adequate metapsychological system must be grounded in a knowledge of organisms – neurophysiology, and so forth – and it must be grounded in the social sciences as we know them – the sciences of those parts of the world suffused with human value: politics, economics, and so on. But in itself, metapsychological science belongs neither to the science of that human world nor to the science of the

natural world, but occupies the space where the two worlds
are related to one another.

In order to explore this region, we have to be careful about
our terms. The existence of the unconscious reflects the split
between the human and natural world. The unconscious
itself, however, should not be thought of as a simple unmediated representative of 'nature'. That would only bring us
back to the predicament of the natural-science metapsychology. True, *thing* presentations are relatively remote from
the influence of civilization when contrasted to *word* presentations. That, however, does not make them the immediate
registration of biological instincts, as a simplistic id
psychology would have it. The *thing* presentation refers to
an event going on in a human mind, which, because it is a
mind, is an entity that has already broken with nature. The
thing presentation looks back at nature across the gap created
when the self defined itself as distinct from its 'natural'
primordium. It is a human, mental event, protosymbolic
because it cannot be named, but none the less outside the
scope of natural science.

As our argument proceeds it becomes increasingly difficult to take 'nature' for granted, or to regard it as an entity
independent of human activity. The latter assumption is the
backbone of natural-science method, the first step of which
is to choose some part of the world and strip it of human
value – that is, see it as it is outside of our care about it or
influence over it. For some parts of the world – for example,
galaxies in outer space – this kind of reduction works quite
well, since the object under study is in fact quite indifferent
to human value. For other parts of the world – for example,
forests – the reduction can work tolerably well as long as it
is kept in bounds, that is, so long as we do not pretend to
be making a complete statement about the forest as we might
about the galaxy, but recognize that there is an extent to
which the forest is different because man has acted on it and
is still acting on it. For yet other parts of the world – for
example, the economic role of the state – the reduction yields
slim results because of the heavy influence human value
and choice has at every level of economic activity. Indeed,
the use of quantitative, natural-science models at the level
of economic description often serves to mask the reality of
the situation for ideological purposes (see Letelier, 1976).
And finally, there are parts of the world – for example, the
subjective lives of persons – where a reduction to organ-

ismic functioning in fact bypasses the phenomenon to be comprehended.

In none of these examples is a component of 'nature' absent. Yet in each of them we determine the degree of naturality not by reference to an absolute standard but in relation to the degree of human value that is in fact embedded in the phenomenon. When this degree of value drops out for practical purposes, we go ahead and declare that part of the world 'nature' and use natural-science methods to study it. Since we assume that such parts of the world pre-dated us with our values, and since natural-science method has yielded so much mastery over nature (whatever value may be placed on such mastery), there is a tendency to think of nature as the basic category and the value-saturated parts of the world as somehow secondary or derivative. But in truth, though we are undoubtedly rooted in nature, and may only be secondarily estranged from it, whatever this nature is can be approached only from the position of a value-laden creature. Any part of the universe man has called 'nature' has already been tramped over by him. It has been gazed upon, named, and cared about to begin with; only secondarily may it be considered free from us.

For this reason, when we are dealing scientifically with those parts of the world – such as economics or psychology – where 'nature' and value are in fact mixed, we need a different standard to describe the natural aspect from that used in the natural sciences, where reduction could be made with little or no loss. Here a reduction wrenches the natural aspect away from that relationship to the human which in fact constitutes the essential feature of the phenomenon to be understood. Behaviourist psychology and so-called 'value-free' economic theory stand as grotesque monuments to the damage done when the natural and the human are severed from their true relationship to each other. I have already concluded that the prime theoretical task for a psychoanalytic metapsychology consists of appreciating the interface between the natural and human worlds as this works itself out subjectively. Now it may be possible to describe a way of looking at this relationship that does justice to psychoanalytic evidence.

Mysterious as it may be in an ultimate sense, from the standpoint of human practice, nature in all its myriad forms always has one property: it stands for what *comes before and is to be overcome by human activity*. As a result of human activity, the 'natural' balance is altered. The parts of it that actually change and are drawn into the human balance lose their standing in nature and become 'civilized', while what remains outside of the net of civilization remains 'natural' . . . *until* it is subjected to the next wave of human activity.

Just how oppositional civilization and nature need to be is a matter of profound concern. Freud, as is well known, took a harsh view and saw the antagonism as immutable and immortal: '. . . the principal task of civilization, its actual *raison d'être*, is to defend us against nature' (1927, p. 15). Other, more harmonious views can and, in my opinion, should be taken of the relation – but whatever they may be, we know nature as that which meets our activity and stands outside it, whether this be the wind and stars or our own death.

If, from the standpoint of civilized activity, nature comes 'before', then civilized activity itself comes afterwards. In other words, temporality, the passage from earlier to later, is an ingredient of the nature–civilization dialectic. From the standpoint of human activity, nature is the *past*, and civilization is the continuously emergent product of over-coming the past. Civilization, then, must be grasped as the summation of all its moments of overcoming nature (whether through harmony or opposition). In short, civiliz-ation with respect to nature is given in *history*, and the boundary between the human world and the natural world is a historical boundary. Since the study of this boundary is essential for the development of an adequate metapsycho-logy, it may be said that such a metapsychology needs to be informed by a *historical point of view*. This does not mean that either psychology or metapsychology is to be reduced to history (any more than to biology), but that they must be grasped from a perspective which views human life as subject to the forces of history.

In so far as we regard anything from a historical point of view, we are saying in effect that we are considering its various aspects with regard to their different relations to history in general. In the case of psychology, for example, it must be the case that the human mind as a whole is subject

to historical development, since in 'prehistory' there is little
that is recognizably human. On the other hand, it is obvious
that not all aspects of psychology change in the same way
or at the same rate. Certain features evolve relatively quickly
in relation to society itself – for example, what is termed
'super-ego'; others – one thinks of instinctual structures –
show a much more sluggish rate of change. Indeed, it is
these latter that have been popularly termed 'human nature',
entirely in accordance with the view that nature is what
resists history.

It would seem, therefore, that the historical point of view
works in a relational way with a pair of categories, one
designating what is in synchrony, so to speak, with the
historical development of society, the other referring to what
is relatively invariant across historical time. Let us call
these the *historical* and *transhistorical*, respectively. I must
emphasize that these terms are not absolutes, that is, that
everything human must be regarded as having both
historical and transhistorical features. The categories are
simply a way of calling attention to the need to analyse
each instance concretely so as to determine its particular
historicity and transhistoricity. The historical point of view
is essentially a reformulation of the nurture/nature polarity
in order to analyse it more rigorously. The transhistorical,
then, corresponds to nature – not a nature outside of us, but
a nature as it has entered into the human situation and
become related to history. This is the necessary step that
must be taken if any account of nature versus nurture is not
to become mechanistic or trivial.

It is assumed widely – and undoubtedly correctly – that
both social and biological factors are essential ingredients in
being human, that is, that neither *nature* nor *nurture* alone
suffices to explain what makes us who we are. What is
generally overlooked, however, is that these 'factors' cannot
be simply or linearly considered to react one on the other,
as they pertain to different states of being, or ontologies.
The 'biological' cannot itself interact with the 'social', any
more than fish can interact with interest rates. In the practical
attempt to relate nature and nurture to each other in the real
life of the human being, one category will become subsumed
under the other unless each is translated into an intermediate
discourse responsive to the dialectic between their
respective ontological forms. In ego psychology as it is
generally construed since the seminal work of Hartmann,

for example, an ambitious attempt is made to unite social
and biological 'factors' in the theory of adaptation. In the
real practice of ego psychology, however, such a union is
little more than an abstract possibility. It turns out that
the leading categories of Hartmannian ego psychology are
prearranged to give greater weight to the biological, for
example, the notion of 'ego apparatuses', which is inherently assimilable mainly to a physicalistic, natural-science
model. Accordingly, the social interactant loses its own
dynamism; it becomes necessarily washed out into the
'average expectable environment', within which the intricate realities of social conflict and history are turned into a
common reagent for the physicalized ego.

This brings us once again to the historical point of view as
a source of the intermediate discourse necessary to restore
a genuine dialectic between nature, the individual and
society. By introducing the distinction between the *historical*
and the *transhistorical*, we are able to take into account
the *tension* between society and biology without having to
collapse one into the other. This is faithful to the empirical
base of psychoanalysis – the lived life of the human. In the
concrete living of life it has been well established that there
is no independence between biological and social factors.
In the words of Maurice Merleau-Ponty, 'in fact and in
principle, it is impossible to establish a cleavage between
what will be "natural" in the individual and what will be
acquired from his social up-bringing. In reality the two
orders are not distinct; they are part and parcel of a single
global phenomenon' (1964, p. 108). To cite but two
examples: Stoller's (1968, 1976) work on gender identity
demonstrates that what is socially made of protoplasmic
gender is operative from the earliest days of an individual
life; while from the other side it has been experimentally
demonstrated that, even for that most 'cultural' of products,
speech, the infant is born preadapted to respond to sounds
of human origin (Friedlander, 1970).

At no point, then, does it make sense to say that a person
has passed from an 'animal' – for example, biological – phase
to a socialized one. Nor is it more than a metaphorical
manner of speaking to say that we have an 'animal' id and
a 'social' ego. On the other hand, it is equally unsatisfactory
to obliterate the distinction between an element that is
relatively close to what society construes as dominant
interest and one that lies remote from that interest. The latter

category is what we call 'nature'. Note that the distinction is posed from the social side, as being one of a greater or lesser conformity to socially determined standards. This is because in life as it is concretely lived, the issues that devolve on to the nature/nurture split are always matters of political concern. And they are of vast social import. Whatever the source of the distinction between 'natural' and 'social' elements, a great deal that is of social significance, from sex and race to morality and madness, is defined in such terms.

But it is of *social*, not biological, significance: hence the need to introduce the historical/transhistorical split as a way of describing the distinction – within the unity of human experience – between what is immediately linked to dominant historical-social interest and what is relatively resistant to such interest. Put abstractly, it can be said that in all cases social and biological factors are involved. The historical point of view, however, allows us to bypass the separation of elements immanent in abstract characterization, and to confront instead the actual dialectic between 'nature' and 'society' as it is lived in everyday life. From this standpoint we can regard development as a continuous gradient from the relatively transhistorical mode of early infancy to the relatively historical (or historicized) mode of adult life.

VARIETIES OF HISTORICAL ANALYSIS
The senses in which I use the concept of history must now be elaborated and made more specific. They are three, although springing from a common conviction.

First, I mean to introduce the historical as a broad designation of the type of endeavour to which psychoanalysis belongs. I mean it here in the sense that Ricoeur (1970) employs when he writes that 'Analytic experience bears a much greater resemblance to historical understanding than to natural explanation' (p. 374), or 'analytic theory is not to be compared with the theory of genes or gases, but with a theory of historical motivation. What differentiates it from other types of historical motivation is the fact that it limits its investigation to the semantics of desire' (p. 375). That is, analysis is a historical mode of investigation, not of society, but of the subject. The introduction of this perspective was what, more than anything else, constituted Freud's break with the organicist psychiatry of his day. It persists in the 'genetic' point of view in metapsychology, and is given theoretical space in Hartmann's adaptational point of view and Erikson's psychosocial theory. It is my contention, however, that the historical point of view has been played down and/or distorted as prevalently construed by psychoanalysis. It would be distracting to pursue the critique in any depth at this point. For now, all that need be said is that the genetic point of view, while indispensable, does not begin to take the weight of a historical approach seriously enough, since it remains bound to the individual person and forsakes any real investigation of the social matrix within which individuality is defined.

As for Hartmann, he tended to discount the importance of historical analysis altogether and his approach was heavily weighted towards the biological and natural-scientific. Thus (from 'Psychoanalysis as a scientific theory'):

while I just spoke of the study of the individual's 'life history', it would be misleading (though it actually has been done) to classify this aspect of analysis as a historical discipline. This misinterpretation may be traceable to its comparison with archaeology, which Freud occasionally uses. It is true that most analytic knowledge has been gained in the psychoanalytic interview and that the concern with developmental problems refers primarily to the history of individuals. But this should not obfuscate the fact that the aim of these studies is (besides its therapeutic purpose) to develop law-like *propositions which then, of course, transcend individual observations.* (1959, p. 324; my emphasis, placed to indicate how Hartmann raises a certain ideology to a self-subsisting fact, and moreover gives the impression that historical science is incapable of developing law-like propositions)

Finally, as to Erikson, I have already attempted to demonstrate (see page 68 above) how his psychosocial theory is mystifying from both a psychoanalytic and historical standpoint, from which it may be concluded that psychosocial theory is in need of a fresh start.

The second sense in which I use the concept of the historical here pertains to the above-mentioned fresh start. To be more exact, I have in mind a return to a perennially radical departure that was made before the birth of Freud. I refer to the only systematic and scientific view of history worthy of apposition to psychoanalysis, namely, Marxism. I have written elsewhere of Marxism's suitabilities and limitations for such apposition (Kovel, 1976), and there is no need to detail the arguments of that essay here, especially as some of the points will return as we proceed. It should be pointed out to the reader who may not have had the opportunity to familiarize himself with the development of Marxist thought, however, that what is advanced here as a Marxist view of history is not the same as what we in the West have come to identify with the name of Marxism. This latter view, which Holt (1965), in one of the few American psychoanalytic articles even to mention the subject, characterized as being one of man as 'a pawn in an economic process' (p. 152), represents in fact an attenuated and vulgarized variant of Marxism – one implicated in many real historical developments, but by no means to be confused with the essence of Marx's view of history.

For Marx, man has indeed *become* a kind of economic pawn, but is not to be considered as such in his essence. This essence is that of a socially self-transformative active agent, one who acts on nature to make the world and is dialectically made by it. The record of man's self-transformation is history. Thus Marxism is, before anything else, the historical vision as such. We do not become what we are outside of a historical process. That this process should turn on class struggle happens to be the factual content of history. It is, however, logically secondary in Marxism to the historical point of view as a determinative framework. The historical dimension of Marxism is the successor, within the terms of scientific discourse, to the vividness of the animistic world-view. The bourgeois revolution deadened the world and froze it into an ahistorical world of a Kantian 'thing-in-itself' and a knowing subject transcendentally removed from materiality. It took Marx to restore a sense of motion to the things of the world – a trajectory given by concrete human activity, or praxis.[2]

Freud's thought is also saturated with a sense of history. But in contrast to Marx, it is a fatalistic history shaped by a kind of prearranged destiny, that of the primal crime and its long shadow of guilt. For Freud, history is the eternal return of this sense of guilt, modified only by the still small voice of reason. For Marx, on the other hand, history is a process that is continually under way, albeit with periodic revolutionary transformations.

Our investigation now is not of society but of the self; and we are interested in exploring the extent to which our 'psychology' can be said to be comprehensible in terms of Marx's principle of historical development. Despite a certain psychological indifference and short-sightedness – which in

my opinion has cost Marxism dearly as a social theory –
Marx leaves no doubt that our psyche, along with everything
human, is to be regarded as a historical product. Indeed,
even that which we call sensory input, and which Freud
regarded, and we generally regard today, as biologically
given, Marx saw as the outcome of history: 'The *development*
of the five senses is a labour of the whole previous history
of the world' (1844a, p. 309).

It is far from my intention to subsume psychoanalysis
under a Marxist perspective, or to regard the historical
perspective as a shibboleth. For one thing, even though
Marxism is in my opinion clearly superior to other social
theories, it is not itself either a finished product or a total
system of explanation capable of subsuming all else. Moreover, in its very incompleteness it stands in as much need
of the psychoanalytic point of view as psychoanalysis does of
it. My working hypothesis is only that the various theoretical
dilemmas within psychoanalysis outlined above stand a
greater chance of resolution if a Marxist historical perspective
is kept in mind.[3]

This brings us to the third and most critical sense in which
I shall be using the concept of history. Critical, because it is
the attempt to ground history concretely in the immediate
flux of life, and from there to see it manifested in the
categories of psychoanalysis. It is not enough to invoke
macrohistorical structures such as class. An analysis must
comprehend how the various large-scale forces of history
define everyday life as it is lived at work, in the family,
through childhood, and, indeed, in the life of the body.
What we learn psychoanalytically is the *subjectification* of
everyday life – the way immediate social existence is registered subjectively under the peculiar conditions of human
psychic representation. From the standpoint of the psyche,
the conditions of everyday life provide the objects of desire
(including the body). What Marxism provides in the way of
a dialectical history has to be transcribed, then, into a
dialectics of the objects of everyday life, suitable for representation in the dialectical psychology of psychoanalysis.[4]

In this way the particular historical/transhistorical
configuration of psychoanalytic concepts can be explored
beyond the confines of clinical theory without falling into
biologism. Consider, for example, the family, and those
elements of mental life that reflect human relations within
the family. We know that some sort of family has existed

PSYCHOHISTORY transhistorically, but that major alterations in the type of   112
family have occurred according to the exigencies of each
historical epoch. It is essential to realize, moreover, that the
historical changes in family structure are only in part – and
secondarily – determined by psychological or 'biological'
factors. At the risk of oversimplifying a highly complex
relationship that deserves much fuller treatment than the
scope of this essay can provide, we can say that family
structure varies according to what might be called the
prevailing relations of production. Production here refers to
the aggregate of ways a society has for transforming nature.
Each society is organized around a particular mode of
production based on a number of primarily non-psychological factors – for example, the source of wealth, the
level of technology, the structure of social domination and
legitimacy, and so forth. Thus the family structure of a pre-
industrial agrarian society (extended patriarchal) is different
from that of, say, early industrial capitalism where
production is based on wage labour (and the family becomes
'nuclear', and patriarchal control slackens); and this in turn
is distinct from a contemporary or late capitalist structure,
where production is largely carried out by machines and the
consumption of commodities is emphasized (and the family
becomes child centred and concerned with the cultivation
of desires).

Now there is more to the relations of production than
these economic factors, and there is more to the family than
its role in the relations of production. But the particular
configuration of human objects provided by the family to
the developing child is determined by the historical as
well as the transhistorical. Indeed we find that the given
dialectical tension in any era between the historical and
transhistorical is what determines the structures of
emotional conflict – and hence the content of unconscious
fantasy and the organization of instinctual life. From this
standpoint, the Oedipus complex is no simple universal,
but a universal determined by the particular tension between
the transhistorical function of the family – given here as the
formation of a differentiated self – and its historical role in
the provision of objects of power, sexual choice, idealization,
and so on.

The transhistorical functions of the family are reflections
of what is 'natural' or 'biological' in us, namely, infantile
helplessness, the need for attachment, separation–individu-

ation, and so forth. While each of these functions is greatly
influenced by the way the prevailing form of social organization affects family life, they are none the less primarily
transhistorical, in that it would be inconceivable to think of
a human being growing up and becoming human without
undergoing these experiences. The transhistorical, roughly
speaking, defines our needs. A measure of whether a need
is transhistorical would be an absolute inability to adapt to
its absence. This would occur, for example, in the case of
food. The case of sexuality and needs for human contact and
attachment are of course much more complicated. We see
the transhistorical clearly at work, however, in instances of
hospitalism, where lack of interpersonal contact at a certain
age seems incompatible with becoming human. It is the
transhistoricity of factors such as this that makes the 'biologically' organized studies of, say, René Spitz (1965) scientifically convincing.

It may also be claimed that the symbolic function itself,
including language, as well as the structuralization of the
mind into conscious, preconscious and unconscious
regions, is transhistorical. We can say this empirically, since
human culture in all times and places is incomprehensible
without assuming the universality of language, symbolism
and the unconscious mind; and we can say it deductively,
as these functions can be shown to be dependent on other
transhistorical structures.

With respect, for example, to language and the symbolic
function, we can postulate two broad transhistorical precur-
sors: (1) inborn brain structures, including those generative
of grammatical patterns; and (2) early object relations,
including object loss, which spurs the symbolic-linguistic
function as an effort at reunion. These provide the scaffolding upon which *thing* and *word* presentations are strung,
the former pointed towards the pole of nature and the latter
towards history – without either *thing* or *word* belonging
fully to nature or history as such.

This halting attempt at theory is directed at giving us a
way of talking about the unfathomability of language
without being mystical or scientistic. For it is language as
the register of human subjectivity which comprises the field
of psychoanalytic inquiry. Psychoanalysis is about words –
and about not being able to find the right words. Even when,
in good clinical work, we feel we have come upon the truth
of the unconscious, we are more truthful still when we

recognize the dropping-off point where language descends
into the *thing*-world.

Such a moment is a finding of the right words, words that most closely describe the truth of the lived situation. But at the same time these words, or, rather, their utterance, indicates an emptiness, a negative – a space within experience whose circumference is describable in verbal terms but whose inmost regions lack any form of known registration. To discover the unconscious is like hacking one's way through an impenetrable jungle only to come at once upon a precipice beyond which is an unfathomable drop. It is a moment of absolute lucidity joined with absolute ignorance. In this way we say that *word* presentations are representations of *thing* presentations – that is, the unconscious is known through its derivative representations. Here the word 'representation' deserves a close look. The prefix 're' indicates 'backward', 'turned around'. Thus the representation is the negative of the presentation. It is the union of identity with oppositeness.

The lucid element of this dialectic, its circumference, can be given in words. They are organized into propositions the contents of which are as variable as the human spirit can devise – and there seems to be no limit to this.

The *thing*-presentational derivatives are what we glimpse as we look over the precipice to which analytic work brings us. They are fragments of a discourse – verbal shards without grammar – which is to say, without the logical relations that ordinarily align verbal discourse with the real, external world. In these *thing*-presentational derivatives discrete boundaries between the elements of the *word*-presentational reconstruction disappear: the self, the other, and their respective bodies merge. Moreover, each element fuses with the external world. Instead of grammatical discourse we get a flux depending on the shifting immediate impact of the patient's consciousness with the surround defined by the analytic setting. In the work of the analysis – and, it can perhaps be added, in any creative process – the fundamental task is to reformulate a more adequate representation in words once the *thing*-presentational fragments have made their impact on experience.

This is of course an intersubjective and empathic project, and not a technical job of transliteration. It is also – as befits the domain of the *word* – profoundly historical in its own

right. But this brings us to matters we can no longer pursue   115
here.

NOTES

1. Freud first dealt with the notion of the *thing* in his pre-
psychoanalytic monograph, *On Aphasia* (1891). The relevant
passages are cited in an appendix to 'The unconscious' (1915b,
pp. 213–15). There are also numerous insights into the concept
scattered throughout the 'Project for a scientific psychology'
(1895; see especially pp. 327f, 331, 365–6, in which he introduced
the intersubjective dimension and the communicative role of
speech as the source of *word* presentations). He returned to the
matter in *The Interpretation of Dreams* (1900, pp. 295–6) but did not
elaborate it again until 'The unconscious', where he used it in
the understanding of schizophrenia. Other references in his later
writings show no development of the concept.

2. For an elaboration of this insight, see Lukács (1923).

3. There is little chance of offering a workable guide to a field as
vast and controversial as Marxist writings within the limits of
this essay. Marx's writings themselves are a difficult, if
indispensable, source. The reader should consult *Writings of the
Young Marx on Philosophy and Society* (Easton and Guddat, eds,
1967), for his early, or 'philosophical', phase, and *Capital* (esp.
vol. 1, 1867) for his later, or 'scientific', writings. Two good
modern introductions are Ollman (1971) and Avineri (1968).

4. Among the many works that have advanced this conception of
psychoanalysis those of Otto Fenichel are of particular interest,
coming as they do from a pillar of Freudian orthodoxy. Fenichel
was, however, also a Marxist who made a number of important
contributions to the line of thought developed in this essay. See
his 'The drive to amass wealth' (1938) and 'Psychoanalysis as
the nucleus of a future dialectical-materialistic psychology' (1967).
See also Wilhelm Reich, 'Dialectical materialism and
psychoanalysis' (1929), and my 'The Marxist view of man and
psychoanalysis' (Kovel, 1976).

PART THREE

THE POLITICS
OF 'PSY' PRACTICE

IN HIS first thesis on Feuerbach, Marx defines revolutionary activity as 'practical-critical'. It is no exaggeration to claim that everything in Marxism stems from this principle, which demands that we consistently examine everything we *do* from the standpoint of its role in history, which is to say, class struggle. It is also no exaggeration to claim that the prevailing 'psy' professions (the term is drawn from Castel, Castel and Lovell, 1982) of psychiatry, psychology, psychoanalysis, psychiatric social work, and so forth, consistently refuse to carry out this examination. Indeed, an opacity to the actual social basis of psy practice is one of the defining features of these professions. Generally speaking, this deficit is covered over by a thick membrane of technocracy, which deflects any questioning in advance, indeed, rules out the possibility of questioning, the 'pure, value free, and scientific' pursuit of Mental Health.

The essays of this section comprise various attempts at a Marxist critique of psy practice. They were not greeted with wild enthusiasm by the centres of psy power in the United States. The first, 'Therapy in late capitalism', picks up the themes of my second book, *A Complete Guide to Therapy* (1977), and moves them in a more radical direction than the scope of that work allowed. The essay was my first extended article for *Telos*. It also manifested (as note 1 indicates) a collective project organized around the aim of founding a journal of radical cultural studies. The journal never saw the light of day, but the extended series of discussions we undertook to prepare it proved an invaluable experience. In fact, this was my first 'seminar' in Marxist theory, which appears in the first part of the essay as turned towards the critique of subjectivity. 'Therapy in late capitalism', may also be read as preparatory for *The Age of Desire*, the writing of which began some two years later.

'Values, interests and psychotherapy' was originally given at a panel discussion before the American Psychiatric

Association annual convention in 1980, and subsequently published in the journal of the American Academy of Psychoanalysis. It appears now with some additional material from two other essays, 'Psychoanalysis today', and 'Psychoanalysis and politics', which dealt with similar topics. The common focus was on the therapist's value position. A great deal of lip-service is given to acknowledging values in psychotherapeutic practice. The problem is that to do so opens a Pandora's box. In my experience, therapists and analysts would much rather discuss sexual fantasies than whether they have been bought off to console people and adjust them to an atrocious reality.

7 THERAPY IN LATE CAPITALISM[1]

A RADICAL approaching the institution of psychotherapy often feels inclined to impale it with a barb updated from Marx's judgement on religion: where once was the opium of the people, here stands their heroin, a new, synthetic addiction, concocted out of the brew of late capitalist culture. The hostility is understandable, since therapy has in some respects been even more successful than religion in deflecting energy from the need for radical social change. Religion at least threatened capital with its immanent critique; like a superannuated retainer it reminded its master of a time when his power had not yet come to be, and therefore of one when it would pass away. Therapy, on the other hand, appears seamless: even when pretending to be transcendent, the reward it dangles is no eschatological grappling with ultimates but an ultimately mundane, 'sensible' happiness, quite eligible for commodification. What is needed is a concrete and precise analysis of the many-sidedness of the phenomenon, situating it within the totality of its society and drawing attention to its liberating elements. In short, we must unearth the latent critical content of therapy and set it against its more obvious conformism.

Therapy, however, does not exist apart from the neurosis it is supposed to remedy. The relationship is dialectical, for just as the variants of psychotherapy arise in response to the actually existing forms of neurosis, so do they serve to label, identify and ground neurotic experience in their own terms. Further, neither therapy nor neurosis should be seen as remote from the entire flux of capitalist relations in everyday life, within the family, or in mass culture. Despite the reciprocal relation of neurosis and therapy, it is necessary to begin our analysis from the standpoint of the disorder, neurosis, rather than from the remedy, therapy. We do not choose to be neurotic, but we choose to do something about our neuroses – to ignore them, to subsume them in some kind of activity, to seek therapeutic help for them – or some combination of all these. Thus although neuroses enter the realm of political activity – usually, as we shall discuss below, in a negative way – therapy (or no therapy) is in itself a political act and can only be grasped in relation to the material conditions it seeks to alter.

Objectively we understand a neurotic person to be failing in tasks of adaptation to the environment through the compulsive repetition of inappropriate behaviours. But what makes the behaviours inappropriate is another, subjective dimension of compulsion: the intrusion of incompletely repressed fantasy. Every neurosis then can be considered a structure grounded in a nodal point in subjectivity and extending beyond the individual to encompass the entirety of his social relations. And at the subjective point of origin, a state of desire, hatred and fear emerges that is intolerable to the self and against which the most elaborate measures have to be taken. These measures, whose nature is socially determined, form the behavioural surface of the neurosis.

It might be helpful at this point to distinguish between two categories of neurotic experience, the normal and the clinical. *Normal neurosis* may be roughly identified with the neurotic character; it is the standard pattern of neurotic experience imposed by the established conflicts of everyday life, and adapted to them. The normal neurotic pays little attention to his characteristic rigidity and irrationality, for this is the way one is supposed to be. Thus his or her inner subjective compulsion becomes cloaked in the veil of common sense. Neurosis becomes *clinical*, by which is meant potentially treatable, when the individual becomes aware of a certain intolerable degree of suffering and/or is made to feel that his or her disturbance lies outside the perimeter of what is socially acceptable. These two functions – the felt suffering and the label of deviance – are tightly but not necessarily coupled. When we feel clinically neurotic (by becoming grossly depressed, suffering through some repetitive pattern of failure in love, or developing some classical symptom such as a phobia), we are generally experiencing more of the subjective imbalance and compulsiveness that is the essence of neurosis. At the same time we are judging this worsened state of affairs in accordance with standards of well-being internalized from the culture. These factors, each culturally rooted, develop along separate paths that meet on the field of neurosis. One may be severely neurotic yet be considered normal so long as one lives within the parameters of what is acceptable. Similarly, a person may be labelled neurotic – and accept the labelling as valid – when the degree of subjective neurosis is actually outweighed by distress stemming from objective social forces. In this society at least, virtually everybody suffers to some degree from normal neurosis. Indeed, just as capitalism universalizes the commodity relationship, so does it impose, in a quite necessarily related way, a universalized neurotic experience among those who must live according to its terms.

In order to ground this insight we need to demonstrate, first, that conditions of life under capitalism necessarily lead to neurosis; second, that the forms of neurosis bear a definite relationship to the historically evolving relations of capitalist production; and finally, that the presence of neurotic structures in the population plays an actual role in the evolution of capitalism itself. Note that it is not being argued that capitalism creates neurosis as such. Such a thesis would be just as one-sided and inadequate as its vulgar-Freudian converse, that neurosis is generated out of fixed biological dispositions. It is necessary to recognize that inherent dispositions exist which, if not strictly biological, are at least transhistorical and thus universal: infantile helplessness, the need for attachment and separation, the unstructuredness of instinctual drives and the potential for ambivalence. These characteristics are, after all, what make us human: they give rise to fantasy, symbolism, and subjectivity and value itself; and they put the human in a state of tension with nature, leading to that transformation of the natural, given order which comprises the basic dialectic of civilization. Moreover, they give rise to neurosis as well – but never in themselves, only as they are twisted against a definite social order and turned inwards, bearing the imprint on its particular forms. Neurosis is living proof of the tension between the human subject and the objective social order; it only comes into existence so far as these are incongruent, which is to say, within history.

The social conditions in which neurotic development can flourish are those of domination, of a social fabric composed of conflicting groups organized along lines of class, sex, race, and so on, and where the division of labour reflects the power of one group over others. In such a setting, in so far as the production of a surplus allows a passage beyond brute necessity, the contradictions between what the social order is and what it can be will eventually settle within the self as one form of neurotic distortion or another. The description just given can, of course, fit nearly every form of social order, and if capitalism is only one among all other social orders so far as generating madness goes, it has none the less managed to produce a rather unique form of neurosis, one which reflects the peculiarities of its history.[2]

A most striking feature of neurosis within capitalism is its ubiquity. The reason for this lies in the particular form of reality principle developed by capital – the fetishism of commodities. The commodity relation is, of course, predicated on the creation of objects of exchange, and of a universal standard, money, by means of which their value may be compared. As Marx consistently pointed out, to place something into a system of exchange means that it has to be abstracted and objectified – that is, placed within a rationalized and calculable context. But this necessarily implies that the commodity relation must also include the creation and sustenance of a *subject* who performs the exchanging – a subject who, first, possesses a universal standard of objective rationality by means of which he can attend to the existence and exchange of objective commodities; and second, who is unable to perceive that these commodities are other than what they seem to be – that is, who is prepared to accept their fetishization within the dominant system of value and exchange.

The neurotic individual, normal or clinical, fits the bill exactly by virtue of the split between the deeper layers of his subjectivity and his internalization of the rationalized reality principle of abstract commodity logic. What makes a person neurotic is not hate or fear *per se*, but intrasubjective conflict between the demands of reason and those of desire. A social order, like capitalism, that imposes a universal imperative of rationalization will therefore universalize neurosis, for the simple reason that desire cannot go its own way to work out idiosyncratic solutions, but must be forever hurled against rationalization. In pre-capitalist society, people were amply crazy – the degree of brutal traumatization and privation saw to that. But there was no category of neurosis in which they all had to be inserted, precisely because there was no universal standard of reason in terms of which their madness appeared as negativity.

It would, however, greatly flatten out the historical process to confine capital's role in neurosis to the mere imposition of instrumental rationality. For one thing, we must always bear in mind that what capital has imposed in the way of reason contains the severest contradictions even on an objective level. And for another, we would miss much of what capitalism is about if we overlook its role in restructuring and marketing desire and impulse themselves. The contradictions within reason as well as the new forms of desire (new needs) each enter into the history of neurosis. More, they become elements in the development of capitalist society. In order to grasp this flux, however, it is necessary to consider two moments within capitalist development which represent the early and contemporary phases of its trajectory and which reveal themselves in developments in personal life having to do with the altered nature of work and consumption.

In the early phase of capitalism, most of its energy went into the production and accumulation of commodities. This process required the transformation of productive activity into abstractable labour power. The alienation which resulted cost the individual control of his vital activity and made his productive capacity into a commodity that not only could be bought and sold, but was also subject to an inexorable process of domination by capital. Yet, alienation stopped short of the subjective world itself, except in so far as this became stunted through separation from the means of existence. And this was not due to any grace on capital's part, but simply to the fact that the inner sphere had only been partially developed as an organ of capitalist relations. It mattered little what subjective variations obtained within the time of labour's activity. From the standpoint of capital what counted was the simple reproduction of the work-force and its controlled delivery, like so many draught animals, to the work-place. Around this need there arose a religion and culture of asceticism, submission and a crude, severe rationalization.

To assist the reproduction of labour, a family structure was emphasized that would generate an ample supply of fresh children to take up the slack of increased commodity production and which would moreover keep these children under control. For this latter function a line had to be maintained between the patriarchal dominators at the top of the social pyramid and their symbolic representative, the father within the family; this line passed through the individual conscience and bound each man and woman of society to church, state and, ultimately, capital.

The basic work relation of early capitalism, the abstraction and expropriation of labour-time, becomes even more expansive within the social world of late capitalist relations. Its forms become greatly complicated by subsequent developments in the relations of production. As capital proceeds down the self-ordained path of growth for its own sake and not for humanity's, it necessarily expands its productive power past the point at which simple accumulation serves its purposes. We may summarize these developments as the addition of a moment of disaccumulation – that is, of the liquidation of surplus – occurring *pari passu* with the continuing expansion of the productive process (see Aronowitz, n.d.).

This occurs at a point of transition, developing in an uneven manner across the Western world towards the close of the nineteenth century and the beginning of the twentieth, a phase during which machinery and the technical apparatus in general – fixed capital – outstrips the productive role of human labour – living capital. And as the machine takes over, writes Marx, 'Labour no longer appears so much to be included within the production process, rather the human being comes to relate more as watchman and regulator to the production process itself. (*What holds for machinery holds likewise for the combination of human activities and the development of human intercourse*)' (Marx, 1859, p. 705; my italics). And again, 'In this transformation, it is . . . the appropriation of his own general productive power . . . in a word, the *development of the social individual* [my italics] which appears as the great foundation-stone of production and of wealth. The *theft of alien labour-time, on which the present wealth is based*, appears a miserable foundation in face of this new one, created by large-scale industry itself' (1859, p. 705).

Two dialectically intertwined trends are intensified by the development of the social individual as a prime instrument of capitalist relations. Appearing in the unitary moments of production and consumption, they eventually come to reside within the subject, defining a 'human nature' which is neurotic in capitalist terms.

From the side of production the social individual is a creature whose work becomes increasingly differentiated and remote from any comprehensible productive process. These trends are manifest in the rise of technocracy, the

bureaucratization of work and, of particular concern for our
analysis, the immense development of service occupations.
Increasingly, work becomes the cultivation and delivery of
human relations themselves. And from these qualities it
follows that human relations become technical, swaddled
in instrumental logic and prepared for commodification.
Rather than being freed by the development of science
and productivity, labour becomes degraded owing to the
entrapment of productive reason within capitalist imperatives (Braverman, 1974). The 'watchman and regulator' of
the production process becomes just another instrument
within it: the human becomes mechanical and accordingly
assumes a machine-like form of reason to the terms of which
all living relations become subsumed.

Meanwhile the pace of production and the hunger for
profit impose equally far-reaching alterations in consumption. What could be assumed automatically in an age of
scarcity and accumulation becomes both more problematic
and more compelling in the light of disaccumulation. Now
there is a surplus to be sold, though it is not to be simply
disposed of, but simultaneously wasted and revalued so
that capital keeps moving. The consumerist imperative in
late capitalism demands the cultivation of new forms of
desire, and this desire is to develop intertwined with the
equally contradictory moment of rationality.

Capital no longer regards the social individual as a *mere*
means, but rather as a means to be actively controlled with
all the forces at its disposal. Indeed the contestation for the
soul of the social individual – whether fought out on the
field of daily life, in mass culture, or, as we shall touch upon
shortly, therapy – has become a principal political struggle
of advanced industrial society. It is a contest which compli-
cates, perhaps decisively, all previous forms of class
struggle. The measures capital has undertaken in order to
undercut the immanent threat from the very reason and
desire it itself has brought forth into the world define in a
broad sense these new forms of struggle. The twisting of
reason into instrumental logic and the fetishization of desire
are only the most general ways of viewing these 'remedi-
ations'. Their effect has been to create new kinds of social
battlegrounds. The fracturing of modern society demands a
series of analyses of the specific forms taken by the contest
for the social individual, whether these be advertising,

education, bureaucratic rationalization – or, as we shall now consider, the subjective life itself.

The changes we have been describing take place within the historical development of the institutions of everyday life, the most critical of which is the family. The family becomes crucial because, in its attempt to fulfil its assigned function of reproducing the individual demanded by the social order, it succeeds mainly by transmitting the contradictions developed within that order into the spheres of personal life (Zaretsky, 1973; also, Ewen, 1976). The need of capital for a 'social individual' is another way of saying that capital must intensify and enter into the terms of family life. The space for this was cleared out by the productive surge of late capitalism. As the moment of disaccumulation was reached, the demand for labour-time began to drop below the level at which child labour was needed. Meanwhile the practice had come to seem odious, owing to the progressive development of the reformist impulse during the nineteenth century. The combination of these factors led to the abolition of child labour in late capitalism and the freeing up of childhood as a separate period. This was essential, for only a child can develop differentiated desire, and only a child can be trained for rationality, an enterprise which was undertaken by general public education.

Alongside this occurred a rapid decline in infant mortality as the result of advances in sanitation and public health. Thus, children came to stay around long enough to be valued and cultivated; and, as their labour was no longer necessary as it was in peasant or early industrial society, they emerged into the disaccumulation phase as a whole new class of consumers, the satisfaction of whom became a new task for the family. A related development was the dissociation of sexuality from reproduction, which freed the former as a source of pleasure and desire. Meanwhile, family life was being buffeted about as a result of the increasing erosion of traditional sources of legitimacy. With the advance of alienation the family became a personal refuge for great masses of people who could otherwise find neither meaning, gratification nor power within community life. Yet, the cultural ties between the individual family and the larger community were becoming ever more attenuated, thus depriving personal relations of a coherent social framework. Authority itself became more and more impersonal and decreasingly mediated by kinship or community.

As a result, people looked for something within the family
only to be frustrated. For the father, promised authority by
virtue of his cultural heritage, yet denied it everywhere,
family life became not the simple dream of a *paterfamilias*,
but a hoax. For the mother, denied authority by phallic
culture, she now unwittingly acquired the burden of
becoming Mum – inculcating the categories of childhood,
assuaging the hurts of her increasingly impotent husband
and passively transmitting the values of consumerism as
though they were instilled into her very milk. At the same
time, the split of sex from reproduction opened up for her –
even more than for the male – the possibility for gratification
that had long been concealed beneath the triple burdens of
domestic toil, child-bearing and the ascetic femininity of
patriarchal lore. With the masculine monopoly of sexual
power becoming seriously eroded from one side, and feminine masochistic submission cracking from the other, the
result could only be the release of hostility and guilt into the
matrix of the 'social individual'. And it is the incoming
children who inherit this cauldron of emergent hope, pent-
up rage, confused longing and incoherent values.

In this context we can appreciate the achievement of
Freud, who did no more than map out a subjective terrain
that history had brought into view. And it is quite significant
that the most prominent features of this landscape were the
neuroses – no less significant than Freud's insight that
neurotic development was entirely continuous with the
normal. The nucleus of Freud's discovery was no mere
residual category – an excretion of bourgeois relations, as
Marxists have often claimed. Consider that Freud's first
appreciation of the causes of neurosis lay in the practice of
coitus interruptus, an economically necessary yet technically
inefficient form of birth control widely practised at the time;
or that one of his first cases was the adolescent hysteric, Dora,
who was enmeshed in a covert erotic situation involving,
among other things, rebellion against her father (Freud,
1905). In these and other instances, the neurosis can be seen
as the binding of a potentially liberatory impulse through
entrapment in infantile conflict – structures universalized
by virtue of the growth of the notion of childhood, and of
the contradictory reason and desire embedded within it.

Neurosis is the self-alienation of a subject who has been
readied for freedom but runs afoul of personal history – a
personal history whose particular terms from childhood on

are both individually unique and determined by the general historical process. Neurosis therefore is an auxiliary form of inner domination which reproduces external domination on the realm of the unconscious. It was on this territory that Freud made his authentic achievement: the discovery of the lost infantile body revealed in the qualities of deep subjectivity itself – an infinitely fluid yet irreconcilable language of desire, terror and hatred which peels the boundary of consciousness away from the registration of the material object and drapes it over phantoms of objects lost. To account for repression, Freud needed the hypothesis of instinctual drive, or *Trieb* – the dialectical non-identity between unconscious fantasy and official, waking thought. And to sustain his realization that repression was a radical process, Freud had to ground the concept of *Trieb* materially – that is, the body had to be granted a real and disjunctive input with respect to the demands of culture. While he largely succeeded, Freud remained to some extent trapped in the terminology of the positivist neuropsychiatry whose assumptions he was demolishing. As a result, he left a legacy of difficulty in mediating psychoanalytic concepts with a genuinely historical social theory.

Every system of domination ensures that potential subjective conflict becomes actual – and maddening – through the class imposition of real suffering and deprivation. Capital's distinctive contribution to this schema was the binding of time through the regimentation of labour-power into an exchangeable commodity. The binding of real time and its eventual translation into the mediating categories of infantile life set forth the principal dichotomy within modern subjectivity: time bound versus Promethean desire. Add domination and the patriarchal family, and we have the forms of the Oedipus complex under capitalism, which Freud read in his consulting room.

Thus capital ensured the universalization of a normal neurotic structure. Quantitative variations – too much infantile trauma, biological variations in resistance, and so forth – would suffice, as had always been the case, to bring out one or another clinical variety of 'mental illness'. To the extent that such afflicted individuals became unsuited for the social process, they would have to be dealt with in one way or another; and although we know that for centuries the fate of the mad had concerned society, it was also the case that only in the early phases of capital and the

Enlightenment, as Foucault (1965) pointed out, was there any general differentiation between the 'mentally disturbed' and the other assorted misfits who had eternally collected around the base of society.

Early capital may have set the stage for neurosis as a category through its industrial binding of time and universalization of reason, but otherwise it had little use for the problem. And this was because its control of the human world was mainly applied at the point of the quantification of labour itself. With the development of the 'social individual', however, the essentially qualitative subjective world becomes necessarily an additional object of control, and neurosis finds itself increasingly at the centre of culture. In the new order, dominated by technology, service work and the commodification of the human relationship, the *way* a person behaves on and off the job becomes an essential aspect of the economic process. Thus the presence of neurosis takes on a significance unthinkable in the days of yore, when sturdy backs, sobriety, faith and thrift would fit the bill. But of deeper interest yet is the fact that the structure of the neurotic experience itself is decisively affected by the ways of advanced capital.

In the early phase of capital neurotic discord can be ideal-typically regarded as between an external, directly dominative force that attempts to bind time and an impulse which resists such binding. Since neurotic conflict is never simply between objective and subjective forces, but involves subjective representations of what is real, there must be an inner registration, or internalization, of the external, directly dominative force. Put simply, the individual has to believe that father is there, backed up by God and state, to ward off impulse; and it is his belief in the image of such authority that enters into the neurotic conflict by becoming linked with infantile representations of the same. To continue the model, then, we would say that the suppressing force in early capitalist normal neurosis consists of a more or less direct representation of an actual authority.

In late capitalist neurosis this picture becomes altered by the diminution of direct, immediate authority, whether religious or secular, and its replacement by the instruments for the control of the social individual. This means the installation of an internalized administration of one's own reason and desire. It is essential, however, that the reason which performs this function be of the kind that is instru-

mental and that fetishizes desire. Otherwise these agencies
would go over to the side of impulse and freedom – that
is, they would lose their legitimating tie to the external
administration of capitalist relations.

It is important to note parenthetically that the above
argument, while heavily indebted to Marcuse's 'obsolescence of the Freudian view of Man', departs from it in a
significant direction (Marcuse, 1970, pp. 44–62). By con-
verting the regulating systems of the psyche to internalized
reproductions of the prevailing administration, Marcuse
made one powerful point but lost another, and with it a fully
dialectical analysis: he severed too completely the social and
the personal orders. By abandoning the concrete mediations
of everyday life, the family and psychology, Marcuse unin-
tentionally returns Marxist dialectics towards the economism from which critical theory had tried to rescue it.

In contrast, the analysis developed here seeks to
encompass the very non-identity between psyche and
society which reflects Adorno's observation of the actual
fracturing of advanced capitalist society (Adorno, 1967).
Because of non-identity a space has to be cleared away
within the self for a phenomenologically determinable core
of self-experience which is mediated by actual social
relations, yet which contains the capacity to resist them. In
short, the sixth thesis on Feuerbach needs to be amended if
it is to become worthy of Marxism: the self is not a simple,
Lockean 'ensemble of social relations' (Marx, in Marx and
Engels, 1968, p. 29), but reveals as well the entire Freudian
dialectic. The model that emerges is complex yet capable of
registering the actual state of contradictoriness. It includes
the fact that essential choices in life have passed into the
alienated hands of an impersonal administrative apparatus
which attempts to impose unidimensionality upon the
human world, but also that the same administration needs
to consume the time of a social individual whose personality
has been cultivated via the mediations of the family and
childhood – a personality locked ineluctably in conflict with
the impersonality of the whole.

When one factors out the invariant or trivial elements and
arrives at the ultimate historical basis of conflict, it may be
seen as the struggle between the inviolable space within the
subject and the intrusions of administered necessity. These
terms can be mapped into Freud's formulation of the clash
between the sexual instincts and civilization, since it is

infantile sexuality, viewed in its fullest sense as Eros, time-less and uncommodifiable, which constitutes the core of subjectivity left over after all the taming measures have had their due. None the less, the conflict is still experienced by the subject in terms of the actual people – lovers, bosses, co-workers, teachers and toll-takers – who have come to play the crucial mediating roles between Eros and the administration. Without the concrete mediations of everyday life, there can be no symbolic scaffolding upon which the structures of consciousness, whether false or true, can be built.

The non-reducibility of self-experience to either social demands or biological need is the pre-condition of neurotic conflict. The conflict itself, then, is always conducted through mental representations of real people which become split and tossed hither and yon as the subject vainly tries to synthesize the opposed trends within him or her. But for this to be so, the social world has to provide fundamental contradictions of its own such that an inner synthesis cannot be achieved. Thus from the standpoint of whether neurotic development occurs it is all the same if the father exists as an actual suppressing authority or whether he is functionally absent and his power usurped. The *form* that the neurosis takes may be different of course – in the first instance we might, for example, expect a hysterical flight, while in the second the picture is more likely to be some kind of narcissistic or schizoid disturbance – but neurosis will take root in both cases because real objects see to it that desire is both unfulfillable and dangerous.

A person growing up under late capitalism will be materi-ally cared for and educated into instrumental reason regard-less of whether he or she be working or middle class. Prolonged and nurtured childhood will have succeeded in stimulating desire well beyond the possibilities of any controlling structure to discharge or bind. Indeed, the very weakness of immediate parental authority, its steady usurp-ation by remoter expertise, guarantees that desire is both unchecked and ungratifiable. The parent can neither stop children nor be adequate to their yearning. And, the non-provision of a worthy object becomes just as potent a repressing force as the actual threat of castration. In both instances the subject is left helplessly suffused with hate, at the mercy of desire, and driven to falsify consciousness.

In late capitalism, as throughout the history of the human species, the deeper body of alienated infantile feeling is relegated to the unconscious. However, certain auxiliary measures have been added to channel the highly developed surplus desire which flows into contemporary culture via the social individual. The principal structure which accommodates this process is instrumental reason itself. For all the circumstances which tend to stimulate desire do so under the sign of the reasonable imperative. The little children who learn to be creative in their progressive school learn too that the school is an administered entity in which one gets ahead by being creative (within limits, of course). And if the child is not privileged enough to get the point in such a setting, he will when he goes home and is told by some television ad to 'feel free' in the interests of a soft drink.

Advanced capital has worked diligently at colonizing the new subjective territory its advance unearthed. The very usurpation of parental authority which plays so large a role in introducing alienation within the subject is itself a measure of this colonial administration. The parent either joins up – becoming, so to speak, a civil servant in the regime of mass culture – or is swept aside to be left screaming in impotent rage, an object of scorn no less than covert yearning.

And like any proper colony, instrumentalized subjectivity provides raw material for the metropolitan region: commodifiable desire. The inchoate longing of childhood bubbles up out of the primary region of self-experience. From earliest infancy it passes through the refinery of instrumental logic as it enters the human world. And there it is named, sorted out, categorized, told – in the fundamental operation of instrumental reason – that it is not part of the subject, that it exists 'out there' in abstractable, quantifiable, ultimately commodifiable terms. If, by definition, we term the forms of experience that have been instrumentally severed from subjectivity the secondary symbolic values, and correlatively we term that from which they have been severed primary symbolic values, then it may be that secondary symbolic value becomes valued over the primary. Otherwise the figure will become drawn back into the subjective world and out of the clutches of commodity relations – for *only secondary symbolic values can be exchanged*. It may be that this kind of operation is at the heart of reification.

The simplest notion of the secondary objectification of fantasy in everyday life is the day-dream: a controlled exercise in wish-fulfilment whose energy derives from unfulfillable unconscious desire and the objects of which are given by the dominant culture. In this sense capital entails the commodification of day-dreams. Such conceptions develop a truth if they are believed in; at least they remain stable enough to enter the market-place where they acquire a more material grounding. And the developing person comes to believe in them because repression of infantile terror is made the easier thereby; and because, simply, to reify desire makes fulfilment seem nearer, since that which is materializable is also possessable, even on the instalment plan.

The same configuration that serves the neurotic character structure becomes increasingly essential for the disposition of the surplus. From this standpoint it would seem that neurotic alienation is necessary in order to develop a primary subjective core which turns out fantasies suitable for skimming by the instruments of capital. The neurosis is the irritant, like the grain of sand to the oyster, that keeps a natural process in a state of chronic disequilibrium and so sustains another dislocation at a different point. Similarly the sludge of secondary symbols accumulated as a result of the endless reification of mass culture obscures the basic disequilibrium even as it irritates it and keeps it going. Thus the various rationalizations which have come to surround neurotic experience in the post-Freudian era have only served to secure the basic neurotic disposition of the times. Were it otherwise, were people either happy or clear about what they wanted, then capital's ceaseless expansion would be endangered.

In addition to churning out saleable desire for the age of consumerism, neurosis has a number of other basic functions under late capitalism. Neurosis is perhaps the only way one can develop a rationalized subject suitable for doing the work of the social individual, who at the same time does not know what he or she wants, that is, whose capacities to resist are compromised. The simultaneous efflorescence of infantile impulse and fear of a non-instrumental expression of the same makes it that much harder for the neurotic to experience outrage over oppression without lapsing into crippling self-doubt. Similarly, though the parricidal nucleus of the Oedipus complex persists as a spur to rebellion, so long as it remains under the aegis of a preponderantly neurotic organization the rebellion will almost surely be self-destructive and lead to a new round of submission. All in all, normal-neurotic character structures are one of the best ways for an oppressive order to maintain its domination without an embarrassing and economically stultifying overt authoritarianism. Further, designating the normal neurosis as one or another category of clinical neurosis both serves the labelling process so dear to instrumental reason and preoccupies people with reified or individualistic explanations for their unhappiness. And when one adds to this highly abbreviated presentation the reflection of how ruinous neurotic bickering and subjectivism (Jacoby, 1971) have been to Left politics, it will not be hard to see how loyal a servant neurosis has been to its master, capital.

But slaves have been known to turn on their masters. The labelling of 'psychopathology' represents, to be sure, one way of forestalling awareness of a fuller truth. But the opportunity to do so only exists because of the actual presence of a colossal burden of neurotic misery in the population, a weight that continually and palpably betrays the capitalist ideology, which maintains that commodity civilization promotes human happiness. If, given all this rationalization, comfort, fun and choice, people are still wretched, unable to love, believe or feel some integrity to their lives, they might also begin to draw the conclusion that something was seriously wrong with their social order. Moreover, the threat posed by neurosis is not limited to the betrayal of ideology. For impulse is antithetical to administration, while neurosis represents a kind of synthesis between the two. But it is a false and uneasy synthesis, owing to the partial breakthrough of impulse and its inherently sluggish educability. Thus the hidden unconscious forms of impulse become ever more threatening, not just to the individual in neurotic distress, but to the social order whose fundamental irrationality has to be cloaked in a film of rationalization. Neurosis is not only unfreedom; it also contains within itself a thrust towards freedom. Clinical neurosis should be regarded as a twisted effort at cure, yet one which still contains somewhere more hope for freedom than the normal neurosis it replaces.

Consequently, the various forms of therapy have arisen as new forms of mediation – re-mediations or *remedies* – to be inserted into the increasingly uneasy neurotic syntheses. The therapies are in this sense like a kind of mental Keynesianism resorted to by capital to iron out another type of endemic crisis; and like the economic analogue, they suffer

from a tendency to inflation, now manifest in the running
riot of a whole Babel of schools.

The concept of what psychotherapy can be has come a long way from Freud's initial insight that making the unconscious conscious may relieve neurotic suffering. It has both retrieved its pre-Freudian roots in suggestion, religious healing and, indeed, shamanism, and branched forward in countless novel directions. In all of these methods, however, one common condition obtains: the individual whose personal distress has been defined as neurosis undergoes an experience in which certain elements of his or her neurotic structure are reproduced, and as a result he or she becomes reunited with some portion of an existence that had been denied by neurotic splitting. Thus disequilibrium proceeds to re-equilibration; disunity to unification, always under the sign of self-appropriation. The therapies speak then of developing 'insight', or of learning 'appropriate behaviour', of discovering one's 'true self', or, as in family therapy, of re-establishing broken and chaotic family communications. The modes under which self-appropriation may occur are exceptionally varied but always involve some element of subjective belief or goal that the therapeutic method validates, as well as some objectification of this in the person of the therapist.

The therapy, then, is the dialogue within which these elements are related to each other. The belief, or value system, of the therapy, establishes the vector of self-appropriation, while the actual therapist offers a concrete model for incorporation, a framework around which the self-appropriation can take place. Thus in Freud's method the analyst imposes the value of reflective truth-telling and offers his accepting yet disengaged attention to break the neurotic cycle; while in Jung's version, belief in a transcendent unconscious force is held out and the analyst becomes an active guide promoting symbolic reunification; or in Gestalt therapy, immediate contact with current awareness becomes the goal; or in behavioural treatment, altering learned, objectifiable behaviour; in transactional analysis, appropriation of a reasonable standard of self-esteem in a group setting; and so forth.

Note that anything can work, at least for a while, in the therapy of a neurosis, so long as it is believed in and backed up with a real therapeutic presence that succeeds in objectively establishing some kind of dialogue with the inner structure of neurosis. The objective factor makes it impossible airily to dismiss the value of some supposed cures as bubbles destined to burst upon disillusionment. Illusions they might be, but no more so than the false consciousness imposed by class domination. While it is true that neurotic contradictions will not be ushered out of existence by therapeutic mumbo-jumbo, this is not the same as claiming that a person will not be *convinced* that they have subsided.

Of course, the two dialectics – the therapeutic and the societal – run together. Indeed, it is just the social dimension which provides an essential framework of objectification around which therapeutic goals can crystallize (for example, Jungian treatment works best for those whose life has prepared them to accept a religious world-view). Because of the non-identity between individual and society, however, no absolute fit between personal *telos* and an objectified social framework can be obtained and a great range of partial solutions, each with its own ideology, is possible.

We are thus in a position to attempt a critique of the differing possibilities for therapy according to two criteria: (1) the degree to which they objectively address themselves to the neurosis, as against blurring the realities or indulging in illusions; and (2) the values inherent in the kind of change they offer, both with respect to their respective methods and goals. Are the resistant powers within the subject employed for this end, or does the therapy attempt its unification on terrain that has already been colonized by capital? In other words, does the therapy become an immanent critique or a new form of fetish? Let us turn to a few examples for clarification.

Critiques of inner and outer worlds have to be made in the language of each sphere. Thus therapies which attempt to apply advanced political insights to emotional disturbances are only imposing another form of false consciousness. This is precisely the problem with so-called 'radical therapy', with its naïve illusion that neurosis and oppression are directly connected so that, for example, a woman becoming conscious of her actual oppression as a woman would also be adequately dealing with neurotic distortions of her sexuality. The spontaneous activity of the subject generates a consciousness that is false by the standards of class consciousness. Yet it is also anchored in definite unconscious fantasies, which, though they may stem from a real child-

hood generated out of late capitalist contradictions, have
been cut off by repression from political categories. Thus
there is a false consciousness of both the objective and
subjective dimensions, and it is deceptive to blend them
together.

This is a dangerous question to overlook. It is not a
mere intellectual failure to apply political categories to a
therapeutic situation. For therapy mobilizes the neurosis in
order to resolve it; but while mobilized, neurotic thinking,
with its transference wishes of submission to therapeutic
authority, will drag the most advanced political ideology
back into domination and compulsivity.

Similarly, though mental patients are blatantly abused by
society, they do not cease thereby to be troubled on their
own. The labelling which defines a career for them as
psychotic has a real and deleterious effect on their inner
subjective life, but does not occupy the whole ground of
subjectivity. To regard people as defined by their oppression
flattens the humanity – and the ultimate powers of resistance
– out of them, and is no better than the crude categorization
that passes for a medical model.

In this regard it should be pointed out that the subjectivity
of psychotic people is radically isolated; both world and self
are petrified into an objectification of far greater extent than
the prevailing degree of capitalist reification. Thus they are
lost even to the given state of unfreedom and correspondingly objective measures, such as drugs and restraint, may
at times (although far less often than prevailing medical
orthodoxy would have it) be necessary as a humane expedient. Here we may be able to appreciate the weakness of
Laing's synthesis of the sixties, which fell short on both
criteria. By minimizing the crippling objectification of the
psychotic, Laing imposed a deep subjective therapy on them
that they could ill tolerate, much less use. At the same time,
as Russell Jacoby (1975) has observed, Laing tended to flatten
the social dialectic by subsuming the alienation of labour
into that of the subject.

Thus a politically advanced position – one mediated
through objective societal categories – is therapeutically
backward; while a therapeutically advanced position – one
that seeks to reclaim alienated subjective territory – is in itself
politically inert. And yet, given the historical relationship
between neurosis and capitalism, therapy cannot be ignored
as a possible element in any overall political strategy. Our

analysis tells us, however, that therapeutic practice should be bracketed from objective political goals. Concretely put, a person should be free to unburden him- or herself in a therapeutic setting without regard for the objective consequences.

In a practical sense, for a therapy to flourish in the world of capitalist relations, it has to generate exchange value. This can be done in two ways (which may be combined in the real setting): the therapy can offer something that is perceived to be of genuine value because it is rare and in danger of being extinguished, like fine handicraft; or it can promise power by promoting unification with the main dynamic of capitalist expansion. With respect to the first type, we have therapy which offers the chance for deep subjective reflectivity and/or an intense, caring personal relationship. Time bought for these purposes will continue to have a premium value in a culture that works to obliterate both of them. To be sure, it is a value reserved for the privileged class. For the rest, therapeutic help will have to come either through a cut-rate compromise or via the second pathway – an already fetishized route. By being fetishized, therapy is able to help the subject defend against his or her deeper anxieties, thus feel less neurotic, indeed, full of 'mental health'.

In today's world the therapist has become a technologist of behaviour and value. Everything there is to know about sex is known. The dialectic of ineffability is abolished by behavioural technology. Masters and Johnson, fresh from their conquest of the orgasm, dance on Reich's grave as the reigning experts on the ways of Eros. Spread out around them are a host of behavioural and cognitive therapists dedicated to the Skinnerian dogma that behaviour is determined by its consequences – that is, purely objectively, undialectically, positivistically, and instrumentally. Systems analysts abound with a somewhat more subtle but equally instrumental vision of people caught hopelessly in a net of communication. And of course the tide of drug treatment continues unabated. Indeed the ultimate is already with us: therapy by computer – and anybody who doubts that subjects have been found who like getting treated by a machine is out of touch with the pace of reification.

Similarly, commodifiable desire – the same that sells deodorants – has been amply mobilized in the interests of therapy. Here a glimmer of the hope set going by capital's democratization – that everyone is entitled to happiness – has become fused with the equation, happiness equals stimulation, into a powerful instrument upon which the neurotically troubled and alienated can seize. The basic thesis of this dimension of therapy is that the neurotic impulse should not be tinged with the hatefulness which is in fact its distinguishing feature. In order to promote this illusion, repression of the hateful side of impulse – the side which wants to possess, devour, castrate and so forth – is necessary; and this is secured by magnifying the image of the non-hateful side – that which just wants to enjoy – out of proportion. Here consumer culture stands at the ready with its cornucopia to back up therapeutic ideology. The Human Potential Movement, with its Joy Therapy and maximization of encountering, spontaneity and impulse, bears witness to the fetishization of this dimension. In the place of an authentic desire which might emerge through overcoming the historically induced split, Human Potential, or post-Freudian psychology dredges up an internalized Manifest Destiny: nothing should be too much for these Americans who compulsively gobble up experience as though it were choice mineral rights. Instead of genuine freedom, then, which would mean an honest confrontation of hatred, evil and madness, fetishized therapy offers us a Disneyland of the mind. And it should be noted that the therapy of an unreflective spontaneity bears more than a haphazard resemblance to the politics of spontaneity. The infantilism that afflicted Left politics of the 1960s – the 'gimme-now' variety – becomes swiftly retooled into the therapist of instant breakthrough (namely Jerry Rubin).

All of the strands of bourgeois reification get rewoven in fetishized therapy. Its mystification returns through the adoration of the latest guru or in the cultivation of 'pure' consciousness through meditation. Its idealistic naïvety crops up cloaked in the preachings of a Carl Rogers or an Erik Erikson.[3] And its latent puritanical authoritarianism marches again dressed up, coyly enough, as the Reality (sic) Therapy of William Glasser. In sum, any ideological stance which preserves the split in bourgeois culture can be used to promote unification between the neurotically split subject and the alienated world. Thus it can be inserted into the neurotic disequilibrium where it will serve repression and reconvert a clinical into a normal neurosis.

Given the increasing alienation of bourgeois culture and its steady commodification of the subjective world, even this tenuous balance is hard to sustain; and the half-life of therapies now comes to resemble that of schools of art or rock groups. With progress in alienation, therapies have had to shout louder and promise more to get a rise out of their increasingly jaded subjects. As a result of these trends – which match on the cultural scale the development in the individual of forms of neurosis which lack clear lines of internal repression and hence lack classical symptoms – there has come to be a gradual coalescence of therapy with other forms of mass culture. Consider the case of Transactional Analysis, one of the most successful of the new therapies, and the first to be clearly modelled on the soap opera or situation comedy, with its apparatus of games, scripts and so on. TA is unabashed about its congruity with consumerist culture – neurotic patterns, for example, are said to earn 'trading stamps'. This not only helps to account for its success as a therapy but also for its lead in the assimilation of the categories of therapy to those of social control on other levels – namely, its widespread use, along with other group therapies, in corporations, the military and other arms of the bureaucracy as an instrument to help people get along with each other and the order of things. Thus work, therapy and everyday life each become suffused with the ethos of 'human relations' – the model of a 'social individual' suitable as a means of production and consumption and disinclined to resist the order of capital.

It should be emphasized that in actual practice, especially as it evolves over time, no therapy fits any category of fetishization in a neat fashion. Nor, except in rare instances, can any practice be assigned wholly to the camp of domination. A brief glance at the tangled path of psychoanalysis may show why.

The main theme of the history of psychoanalysis – a history, it should be added, not yet adequately written – is that of the absorption of critique by the dominant culture. The heart of psychoanalytic therapy is restoration of integrity through the appropriation of reflective powers lost by neurotic splitting. But this is an attack at one of the points where neurosis buttresses the reification demanded by capitalist culture. Self-reflection counters the instrumentalization of reason so essential to capital. A reflective subject is a critical, resistant subject. Moreover, psychoanalysis in its critical form reveals both the existence of Eros and the actual shambles made of erotic prospects for human liberation by the bourgeois world. To be sure, it also plunges into the twisted hate which is the subjective tracing of outer domination, and so tends to discourage ready-made solutions to the human dilemma. But at its heart is a search for the truth, which necessarily serves the quest for freedom, as Marxists from Reich and Trotsky to Adorno, Marcuse and Jacoby have observed.

Consequently, in its initial phase (up to 1920), psychoanalysis was a fundamentally revolutionary doctrine, although Freud's ambivalence towards the critical potential of what he had discovered left the way open for a number of courses. After 1920 the battle for the future of psychoanalysis began, with Marxists, Surrealists, and so on, on the one side and bourgeois culture on the other. We cannot recount these struggles except to note that they took a decisive turn towards the bourgeois side when Stalinism forced anything critical out of Marxism and Nazism uprooted the psychoanalytic movement *en masse* and drove most of it to America. Before the emigration, the way had been cleared for the bourgeoisification of psychoanalysis with the realization by mass culture that in the new science a weapon had been handed to them for the exploitation of their new subjective domain. Significantly enough, it was Edward Bernays, Freud's nephew and the founder of public relations, who spearheaded the appropriation of psychodynamics by advertising and the mass media in general. Meanwhile, the first among neo-Freudians, Alfred Adler, was disseminating his consciousness-bound version of psychoanalysis among the educational and social-work establishments.

In general, in order to catch hold in American culture, a psychoanalytic idea had to be stripped of its dialectical thrust, as with the neo-Freudian de-emphasis on the unconscious. By the same token, orthodox Freudianism held on to the unconscious but grounded it in an unmediated id psychology safe for bourgeois culture. In this guise psychoanalysis portrayed people as Hobbesian animals needing to be trained, an ideology compatible with historical formulations such as 'capitalism exists because of anal-sadistic instincts' or 'the police exist because of the masochism of the masses'.

Then in the 1930s the ego psychology of Heinz Hartmann (1939) began to hold sway. As Adorno (1967) pointed out,

Hartmann's work was in a basically correct theoretical direction in so far as it restored the principle of non-identity
within the subject (ego reflecting reality and id reflecting
desire) and so tended to rescue psychoanalysis from the
undialectical morass into which it had fallen. But the same
deadly biologistic flaw inhered in Hartmann's ego, which
was handed the job of 'deinstinctualizing psychic energy'.
Given the class position of psychoanalysts and the need of
the Second World War and post-war culture to justify the
ways of the bourgeois god to man, it was an inevitable path
to yet another flattening of the critical dialectic, this time the
enshrinement of ego-reality over id-desire. Co-ordinated
with this was the absorption of psychoanalysis into medical
orthodoxy and psychiatric education as an avatar of truth
about mental illness. The result was its transformation into
an adjustment psychology that found itself trussed up in
conformist thinking and upper-middle-class mores when
the crises of the 1960s reopened the question of Marxist
liberation.

Psychoanalytic practice – a term which embraces a goodly
variety of pursuits – reflects the history of the doctrine. Thus
psychoanalysis may be used as a mode of therapy in which
the instrumental reasoning of ego psychology can be
imposed as an ethos of intellectualized self-administration;
or the conformism inherent in any undialectical psychology
can appear as moralization, with all unconventional and
protest activity being dismissed as 'neurotic acting-out'; or
a caricature of its original, unmediated depth-psychology
can persist as rampant subjectivism, the old idealist myth
that passive contemplation is praxis enough for life's problems. All of these forms may be expected to crop up in one
guise or another, simply because the therapy has been
rooted in bourgeois culture as long as it has.

But just as that culture continually creates possibilities for
its own overcoming, so can psychoanalytic practice touch
from time to time its critical origins. Several conditions
remain indispensable for this. One is the eschewing of any
liberatory, radically curative or transcendent goal which is
to emerge from the therapy itself – that is, there should be
no superordinate value to what is going on, no pretence that
a short cut through history has been found, nor that a 'true
self' will emerge at the end of the treatment. Another,
related condition is the bracketing out of objective and
political considerations during sessions, in the interests of

permitting the emergence of even the most violent and forbidden thoughts (since, as in a dream, there would then be no realistic consequences). Yet another is the recognition that, under the sway of neurotic subjectivity, political thinking will degenerate towards domination, since it is the child-mind which is mobilized by the therapeutic situation. And finally, a certain respect for the integrity and worth of the person is necessary, no matter how far short of universality this may be – along, however, with the insistence that this individual be truthful concerning his or her warps and blemishes.

Therapy so construed – be it psychoanalytic or otherwise – retains the possibility of critique by refusing to present itself as more than what it is. Its very modesty is its strength. Its refusal to provide the Big Answer opens for the subject the possibility of looking outward. And by moving negatively, refusing to give answers and drawing in the limits of its judgement, a critical therapy draws a line against the colonization of the subjective world which defines late capitalism, and thereby works towards the restoration of the dialectical mode of resistance. In concrete terms, the person who emerges from therapy conducted as critique is no True Self, nor even free of normal neurosis. But he or she has widened the scope of the choices that can be made, while a certain part of locked-in subjectivity has been freed to make real demands upon the world. In sum, they are more ready for love and the politics of liberation.

Whether these choices will be actualized depends ultimately on the nature of their objects. Here the future poses a whole new conjuncture of possibilities. For if capital is moving into a new phase of scarcity, with a heightened legitimation crisis and the real possibilities of an intensified authoritarianism, then the conditions under which subjectivity both grew and became neurotic will be drastically altered. The terms of our subjectivity were forged within a capitalism undergoing more or less incessant expansion. Our child-mind is a creature of the age of surplus: commodified desire is part of consumerist society; and instrumental reason requires delay, leisure and an elaborate educational process. Clearly, all these conditions may become upset in the years to come. But if so, then the resistive powers immanent within the therapies will need all the more to be rescued and drawn into new forms of praxis for the struggles ahead.

NOTES

1. This essay was prepared in collaboration with Carol Lopate, Stuart Ewen, Stanley Aronowitz, Rosalyn Baxandall, Elizabeth Ewen and David Nasaw. Without their input, it could never have come to be. I am also grateful to Russell Jacoby, Brigid Marcuse, Bell Chevigny and Jean Elshtain for their editorial advice.

2. The question of the extent to which it applies to already established socialist orders is an important one which will have to be deferred for now.

3. See 'Erik Erikson's psychohistory', page 68 above.

8 VALUES, INTERESTS AND PSYCHOTHERAPY

W E SAY, with reason, that we 'practise' psychotherapy. But what does it mean to practise something? Are we talking of the logic of professionalism – that we are the licensed masters of a body of technical knowledge; that we rent space and apportion time in a contractual relationship with someone called a patient, who is to receive the benefit of that technique; and that we obtain a fee, or, in increasing numbers of cases, a salary or a reimbursement, for the application of our technique, which fee we then exchange for the things of our life? No one would dispute that this definition of practise has application to the real world. But we may be talking of something else when we talk of practise – something wider, more universal and seemingly more abstract, but just as real none the less. For is not 'practise' another way of defining that human essence enunciated by the young Marx in his first thesis on Feuerbach: 'sensuous human activity' (Easton and Guddat, eds, 1967), or praxis, or labour itself?

Labour, or practise, here should not be reduced to actual work-in-the-world, although it contains such work, including the work of psychotherapy. More generally, however, it is the active encounter of humans with nature, an encounter which transforms both the person and the object of her/his labour. Praxis therefore is transformative human activity. It includes the play of children as well as the work of adults. And since it is transformative, it is purposive. 'The meaning of labour', writes Sartre, 'is provided *by an end*, and need . . . is in fact the lived revelation of a goal to aim at' (Sartre, 1976). But this goal, the future, does not exist yet: it must be made by us. The future will depend upon what we practise today, that is, how we build it; and what we build will depend upon what we envision and how we direct our activity towards it.

There is a vector between immediacy – what is now, or what we are thrown into – and the conscious, purposive, transforming qualities of labour or praxis; and this vector 148 deserves a name: the name of *value*. What we value is not simply what we want, but what we are willing to do something about. Value is a material element of practise. It is the ingredient of orientation – our appreciation of what we want that is not here; and our willingness to do something in a direction to bring it about. If I value rare stamps, I am willing to look for such stamps and exchange money towards their possession. If I value freedom of speech, I am willing to do something to secure said freedom. If I value the status quo, then I act in such a way as to maintain it. And note here that I may or may not be immediately *conscious* of my values. And further, the consciousness one has of them may be false. A man who says and thinks that he values freedom, yet acts so as to reduce it, has such a false consciousness.

Needless to say, a great portion of our values are neither particularly interesting nor problematic. They become so when they are caught up in social conflict: in terms of our definition of labour, or praxis, when the object of labour is not merely nature in the raw, but includes some other person, with values of his or her own. And to allow for the reality that this other person presents, we need another term which defines the real differences people experience within history. Such a term is *interest* (Habermas, 1971). Our social interest is our real investment in the historical world. Without the concept of interest, the value problem becomes abstract and meaningless. When two people involved together have the same interest, then there is no conflict and no problem of values *between* them. Interests in turn are the function of real social practices and reflect our material relation to the world. The sexual division of labour within marriage, for example, can result in situations where husband and wife share a common interest – say, in the health of their children – and in other situations where their interests may diverge – say, in the husband's need to expand his power in the world by forcing the wife to play the role of domestic functionary and narcissistic supplier – that is, through a suppression of her individuality. Here conflict will not erupt, despite a real difference in their interests, so long as society sees to it that the woman's consciousness will itself remain stunted and basically submerged in her husband's. If, however, society goes through a process of historical development so that her value becomes enhanced, then the real conflict between their social interests will

surface and problems will ensue. In the course of the conflict,
new value relations will emerge for both of them.

To sum up, our values are indications of how we orientate ourselves in a real historical process. Though they are manifest psychologically, they can in no sense be reduced to psychological relations. And the concept of interest stands to remind us of this. The one secure generalization we can make about psychotherapy on the basis of the above analysis is that it is a profoundly value-embedded practice. Indeed, since so much of therapy concerns consciousness and choice, and plays so heavily upon moral themes, values may be said to be at the very centre of it. And just as we expect of a patient that her/his value orientation be internally coherent and consistent with real practices, so must we expect the same of therapists. In other words, the therapy we practise cannot be sharply demarcated from the life we lead. We do not sit in a consulting room for x hours a day and live separately for $24-x$ hours. How we practise during the x hours has a lot to do with what we are during the rest of the day; and what we do during the $24-x$ hours reflects back profoundly into the time spent in the consulting room.

In fact, the entire question of time has to be thoroughly rethought within the framework of psychotherapy. For there is a serious contradiction here. Therapy time is – or should be – 'free time', that is, time within which the patient is free to unburden her- or himself, express all kinds of outrageous thoughts, and so forth. Yet as we all know bitterly well, time in capitalist society is anything but free. The measure of value, rather, is the amount of time to be converted into money. As a result, free time is like a free press: free for anyone who is rich enough to buy it. The situation is worse in the United States than in Britain, but the basic relationship applies wherever therapy is practised in the modern world: the therapist's control over time is a function of her/his class position; the patient's search for time is a function of her/his desire to find a space for self-expression – a space, finally, for desire itself. When Freud wrote that the unconscious is timeless, he was expressing this truth. However, therapeutic work takes place in a temporality that is firmly bound. Depending on the patient's class position, she/he is enabled to control time as well. This is another way of describing the difference between the reality principle and the pleasure principle; but it calls attention to the way this difference devolves into structural differences between therapist and patient. These may be subtle, and of course, they are easily mystified.

Thus many ambiguities may be concealed within the supposedly disinterested therapeutic relationship. And yet the disinterestedness of this relationship is a vital condition for therapy, one which requires a suspension of ordinary judgements. After all, therapy has to be different from the rest of life, or there is no point to it. And one of the fundamental tenets upon which therapy is built is a respect for the individuality of the patient. In practical terms, this respect, which is, to be sure, a very important value of its own, means a capacity to suspend or at least modify ordinary value judgements where the patient is concerned. For example, if the therapist is personally devout and the patient an atheist, it would be essential for this position of the patient to be respected. In other words, the patient must be taken on his or her own terms, and not ours. Thus the therapist needs a certain reflexivity in his or her value structure. This is associated with the ability to empathize. But empathy is a subjective state, while value, as we have observed, contains much more of a person's practical orientation to the world. We cannot therefore invoke a purely psychological function to account for the ability to respect another's values. A more complex analysis is needed, one which takes into account the therapist's entire position in the world. Consider some terms used to describe this faculty of the therapist.

We say that therapists should be *objective* and *neutral* with respect to the patient. But in actual fact there is something very slippery about these seemingly innocuous terms. How are we to be objective about another human being? To be objective means to be attuned to full reality as against whim or fancy. But who is to say how to define the reality that is human? Is it being objective to treat a person as an object, that is to say, a *thing without value*? Objects have position in time and space, and nothing else. They do not remember and they do not anticipate. And they value nothing. The whole of scientific medicine is built intellectually on the premise that useful knowledge about human beings can be obtained if we momentarily reduce them to object status – concentrate on the cells of their liver, the pH of their bodily fluid, or the structural integrity of their bones. We know that this is less than the whole person, and we know that physical medicine, and psychiatry when it models itself after medicine, has troubles as well as triumphs with its organic reduction. But without exploring this further at present, we understand the basis for this reduction heuristically: there are occasions when object-status overtakes us and when, therefore, the object-reduction applies to a real case. If I slip on the ice and fall on my outstretched hand, gravity, mass, and the mechanical properties of my bones hold sway, and value considerations are for the moment irrelevant. But when I go to a therapist's office, I am not bringing in my disease like a broken watch for repair; it is I, myself, a knowing, willing, resisting, value-laden subject, who goes in there. If the therapist is to be objective about me – that is, treat me as I really am – then she/he cannot treat me as an object. To be objective about another human means recognizing her or his subjectivity with its values as a real agency. But one cannot recognize subjectivity at a distance: it has to be encountered, engaged. And how can we really, truly be *neutral* in such a case? For if I am neutral, then I am disengaged. Neutrality can be read as not caring. I am reminded of an occasion when, in order to get an extremely resistant, though superficially compliant, patient unstuck, I pointed out to him that he was free to continue in his inert and self-destructive ways. He was, and I was right to point this out. However, I must have been exasperated, as well, for he interpreted my comment as a brutal rejection. 'I know I am free,' he retorted, 'but you are here to stop me and change me. You can't just let me get away with this. After all, that is why I see you . . . to stand for something different.'

Those who try to hide behind the mantle of pure objectivity, then, are deceiving themselves and short-changing their patients. We hear much talk about 'technique' in therapy. But this is a word, in my opinion, which should be subjected to relentless scrutiny. If technique means, 'according to the principles of work as defined in the beginning of this talk', then there is no problem with the term. However, if it means, as it often does, a disengaged, purely instrumental approach, an approach that can be assimilated to, say, a training manual along the lines of, 'if patient does *A*, say *B*', then the technical becomes a term for the mechanistic treating of another human, the reduction of her/his subjectivity to a predictable, controllable and ultimately quiescent object. It only remains to be added that the seemingly value-free position subsumed into a purely technical approach to therapeutics has in reality a profound, if unspoken, value embedded in it, namely, that very value inherent in reducing a person to a controllable object. The therapist, then, who hides behind a shield of seemingly detached and technical neutrality is in fact asserting a highly authoritarian value position.

There is a superficially tempting way out of the problem of neutrality, which is to draw a line between value positions and to say, in effect: those on this side of the line are 'health values', such as intimacy, spontaneity, insight, and so on; while those on the other side are not germane to mental health – for example, matters of religious or political conviction. The one group states, according to this line of reasoning, 'I will engage in my role as therapist'; the other, 'I will let be out of respect for the individuality of the patient.' However this pathway is as misleading as the one of pure objectivity. It assumes falsely that values can be neatly segregated or unambiguously defined, that a person's politics, for example, are unrelated to her/his human relations, or that 'health' is an apolitical concept. In truth, however, unless we reduce politics to the meaningless consummatory act of which lever to pull at the polls, it must be regarded as profoundly interrelated with all of the passions and human attachments to which a person is subjected and which are themselves bound to become implicated in any real therapy. Furthermore, 'health ethics' *per se* – that is, the reduction of all value questions to matters of sickness or well-being – is political precisely in its seeming apolitical nature. Surely, withdrawing value from the political arena by a process of medicalization is a political act of deep significance. In truth, if the therapist is engaged in one aspect of the patient's life she/he is necessarily engaged in all others. The predicament still remains: how to be 'for' the patient, yet involved in a real way; or, how to be with another without losing oneself.

In this process there is no way of evading reality. All concepts of 'mental health' are historical statements. For example, the insight for which psychoanalysis toils has a complex and problematic relation to states of well-being. What is indisputable, however, is that insight entails historically determined value positions. Not all cultures value insight or the practice of introspection, which is necessary for its realization in analysis. And within our culture, introspection signifies participation in a particular class and social relation. It is not, after all, something encouraged or held out as part of working-class life. I am not saying that working-class people do not develop insight, but for them to do so in analysis means pursuing an activity foreign to their experience of the world. Therefore its attainment amounts to more of a dislocation than would be the case for someone whose class-experience involved the categories of reflection. Nor is insight a goal to be pursued in isolation. It is always something that occurs in conjunction with a privileged relationship. One does not acquire insight in the abstract, but as an analysand, just as one acquired forgiveness from sin in an earlier era as a penitent in a confessional.

The same goes for all therapeutic goals, including symptom-relief or freedom from pain. In other words, one cannot evade the value problem by saying, in effect, I'm simply doing my job as a physician to relieve suffering. For the suffering we deal with inevitably has a moral and social quality. I myself think that most suffering is needless; but I am also prepared hotly to defend the thesis that some degree of suffering is inherent in consciousness. We are sentient creatures who suffer from desires. The mystic says: eliminate desire, then you will suffer no more. I counter: to suffer is to be alive, to experience the historical incompleteness of the world. Given the degree of injustice and barbarity actually prevalent in the world, not to suffer would mean a kind of deadness, an unconscionable betrayal of one's fellow humans. Would one want to remove the pain, for example, of a Simone Weil, clearly a 'troubled' woman, full of 'psycho-pathology', whose sufferings had the stamp of genius on them and were turned towards human emancipation (Petre-mente, 1977)? Of one thing only I am sure: therapy has no simple equations for such a case. That is, of course, an expression of my value position, just as the mystic's statement was, just as a 'feel-good' therapist's who practised, for example, by pumping his or her patients full of euphoriant and narcotic drugs, would be of his or hers. We can argue the respective merits of these values. What is indisputable again, however, is that our most elementary function as a therapist, the removal of pain, is subject to a very subtle value analysis.

Nor can one rest with the evasion that we merely give the patient what she/he wants, that is, pays for. That this is an evasion can be shown by a very simple example, for I do not think that there is any reader who would, for example, accept a man for treatment who came with the complaint that he suffered from some anxiety and guilt when he raped small boys, and asked for help in removing these unpleasant affects. You might argue that that is an extreme and rare case and that in the vast majority of real instances one has no difficulty in at least trying to give the patient what she or he wants. This may be factually true, but it does not invalidate the proposition that the choice to help someone at all, no matter how elementary the request, is a function of our values.

To illustrate this in a somewhat more complex and marginal way, let me tell you about a woman whom I recently declined to treat. I had seen her briefly a few years ago, at which time it had become clear to me that a substantial part of her difficulty lay in her objective social position. It was not that she was poor or deprived: quite the opposite. Rather, she belonged to the upper strata of society. And I use the word 'belong' advisedly. For she was one of those corporate wives who function as adornments to their husbands. They have to keep the right kind of houses and are allowed by the more progressive corporations (of which this was one) to travel with their husbands to conventions and meetings, where there are special therapeutic events for wives. This woman's husband was a relentlessly ambitious man who refused to come in for treatment. He obviously doted on his wife and provided her with powerful material rewards as well as a kind of protection against her relatively unbridled impulses, of which she had many. In addition to this, she had three daughters, to whom she was very attached.

She came in for help suffering from that kind of endemic and poorly defined 'depression' characteristic of so many women in her station. I had the opportunity to treat the case as an intrapsychic affair and to help reconcile her to the security of her position. But it seemed that to do so would be a violation of the truth and of her real potential as a woman. So I told her instead, in effect, that along with her many unresolved infantile conflicts she was caught in a predicament that could not be overlooked. For the truth is, I said, 'you are a bird in a gilded cage'. She was, to be sure, not *only* such a creature, but enough of one to make it an ineluctable feature of her suffering. She agreed with this – and it made a difference to her – but not very much could be done, for the next thing that happened was the ubiquitous corporate transfer, this time to Africa, where the husband was to play a major role in steering his company's fortunes. During her years overseas she came back from time to time. Her situation had by now led her to take a lover as a diversion, but she evinced no intention of making a serious change in her comfortably miserable state.

In the meanwhile I had ample time to reflect. The husband's corporation was not simply a cultural arrangement to keep wives suppressed. It was a powerful historical reality engaged in activities in southern Africa of a sort that I happen to find abominable. In blunt terms, it was sustaining the apartheid regime of South Africa. And the husband, not malevolently perhaps, but as an objective consequence of his ambition, was furthering this in a definite way.

Eventually the family returned, set up house in a wealthy suburb of New York City, and plunged our patient back into an existence she knew only too well as a source of despair. At this point she made two decisions: to jettison her lover and return to therapy. This time, she said, it was to make a real change in her circumstances. Just getting a job wasn't enough; she wanted to confront 'the whole thing'.

I agreed that such a confrontation was a good idea, and that therapy was a good idea, too. But I declined to offer myself as the therapist, despite – or rather, because of – the previous contact we had had. And, not unexpectedly, she declined my offer of a referral.

What had happened here? It is a complex matter, but no more so, perhaps, than any human relationship. There was no question of her being trapped, and although I remain loath to predict what real change would be best for her, it seems to me, now as it did then, that some change had to take place – either reconciling her to her limits, which some might advocate as the path of wisdom, or a more imaginative confrontation of them, with the sobering possibility of family breakup. Now there are values inherent in both choices, and although I think that mine would have inclined towards the latter choice, I think also that I could work with either outcome – in other words, I could have let her be herself in that decision. But such a decision could not be made in isolation. Therapy goes beyond any particular decision; it is also a material relationship. I had to be paid for my time, and she, being objectively dependent upon her husband and the corporation, would have had to use money generated by them for the purpose. And this I could not accept, partly because the corporation was obnoxious to me, but mainly because this revulsion of mine could not but ruin the treatment. She knew at some level how I felt, though I had never exhorted her on such subjects; and there was no escaping therefore the material implication that she would be taking money from her husband in a situation that was prearranged to betray him. There is still more. Her lover had been a physician, and an outsider; and he was but the next-to-last in a series of infatuations with mysterious and, so to speak, dark men. I was clearly in line for the final position. There being no way to resolve this within the configuration of roles, values and interests we had each assumed, it seemed to me the case that a genuine therapeutic relationship would be impossible to arrange. And so I bowed out, provoking her rage and, unfortunately, her spite, for she seemed bound to deny herself the benefits of treatment along with its forbidden fantasies.

To summarize, I found myself unable to continue working with her because the real configuration of our interests and values precluded my letting her be herself. From another angle, the real value problem made itself felt in a rigid-ification of the transference.

Now it may be claimed that I was acting in an overly opinionated way here – and that moreover my particular set of opinions or values are bound to get me into trouble with a significant proportion of the clientele who can afford private psychotherapy. That is, to be sure, my problem. But there is also a related problem for the mental health professional in general. For the antithesis to my position, which is to have or espouse no political values whatsoever – that is, to keep a low, suitably detached 'professional' profile – is impossible and self-contradictory. In fact, of course, the mental health professional has a set of values like everyone else, which develop through cultural indoctrination and which are rooted in material economic interest. The calls for the political detachment of the professional are made from the assumption that there is no distinction in class interest between patient and therapist. This may in fact be the general case, but to the extent it is, it is a fact correlated with the capture of psychotherapeutics by white male bourgeois ideology. And this has serious, and by no means salutory, consequences.

The core of therapeutics is care, and care is a universalizing quality of relationship. Class interest, on the other hand, is particularizing and delimiting, the more so as it becomes the interest of the dominant class, which invariably attempts to impose its own view of reality upon everything in order to keep itself in power. The result of this delimitization, evident on a massive social scale, is social alienation, or estrangement. Care, by contrast, is the antidote to alienation. If we care for someone we are *for* her or him no matter what she/he may be. And by caring we accept a flexible set of therapeutic goals according to the needs of the patient. This is, as we well know, an extraordinarily demanding job, and it is important to remind ourselves of how it came about historically. For the rise of psychotherapeutic movements, and I am here lumping all of them together, is on the societal level precisely a reaction to massive social estrangement and the associated splitting-off of a privatized inner world where personal life is to take place. Therapy is the reaching into that estranged inner world by a new class of professionals. And the capture of that professional class by dominant bourgeois ideology is therefore a way of maintaining alienation at the precise moment of its supposed dissolution.

The above line of reasoning was carried out on an abstract plane. However, it should not be thought that it is without application to the most mundane details of practice. How many of us, for all that we supposedly know better, have said on referral: 'I have a *good* patient for you . . . he can pay a full fee', or better yet, 'he has a full insurance policy'? The issue before us is not whether this attitude keeps psychotherapists from treating the poor (it, of course, does), but how it determines the way psychiatry treats everyone. In other words, economic interest is never merely a matter of crude wealth. It is also a mystique, a way of life, a culture. And concretely speaking, it is a profound regulator of practice. In order to stay afloat, the psychiatrist must not only treat people who can afford him/her, but must treat them in such a way that they can continue to afford him/her. But there is also a language in this, and a way of listening to, looking at, and being with another person. Health values, far from being morally neutral, have to be accommodated to the dominant morality of conventional success. And this applies to rich and poor patient alike. For example, a penniless woman of my acquaintance sought help from a prominent psychiatrist. The doctor cheerfully accepted her for treatment, and told her not to worry about the fee, because with treatment she would not only be over her depression but would be earning a fancy income as well in six months. This therapist was only being candid, for most psychiatrists, like good, bourgeois parents, have every reason to value the worldly success of their patients. And this does not have to be done by exhortation. It is contained in the very categories of treatment. Consider only how basic psychoanalytic technique, by stressing delay of gratification, intellectual mastery, and so forth, is a recycled version of the basic Protestant value system for the accumulation of wealth. It is true that analysis also works with spontaneity, but in the balance between spontaneity and control, the weight of economic interest is placed on the side of the latter. At the simplest level, the patient who rebels and goes his or her own way, leaving the stifling job or the confining marriage, often faces loss of the therapy itself, for rebels and freer spirits are distinctly less likely to have good insurance policies than the citizen who stays put. This may seem so elementary as not to require notice, yet it is the very substance of how psychiatry becomes an intellectually timid and conformist profession that functions to reproduce the existing order of society.

The response to these various dilemmas need not be cynicism or a retreat from any particular value, including the much-battered one of neutrality. It is to recognize instead the necessity of a superordinate and universalizing viewpoint within which these values can be realized. I do not wish to leave the impression that I identify this viewpoint with what ordinarily passes for a radical political stance. In the real world, for reasons we need not explore here, many political radicals are tuned to the social collective and remain obtuse and uncaring where individual people are concerned. On the other hand, many a so-called 'bourgeois' therapist breaks, consciously or not, with her/his class position in the direction of a caring attitude. For this attitude still exists as a remnant of the broken promises of the capitalist era. The issue is not immediately political in a narrow sense. Rather is it one of finding the foundation for a value position adequate to a therapy which must respect the individual and care for her/him, while being carried out in class society. For present purposes let us call this the perspective of a critical intelligence. Such an intelligence recognizes the determination of any practice by the social order of which it is a part; and in so doing, moves to transcend that order. It lives in reality but does not accept it blindly, recognizing instead that the world is an unfree place, and that all of its official categories are likewise unfree. Critical intelligence differentiates, and distinguishes sharply between surface and depth, actuality and potentiality. It sees the heights and the depths as manifestations of one reality, and has the sensitivity therefore not to resort to manipulation or crude exhortations. Freud at his best was a critical thinker *par excellence*; and what is to be most valued about psychoanalysis remains its appreciation of the radically repudiated underside of bourgeois existence. This discovery of Freud's enables us to regard any person, including ourselves, as an unfinished project, one whose real powers can transcend the given state of affairs. By postulating these powers we are enabled to be *for* a person while critical of that state of affairs, in both its internal and external aspects – its neurotic crippling as well as its social backwardness. The therapist's paramount goal remains the individuation of the patient. Individuation is not individualism, each person narcissistically for him or herself. It is the development of human power in a social context. It requires, therefore, a grasp not only of how we move from infancy to adulthood, but equally, a critical appreciation of the actual state of unfreedom ingrained in family and society. For in this society people are not allowed to develop their individuality except at the expense of others; which is to say, they cannot develop that universal quality which is the heart of individuation. Caring, that kernel of the authentic therapeutic attitude, is, it may be added, a form of praxis in the interest of individuation. That is why it, too, has a universalizing quality, a movement towards the affirmation of what a person can be – and has, as well, a latent critical content, directed at what suppresses human capacities. But since full individuation is impossible under the given arrangements, therapy must remain partial and preliminary. Recognizing this might save us from the sectarian squabbles which infest psychotherapeutics and which are all foreign to the critical intelligence.

One last clarification may be in order. Though a political stance and a therapeutic one are different, this need not be taken to mean that the therapist should shy away from politics or public life. Indeed, it should not mean so, in my opinion. Given the state of the world, everyone has an overriding interest in political involvement, and there can be no excuses for disengagement because of so-called neutrality – any more than there would be if a fire broke out in one's office during a session. Of course, the situations are deeply different, in that political engagement is an ongoing and not necessarily an emergency process, and needs to be integrated into sound therapeutic practice. The question arises, for example, as to whether public political activity by the therapist outside the office may affect the transference. Indeed it may – but so may everything else, including anonymity and the absence of political involvement. Whether it affects transference in a constructive way or not depends not on the public position taken, but on the quality of one's therapeutic behaviour. Here it is essential that the therapeutic session not be converted into an occasion for indoctrination or proselytizing. The therapist's politics are to be neither affirmed nor denied within the confines of the session. Should they become known, they should be acknowledged and then made into an occasion for the active confrontation by the patient of his or her own political values and relation to public life. However, this confrontation should go on, in any case. The political dimension of life should be actively engaged in therapy, as a part of personal reality no less real and no less subject to neurotic distortion than sexuality. In this regard, the therapist should be able to convey respect for differences in politics, so long as those differences are consciously articulated. What should not be tolerated, in therapy any more than life outside, is political unconsciousness and automatism – a politics passively received and blindly reproduced.

All this is part of the critical approach to therapy. It cannot be taken lightly, given the way therapy has become institutionalized. For the spirit of professionalism, and therefore the real interests inherent in that spirit, are also foreign to the critical intelligence. Those who undertake to develop it have a struggle ahead of them, a struggle against internalized attitudes no less than entrenched material forces. However, conflict is one thing which should not be foreign to the psychotherapist – and this conflict in particular is to be greatly valued.

PART FOUR

MARX AND FREUD

THE ESSAYS of this section are a miscellaneous group, all moving within a theoretical space defined by psycho-analysis and Marxism. I never had any strong impulse to form a synthesis between Freud and Marx, in which their particular identities would dissolve. It seemed then – and seems now – that this does violence to Marxism and psycho-analysis alike. I use Marxism and psychoanalysis rather as methodologies, each turned critically towards the other, and both directed towards various problems in subjectivity and society.

A word or two about 'Marxism' might be in order, since if you call yourself a Marxist it does not mean anything more specific than-if you call yourself a Christian. Broadly speaking, the Marxism I had in mind from the early seventies until the early eighties was 'Western', 'Hegelian', 'humanist', 'anti-Stalinist', 'anti-bureaucratic', and 'non-Leninist'. That is to say, I was hostile to the idea of a strong and centralized party as the vanguard of the revolution, because of the potentially authoritarian character of such a body. I saw the revolutionary path within advanced industrial societies moving through a kind of Luxemburgist route, that is, the spontaneity of the masses, workers' councils, decentralization and so forth. It would be fair to say that I have strong anarchistic tendencies, stemming from a deep-seated distrust of authority and a love of spontaneity, the individualism endemic to Americans, and the legacy of sixties' radicalism. In this period, I suffered yet another split, between an anarchist heart and a Marxist head – and perhaps another illusion, that these two could be put together within the conditions of our time.

A number of these tendencies found a home among the group of intellectuals around the journal *Telos*, the same which had launched my Marxist career with its review of *White Racism*. By 1974, I had become an editor, and while I cannot say I contributed greatly to the journal, it is certainly

true that its heady brand of radical intellectuality – so much
against the American grain, it has to be added – contributed
greatly to my development, and gave me a secure reference
point for almost a decade. The dominant tendency within
the *Telos* group was the critical theory of the Frankfurt
school. This proved congenial to me, especially the thought
of Marcuse, Adorno and Horkheimer, all of whom had
combined Marxism with psychoanalysis. For some time I
would identify myself as either a Marcusean or an Adornian,
depending on whether I was feeling optimistic or pessimistic
about social transformation.

'The Marxist view of man and psychoanalysis' was my
first formal statement of the Marx–Freud problem. There
have been a number of others over the years, but this is
representative of the lot. (However, compare it to 'Marx,
Freud and the problem of materialism' (page 306) to see how
my thinking on this subject underwent a change in the
eighties.)

'Narcissism and the family' appeared in *Telos*, and reflects
its influence, as well as that of the Frankfurt School. It also
signals a direction to my thinking which was to culminate
in *The Age of Desire*. As in 'Therapy in late capitalism' (page
121), the article uses Marxism and psychoanalysis in the
study of what might be called civil society, or everyday life.
In contrast to the earlier essays, there is now a definite
conception of late (or monopoly) capitalist society as a
totality, a prominent feature of which is the production and
administration of personal life and subjectivity. Closely
related to this is a strong awareness of mass culture as
the predominant means by which the corporate structure
administers desire in the interests of promoting consumption and depoliticizing the population. The special role of
psychoanalysis consists of its unmasking of a subjectivity
distorted by an intractable crisis of the family. It is therefore to
the family, the mediation between subjectivity and history,
that the essay turns as a point of entry into the totality of
late capitalism. The essay also returns to more explicitly
psychoanalytic ground. As a participant in a 1980 *Telos*
symposium on narcissism in late-capitalist society, I felt my
contribution would be greatest if I stuck to what I knew
through practice. The issue of narcissistic disorders had
surfaced in psychoanalysis, while Christopher Lasch and
others had advanced the term as a way of accounting

for late-capitalist culture as a whole. I tried to put both dimensions together in a historical manifold.

The next two essays reflect another major association, with Stanley Diamond and the journal *Dialectical Anthropology*. I did not meet Diamond until 1980, but there was an immediate resonance and affinity, and from then on his notion of the primitive as a zone of lost and partially recoverable wholeness has played a major role in my thought. There has always been a Utopian element to my world-view, occupied variously by the figures of Blake, Reich, Marcuse and Marx, and serving as a counterpoint to my critical tendencies. I found in the idea of the primitive – and the anthropological ground of that idea – a singularly fruitful realization of Utopian possibilities.

'Mind and state in ancient Greece' was originally to be a chapter of *The Age of Desire* demonstrating the essentially historical nature of the psyche. The idea first came from discussions with Bennett Simon, psychoanalyst and classicist, and I had mulled episodically about it for years before setting it down in a draft of the book. It didn't quite work there, so I lifted it out, went over it with Diamond and placed it in *Dialectical Anthropology*. Despite its amateurishness, the essay has always been one of my favourites.

'Marx on the Jewish question' was written for a special issue of *Dialectical Anthropology*. The article provided a double challenge: to make sense of the darker side of Marx – and radical discourse in general – and to come to grips with my own 'non-Jewish Jewishness'. Both are vexing questions. The opacity of Marxism for subjectivity and the tragic side of human existence is a major shortcoming. My speculation here is that this is not unconnected to Marx's anti-Semitism. From the other side, a major conflict in my own life has arisen from my perception of the decay of Jewish radicalism and its replacement – I speak here of the United States in particular – by rampant embourgeoisification and Zionism. All of which provides a good deal of tension for the essay, and an opportunity to dust off some literary material.

Finally, 'Why Freud or Reich?' resumes on the ground of polemic. I had been asked to write an introduction to Janine Chasseguet-Smirgel and Béla Grunberger's *Freud or Reich?* (1986). The authors refused – sensibly enough – to have it appear in their book, and so I touched and toughened it up and ran it in *Free Associations*. I have often pledged to myself

not to get involved in polemics, and just as often have
broken that pledge when I found something about which I
could not remain silent. In any case, *Freud or Reich?* epitomizes psychoanalytic discourse turned to frankly reactionary ends. More, it says some true things about Reich,
but in such a destructive spirit as to demand a response. Most
important, the essay gave me an opportunity to address the
question of this tragic genius who so inspired me and
affected my life. I fear it will please neither the true believers
in Reich nor those who see him as a crank and madman.

9 THE MARXIST VIEW OF MAN AND PSYCHOANALYSIS

Any attempt to comprehend the different views of man developed by Marxism and psychoanalysis must begin with the questions: which Marxism and which psychoanalysis? Or, better, whose? The problem is not merely the one – significant enough – of reducing an immense topic to manageable size. At a deeper level it reflects the truth that Marxism and psychoanalysis are in fact trends; put another way, intellectual booty that has been fought over, dispersed, buried, and transmuted by the very historical interests Marx and Freud subjected to critique.

And so a minimum condition for an essay of this sort is the specification of its author's own interests. Let me put them negatively. I shall be scarcely considering the possibilities of mediation between psychoanalysis and what has been aptly called vulgar Marxism – that doctrine which serves the interest of despotic state bureaucracies and sectarian Left-splinter parties alike by interpreting Marx's thought in a narrowly economistic way and without the category of freedom so essential to it. Nor shall I be much interested in pursuing the prospect of mediation between Marxism and any version of psychoanalysis that waters down Freud's insistence on the centrality of repressed infantile sexuality, whether it be Erik Erikson's inflation of the identity concept[1] or Erich Fromm's reformulation of the problem of drive and repression.[2] Justice is done to Marx or Freud only by recognizing the profound contradiction they pose for each other.

Marx and Freud were most alike in their insistence that the human world be viewed from the standpoint of contradiction. Refusing to accept the given fact as self-constitutive, each saw 'reality' as emergent from the interplay of forces that had been split off in a historical process and were struggling towards a surface that worked actively to confine them. For both men, the activity itself – the splitting-off, the struggling, the working to confine – was ultimately referred to the categories of real *domination*, expressed in the forced division of labour, or the Oedipal situation within the family. As a result of this unremittingly dialectical and hierarchical interpretation, each theory becomes harshly critical of the existing order and hence a problem for those institutions within the established order, such as universities, which have to live in an uneasy balance between the needs of power and those of critical truth.

Often rejected because they do not meet the standards of positive or 'normal' science, just as often accepted on condition they be de-fanged, the two critiques have refused to go away. Marxism in particular has been difficult for academia to swallow, since it insists upon the material transformation of all social institutions and sets itself up as a permanent de-legitimator of the bourgeois world. Psycho-analysis, on the other hand, was more readily tamed, since it placed prime emphasis upon the subjective. Indeed, it has become appropriated by American medicine and psychiatry as a quasi-official theory of the mind. Whether this theory is truly psychoanalytic is a problem that has to be considered, but in any event the appropriation itself provided an anch-oring of psychoanalysis in bourgeois culture. It remained, however, for the legitimation crisis of late capitalism to bring Marxism back into academic view, where it presently challenges and is challenged by other intellectual forces, including the psychoanalytic.

The areas of homology noted above between Marxism and psychoanalysis could be multiplied (compare Heilbroner, 1975, pp. 414–32). Why, then, the sense of profound contra-diction? One is tempted to say that it is because Marx was a Utopian, Freud an anti-Utopian sceptic; or that Marx kept his eye on the species, which has a chance to live and is swept up in Darwinian progression, while Freud looked at the individual, who must die, and whose happiness is so easily sacrificed for that of the collectivity; or that Marx sustained a role for the future and active striving, while Freud was obsessed with the past with its passive pull. All these points indicate the conflict between the two systems, but they do not, in my opinion, explain it in any way that opens up the possibility of overcoming that conflict within its own terms. For this purpose a more penetrating methodo-logical critique is needed, an examination of the actual domain encompassed by each theory as it constructs a vision

of man. Moreover, such a critique has to include the historical   169
dimension of that domain.

THE MARXIST VIEW OF MAN

It has become a truism by now that Marx overturned
Hegelian idealism to insert, not the idea, but concrete
practical activity – the labour process – as the motor of
society. It is, however, anything but a simple step to get
from this fundamental point to a comprehensive view of
man. It is true that many Marxists have tried to make it a
simple step: Man is *Homo laborans*, defined by his situation
in the labour process; his psychology is defined then by such
traits as would make him want to work, productively to
transform nature, or to exploit those who do work.
Depending upon the objective situation, one or another side
of these propensities will come to the fore, giving to Man
his place in the class struggle. To this view – which of
course corresponds to the term 'vulgar Marxism' – all other
attributes are mere incidentals, residual categories at best,
or positive mystifications. To such an eye, man is a passive
creature whose consciousness is simply determined by the
impingement of material forces.

As soon as one abandons such an extrapolation of *Homo
laborans*, whose very linearity is profoundly un-Marxist, the
way is open for a richer conception of the Marxist view of
what is intrinsically human. Indeed, the linear view falls of
its own weight, since it is totally unable to account for one
of the main elements of Marxist doctrine, the revolutionary
role of the proletariat, without introducing *ad hoc* motivations
– that is, forces *within* the person that are mysterious and
out of reach of society. Put differently, if people are simply
determined by material conditions, why do they resist
oppression? Vulgar Marxism would like to keep any such
questions out of view, since they create embarrassing
complications for the new socialist order. Vulgar Marxist
man is a robot as ripe for the domination of bureaucratic
socialism as for that of corporate capital.

To be sure, some Marxist thinkers have been aware of the
dilemma posed by a strictly materialist conception of human
nature; and they have been able to demonstrate a current
within Marx's thinking which opens on to a more recognizably human view. According to this interpretation, which
may be identified as that of socialist humanism, Marx does
not see man as inexorably bound by material conditions but

as an inherently active and self-appropriating agent. What is distinctly 'Marxist', however, is that this self-appropriation can come about only through the universalization of the self in society. This in turn requires the overcoming of class society and its alienation of human power in the labour process.

In the humanist view, therefore, *Homo laborans* – man defined by the labour process – is not man as he really is but man stunted by capitalism. Vulgar Marxism, it follows, mistakes the critique of man as he has become under capitalism for the essence of the human. Under capitalism, however, this human essential exists only in a potential form, at least in the mass. It is there – but to be created, not as it will become. Hence Marx's insistence on concrete praxis as the self-formative principle. Entailed in this too we see his profoundly historical perspective. We are not merely determined by what has gone before but by what we are to become through our social activity.

The role of society cannot be stressed too strongly when considering Marx's view of man. The matter is stated very clearly in 'The sixth thesis on Feuerbach': 'The essence of man is no abstraction inhering in each single individual. In its actuality it is the ensemble of social relationships' (1844b, p. 402). Marx wrote little to elaborate this nuclear proposition concerning human nature, although every line of his work is consistent with it. No doubt he felt it to be self-evident and, regarding the social impediments to full human individuation and freedom as primary, expended his energy on their delineation. Here is another version, from a footnote to *Capital*:

Since he comes into the world neither with a looking-glass in his hand, nor as a Fichtian philosopher, to whom 'I am I' is sufficient, man first sees and recognizes himself in other men. Peter only establishes his own identity as a man by first comparing himself with Paul as being of like kind. And thereby Paul, just as he stands in his Pauline personality, becomes to Peter the type of the genus homo. (1867, p. 52)

The point again, however, is that men do not exist in a passive material relation, simply absorbing and reflecting social impressions as the earth absorbs sunlight. Rather human existence is an active process, one that involves a certain postulated formative power as well as a need for objects in the world. However, neither these powers nor these needs are to be seen as fixed or rigidly structured. What is 'natural' in human nature is only the willingness to make, and the necessity for the 'ensemble of social relations'. The needs and powers are mutually created in the making. It is this broader image of Man the Maker, *Homo faber*, which constitutes the heart of the labour process. As Marx writes:

'Man' opposes himself to nature as one of her own forces, setting in motion . . . the natural forces of his body, in order to appropriate Nature's productions in a form adapted to his own wants. By thus acting on the external world and changing it, he at the same time changes his own nature. He develops his slumbering powers and compels them to act in obedience to his sway. (1867, p. 177)

And this form of labour is 'exclusively human'. More, the active, exclusively human work relationship presupposes and, we are led to believe, creates the conditions of consciousness itself:

What distinguishes the worst architect from the best of bees is this, that the architect raises his structure in imagination before he erects it in reality. At the end of every labour-process, we get a result that already existed in the imagination of the labourer at its commencement. (1867, p. 177)

To sum up, that which is definitively human for Marx is purposeful and intentional activity which transforms nature and so becomes social. Nature should be seen here as what is passively given, the social as what actively transforms it in a human way. The 'labour process' is thus the human essence of the human condition itself. If Marx seems to some critics to be riddled with the notion of labour as productive economic activity (for example, Adorno's remark that he wanted to make the world into a gigantic work house – reported in Jay, 1973, p. 57), it is because he is preoccupied with what has become of this innate, transhistorical capacity over the course of history. 'Men make their own history, but they do not make it just as they please; they do not make it under circumstances chosen by themselves, but under circumstances directly encountered, given and transmitted from the past. The tradition of all the dead generations weighs like a nightmare on the brain of the living' (Marx, 1968b, p. 97). What is given is the nightmare of toil and domination. And Marx sets out to look at the given, with that concentrated power which is the mark of his genius, in

order to resolve its 'givenness' into the product of what it
has been and what it might become.

Hence the insistence on concreteness and praxis – that is, on a method that restores motion to phenomena which might seem otherwise frozen, and specificity to that which is abstract. This explains why Marx wastes so little time with the concept of 'Man', and why Marxist humanism remains problematic unless it rids itself of the hypostatized notion of Man to which academic discussion is so prone. Not in Man but in men and women in their real historical activity resides the Marxist view of man.

Within Marx's conception, the preservation of the moment of the future within the present deserves special attention. By placing intentionality and purpose at the centre of its view of man, Marxism retains a critical function along with its concreteness. Everything is to be studied exactly as it manifests itself now, but that very manifestation pushes forward into immediacy that which has been bound down by the past. To be sure, Marx cannot hold that this future is rigidly determined – that it will inevitably turn out to be communistic – without losing the concept of freedom embedded within his idea of praxis. To the extent that he lapses into deterministic and naïvely Utopian statements he demands criticism. But by and large within Marx's writings the concept of the future is not to be read as 'that which will come to be' but as the 'non-necessity of what is'. Thus the future means potentiality and, more to the point, a rejection of immutability within any historically defined category.

Here is the power of the Marxist view of man for any of the human sciences, psychology included. The Marxist view of man is not a psychology; indeed, it cannot in itself generate one, for reasons we shall shortly elaborate. Rather must it remain a superordinate critique of psychology and all the rest of the individual human sciences, holding before them the reminder that the object of their study, Man, is an unfinished and fractured creature, and that their specific discipline picks up but one of the pieces at a time. A real piece, no doubt, yet a shard that cannot be fully grasped outside the process of societal transformation. Accordingly, any standard of measurement established by the prevailing social order is as subject to critique as are any of the deviations from the standards of the prevailing order which form the ordinary subject-matter of academic discourse.

From the standpoint of psychology Marx reveals this

principle in a way most telling when he describes the 173
relations between the miser and the capitalist: 'This boundless greed after riches, this passionate chase after exchange-
value, is common to the capitalist and the miser; but while
the miser is merely a capitalist gone mad, the capitalist is a
rational miser' (1867, 1: p. 153). Specifics aside, what is
striking about this passage is its refusal to locate madness
or reason outside each other. The point goes far beyond
establishing the labelling of deviant behaviour, or the truth
that there may be a core of reason in madness. It also crucially
implies that we cannot take reason itself for granted, that it
does not exist without a core of madness, that it and madness
alike develop within history.

THE LIMITS OF MARXIST PSYCHOLOGY

This is a point that has been almost wholly lost to psychology,
including that most dialectical and critical of psychologies,
psychoanalysis. For all that his work remorselessly undermined the pretensions of reason and common sense –
indeed, showed them to exist in precisely the same kind of
emergent relationship to the repressed past that Marx had
shown for historical activity in general – Freud stubbornly
affirmed the transhistorical nature of a standard of rationality
and morality which had in fact been handed to him by
historical development. Consequently he could not see his
own history for what it was and turned to biology as the
source of explanation. Since reason was apprehension of
reality, and reality was always there – that is, not emergent
in history – reason had to rest ultimately on the rock of
material, non-human substance, on the movement of matter
through space and time and the laws of thermodynamics.
The sense of profound conflict between reason and desire
which Freud discovered in the human heart could find its
analogue therefore only in an equally profound schism
between the rational-human and the irrational-natural
worlds.

Moreover, as he resolved the essential conflict further,
Freud, lacking a vision of any dynamism within history
itself, had ultimately to locate it within warring trends of
nature: the reality and pleasure principles and, finally, Eros
and Thanatos. Society's splits were thereby subordinated
theoretically to those of nature. They resulted from efforts
to tame one part of nature – the death force – in the interest
of securing the goals of another part – the life force: efforts

which were bound to fail because of the weakened binding
power inherent in aim-inhibited libido.

Although reflective of the endemic spirit of crisis hanging over the Western world, Freud's social generalizations have proved at best sterile. I am here referring to large-scale societal generalizations, not his observations on, say, group psychology, which have been enormously fruitful. When applied concretely to problems of historical character, Freud's grand theories led to clumsy and positivistic biologizations of complex phenomena (for example, the inference of the Primal Crime as an actual event with genetic consequences); while from a theoretical side the lack of a historical critique left no resistance to the eventual conformism of psychoanalytic thought to the bourgeois order of things.

This weakness has persisted in the writings of the ego psychologists. However meritorious their work has been from the standpoint of theoretical refinement, in particular the avoidance of gross biologization, Freudian ego psychologists have continued in the master's tradition of opacity to historical dynamism. Heinz Hartmann, for example, brilliantly described the ways in which reason and morality are grounded within the psyche in relation to conflict (Hartmann, 1960). Yet one searches his writings in vain to find any awareness of serious contradiction within the categories of reason and morality. As with Freud, these are somehow there, ahistorical givens which the individual may or may not assimilate. There is no sense of their own problematical and conflict-ridden development within history; nor is cognizance taken of the truth that the so-called 'mental apparatus' has to be something that is evolving as humanity itself evolves – that is, that the psyche is as much a historical as it is a biological entity. Thus the grand systematization of metapsychology carried out by David Rapaport and Merton Gill omits consideration of a historical point of view in their canon of basic psychoanalytic operations (Rapaport and Gill, 1967).

To admit such a point of view would mean, to be sure, an exposure to Marxism. As *outré* as the prospect may seem, it does not in reality go beyond the existing structure of psychoanalysis. Every discipline has a domain within which its method generates knowledge and outside of which it must articulate with other disciplines that focus on other aspects of reality. These cross-disciplinary relations are of considerable theoretical importance – for example, the theoretic fruitfulness for biology of its relations with chem- istry. Just so has psychoanalysis been related to biology, albeit in a one-sided and limiting way. This one-sidedness is co-ordinated with the fact that its social articulations have been by and large a dreary hodgepodge. All that is proposed then is that this hodgepodge be replaced with a dynamic social theory worthy of the dialectical content of psychoanalysis. And despite the radical overhauling this may spell for many psychoanalytic categories, from the basic theoretical standpoint it would seem quite possible in view of the many striking homologies between the Freudian and Marxist systems of thought.

The question arises, however, whether Marxism is ready to be utilized for such a fertilization. For now we are not talking of a 'view of man' which can serve as a superordinate critique of the human sciences but of the Marxist conception of real men and women. We are suggesting a view, that is, which must retain the spirit of historical transformation while opening itself to the insights of psychoanalysis.

Is Marxism ready for such a view? The answer to this question has to be: not yet. The difficulty begins with the fact that Marxism cannot generate a psychology of its own. To be more exact, the terms of its own discourse, the very method which Marx employed with such power, demand that human motivation be appreciated only in so far as it eventuates in an activity – that is to say, as some event in the objective world. For only such an event can be abstracted and drawn into the money relationship which is the primum mobile of political economy. 'The money-form attaches itself either to the most important articles of exchange from outside . . . or else it attaches itself to the object of utility that forms . . . the chief portion of indigenous alienable wealth' (Marx, 1867, 1: p. 88). Only the alienable object can enter the exchange relationship, where it becomes further objectified into the commodity form. And so Marx makes plain that he is excluding the subjective side on the very first page of *Capital*, whose 'investigation must . . . begin with the analysis of a commodity', 'an object outside us, a thing that by its properties satisfies human wants of some sort or another. The nature of such wants, whether, for instance, they spring from the stomach or from fancy, makes no difference' (p. 35).

Thus the method of Marxism holds subjectivity in abeyance, and focuses only on that which is 'alienable'. It follows

therefore that only those aspects of mind which directly
mirror the objective world can be regarded as psychologically crucial. Consequently, even a humanist Marxism
cannot escape the trap of psychological one-dimensionality
if it is to be methodologically consistent. In other terms,
Marxism by itself cannot generate a psychology other than
one which confines itself to objectifiable events as determinants of behaviour. This helps to explain the predominance
of behaviouristic theory in the Soviet Union, and in many
orthodox Marxist attempts to describe psychological
relations. But behaviourism is a disaster for Marxism, since
it cannot escape the mere instrumentalization of psychology.
Behaviourism can never postulate a psychological force
which refuses to accept the immediacy of the given fact, and
it must consequently remain chained to the established
order. The concretely repressive uses to which behaviourism
has been put are but the manifestations of this fundamental
flaw.

The trap in which Marxism finds itself in relation to
psychology – caught between a subjectivism it cannot use
and a behaviourism from whose implications it must recoil
– is no trivial matter. It cannot, for example, be remedied by
tacking on fantasies and feelings to objective sources of
motivation with the homily that they are 'also important'.
The conjunction 'also' here implies that the subjective state
is simply additive and of the same conceptual value as the
objective.

But once such a principle is granted, Marxism collapses
like a house of cards. For Marx's entire *œuvre* rests upon the
consistent apprehension of a dialectical, not an additive,
relationship between subject and object. His insight was
that the objective commodity world arises through an indifference to subjective states except in so far as they could
become objectifiable. He saw, further, that this 'objectified'
subject became the regulating principle of social life through
the dialectic of domination. And last, he perceived that the
social life so produced became the condition for the further
development of the subject, the 'ensemble of social
relations'. Hence subjectivity in itself is intrinsically false
under the existing order. It comes immediately under the
sway of the 'fetishization of commodities', that objectification of human relationships whose contradictions define
the trajectory of history.

In other words, consciousness, or immediate introspection, is a profoundly unreliable guide. Put more decisively, the Marxist believes in an unconscious, but not one within the mind. As Rosa Luxemburg wrote, 'the unconscious comes before the conscious, the logic of the objective historical process before the subjective logic of its bearers' (1971, p. 293). Marx holds to this principle from the *German Ideology* onwards, and without it his system loses its identity.

In order then to account for the human capacity to point beyond the existing order, without relying on the falseness of subjective data, later Marxists, beginning with Lukács and Korsch, sought to deepen the dialectical roots of Marxism (Korsch, 1970; Lukács, 1923). In doing so they returned to a Hegelian philosophical analysis which Marx himself had embraced in his early phase but which had been steadily weakened as the focus of Marxism became increasingly economistic and Darwinian. Despite their bold insight, however, these later ventures failed to meet an essential standard of a truly Marxist approach: concrete specificity. The philosophical Marxists could demonstrate that a crudely materialistic Marxism failed to embrace the revolutionary aspirations of the proletariat and hence was no real Marxism at all. None the less, they could not recapitulate Marx's own movement beyond his Hegelian roots into the realm of concrete reality. Here it is worth noting that Lukács and Korsch were coming to the realization of a need to go beyond the materialistic limits of Marxism at a time when the discoveries of Freud had challenged the world-view of European thought. More to the point, they specifically rejected psychoanalysis, the one psychology specifically suited to explore falsified subjectivity and behaviour arising independently of conscious will.

THE COMPATIBILITY OF MARXISM
AND FREUDIANISM

The rejection of Freud by Marxist theoreticians would at first sight seem scarcely to need explanation, since psychoanalysis boldly asserted that the true motives for behaviour were infantile impulses of a sexual sort and not anything which primarily resided in the social, objective world. Nothing could be more foreign to Marxism. Moreover, the Freudians had by and large asserted their allegiance to bourgeois society, a turn of events to which Marxist thinkers could point as evidence for their conviction that psychoanalytic theories were rationalizations of the status quo.

However true this latter point from the standpoint of
practice, a truly dialectical eye need not have turned away
so quickly from a doctrine that seemed Marxism's very
reversal. Indeed, a closer look would have disclosed something remarkable. For Freud, through a series of developments that owed nothing directly to Marxism but which had
been shaped none the less by the history of capitalist society,
had arrived at a method which was as dialectical as Marx's
but which entered the totality of the bourgeois world in an
opposite direction. Where Marx's method held the subject
constant and considered only its objectifications, Freud's
was to hold the object constant and consider only its
subjectification.

Psychoanalysis is as unthinkable as Marxism without its
specific method or praxis. The entire body of psychoanalytic
knowledge is generated through the simple device of lying
down, out of view of an analyst-object, without recourse to
activity in the external world, and, with the objective world
thus held still, agreeing to the imperative of saying whatever
comes to *mind*. Speech here is the only path out of the
subjective realm, the content of which is manifested then,
not as a matter of needs – that is, dispositions with a material
base – but as wishes whose goal may as well be immaterial
as material. Indeed, precisely homologous to Marx in the
opening page of *Capital*, Freud asserts from the outset
that the nature of such wishes, whether they have real
consequences or not, 'makes no difference'. Only by disreg-
arding the reality-ego will the forms of the subjective world
come into view.

The ground of psychoanalytic knowledge is thus subjectivity. Only in this realm are its observations concrete and
empirical. Freud appreciated this; yet he went critically
further. In his original and most profound synthesis of
chapter 7 of *The Interpretation of Dreams*, he held that the
subjective world was itself created through the non-appearance of a needed object. A wish is an impulse that seeks 'to
re-establish the situation of the original satisfaction' (Freud,
1900, p. 566). Based upon an unmet objective need, the
mind strives to gratify that need, first by raising the memory
of satisfaction to the level of a perception, and later, when
the wish is unfulfilled, to find new objects in the world.
However, owing to the emergence of the wish along with
the need, new objects are never simple gratifications of

current objective requirements but always the requirement   179
of a fusion of wish and need.

Organized wishes of this sort are fantasies. Thus Freud
locates fantasy, the wish for lost gratification, at the heart of
human subjectivity and thought. All the elaborate constructions of psychoanalytic theory, with their problematic
relation to biology, are essentially attempts to explain this
fundamental finding, generated within the stilled activity of
the analytic situation.

This analytic knowledge, extracted from an artificial
setting, should never be used to comprehend the human
totality, as vulgarizations of psychoanalysis have attempted
to do. Yet it is as deep as the Marxist insight gleaned through
the quieting of subjectivity. And it poses a massive challenge
for the Marxist view of man.

This challenge may be seen to have several aspects. From
the formal side, psychoanalysis has discovered in each of us
a spontaneous well of subjectivity that simply does not
contain in any immediate sense the categories of political
economy yet plays a powerful determining role in social life.
Under the conditions of free association addressed to an
object outside of one's perceptual field (that is, the analyst),
the subject turns to the field of imagination, on which
soon enough appears, with amazing forcefulness, a host of
fantasies concerned with the body, self-regard and
immediate love relationships. In the spontaneous phenomenology of the subjective world the pursuit of economic
power, indeed everything Marx comprehended as the
labour-process, becomes rapidly drowned out by a flood of
narcissistic and sexual concerns. Subjectively, a man who
may spend most of his waking life maximizing the rate of
profit will turn out to be more intensely concerned with
whether the colour of the shirt he just bought makes him
look manly than with the big deal he just consummated.

Marxists may counter that what counts is how he behaves
objectively with respect to the production process, or that
the purchase of the shirt is a clear example of the cultivation
of false needs by advertising, media and other agencies
of capitalist ideology. They will never penetrate into the
concrete phenomenon, however, unless they recognize that
the behaviour in question is as much the product of a
complex of wishes, deriving, let us say, from an unconscious
homosexual conflict and pressing itself spontaneously into
mind, as it is the result of objective needs, true or false. It is

quite true that the production process maintains itself by 180
creating conditions of life which reproduce individuals suitable for working within it, until its own internal contradictions force a shift. It is not true, however, that the totality of
the production process can be comprehended through the
direct imposition of its imperatives on the minds of such
individuals. The man in question, for instance, may be
driven inwardly to work for the maximization of profit
despite a realization that such activity is destructive to his
own health or to humanity's well-being. A Marxist looking
at this will see objective material conditions overriding
consciousness, and he will be right – in part. A psychoanalyst
meanwhile will see the unconscious conflict about homosexuality at work overriding consciousness, and he will be
right, too – in part.

It is not a matter of either/or; neither, critically, is it a
simple matter of both/and, of each level being equally valid,
as though they could be lumped together. No, the truth
is dialectical, because the two levels are *disjunctively* tied
together. The objective-economic imperative will be used
to deny the unconscious meaning, to defend against its
conscious realization; while the pressure of the unconscious
complex will be used to deny the objective-material reality,
the overturning of which would lead to a threatening
increase of instinctual pressure. Thus our subject is more
consciously preoccupied with the derivate situation of
buying the shirt than he is with the main, material reality of
his work process.

In consequence, the objective level is in part constituted
out of the active negation of the subjective; while the
subjective level is equivalently constituted out of the active
negation of the objective. And the negations in each case
affirm what is denied, hence sustain its existence. In other
words, if the unconscious complex which underlies the
subjective phenomenon is realized – made conscious and
self-appropriated – it will lose its power. Hence its denial
(including the denial by orthodox Marxists who refuse to
take the unconscious seriously) only serves to sustain its
power. Similarly the denial of objective relationship imposed
by the need to keep an unwelcome social reality unrecog-
nized serves only to retard appropriation of that reality
through revolutionary praxis and hence sustains the existing
order – and with it, repression of threatening fantasy.
The extent to which such processes have impeded class

consciousness and revolutionary activity is an important political question which has received scarcely any attention since Wilhelm Reich opened the topic up more than forty years ago (Reich, 1972b).

It should be re-emphasized here that the reason the levels of knowledge are disjunctive is that they arise from fundamentally different praxes. This finding is compatible with both Marx and Freud, each of whom held that what one knows is a function of what one does. Thus Marxism postulates that the non-recognition of social reality develops within productive activity – in other words, where the self, or subject, is actively engaged in transforming the object for the purposes of exchange. In these circumstances part of the self is projected into the object, and the real fate of that object – whether it is bought or sold, conserved or destroyed – becomes of decisive importance. The screening or distorting function occurs, however, outside of the self through the autonomous workings of the exchange principle, whose masking effect on social reality Marx detailed with genius. The exchange dynamic works, however, only in so far as the self is engaged with an object that can be altered through activity – which is to say, in the great range of everyday life situations.

Freud's inspiration was to recognize in neurosis and the dream an 'everynight' life situation wherein these conditions did not obtain; and to devise a method, or praxis, which generated knowledge by preying on the waking mind's proclivity to sink into its nocturnal meanderings. It turned out, moreover, that the path disclosed by the analytic method led invariably to the forgotten world of childhood. This fact is too well known to require detailing. Indeed, such Marxist attempts as have been made to comprehend psychology and the world of daily life have generally recognized that the psychoanalytic discovery of the importance of infantile experience opened up a vital area (Zaretsky, 1973). To return to our businessman-friend for a moment, the reason that his unconscious complex plays so powerful a role in current life while yet being disjunctive with it is that the *wish* points backwards in time to his father and his childhood sexual attitude towards him, while the *need* is expressed in a setting of adult, rationalized thinking the objects of which are current figures. Thus the mind always contains levels out of phase with current reality. True, contemporary objects are symbolically linked to the past, but the symbolic tie takes on value only because the real one has been lost. In short, a father figure cannot be a father; the infantile is the lost. It may be true in an ultimate sense, as Marxists claim, that the father complex is generated out of the reproduction within the family of capitalist social relations. Still, the child perceives this reality in terms of the immediacy of his desire and not according to ultimate realities. And repression splits that immediacy away from more mature presentations of the world and so introduces a permanent schism into subjectivity.

Marxism, rather than flattening subjectivity, could serve to deepen our understanding of the schism within it. Marx made no more basic discovery than the universalization of the abstract, rational calculating attitude in the capitalist exchange relationship. It was capital that bound time in the labour process, thus creating labour power and the conditions for the extraction of surplus value. Half a century later Freud realized that the radical split between primary and secondary processes – that is, between childhood and adult thought – is created by a similar binding of the free, mobile discharge of psychological tension. The universalization of the quantitative element in the 'reality-principle' specific to capital sees to it, however, that infantile, primary-process thought, being non-objectifiable, stays without exchange value. In other words, reality, in so far as it is valued, is constructed so as to exclude the realization of desire, myth and mystery – all of the concomitants of the human imagination and childhood. This is but another way of describing the fundamental subject/object split so basic to the world of capital yet so imperfectly grasped by the Marxist view of man. In order to begin to appreciate it, Marxism will have to go beyond the limited vision of the self presented by Marx. For in 'The sixth thesis on Feuerbach' and the quotation from *Capital* cited above, Marx contends that the structure of the self is not intrinsically problematic: it is the 'ensemble of social relations' and the mirroring of one's self in others. All of this, however, is presented from the adult point of view, as though a fully formed *Anlagen* of the self emerged all at once from the womb, ready for socialization. In broad outline, of course, there is a deep truth to Marx's view: all that we are is formed in the social process. But it is not formed directly. Rather, it is mediated through the categories of childhood, whose primary-process mode of thought retains the capacity to dissolve each aspect of the

self into the whole world and vice versa. In its innermost 183
core, the self is no unity but a sea of contradiction. No one
who has looked deeply into his or her self can fail to
be impressed with the anarchy that reigns there. Only
repression of the infantile, self-dissolving imagination can
in the ordinary course of life sustain a sense of unity, a fact
that in itself accounts for the permanently uneasy role
psychoanalysis has to play in culture.

The finding that self-unity is inherently problematic is not
necessarily bad news to Marxist theory. Indeed, a moment's
reflection reveals that such a concept is essential for any
doctrine which insists upon a revolutionary transformation
of society as the means of liberation. By contrast, the neo-
or post-Freudians who hold out the possibility of some
intrinsically psychological self-formative process – Horney's
concept of the True Self, Erikson's identity theory, Maslow's
self-actualization, and so on – are also disputing any
necessity for radical social change. Instead of overturning
power and property relations, the preachers of self-transformation imply that some form of therapy is the answer.
Freud, by contrast, indicated the fracture and left the way
open for a non-psychological cure.[3]

MARXISM'S FAILURE TO APPROPRIATE PSYCHOANALYSIS
Were Marxism to appropriate Freudian psychoanalysis –
even a version stripped of its reactionary accoutrements – it
would no doubt become seriously altered, at the least in
having to consider the realm of everyday life and the family
as a major ground of social contest alongside the work-place,
and perhaps in more fundamental theoretical ways as well.
But the effort would seem worth while in view of the
potential gain. After all, here is the vision of man Marxism
needs: a concrete, dialectical psychology, not bound to
conscious subjectivity yet postulating a subjective core of
resistance; an inner realm which cannot be counted down
into exchange value; one, therefore, that contains the wish
to be free.

True, what Marx locates in the thrust towards the future,
Freud finds in the shadow of the past. But the gap between
them is much less than between either and a conception of
mere immediacy, whether it be called positivism or common
sense. And it is a gap that can be looked across if not bridged.

From another angle, the refusal of psychoanalytic thought

to be bound by the judgements of consciousness opens up
theoretical space for Marxism. Setting aside the hubris of
analysts who think they have penetrated the mysteries of
existence with their calculus of the subject, psychoanalysis
postulates a view of mind in which the alienable world of
exchange is not only resisted at one level but swallowed at
another. Preoccupied with its unconscious urges, the mind
is only too willing to accept the fetishism of commodities.

Why then has the appropriation not come about? To pass
off the trouble as intellectual inertia only begs the question
– and makes it non-Marxist and non-Freudian as well. The
reason is a more dynamic one, and it seems to me to be
one of the most profound and intractable problems facing
Marxism. It may be simply stated as the horrific character of
the unconscious.

If the wish Freud discovered to be the unit of mental life
were only the trace of past satisfaction, there would be no
problem. Nó doubt such a component exists. The memory
of lost infantile pleasure cast forwards becomes the core of
the Utopian impulse – and this, combined with capital's
betrayal of its own promise to provide material gratification,
becomes a real part of the class struggle, one quite compatible
with traditional Marxist thinking. But Freud saw something
else. He observed in the deeper subjective zone of the mind,
that layer generated out of infantile experience, a profound
antipathy to pain: 'The first ψ-system [that is, primary
process thinking] is totally incapable of bringing anything
disagreeable into the context of its thoughts. It is unable to
do anything but wish' (Freud, 1900, p. 600). But we do not
live by the primary process. Some other mode of thought in
contact with objective reality is needed. And, writes Freud,
the '*bitter* experience of life must have changed this primitive
thought-activity into a more expedient secondary one'
(p. 566; my italics).

What is bitter about this experience? Not – here at any rate
– the disposition of real objects by political economy. No,
simply the non-appearance of the breast (used as a metaphor
for the whole transaction between the child and the parental
world), an absolutely transhistorical experience, entirely
necessary for the generation of a dialectical creature who is
to create history. Now the actual, historically determined
structure of family life determines much about the non-
appearance of the breast, and so enters into the degree
of frustration and bitterness, the degree of hatred and

passivity, and so forth – in short, the real way people behave.
But the thrust of Freud's thought was to develop a theory
of mental repression, not real behaviour, and it is with
repression that the deepest complications arise. For Freud
noted that in order to make any use of the primary wishful
system, the secondary, realistic system of thought must
undertake a *falsification of experience*. In Freud's terms: '*The
second system can only cathect an idea if it is in a position to inhibit
any development of unpleasure that may proceed from it.*' And
this concept 'is the key to the whole theory of repression'
(1900, p. 601; Freud's italics).

These passages from *The Interpretation of Dreams* are among
the most difficult of Freud's theoretical writings. None the
less, what they attempt to explain is one of the most simple
and regularly revealed facts of the psychoanalytic method.
This is that people are terrified of their inner selves. More,
it would seem that if they could stand a full consciousness
they would cease to be human, that is, would cease groping
in the real world to find new constructions, indeed, would
cease to undertake the labour process in a genuinely transformative way. Humans have been hag-ridden by their
dreams since they became human, and what they transform
during the day is a flight from the dark as much as it is a
product of a hidden objective law. Finally, what is only a
minor trauma from the objective standpoint is responsible
for this divided subjectivity. And this trauma, 'separation',
is not to be taken away, since it is objectively necessary for
the formation of a social self.

The truth underscored by this relationship is that the
split in subjectivity not only denies the fantasy world but
overvalues it and institutionalizes madness in normal behaviour. Goaded by phantoms, men have resorted to the sadism
and domination which runs like a steady stream through
history. This line of explanation is not as harsh as one which
resorts to a biological instinct of aggression. Indeed, since it
posits at every point a co-determination between objective-
material cause and subjective-fantasy, it allows for historical
modification. And it can potentially encompass phenomena,
such as the domination of women, which traditional
Marxism has been unable to adequately grasp.[4] None the
less, it has proven largely intolerable to Marxism so far –
perhaps because it so radically undermines that confidence
in the capacity clearly to discern the objective situation which
is central to the faith of Marxism, but perhaps, too, because

it undermines faith itself. Faced with the reification of capitalist culture, in which everything is fixated in plastic objectivity, Marxists have to strain all their powers to envision a revolutionary class-consciousness as the bearer of the future. Any notion of deep contradictions within the subject who is to bear this future has proven anathema to them.

Yet it has been a crippling omission. The weaknesses in the Marxist analysis of the oppression of women or of the sluggishness of class-consciousness have already been noted. It remains here briefly to mention another, even more pervasive weakness of Marxist analysis evidenced in the aversion to deep subjectivity, a weakness that affects the structure of political economy itself.

Instead of excoriating Freud for his bourgeois defects, Marxists could have been asking themselves, and in a Marxist way, about the pre-conditions in capitalist society which permitted the emergence of psychoanalysis as a body of thought. In other words, Freud discovered something real, the laws of subjectivity. These were present throughout history, like the laws pertaining to the division of labour; yet, as with Marx's discovery, it took a particular epoch to bring them into view. It must have been the particular form which subjectivity took in Freud's time that heightened its inner contradictions and so made it visible. This form, however, was itself determined by the working of capital.

In general terms, I suggest that the visibility of subjectivity was the outcome of capital's false promises. Having developed the productive process, capital systematically created hopes and just as systematically betrayed them. It was capital that created a nuclear family divorced from the workplace as the source of humanity in an inhumane world; and it was capital that delegitimated the authority of the family in order to promote a mobile force of workers and – because of the glut of commodities – of consumers. The broad result was the cultivation of a limitless yearning for 'goods' and an equally powerful type of technical rationality – each false and each destined to contradict the other. In sum, the contradictions within subjectivity are in every sense a historically conditioned entity; and Freud was nothing more – or less – than an inspired reader of the mind of late capitalist culture.

The significance of this relationship for both Marxism and psychoanalysis has yet to be probed. For Marxism the

exploration bids to help it comprehend the reality of an age
where subjectivity becomes strategic terrain in the contest
over the social individual, territory bounded by the phantoms of the unconscious world at one extreme and the
instrumental manipulations of mass culture at the other.
If this seems too immaterial to Marxists, they should be
reminded that Marxism is concrete and deals with full
human events, not the crude material quantities which
result from the reification of repressive thought, whether
state or corporate capitalist. Capital itself is not a thing
but a relationship in motion, recognized by Marx to have
monstrous vitality – 'value that sucks up the value-creating
power' (1867, 1: p. 571). We should now be able to recognize
that his frequent use of such metaphors may not have
been a mere rhetorical flourish but an as-yet-unformulated
insight. Marx's analysis of the commodity, which began
with the indifference to 'fancy', was the analysis of social
pathology. As far-reaching as it went, it should never be
identified with the actual totality of society, any more than
Freud's inspired excursion into subjectivity. Each man saw
something which twisted that totality into the forms of
history. What they did not include – but which is there for
us to see – is the extent to which the subjective and objective
worlds each move against the unseen other.

NOTES

1. See 'Erik Erikson's psychohistory', page 68 above.

2. See Fromm (1966). In the case of vulgar Marxism, mediation
has simply been defined out of the picture in advance through
the relegation of any subjective analysis to a mere residual
category. And as for the various neo-Freudian positions, it is
made trivial and uninteresting by redefining the terms of
subjectivity. When Fromm, for example, writes, 'Freud believed
that the effective *cause for repression* (the most important content
to be repressed being incestuous desires) is the fear of castration.
I believe, on the contrary, that individually and socially, man's
greatest fear is that of complete isolation from his fellow man,
of complete ostracism' (p. 241; Fromm's italics), he is in effect
greasing the skids for psychoanalysis. He is also, in my opinion,
not looking closely enough at what goes on in people's minds.
And most important from the theoretical standpoint, he is losing
the thread of dialectical thought, that species of inquiry without
which neither Marx nor Freud are themselves.

3. For a wide-ranging discussion of this issue, see Jacoby (1975).

4. For signs of a change in Marxist thought, see Zaretsky (1975).

10 NARCISSISM AND THE FAMILY

To pursue the psychological and social relations of narcissism is to enter a swamp. However, that swamp happens to be a real part of the world. Consider some of its dimensions:

– Narcissism is an aspect of personal life without which human existence would not be thinkable. One treads softly about the word 'normal' but in this case we must assume that narcissism, as the location of desire in the self, is ubiquitous, and indeed transhistorical. Moreover, when we talk of a 'healthy narcissism', we are not positing an idle or meaningless value.

– An exaggerated narcissism is an aspect of real, if difficult to conceptualize, disorders. Psychotics are invariably narcissistic, by which we mean inordinately self-preoccupied, as are adolescents at their most unpleasant. Further, there is a host of character types whom one must call 'narcissistic'. These people may not be formally neurotic or psychotic, yet are marked by a peculiar self-organization. Prone to disturbances in self-esteem, they are variously cold, remote or empty in their relations. At the end of 'normalcy' they slide with imperceptible gradualness into something that is best called 'alienation', or estrangement.

– Narcissism, or desire located in the self, is never self-contained. It is always referred rather to something besides the self, the *other*, or object. To be exact, we regard the *other* as the figure (or ground) in the world against which the self is drawn, while the object as such is the terminus point of desire. In general, we may regard the *other* and the object as two aspects of the same entity. Their existence reminds us that the self is actively and socially constructed. In Marx's words, it is indeed the 'ensemble of social relations' (1967, p. 401).

– But Marx did not take into account the decisive feature by

means of which the self–*other* dialectic takes its varying
forms: the ontogenesis of the self in infantile experience,
and of the *other*, therefore, as being composed in some way
out of the infant's body and his/her key real others, the
parents. In other words, narcissism is concretely rooted in
the family.

– Narcissism is a mythic structure celebrating and yearning
for ripeness. It is an essential element, as developed by
Marcuse (1955), in Utopian and transcendent thought.

– Narcissism is also necessarily political in an immediate
sense. That is, it is as historical as it is transhistorical. And,
as this conference [on narcissism] testifies, it is a focal issue
of contemporary society. Lasch's recent work (1978) is but a
manifestation of this centrality. There is ample evidence
that something akin to the 'culture of narcissism' pervades
contemporary American life, and that it plays a powerful
role in the fortunes of capitalism. Substantial questions
persist, however, as to just what that role is; moreover,
the articulation between several dimensions of the matter
remain largely unspecified. For even a swamp has its real
composition.

We may begin with a review of so-called 'normal'
narcissism,[1] then proceed to consider the narcissistic
character and its relation to narcissism on a historical scale.
As stated above, the ubiquity of narcissism cannot be
doubted, although the multiplicity of its forms requires
some elaboration. Narcissism is the fundamental quality of
all relationships in which the orientation is such that the
other imparts value to the self. It includes ordinary selfishness
or self-centredness, then, but is by no means limited to these
traits. For the self and its *other* can take on many guises.
Narcissism involves all matters of self-regard and evaluation. It is contained in the relations of the self to the outside,
as in questions of pride, vanity, dignity, self-adornment and
so on; and it is contained in relations of the self to itself, as
in the area of self-regard, ideals, goals and, indeed, in values
themselves. In these relations, one part of the self plays the
role of *other* to the remainder. In psychoanalytic parlance,
then, we speak of the *ego-ideal* or *super-ego* as invested
narcissistically. This is another way of saying that they are
internalized states of the *other*. Religious belief has a strong
narcissistic component, with the deity as the integral of all
others, and so does political belief, with party or the classless

society playing the same role. Whether or not something entails narcissism, however, is only loosely coupled with its validity, although the 'fit' between the narcissistic value of a thing and its objective quality is a matter of some importance. Fervour of belief, of course, can have powerful real consequences, even if the belief be in something absurd or destructive. On the other hand, the obvious and politically significant fact that socialist and egalitarian goals can at times be pursued with highly narcissistic and non-rational purposes does not invalidate the rational core of the goals themselves. Finally, as if matters were not complicated enough already, we should note that the narcissistic relationship never exists in pure form. In the real world it is admixed with object-oriented relata in which the object is desired not as *other* to the self, but *in itself* as a source of gratification. In sexuality, for example, the genital of the other person is usually seen simultaneously from two sides: as object, that is, as bearer of pleasure; and as *other*, that is, as some missing part of the self, to be claimed. The proportions of object-related and narcissistic orientations vary widely in different circumstances; and it is the preponderance of one or the other we have in mind when we say that such and such (for example, a sexual encounter) is narcissistic or not.

That the matter should turn out to be so complicated is due not to caprice but to some basic peculiarities inherent in the formation of the human self. Indeed, narcissism as such is not some quality appended to a prefabricated self-organization. It is rather an essential element of the formation of that self.

Therefore we speak of *primary* and *secondary* narcissism as deployments of desire occurring at critically different phases of self-organization. The first concept, primary narcissism, is somewhat hypothetical yet necessary, for it refers to the infant's investment in itself before any differentiation is made between self and other. In this undifferentiated phase there is no articulation of self as such, although there is a relationship to objects, primarily the breast. The object that is sought, however, is not distinguished from the subject that seeks it. There is no *other*, no self-consciousness and no estrangement. In so far as things are perceived, they are apprehended as being all of a piece, a piece in which there is no special location of an observing, experiencing 'I', or *cogito*. Because of this basic fusion the omnipotence of thought that characterizes states of desire, and which is the

real evidence for primary narcissism, arises. This omnipotence, first delineated by Ferenczi (1909), is the nucleus
of all neurotic and psychotic formations. It is also continued
into all later narcissistic developments, especially those of
the ego-ideal and super-ego.

Secondary narcissism is a clearer matter, although based
on a more complex state of development. It is the investment
of regard in the self as it emerges in a differentiated way
from others. Moreover – and this is key – the regard comes
from a person left behind and is the condition of the
separation. In other words, secondary narcissism is beset
with the hazards of separation. The affection and joy with
which infants are beheld as they mature is in a very real
sense a kind of shielding nest protecting the helpless young
as they traverse the path to individuality. And the narcissism
we develop inwardly is also a barrier against self-vulner-
ability. Freud felt that secondary narcissism was a reflux of
libido: first from the ego on to object, then back from object
to ego. Though this may describe the process from the
vantage of a developing subject, it does not encompass its
full complexity. For narcissism is not simply an instinctual
matter; it is also the internalization of a real relationship.
The baby develops a notion of self charged with the actual
regard she/he has received from the parent. Our self-esteem
is, it is said, but the internalized gleam in our mother's eye.

Any separation between inside and outside, between,
that is, the subject's desire and the object's regard, is
highly artificial. It is, ultimately, desire that becomes located
narcissistically. But this desire is itself determined by the
objects to which it is directed. Infants come to love themselves if they loved the parents who loved them; only then
is the gleam in the eye, and later the parents' praise,
internalized as a healthy narcissism.

A host of things can go wrong with this scheme. The
conjunction of omnipotence of thought and infantile helplessness guarantees narcissistic vulnerability to the human
species. This vulnerability is particularly extreme at the
primary end, when the omnipotence of ideas is at its zenith
and no realistic appreciation exists to modify the impact of
unpleasant stimuli. Anyone who watches the catastrophic
reaction of a little baby to hunger or a wet nappy will
understand what I mean. The infant is provided at first with
little but an all-purpose distress signal. Everything else is
left to the adult who is roused by this call to do something

about it. The dyad (baby with scream – effecting adult) is
the original unit of competency, to be replaced later by the
grown individual's full set of powers. However, narcissism
lingers as the record of transition from the dyadic person to
the individual, remaining as a kind of inverted testimonial
not to the real objective weakness of the baby but to its
grandiosity and omnipotence of thought. Thus, the internalized *other* is a composite, derived in part from the figure
of the effecting adult and in part from the infant's own
grandiosity. We have here the basis for the absolutism of
conscience and ideal. It is a profound irony that infantile
omnipotence is so closely related to real human power. The
balance is a delicate one: without the impetus of omnipotent
thought, power would not assert itself. Yet the real power,
once achieved, also tames, or at least walls off, the sense of
omnipotence. This is as true for small children as it is for
adults. And a failed power is also a failure of that barrier,
being accompanied by a reflux of infantile omnipotence. We
see this most strikingly in the psychoses, but the relationship
exists elsewhere.

It follows that bridges of transition need to be provided
lest narcissism remain in its raw and destructive early
infantile form. From another angle, mere parenting is not
enough: a widening zone of social objects must be provided if
human powers are to be realized. In sum, a real community,
which is to say, one grounded in unalienated work and
social relations, is the path from infantile omnipotence to
adult power. This is by way of saying that the individual
who replaces the infant is no monad, either. In place of the
original effecting parent, the individual now is an effective
member of a community.

So much for the ideal case. To see what has happened in
real America, we may turn to a closer examination of the so-
called narcissistic characters in accordance with the principle
that mental pathology, like the prison, provides a true
indication of the level of civilization achieved by society.

No statistics exist for these matters, yet it is fairly clear
from the informal reports of psychoanalysts that, at least for
the bourgeoisie, there are increasing numbers of patients
who present disorders of narcissism. Indeed, the concept
scarcely existed in the early days of analytic practice, whereas
now it is a leading category. Psychoanalysis, to be sure,
plays a highly ambiguous role in the naming of disorders.
No less a shaper of rules of discourse than a reflector

of reality, psychoanalysis is thoroughly immersed in the
totality it seeks to comprehend. But this only underscores
the significance of its surging experience with narcissistic
patients.

The appellation, 'narcissistic character', is not an easy one
to grasp, and no progress will be made at all if it is viewed
in the same light as the symptom neuroses, or, indeed,
along the lines of other disturbances of character. It is not,
for example, the same thing as excessive vanity or 'egotism',
that is, those states of character in which narcissism is, so to
speak, worn on the sleeve – and in which, correspondingly,
deeper structures of the self may have different and less
narcissistic qualities. Disturbed narcissism is rather a
separate dimension of its own; it can coexist quite well with
the classical neurotic syndromes and character problems.
What is peculiar about it lies not in any particular pattern of
functional distress, but rather in a troubled form of human
relationship. This is often masked at first, so that, typically,
problems of narcissistic pathology do not become manifest
until the treatment is under way. What one learns then
is that the individual suffers from a kind of *emptiness*.
Experience seems drained and lifeless, without real texture.
It is not that things are not perceived sharply – for usually
the narcissistic character is if anything hypersensitive – and
it is not that correct functioning is impossible – for quite
often, the world being what it is, the individual functions at
quite a high level. It is rather that, in the zone of felt
experience between perception and action, a kind of cold
hollowness transpires. The fit between such people and the
world is never perfect, whatever the high level of functional
adaptation they may evince. For no matter how they *do*, the
narcissistic nature of the problem is revealed by an inordinate
vulnerability in the area of self-regard. Sometimes manifest
by grandiosity and arrogance, at other times by feelings of
worthlessness and inadequacy, and often enough sliding
into a kind of depression that differs from classical
depressions in its admixture of numbness – the narcissistic
individual earns his/her label.

It is an odd feature of this disorder – and one that makes
it a curio so far as public-health measurements go – that the
diagnosis can only be made in a psychoanalytic setting. Any
other context is simply unable to penetrate through the
wall of pseudo-functioning thrown up by the narcissistic
individual. In the analytic relationship, however, the charac-

teristically cold and bleak personal quality soon enough comes to the fore. And with this we learn some other things as well. The narcissistic character is not indifferent to people, or withdrawn from them, as so-called schizoid individuals are. The other person is generally quite essential for them – but only as a bearer of supplies, in short, as a virtually pure *other* to the narcissistic self. At the same time, this *other* is regarded with a good deal of hostility and contempt. For the narcissist, personal relations are in terms of power. The narcissist cannot tolerate weakness in the self and seeks it constantly in others, bringing it out in them if necessary through an artful process of belittlement.

Otto Kernberg (1975) and Heinz Kohut (1971), the leading psychoanalytic investigators of disturbed narcissism, agree that the best way of making sense of this picture is to postulate the existence of a so-called 'grandiose self' – a distinct organization of self-experience intermediate between the official persona presented to the world and an innermost state of affairs against which it defends. In the grandiose self the omnipotence of early infancy is attached to an *alter ego* whose existence may not be avowed by the individual who bears it. This alternate subject is positioned behind the official persona and guides it, therefore, without having to contact the world itself. It is by maintaining this split in self-experience that the sick narcissist is able to avoid psychosis, and often enough, detection, either by others or oneself. Kohut and Kernberg have major differences, however, concerning the significance of the grandiose self, the former regarding it as an aberration of normal self-organization while the latter sees it as an entirely pathological formation. These differences are of little concern to us here and can be most usefully referred to different portions of a spectrum; Kohut's notion being rather more applicable to people on the normal end, and Kernberg's to those who are relatively greatly estranged. Of the two, I regard Kernberg as the trenchant thinker inasmuch as he gives real credence to the role of hostility and hatred in the narcissistic character, while Kohut seems prone to an idealistic rendering. My own experience, in any case, supports Kernberg's basic formulation, and goes as follows: once we, so to speak, discover the grandiose self we learn that it, too, has a defensive position. The narcissist's posture of grandiose coldness, the retreat from real human contact, masks a deeper layer of self-experience which is, in subjective reality, painfully weak. This underside of the grandiose self is the experience of a ravenous infant, beset with a diffuse type of oral rage that bids to devour everything in sight, and, indeed, annihilate the subject, along with the object, were it exposed. The grandiose self is, then, a negation of this deeper aspect, and serves to keep the narcissistic individual away from situations where this weakness and desire would become exposed. And this grandiose self is itself masked by a veneer of social adaptation.

The term 'veneer' applies here in a serious way. For while the narcissistic character is often enough a perfectly well-functioning citizen, one finds on a closer look that the flaws in the narcissist's character have exacted a peculiar, and quite specific, toll. For their social engagement is, literally, veneer-like. It is without much depth of attachment and quite specifically, without a notion of transcendence or universality. In other terms, the narcissistic character is unable to affirm a unity of project or purpose, a common goal, with other people in a way that goes beyond immediacy or instrumentality. They often do fine with the rules for everyday alienated discourse, but cannot go beyond and are therefore lost to class-consciousness, history and, necessarily, the future. I would call this veneer-like quality of social relation the *de-sociation* of the narcissistic character. It is one of the central features of the problem, and certainly the one of greatest interest to us here. I should add at this point, that I definitely do not regard narcissistic de-sociation as the sole, or even necessarily the principal way that people are cut off from class-consciousness or other manifestations of universality. It is, however, a particularly strategic one in the present juncture of advanced capitalism, at least for bourgeois individuals.

Let us review what has been said: I am claiming, on the basis of psychoanalytic praxis, that there are numerous individuals in our society who suffer multiple and severe self-alienation of a narcissistic sort. A few are troubled enough by failures in love and work – and sufficiently imbued with psychoanalytic discourse – to seek help. We cannot help but assume, however, that these individuals represent a far larger body of narcissistically troubled people – many less troubled, to be sure, and many others as, or more troubled while less inclined, or able, to seek help. Moreover, the conclusion is inescapable that conditions of contemporary American life are bringing more and more of this type of problem to the fore. Recall the two makes of the film, *Invasion of the Body Snatchers*. The 1956 version was saturated with Cold War propaganda and showed the attacked town retaining its integrity, while that of 1978 revealed a total penetration of alien existence into the city. The penetration itself – the taking over of people by alien and emotionally dead forces – was a representation of the type of narcissistic disturbance we have been describing here, while the progression between the two films gives a sense of the rapidly developing history of the disorder. The problem before us now, however, is to describe its mediations in the contemporary family.

The first thing that strikes me about the narcissistic individuals I have worked with closely is the lack of what might be called an overtly traumatic quality in their family experience. This is not to say that they were happy with what happened there, or that they feel close to their parents. Far from it. They are quite generally full of an overweening hatred of their parents – a hatred, however, that never is authentically expressed owing to a persistent dependence upon the older generation. Objectively, this dependence is not to be confused with a relationship that is either close or loving. Often – especially under the scattering conditions of contemporary life – the individual hardly ever sees her/his family, indeed, shuns them. However, they remain dependent in the sense that parental judgements loom excessively large, often causing feelings of panic. Thus the dependence is mainly secured subjectively. The subjective side of this dependence is an extreme, florid and hate-filled fantasy life concerning the parents: indeed it is the very intensity of this fantasy which renders hatred monstrous and prevents its expression.

From another angle, what makes this hatred so monstrous is its lack of reasonable cause – that is, the lack of gross trauma. The parents often fluttered about when they were little, and belonged neither to the brutalizing, punitive, rejecting type nor to those whose contact might carry seduction to the point of incest. This 'contact' – that is, the real nature of the parent–child bond – seems to have itself been of a narcissistic character. The child was regarded as an adornment of the parent, rather than a creature in her/his own right; and this parental concern had the quality of capital invested for a future yield. But this yield was itself

no more – or less – than a 'normally narcissistic' pride or
respect on the parent's part, a pride which was rationalized
because it belonged to the prevailing relations of the bourgeois community and which, being rationalized, was reasonable from the parent's standpoint and carried out with
relatively little fuss.

Relative, that is, to the perception of the child, for whom
every glance of the parent is a sword-thrust of the *other*. The
parent, with a kind of reason on her or his side, regards the
child as 'overly sensitive' even as the latter sees the parent
as murderously intrusive. From the child's standpoint, the
parent cannot win: affection is construed as invasion, and
restraint as gross neglect. We have what is later to appear
as a 'failed' relationship with the primary parental object.
Often the only element of the relationship which resists
failure is the quality of adornment: at least, the two of them
reason, the child can make the parent proud. Or, just as
often, the child can fail in the world and so frustrate the
parent's hopes for narcissistic aggrandizement. But this,
too, is a sign that the narcissistic element is the one that has
'taken' between the two of them; even if used for the
purposes of spite, it still constitutes a real bond, better than
the icy distancing which seems the only other way out of
the cauldron that is the child's growing perception of his/
her relations with the older generation. The narcissistic
dimension is at the same time the plane of cleavage along
which intimate relationships fall apart and the framework
around which they are rebuilt as grandiose self. For in this
self-system the child's primary sense of omnipotence meets
the parent's judging function. The stabbings felt by the
parent's seemingly innocuous signals are in fact promptings
of the child's own imperious self-demands triggered by the
parent. But because the grandiose self is perceived as alien,
these promptings are not recognized as the child's own, and
are re-projected as hatred out into the world where they
fuse with the perception of the anxious, praising and/or
judgemental parent. This process in turn walls the grandiose
self further off from both outside world and the remainder
of the subject: in short, it is the self-perpetuating cycle by
which that self-system is inculcated and grows. And when
it grows too big, or is too larded with hatred, we have
that edge of the contemporary spectrum who are called
'narcissistic characters' and end up in analysts' offices.

We must account for this situation historically, for it is

manifestly a historical state of affairs. Primitive societies do not accumulate persons of this type, nor, so far as I know, do socialist societies, feudal societies or even capitalist societies through the nineteenth century. If we take, for example, the work of an author such as George Eliot for a guide, we will see that in her carefully wrought and expansive treatment of a society that was very much in the grip of capitalist relations, scarcely an individual who meets the description of pathological narcissism, outlined above, is to be found. And while such evidence is by no means 'proof', I think it a fair assumption that this type of individual was not prevalent then, and played no role in the totality of early capitalist society. This phenomenon may have something to do with the atavistic clingings of religious faith which capitalism permitted until quite recently and with the vestigial maintenance, so touchingly recounted by Eliot, of the remnants of an earlier community. However true these observations may be, they remain incomplete without a grasp of their interconnection with the life of the family, and with subjectivity in general.

To return to our consideration of the family, the lack of overt trauma in the family relations of narcissistically disturbed individuals was stressed in order to highlight a deeper point. For when the particular traumas which lend an individual stamp to each case fade out, we are left with the distinct impression that what crushes the developing person under a weight of sick narcissism is *nothing but the family itself*: a family that is itself de-sociated is the breeding ground for de-sociated individuals. For the scission of the family from organic, productive and reciprocal relations with the community forces the energy of that family in upon the developing individual. In the superheated environment which results the person is moulded in the direction of pathological narcissism. One may schematize further: the bourgeois age is, among other things, that age of a family centred upon children. It is therefore the era in which childhood emerges for the first time in history as a distinct category of existence. Pathological narcissism is then fundamentally the outcome when the family, so to speak, is not merely centred on children but collapses upon them as well, crushing them beneath its weight. It is therefore a specific disorder for that phase of capitalist development in which such a collapse occurs. Pathological narcissism is a pox of late capitalism.

Ariès (1962), De Mause (1974) and Shorter (1975), among
others, have chronicled the rise of the bourgeois family as a
child-centred entity; while Poster (1978) and Zaretsky (1973)
have developed the central role capitalism has played in the
process. Through its need for a mobile labour force, through
its usurpation of domestic production, through its whole
philosophy of the individual contract and its promotion of
bourgeois democracy, capitalism knocked the underpinnings away from patriarchy and the traditional community,
and sent the family on the path of nucleation which it is
still traversing. The same movement of development that
created the nuclear family gave to the class in power,
the bourgeoisie, the means of directing its command over
resources towards the nurturance of children. For among
these resources must be reckoned that of time itself. In the
infinitely expansable system of exchange that constitutes
the fabric of capitalist relations, an equation may be readily
drawn between surplus-value and time. The appropriation
of the former by the bourgeoisie is simultaneously an appropriation of the latter. And this freed time, stolen from
labour, is concretely invested in the care of the young. With
increasing productivity and the decline in the need for child
labour, the same gift was belatedly – and with substantial
compromises – returned to the upper strata of the working
class. By the late nineteenth century childhood had become
at least an affordable dream for the bulk of the population.

It may be said that the ideology of a good childhood – at
least a 'better' one for each successive generation –
represents one of the real promises of capitalist society.
Converged in this new category are the twinned hopes for
material abundance and the development of the individual,
with all the notions of freedom so entailed. But it has always
been the case that the freed time with which childhood in
the bourgeois world has been filled is in fact unfree time, time
stolen through the domination of labour, which domination
reproduces itself in everyday life. More concretely, the
family set loose by the breakup of the older extended
community has always been, however ideology may have
it, adrift on an open boat in a shark-infested sea. The
essentially predatory nature of capitalist society, coupled
with the coldness of its exchange-dominated social relations,
forces the family in on itself. An increasingly desperate
defensiveness appears in family relations and saps the very
development of the individual for which the family was

intended. To return for a moment to George Eliot, we observe in *The Mill on the Floss* (1860) that Maggie Tulliver's father loses his family-owned mill and is made to undertake the wage-labour of managing it for the new owner. The humiliation destroys him and his family. Specifically it forces Maggie, who had been his darling for the future, to retreat to the hearth in a vain – and self-crippling – attempt to console him for his losses. I find this situation paradigmatic of the fundamental insecurity that afflicts the nuclear family in a world of capitalist predation – and it specifically pinpoints the burden imposed upon the women who have been assigned the task of consolation at the cost of their own individuation.

It does not, however, prefigure the specifically narcissistic turn of events. So long as the family remains a bastion against the outer world, so long, that is, as it sustains its own integrity, then it may inculcate limitations of all kinds, including the contours of what we recognize as neurosis, but will not introduce the disorder of narcissism itself. For the 'integrity' of a family is simply the integral of the integrity of its members. From the standpoint of the developing child, what this means is that she/he is exposed to a coherent set of behaviours on the part of parental figures. The adult is seen as the same person throughout the range of interactions with the child: gratification is connected to prohibition and control to intimacy. The parent may be dreadful or wanting, but she/he is who she/he is, and is either there or not there. What this means subjectively is that the *other* to whom the self relates in the process of narcissistic development becomes, as the child's maturation allows it, a recognizable human being. And coherence of the object is matched by coherence of the subject.

But coherence of the object goes by the board in late capitalism. It is not my province at this point to explore how this works itself out at all levels of the totality – in the eclipse of reason and the rise of totalizing mass culture under the sway of the sign and logic of the commodity form itself. For our purposes we need only bear in mind that the outcome and integral of the process is the hegemony of the commodity form in late capitalist culture, manifest as disembodied and abstract exchange, and omnipresent as the infinitely transmutable image broadcast by the media. In sum, a non-human *other* has emerged as the dominant cultural form in late capitalist culture, to replace the human personages

which from Pharaonic Egypt onwards had been the
cementing forces of societal narcissism. Now the human
representations are themselves palpably stooges for the
infinite fluid that is the commodity itself; and it is the
commodity – to be more exact, those that realize it – that is
the real master of society.

Our concern, however, is with the actual human bonds
that constitute the individual and which could, if cohesive
enough, shield him or her from the penetration of this social
other. And the point of particular concern is that juncture at
which the bastion that had been the bourgeois family is itself
fractured and entered, leaving the human objects, too, in a
state of disarray.

We do not want to elide a complex historical reality. Except
as a piece of bourgeois ideology, there was never an isolated
family that sealed itself hermetically against the world.
And although this ideology has served to perpetuate the
public–private split that is an essential part of the bourgeois
heritage, it should not be confused with a real historical
accounting. In actual history, the isolated, pure family has
been only a phantasm in the minds of people who yearn for
consolation against the rigours of society and the indifference of nature. The real family has always existed as a
nexus of influences within the whole, a nexus between the
individual and the social totality. Families are regions of
increased social density within this totality, stabilized by the
pinions of transhistorical human need and the exigencies of
socialization. As history lurches along, the configuration of
these pinions changes; different languages become bound
to the family nexus and different material and juridical
relations arise between it and other nexuses within the
totality. It is the sense of such a differentiation that we have
in mind when we talk of the penetration of the nuclear
bourgeois family.

Penetration by what? By the state, of course. Lasch, and
more recently, Jacques Donzelot (1979), have described the
process in some detail. The nuclear family, handed the
task of socialization in a world whose public relations are
dominated by an abstract and inhuman mode of production,
is as self-contradictory a formation as ever to step forward
on to the historical stage. The contradiction is glaring: more
and more socialization must be carried out by fewer and
fewer people; people, moreover, whose autonomous
strength to provide such is constantly being sapped. The

result: an inevitable breakdown, manifest as the intolerable
efflorescence of those behaviours which the dominant order
considers marginal: the perverse, the promiscuous, the
addictive, the criminal, the ineducable, the neurotic and the
outright mad. Worse, when the family fulfils its function
properly it is just as likely to produce individuals who are
too strong – that is, who may rebel, either through deviant
pathways or, of deepest concern to power, collective revolutionary action. In any case the bourgeois order cannot
dream of leaving the family alone. Whether it makes people
who are too weak or too strong, it must be, and indeed has
been, colonized and pacified.

The visible edge of the process has been, as Donzelot has
described, the state's concern with delinquent, ineducable
and unsocializable children. But the development of central
interest is less the discipline of the marginal than the emergence of forms suitable for a thoroughgoing colonization of
the entire institution. This discourse includes psychoanalysis itself – not so much as Freud enunciated it but as it
became integrated into the burgeoning health industries.
And it is ultimately those industries themselves, along with
their ancillae in the fields of psychology, social work and
counselling, which have become the colonial administrators
for the capitalist state in its encounter with the family (Lasch,
1977; cf. also Kovel, 1980).

The phase of monopoly capital has been the decisive
moment for the breaching of the bourgeois family. For here
a number of trajectories have converged, the total of which
adds up to a qualitatively distinct imperative from what had
gone before: (1) We must note the emergence of a massified
state apparatus, essential to iron out the endless crises
of the capitalist economy. Once instituted on economic
grounds, the tendency of such an apparatus is to assume
hegemony over the whole of society. (2) The rise of the
medical establishment becomes an especially critical part of
that state apparatus – economically gluttonous yet essential
for legitimation. (3) The commodification of erstwhile
domestic preserves, such as the production of leisure and
popular culture, becomes a vital feature of the economy and
the legitimation process alike. (4) The increase of productivity and the endemic generation of surpluses introduce an
age of consumerism which cannot but tear families asunder.
For in one motion children cease to be producers and become
consumers. This places them at automatic odds with the

older generation, and also places alongside that older generation an essentially alien power of socialization – the inhuman force of the commodity itself, seeking to be realized in the human heart that must be induced to possess it.

We must add to the above another general feature of capitalist society which has been accentuated in its late phase: the relentless separation of work from domestic life. This would not matter so much if a real community existed to provide care and support function. However, as such a community itself lies victim to capital, it is generally the case that parental work is carried out at the expense of consistent parental contact. For a while this schism contributed to the well-documented 'decline of the father'. However, with the increasingly necessary emergence of the two-pay-packet family, the problem takes on a more general hue.

For all these reasons, and through concrete influences ranging from TV to schools and clinics themselves, the integrity of the parental object is violated in late capitalism and the ground is laid for the development of a pathological narcissism. The state enters by usurping the relations between individuals and by introducing alien intermediaries. This is epitomized by the configuration of a family that relates to itself only by sitting glued together in front of the television. Therefore, despite the depredations of work, the problem is not one of neglect, for the narcissistic individual is less the subject of abandonment than the victim of a kind of cloying attachment. What is missing, however, is the kind of articulated and socially coherent human surroundings necessary for the development of real individuals. Intensity of involvement persists, for this is, in the end, what the nuclear family dishes out best. But such intensity is delivered in one or, more likely, a small series of essentially *dyadic* relationships: baby–mother; baby–father; small child to mother in a different phase, and so on. These relationships are not themselves subject to the break-in of others as in the classic Oedipal triangle, which, whatever its unsavoury consequences, fulfilled the inestimable need of providing a coherent subjective differentiation and so permitted the development of real individuals. The differentiated parent is experienced in a multiplicity of subtle interrelationships. As a result, a rounded, full figure emerges, suitable for internalization as an integrated individual. By contrast, the late capitalist family is a setting in which intense dyadic relations with mother may be linearly succeeded by, rather than differentiated into, intense dyadic relations with father – for mother and father have not that much to do with each other, and what they have to do is broken into by some instrumentality of the state, whether this be the media or a social worker. There is, in the shorthand we have been developing, no *other* to the *other*: therefore that original *other*, the narcissistic influence of the primary object, remains omnipresent, as does primary narcissism with its omnipotence of thought. And from the parent's side, estrangement and the loss of social texture leads to narcissistic over-investment in the child. The developing child cannot as a result mediate her/his grandiose self-system; she/he can only, as a result of the terror induced by ravening desires, wall it off, whereby the grandiose self begins the process of quasi-independent development which eventuates in narcissistic character pathology.

It should be emphasized that I do not draw attention to the so-called narcissistic character disorders to tar us all with the brush of psychopathology. That would be a corrupt and pointless extension of the false ideology of health to a historical situation. It is absurd to claim we are all 'sick' except in the context of a transcendent standard. Otherwise the bench-mark is necessarily accommodation to a murderous and stunting social order. There is no escaping this dilemma within medical discourse. However it is useful to see how a historically significant segment of people are led to develop self-experience of a specific kind – a kind, moreover, that reproduces on subjective terrain the sense of alienation and estrangement which we recognize as the signature of capitalist relations.

In this respect the key feature is the de-sociation of the narcissistic character, for it is this quality, more than any other, that contributes to the reproduction of capitalist relations and so moves to close the circle of narcissistic families making narcissistic people who make a narcissistic society and live in narcissistic families that are products of that society. Bookchin (1978) has pointed out the 'asociality' of capitalist society, its loss of texture and regression to an increasingly hollowed-out, inorganic status in which the bureaucrat is constitutive of the social fabric. The de-sociation of the sick narcissist epitomizes the subjective moment of this development, one which is played out in a myriad of forms and across traditional social boundaries such as class. These are the people – not the shadowy sick

extremes but the vast range who live in the sun of normalcy
– who imbibe and reproduce the culture of narcissism, who
buy well, tend the self and never dream of making trouble;
or who, if they lack the means to buy, simply lapse into de-
sociated self-containment. It would be a mistake to regard
the phenomena in which they participate as the unmediated
result of politico-economic manipulation. No, the savants
of Madison Avenue are not wholly off the mark when they
claim that they basically give people what they want. For
those wants have been instilled, and at a deeper level than
mere conscious manipulation: they are laid down in a
primitive experience that produces an inflated, weak, easily
manipulable self-system, ever at the ready to attach itself to
the non-human *others* devised out of the commodity form.
In this way we may epitomize the narcissism we have been
chronicling as nothing but the subjective reflex of late
capitalism itself.

It would also be a mistake to think that this situation can
be remedied by pressing into service the obsolete nuclear
family. For, in the first place, such a family was never very
much of a bastion to begin with, having been palpably
associated with all that has been miserable and thankless in
the bourgeois character. And in the second place, it grew
the way it did, and retained its character, because of the
concrete form of domination without which it would not
have an identity to fall back upon – patriarchy. Here we
must remember, if we are to be historical, that narcissism,
like capital itself, is embedded in a dialectic, and that it has
a side of resistance as well, a resistance that is articulated
precisely against the weight of patriarchal domination. The
resistance of narcissism is embodied in the myth of Narcissus
evoked by Marcuse. In the capitalist world it surfaces as a
rebellion of the body against its deformation into a machine.
And it takes other forms as well, depending upon concrete
circumstances. It is this resistance of narcissism, for example,
which contributes to the emancipatory force of the gay
movement and accounts for the legitimate hostility with
which gay people (and feminists as well) have countered
the politics which assumes that the foremost way out of
the de-sociation of the narcissistic society is through a
resuscitation of the nuclear family, with the unspoken but
real insinuation that its inevitable sidekick, patriarchy, is to
follow.

This should not be construed either, however, as a call to

continue the smashing of what that family promised in
its emancipatory moment, namely, secure and coherent
intimate human relations. I think these have been established as a transhistorical human need – that is, a necessary
condition for the development of real human power, as
against infantile omnipotence. We understand as well that
sufficient conditions for the growth of that power include
the provision of an authentically socialist society – a society
within which the antique form of the nuclear-patriarchal
family will be relegated to museums. We need not only the
material relations of that society to allow real individuality
to develop: we need the maintenance of its transcendent
promise as well. Our task, in the present state of crisis and
opportunity, is to develop an adequate intermediary, and it
is a challenge worth assuming.

NOTE
1. It is not my intention here to review or provide a guide to the
substantial psychoanalytic literature on narcissism, or to situate
myself with regard to the numerous unresolved controversies
that beset this topic. The reader should of course begin with
Freud's 1914 essay, 'On narcissism', but remember that this piece
is a preliminary foray of Freud's, an attempt to bring the theory
of the libido into line with obviously vital issues of self-experience.
It by no means closes the theoretical books.

11 MIND AND STATE IN ANCIENT GREECE

> The story of the individual, even in ancient Greece, which
> not only created the concept of individuality but set the
> patterns for Western culture, is still largely unwritten.
> Max Horkheimer, *Eclipse of Reason*

THE ATOMIZATION of the individual in Western society
– and the loss of that authentic *individuation* which can
be vouchsafed only under unalienated social conditions – is
inscribed in the notion of 'mind' as a separate, analysable
entity. This illusion has become the professional domain of
psychology, psychoanalysis, psychiatry, and so on.
However it, too, has a history, and origins which it may be
useful to pursue. When and how did men awaken to the
notion of a mind that they possessed, and which deserved
study as a seemingly free-standing thing?

As it was Plato who first devised such a conception of
'mind', it is to ancient Greece that we turn for our study.

If Plato was the first to systematically think about the mind
as a discrete entity, then there were others who went before
him and failed to do so. At this juncture we are faced with
a logical choice. *Either* pre-Platonic notions of mentality are
scientifically backward positions, that is, they failed to pick
up what was real but somehow undetectable; *or* Plato's
concept of mind is a historical manifestation, that is, it is a
description of, and an attempt to master, an emergent form
of experience. According to this position, therefore, pre-
Platonic paradigms of mind were equally authentic manifestations of the age in which they appeared.[1] And if the
second, radically historical, point of view is correct with
respect to Plato and the Greeks, it should be equally informa-
tive about contemporary psychology. Further, if the second
notion of mentality is correct, as I believe it to be, then it
opens before us the prospect of discovering those mediating
elements within society that subserve the dramatically
shifting and highly influential historical notions of self-
experience.[2]

Bruno Snell (1953; and Diamond, 1980), in Vico's mode,
has explored the fact that Homer (or the Homeric bards)
lacks abstract terms referring to the person. Recently,

Bennett Simon (1978) has amplified Snell's study and developed the comparison with Plato. Homer occupies a compelling place as the first Western text. He is also, as Simon points out, at the end of the pre-literate tradition. Therefore the distinctions with later thought may have something to do with the oral mode by which the epics were transmitted. We shall return to this point later. For now what interests us is that Homer, as the first text, is at the same time a leap forward of self-representation and a recapitulation of prehistory. For by the eighth century, Greece had already undergone a millennium or more of history, with attendant, if but dimly appreciated, social transformations.

We may schematize the emergence of the Greek notion of mind as follows:

1. Homeric: prehistoric to eighth century
2. Transitional: eighth to fourth century
3. Platonic: 427–348

1. *Homeric*. There is no generic term for *person*, *self*, *mind* or even *body* in the *Iliad* and *Odyssey*. Three attributes are used to describe mental qualities – *psyche* (the force that keeps men alive and leaves upon death); *thymos* (the generator of motion, or affect); and *noos* (the cause of ideas). These are not integrated in any way. Rather is the person considered an aggregate of independent parts, more exactly as a set of functions arising from an aggregate of organs. Man is an 'open force field' (Frankel, 1978, cited in Simon, 1978, p. 63). Correspondingly, there is no hierarchy of function, no notion of a higher centre controlling a lower one. Finally, motivation and action are accounted for by the visitation of extrinsic forces rather than the promptings of an endogenous self.

It goes without saying that these 'pre-scientific' notions do not prevent Homer from portraying scenes of human reality with unsurpassed poignance and recognizability.

2. *Transitional*. Between Homer and Plato the idea of an inner mental agency took hold. *Psyche* emerges as 'living self'. It takes over the functions of Homer's *thymos* rather than *noos*, becoming the spirited, affective notion of personhood. Body (*soma*) also becomes an integrated term. However, as E. R. Dodds (1951) put it, 'Between *psyche* in this sense and *soma* . . . there is no fundamental antagonism; *psyche* is just the mental correlate of *soma*.' Each term can

mean 'life'; and each can mean 'person'. Most of our knowledge about its use comes of course from writers. However,
there is also the anonymous sixth-century epitaph
complaining that a sailor's life, 'gives few satisfactions to the
psyche' (Dodds, 1951, p. 128).

The Greek notion of personhood is problematic from the
start and reflects an individuality born of separateness. No
sooner are *psyche* and *soma* unified in general usage, than
Heraclitus introduces the notion of their differentiation (by
pointing out that *psyche* has no spatial boundary), and
distinguishes as well as between appearance and reality,
dreaming and wakefulness. A similarly abstract point is
made by Anaxagoras, who employs the Homeric intellective
term, *noos* (Simon, 1978, p. 159). The soul has hidden
depths and tensions; and even, as with Pythagoras (who
incorporates shamanistic tendencies), the capacity for dislocation from the body.

The lyric poets of the sixth century develop the idea of a
person concretely. For the first time, individuals write of
themselves, their passions, longings and – most significantly
– aloneness. Archilochus pokes fun at warrior tradition; and
Sappho depicts (like Pythagoras) the detachment of mind
from place, and union with another in memory. The latter
also introduces for the first time the notion of self-contradictory feeling: 'bittersweet love'.[3]

It is important to bear in mind that the individuality of the
archaic poets remains a relatively unalienated social product.
The other is always included in the address. As Snell puts
it, 'Though the individual who detaches himself from his
environment severs many old bonds, his discovery of the
dimension of the soul once more joins him in company with
those who have fought their way to the same insight' (Snell,
1953, p. 65).

It is important also to bear in mind that at the time of the
archaic poets, Solon's code (594) establishes the foundation
in law of the Athenian *polis*.

3. *Platonic*. Here the notion of individual is fully inscribed.
Psyche is now used in an entirely new sense, as *the self*, or
the seat of consciousness. By drawing all mental faculties
within the orbit of the self, Plato succeeds in isolating self-
experience for study. At the same time, by giving *psyche* the
quality of activity, he provides a philosophic basis for moral
responsibility under the conditions of Athenian society.
Although Plato's theory is consistently argued in a political

framework (mainly in the *Republic*), the distance between individuals, or between subject and society, is much more radically drawn than, for example, in the informal writings of the lyric poets. This is because Plato is systematic: he tells us of the essence of the self, that it has a structure, albeit a non-material one, and that there is a definite entity such as human nature. From another angle, Plato draws the self so sharply because he is the first thinker to confront seriously a tension within the individual between rational and irrational forces. His portrait of the self is sharply etched with the acid of psychological conflict. And as a logical consequence of the high state of intrapsychic conflict, the Platonic self is a hierarchically ruled entity. Reason is not only inscribed for Plato, it is enthroned, and passion, or appetite, or desire, takes that subordinate, and potentially maddening, station which it is to occupy for the remainder of the Western tradition. In contrast, say, to Hippocratic notions of health, which involved the notion of harmonious balance, for Plato, mental well-being consisted of the subordination of the lower portions of *psyche* to the higher. This is consistent with his espousal of contemplation as the highest good.

This brief exegesis of Platonic psychology[4] may serve to indicate the emergence of the object of psychological discourse. Did Plato delineate a 'natural thing'? Clearly not. But if historical, what were the conditions of the differentiation of the entity, mind, out of the remainder of the matrix? Homer had been content to leave mentality embedded in a total force field within which nature, the person and society were in continuous exchange with, and emerge only in relation to, each other. And pre-Socratic thought, though it allowed for a sense of individuality, did not proceed to that notion, mind-as-discrete-structure, upon which the future development of psychology would be predicated. Yet from Homer to Plato there seems to have occurred an inexorable bimodal process: *individualization* – the isolation of a discrete focus of individual subjectivity from the social totality – and *internalization* – the investment of that subjectivity with internal structure of an increasingly problematic and conflicted sort. In this respect the association of the Platonic self with the notion of intrasubjective conflict becomes a logical outgrowth of the process. It is not an idiosyncrasy of Plato's that he invested psyche with so much struggle between 'higher' intellective forces and 'lower' appetitive ones. Rather, the presence of mental

conflict is a condition of, and, in a sense, a motor for, the
process of individualization. A less internally conflicted,
that is, more harmoniously balanced, self would remain
articulated with the society from which it arises. It would be
individuated rather than *individualized*. On the other hand,
the sharply conflicted self develops, as a concomitant of its
intellective functioning, a *consciousness* of itself as discrete.
And the problem for us is to treat this matter historically.

We may begin with one of the more consistently under-
appreciated facts about archaic and classical civilization.
The pre-Socratic's insistence upon the distinction between
illusion and reality is frequently coupled with a critique, at
times a very harsh critique, of merely *popular* belief (Dodds,
1951, p. 181). In other words, by this phase (that is, the fifth
century), there had already emerged a distinction between
high and low culture, between the thought of élites and that
of the rabble. No such notion exists in Homer. By the
time of Heraclitus, however, the debunking of popular
superstitions becomes a consistent feature of thought. And
with Plato, whose antipathy to ordinary people is explicit,
it becomes a dominant one.

What is at issue here cannot simply be the presence of
social class. Homer describes a highly stratified chieftain
society – as does Hesiod (trans. Lattimore, 1959), who comes
shortly afterwards and writes at length about the struggles
of the peasant class with 'barons'. We are dealing rather in
these later writings with the presence of 'masses' – relatively
unintegrated people who are caught up in dislocating social
transformations and whose forms of thought become
thereby alien to the dominant groups who control the means
of expression and literate discourse. One of the conditions
for the emergence of a sharply differentiated self-concept,
then, appears to be the existence of sharply differentiated
social distinctions – between city and country, intelligentsia
and peasantry, élites and masses. And behind these distinctions lies the reality of domination.

The latter point deserves elaboration. Classical Greece
was not, of course, the only dominative ancient society with
high and low cultures. But it was the one with the highest
degree of contradiction. It was the only society which strove
towards rationality and developed a notion of freedom. But
it remained, like other state societies, basically unfree and
racked with class divisions. The oft-made claim that Greek
slavery was a relatively innocuous and permeable institution

is belied by the facts. Athenian wealth came significantly from the mines, wherein the conditions of the slaves were such that death became all they could wish for.[5] It would be foolish to call Athenian democracy a sham – it remains the exemplar of political-civil existence (Bookchin, 1978). But it was embedded in a society of extraordinarily uneven development whose institutional contradictions would necessarily manifest themselves in forms of thought. And so Greek rationality could never develop separately from its dialectical counterfoil of irrationality. The two emerge conjoinedly; and Plato, who lived in an Athens at the zenith of its discord and represents its narrowest, most oligarchic interests even as he strives towards universality of thought, stands at the apex of the contradiction between rational and irrational (Dodds, 1951).

From the perspective of history, what we have been saying amounts to this: that the development of the notion of individual self is closely linked to the emergence of the state; and that the estrangement of that self, both within itself and between itself and others, is a reflection of the alienation inherent in the political processes subsumed by the state. Put schematically, the state becomes a mirror to the mind. Consciousness, looking outwards to reality, encounters the opacity of the state. Reflected backwards, it recognizes itself as mind.

The state's opacity stands in contrast to the relative transparency of primitive society (Diamond, 1974a). Before the state, immediate human relations form the fabric of society. The state necessarily introduces estrangement into social existence. In the words of Max Weber, the state is 'an association that claims the monopoly of the *legitimate use* of *violence*, and cannot be defined in any other manner' (1946, p. 334). The conjunction of legitimacy and violence raises the state above the rest of society, giving it an inherently self-contradictory pair of qualities which is denied to all other individuals and groups. This distinction is most sharply lodged in the contrast between the law of the state and the customs of primitive society (Diamond, 1974b), but it belongs as well to other features of the state apparatus and, by an extension that we need document, to all aspects of life in state-dominated societies. So long as there is a state, the integral of these particular distinctions exists as its *otherness*, or opacity, rendering each person a relative stranger to all others outside of immediate networks of affiliation, and thereby creating the necessary, although not the sufficient, condition for the emergence of estranged and conflicted self-consciousness.

Despite the qualitative distinction between statist and primitive societies there is no clear line of distinction between them, nor should we expect a unifactorial type of explanation to account for the rise of states (Rapp, 1977; see also: Fried, 1967; Krader, 1968; Service, 1971). In part this is due to the fact that almost all known instances of transition have to do with the dynamism of the state and the corresponding influence of contiguous or foreign states upon primitive societies, and not with the endogenous development of primitive communities. Furthermore, the very dynamism of the state, which is what has to be explained, is in no sense the product of a single underlying factor, but rather seems to be the dialectical outcome of a number of specifically interacting elements. In any case, the question of the rise of states is one that has to be settled historically and concretely, and not by the invocation of a grand master-plan.

The study of archaic Greek civilization tantalizes us with a profusion of indirect evidence that drops off into pre-literate obscurity at the point of origin. Literacy and the correlated production of state documents is both the means by which history is transmitted and one of the principal elements in the internal development of the state. For literacy is a technological innovation which makes possible a qualitatively distinct expansion of the means of representation. And the monopolization of this means becomes an essential element of state power as well as a way of extending its necessary legitimacy.

The pre-literate Greek state must have been little different from chiefdom societies as we know them (Service, 1971). These in turn must have arisen at some point from tribal organizations of primitive type. I see no reason to dispute Morgan's original claim (1877) that Greek society was originally organized into *gentes*. According to George Thomson (1967), until the Dorian conquest (c. 1100), there is substantial evidence for a matriarchate, with communal ownership of land. The culture of these earliest forms centred about the notion of *moira*, a term that can be roughly translated as 'share', and which practically implied that all members of the community received an equal portion of the social product. The avenging spirits who punished social transgression, the *Erinyes*, were themselves representations of the archaic mother spirit. (They return centuries later in the *Oresteia*, the trilogy wherein Aeschylus sought to recapture the essentials of the formation of the Greek *polis*.) These spirits were, in the words of Thomson (following Morgan and Engels (1972)), reflections of 'dynastic conflicts precipitated in the ruling class of a matriarchal society by the rapid growth of property' (Thomson, 1967, p. 67). By a means that will doubtlessly remain obscure, primitive Greek society then came under the power of the patriarchal-chieftains of the Homeric age.

That Homeric society was patriarchal and dominative cannot be doubted. However, it was also an intermediary between tribal society and the state, and had not yet acquired the otherness of the latter. The Homeric king ruled; and the Homeric father had enormous authority over women, children and slaves. Land, however, was basically owned by the community (Ehrenberg, 1960), and the community itself was still structured by family. The Homeric legends, as Thomson put it, may have crystallized five centuries of revolutionary change (Thomson, 1967, p. 67), but it was a revolution within a certain type of social order. The lens held up by the Homeric poet to history looked straight back to the primitive community; and the unbounded notion of self we find in Homer is correspondingly the self of the primitive world-view.

The most prominent event in the transformation of tribal to state society was Solon's constitution of 594. This was, however, a nodal point and not one of absolute transformation. It had been preceded by the steady disintegration of the older order through class struggle and the accumulation of large numbers of slaves through debt. Before Solon, one belonged to society through membership in the clan, or gens. But too many people had fallen outside the gentile system. Solon enabled Athenian society to reconstitute itself along explicit class lines on the basis of property, without the intermediary of the gens, and therefore without the tie to primitive culture that had characterized all previous Greek civilization.

The new order provided the matrix for the development of the Greek state in its glory and subsequent decline. The isolated individual appears in poetry and philosophy as the state appears in history. Statism in its early phase fosters the emergence of individuality. The literacy which makes possible the growth of the state is to a great extent the

documentation of particular people for purposes of census,
taxation, military conscription and so forth.[6] Furthermore,
legality, as the specific system for regulating social existence
under the state, is essentially a matter involving discrete
individuals, whether in opposition to another person or in
relation to the state. I do not think it is true to say that the
state caused, or even made possible, the emergence of such
individuality. For it is no less true that individuality made
possible the state. Moreover, there were many despotic
states in which such a category of individual never arose.
However, it is the case that isolated individuality and the
state proved necessary for each other and were inextricably
intertwined – at least in the early and classical stages of
certain special instances.

Between the inception of the *polis* and the time of Plato
lies a tangled skein of history which it would be distracting
to unravel here. The broad outline is clear, however. The
Athenian state did what states based on class oppression
tend to do; it expanded and became imperialistic; and in
doing so increased its contradictoriness, became corrupt and
fell. In the course of its decline, Athens acquired, as states
also do, ideologues who defended its tottering structure and
attempted to patch together its exploding contradictions.
There is no reason why such ideologues should not be men
of genius such as Plato. But all of Plato's brilliance could not
hide the bankruptcy of the Athenian city-state. Rather did
the reverse occur: the political decline he strove to reverse
seeped back into his work, notably the *Republic*, and
corrupted it as well (Diamond, 1974c).

As Thomson points out, the nuclear term *moira*, or share,
which organizes primitive Greek society, begins to coexist
with another culturally organizing term, *ananke*, or
necessity, as tribal society is swept away. For the pre-Socratic
Heraclitus, *ananke* and *moira* are equivalents. But with Plato
the balance is broken: in the *Republic*, *ananke* usurps *moira*.
Moreover, *ananke* appears, fittingly enough, in the guise of
a slave-driver (Thomson, 1967, p. 158).

The *Republic* was written in a time of sharp and protracted
social conflict. An underlying economic problem was a fall
in the supply of slaves, tantamount in capitalism to a fall in
the rate of profit (Winsperar, 1956). The ruling class response
would predictably have been to glorify and legitimize the
institution of slavery, to do anything to squeeze more work
out of the existing slaves and to acquire as many new ones

as possible. There is no way of knowing how consciously Plato devised the *Republic* to foster these aims, but there is little doubt that it functioned so, or that it must have been an admirable text for the instruction of upper-class youth in his Academy.[7] The 'Noble Lie', wherein the rulers of the city are advised to promulgate the falsehood that the different classes of people are so because of essential metallic differences in their nature (Plato, Rouse, trans. 1956, 414–15E), is such a stratagem – and the first known Western instance of propaganda and the deliberate mystification of the masses to preserve a socio-economic order (not to mention racism, of which the 'Noble Lie' is a distant but real harbinger). Similarly, Plato's actively anti-Homeric stance, which ruthlessly banished poetry from the city, was a way of suppressing popular oral culture, and all ties to a past in which *moira* was the dominant social principle. One may even speculate that his celebrated image of the Cave is also a metaphor for, and an attempted mystification of, the mines where metallic wealth was generated.[8]

The image of Plato's Cave leads us to a further inquiry as to the origins of the sense of an isolated self. Plato had not yet reached that stage of discourse in which thought is, so to speak, purified of all imagery and attains a bloodless technicism. Although he seeks to eliminate poetry from the state, his own writing is highly poetic. It is suffused with the very metaphor he seeks to dispel. The Platonic text is therefore shot through with an alternate, and unintended, set of meanings grounded in metaphor and imagery – in other words, in a meta-language rooted in the body and intimate personal experience. In sum, Plato invites a psychoanalytic hermeneutics. This Bennett Simon has done, and has come up with an interesting (and convincingly documented) interpretation of Plato's Cave – or rather, of one line of meaning sunk into this complex, and undoubtedly overdetermined, allegory, and woven throughout the dialogues.

The cave is the place where illusion is imposed. In it prisoners are forced from childhood passively to watch a spectacle, a 'puppet show', projected as shadows upon a wall by unseen exhibitors. Simon interprets this 'as a primal scene fantasy: children in the darkness of the bedroom, seeing the shadows and hearing the echoes of parental intercourse' (1978, p. 178). The interpretation is not drawn from this one image alone, but – as psychoanalytic prop-

ositions need to be – from a theme which variously runs
throughout the *Republic* as well as other dialogues and
generates the inner content of that disordering madness
which hovers about the Platonic state and *psyche*: 'Our
analysis of the themes and images of birth and copulation
and death in the *Republic* leads to a frightening primal scene
fantasy, which seems to be the substrata from which arise
the Platonic notions of evil, madness, and that special brand
of madness which is political rivalry and civil war' (p. 179).
Simon goes further yet. Plato's goal of philosophic contemplation, his very ascent into a desensualized idealism and
his promotion of a guardian class who are also philosophers,
is a negation of this supercharged experience. 'I believe that
an important *unconscious* aspect of Plato's design for his ideal
state is the wish to protect the élite and the guardians from
primal scene trauma and its consequences' (p. 176).

   So much may be true. At least it is supported by textual
evidence. But the question remains for this as for other
psychoanalytic propositions – what is the historical position
of this fantasy structure? Is it compelling for Plato as an
individual, in which case we can regard it merely as a
neurosis; or is it an essential part of the culture of his times?
And if so, what are its mediations? Failure to ground
psychoanalytic discourse historically leads either to a crude
biologism in which an ahistorical instinct generates the
fantasy; or to an equally mystifying idealism in which ideas
generate each other. In either case no critical position can be
taken; the psychoanalytic notion merely reproduces the
historical structure.

   Let us consider another side to the 'Noble Lie'. The lie, at
least that promulgated by guardians, is not accidental but
systematic for Plato: 'Often the rulers will have really to use
falsehood and deceit for the benefit of the ruled; and we said
all such things were useful as a kind of drug (*sic*)' (Plato,
Rouse, trans. 1956, 459E). At the same time, lying reveals
the problematic. Occurring when power can no longer
sustain itself with its own rationality, the lie signals the weak
historical point in the system, the edge of unmediable
contradiction. Plato has the honesty to admit that his lies
are such and to doubt that the people will fall for them.
None the less he proceeds with the following admitted
extravagance: former life was only a dream; men were not
born of actual mothers but were gestated deep in the earth
and delivered completely formed – that is, with all their

social acquisitions, class distinctions, and so on. (The lie here gives us yet another level of meaning for the Cave, which even the dullest eye may recognize as a representation of the womb.) They would thereby – if only they could be made to believe this lie – cease squabbling about their differences and take up the common defence of their earth mother, that is, the imperial Athenian state. This piece of propaganda is consonant with Plato's conviction – which he also doubts the people will accept – that the family should be abolished as such and that the state, or to be more exact, the guardians, should prescribe group marriage and, with an eye to eugenics, collective child-rearing, so that no child should know its true parents and that the fittest might be drawn into ruling circles (457–9E). But the fantasy, aside from its totalitarian implication, is nothing else than a prefiguration of the end of an actual struggle which had been going on for centuries and would continue thenceforward throughout the eras of state hegemony, namely, the essential antagonism between the family and the state as principles of social organization. And closely linked with this struggle, in fact, intertwined with it at every stage, is the struggle between male and female, a battle ostensibly won by the former with the advent of state hegemony but which has been in reality never-ending.

The state grows at the expense of the family,[9] and the male at the expense of the female. The process is intricate and decisively dysphasic, for the state also grows at the expense of the father, under whose power the family falls in the latter stages of its pre-state development, and who also remains titularly enthroned over personal life in all state formations until those of late capitalism (Kovel, 1978). And this is because, as Rapp has put it, 'kinship structures were the great losers in the civilizational process . . . with the rise of state structures, kin-based forms of organization were curtailed, sapped of their legitimacy and autonomy in favour of the evolving sphere of territorial and class-specific politics . . . In the process, not only kinship, but women lost out' (Rapp, 1977, p. 310).

Nowhere was this process more clearly drawn than in the Greek experience (Thomson, 1965). And the history of the individual, including its Platonic realization, is written at the interface between stateship and kinship. The development was clearly spelled out by Gustave Glotz as long ago as 1929:

In reality, the Greek city, while retaining the institution of the
family, grew at its expense. It was compelled to appeal to individual
forces which the original group repressed. For a long time the city
had to fight against the genos *and each of its victories was gained*
by the suppression of some form of patriarchal servitude . . . (p. 4)

The decisive institutionalizing turn came with Solon's constitution, with juridically removed authority from the gens
chieftain.

At one blow the family system was shattered, undermined at its
very foundations. The state was placed in direct contact with
individuals. The solidarity of the family, in its active rather than
passive form, no longer had a raison d'être. (p. 107)

As we noted before, Solon's constitution was a nodal point,
and not a culmination. Just as it had been preceded by
a crumbling of the old order, so was it succeeded by a
furtherance of the process it helped set into motion. Glotz
continues: 'Throughout the whole of the fifth century the
last traces of family responsibility were being progressively
abolished' (1929, p. 258). Plato represents its culmination –
and degeneration – into a totalitarian solution born out of
extreme anxiety. According to this line of reasoning, then,
the proliferation of primal-scene imagery in the *Republic* is
an outcome of the negation suffered by the family in the
course of state development. The imagery reflects the
anxiety of being exposed to the 'lower', appetitive functioning of the family once the restraints of the 'higher',
socially integrative functioning have been dissolved.

It is the nature of the above 'furtherance' which most
concerns us and most eludes us, for there are neither
historical nor psychological tools available to grasp the
interplay between family, state and *psyche*. I do not think
the process was a linear or one-sided one, so that the 'state'
in the abstract, or even its ruling class, simply takes over the
family piece by piece in the interests of 'power'. I suspect
rather that each piece of dissolution of the family introduces
anxiety into the social totality, and that this anxiety is itself
a spur for further controlling and dissolving the family, via
social mediations we are unable to explore here. From this
angle the state's growth takes on a twofold aspect: *positively*
as the successively greater control of territory, resources and
the division of labour; and *negatively* as the repression of the
anxieties set loose by the breakup of the family. I would not

regard either of the aspects as prior to, or causal of, the other. They are mutually determinative dialectical moments that exist in a state of negativity. It is the negative side that Aeschylus grasped when he had Orestes pursued by the Erinyes, spirits of his murdered mother who chased him all the way to Apollo's state-bearing doorstep. And it is the relationship intuited by E. R. Dodds when he asserted that the 'guilt culture' which overcame Athens in the later years of its empire, and which was a main moment in the irrational counterpoise to Greek rationality, had to be explained on the basis of a breakdown in the family, specifically, a loss of paternal authority and a concomitant rise in the anxiety contingent on parricidal fantasies. Dodds introduces us to the interesting fact that undisguised Oedipal dreams were common in late antiquity (1951, p. 61), and reminds us of the larger implication that Oedipus is not primarily an intrapsychic affair but participates actively in history.

Dodds's hypothesis is that the decrease in authority of the real *paterfamilias* led to an increase in need for moral sanction – that is, for an internalized guilt signal. This corresponds with the general tendency of internalization to increase with historical time (Dodds, 1951). It also helps to account for 'guilt culture' as a re-projection, and cultural integration, of an unbearable psychological state. Moreover, it gives us another sense in which the psychological surfaced – for the unbearable also becomes a location of consciousness: consciousness of *psyche* emerges, as *psyche* is set off from the world by projection of its pain and guilt.

That the dethroning of the real father produced anxiety would be evidence, in the Freudian scheme of things, for widespread parricidal impulses. These in turn might be explained on the basis of a supposedly universal 'aggressive instinct'. Such would again fall into the trap of biologism, explaining nothing and supporting authority. More to the point, we must consider the historical evidence that the kind of family which the state overcame was itself a highly dominative and patriarchal one in which the father had, and doubtlessly exercised, rights of life and death over his children. The key transition is not between primitive society and the state, but involves a chieftain–society intermediary (Service, 1971). This society was well ensconced by Homeric times and carried with it all the marks of patriarchal oppression. (After all, Agamemnon was murdered because he had arbitrarily sacrificed his daughter.) Although archaic

Greek society lacked the sense of alienation later imparted by the state, it should be recognized that the classical Greek *polis* was in many respects a progressive development – just as, many centuries later, early capitalism could be seen as progressive relative to feudal backwardness. Yet it remained prey to parental imagos from the archaic past.

One uses the plural here: imagos. The archaic mother stalks about alongside her consort in the Greek imagination. One suspects that, for Plato in any case, the greater anxiety was towards this repudiated female principle, debased in actual social existence and correspondingly monstrified in the imagination. The point, however, is not to choose between Oedipus and Orestes as the inner protagonist of classical Greek development. There is rather no dominant or singular myth. Cultural totalitarianism was antithetical to the spirit of paganism, and had to await the dubious blessing of Christianity. Plato's life work was expended in the germination of a unifying world-view grounded in a totalitarian state. Regarded against the backdrop of what it accomplished at the time, it must be happily viewed as a pathetic failure. But it introduced the germ of essentialism into thought which, applied to *psyche*, made it into an object for psychology.

Psyche, or mind, however, is no independent, free-standing or hierarchically arranged *thing*. It is a *relation* – a nexus of the historical *relata* of subjectivity occurring at a particular time. Mind is constructed; it is not a passive existant, but an active historical force. Its Platonic hierarchization contains and further develops an indwelling contradiction: the movement towards freedom and individuation contained in the Athenian *polis* along with the domination which ruled the actual society of his time. And it incorporates the primitive past of *moira* in a debased form (for example, in the state-imposed group marriages), as if to keep people from remembering and contacting a tradition antithetical to the class society in which they found themselves.

But *psyche* was not merely ideological. It was also constitutive. It was a stitching together of a whole mass of mental fragments set loose by the intrusion of the state into the family. Before there was a state, family and society were conterminous and a unified development between phases of life could be ritually provided. The state introduces an otherness which cannot be mediated through the family. Correspondingly, family-centred operations now take on a life of their own. Childhood in particular becomes problematic for the simple reason that one cannot move smoothly from infancy to mature social existence when elders are replaced with state functionaries as sources of authority. As a result infantile experience sediments intrapsychically. The individual *psyche* is named to be the site of its fantasies. Plato intuits the danger if these should spill over and so constructs *psyche* as a container, holding desire at bay and separating the individual from others and from society. These others are organized into the social classes which embody the positive material development of the state. Those from whom the ruling class ideologue was most radically separated became repositories for a subjective otherness which was projected on to them. The political aloneness of the psyche in statist society therefore becomes critically buttressed through repression. The parts of mind that are split off etch the individuality of the *psyche*. At the same time, projected on to lower classes, they maintain the class system in place. Master and slave become locked together in unhappy embrace, each containing a part of the other that is not to be appropriated, or even known except by the dilutions of abstract philosophic discourse. Just as the state, then, achieves its identity through this differentiation and rigidification of the classes whose activity constitutes it, so does *psyche* achieve its rigid identity through an internalization of these very class distinctions. The two constructions come to mirror one another. At one and the same time this construction establishes in the individual a narcissistic yearning whose object can be represented in the state's otherness. That the state can never satisfy such desire is precisely the secret of its power over the individual and the source of the legitimacy that must be yoked to its violence.

The most stringent caution should be exercised in extrapolating between the forms of one civilization and those of another, in this case, between ancient Greece and our own. On the other hand, Plato is the progenitor of the Western intellectual tradition – and not for abstractly intellectual reasons. Western philosophy may not exactly be a series of footnotes to Plato but it has consisted of the workings out of problems that he was the first systematically to enunciate. Plato is like an armature to what came since: it built itself around him. And from the standpoint of psychology, the resemblance between Freud's view of mind and that of Plato (Simon, 1978, pp. 200–14) is too striking to be set aside as a

chance occurrence. Their views of mind – hierarchical,
conflictual, radically individuated and structuralized – must
be regarded as homologous solutions to a fundamentally
similar set of problems.

We cannot here take up the intricacies of Freudian thought
in relation to its times (which too have been those of an
unstable imperial order); nor consider the various problem-
atics posed by psychology, except to suggest the following:
if the same dialectic pertains to contemporary psychology
as it did to the self-understanding of ancient Greece, then it
will be as true for us as it was for them that *psyche* refers not
to an isolatable thing but to a historically dynamic relation
between a person and the social totality. It is, so to speak, a
kind of aperture between them. And if this is so, then the
consequences for *psychology* are drastic, for it finds itself
without the confident location of an object for its discourse.

This is not a loss that needs to be mourned. The
professional division of discourse is a historical act specific
to the needs of bourgeois existence and not a statement
about the contours of reality. It is well that a science be
reminded that its particular current status should be subordinated to what Marx called for in the '1844 manuscripts',
namely, the need for the future development of a single,
'human science' (Marx, 1963, p. 164). And it is also essential
to register the losses imposed by the conceptual totalitarianism of a Plato and by the scientific compartmentaliz-
ation of the world which followed. Though predicated on
the maintenance of domination, such ideas are not neutral
in their own right, but contribute to 'un-freedom', and
weaken one place even as they strengthen another. For, in
the words of Paul Feyerabend, man 'becomes impoverished
at precisely the moment he discovers an autonomous
"I" . . .' (1975, p. 262). This free-standing, lonely 'I' is
nothing less than the *Ego*, object of psychoanalytic and
psychological discourse – and, as Horkheimer put it, 'the
principle of the self endeavouring to win in the fight against
nature in general, against other people in particular, and
against its own impulses' (1974, p. 105). But it is nothing
more, either, and surely not the individuated self that is the
province of those who appropriate their social existence.

NOTES

1. This is not to deny that Plato's conscious reflection about mind
was a quantum leap from the positions that went before. Just so

does modern psychology change and add to psyche by reflecting 225
upon it. I mean this materially, as in the rise, say, of the institutions
of psychotherapy, all predicated upon the provision of an
intellectual raw material, 'mind', to work upon.

2. In order to develop a theory of these mediations, a certain
Archimedean point is needed, which involves the acceptance of
valid psychological categories of knowledge. In other words, I
am using, say, Freudian ideas while at the same time subjecting
them to historical critique, that is, using psychology *critically*. The
alternative is to historicize mentality out of existence by reducing
it to forms of speech or discourse as, for example, Foucault, tends
to do.

3. *Sappho* (translated by Mary Bernard, 1951). 'The Fragment' (53)
goes: 'With his venom/irresistible and bittersweet/that loosener
of limbs, Love/reptile like strikes me down.'

4. For a more extensive discussion see Simon (1978, pp. 157–215).

5. See the first-century descriptions by Diodorus (cited in
Thomson, 1967, p. 162). Thomson points out that, though we
have virtually no direct evidence on the condition of slaves earlier
than this, there is every reason to believe it was fully as awful
in Plato's time.

6. Literacy is also intrinsically privatizing. It introduces the
relation of self to others mediated by written symbol, as against
direct face-to-face communication. The written word necessarily
introduces the possibility of individual expansion.

7. Some things have not changed. The *Republic* (along with Eliot's
The Waste Land) was required reading during my freshman year
at Yale. Nor was one word heard of its reactionary and élitist
qualities.

8. The men in the cave are fettered prisoners who are there from
childhood, i.e., as those born into slavery would be. The cave itself
has a long tunnel-like entrance leading to daylight (Plato, Rouse,
trans. 1956, 514A–516B).

9. See, for example, Diamond (1951). Diamond's dissertation,
which focuses on a specific historical instance of state formation,
deals precisely with this subject. For a further elaboration of the
Platonic characterization of these processes and the meaning of
this characterization for the Western intellectual tradition, see
also Diamond, 1974a (pp. 176–202).

12 MARX ON THE JEWISH QUESTION

THE PROBLEMATIC relations between Marxism, radicalism and Judaism have not escaped notice. Julius Carlebach's monumental *Karl Marx and the Radical Critique of Judaism* (1978) lists no fewer than ninety-three works directly concerned with the subject, in a bibliography that only goes to 1973. More studies, some of them quite substantial, have appeared since. The justification for yet another does not reside, therefore, in any claim to originality; while the sheer weight of the effort to come to grips with the problem rules out in advance any hope of achieving a satisfactory rēsolution. Where Jewishness is concerned there can be no good answer, only an unending series of contradictions. This is, however, just the point: to wrestle with what cannot be resolved within history in order to understand history more deeply – and to gain some insight into the possibilities of changing it. We are faced, in short, with a kind of *koan*.

It may be framed as follows: how to comprehend the existence of an evidently anti-Semitic streak in the earliest published work of historical materialism? What does this signify in light of the complex relations between Jews and the radical tradition, relations characterized by affinity, alienation, and even, at times, hatred?

In 1843, the twenty-five-year-old Karl Marx wrote for the first and only issue of the *Deutsch-französische Jahrbücher* (of which he was an editor) two review-essays of works by the radical theologian Bruno Bauer, 'Die Judenfrage' and 'Die Fähigkeit [capacity] der heutigen Juden und Christen frei zu werden'. The two parts have come to be known by the title of the first, 'On the Jewish question' (henceforth OJQ) (Marx, 1964a). Except for a gloss on these pieces – and Bauer's reply to them – in *The Holy Family*, OJQ is the only substantive part of Marx's life work to be devoted to the problem of Jewishness. Since Marx was descended from rabbis on both sides of his family, and since his father converted to Christianity just before his birth and Karl was himself

baptised at age six, and since other men of genius who were
in a similar predicament, such as Heine and Lassalle, had
agitated themselves considerably over Jewishness, Marx's
untoward degree of silence concerning a topic of such world-
historical significance strikes one as noteworthy, a matter of
'blockage', to use the term of Carlebach. We shall return to
this point later. For now, what is the evidence of OJQ?

The Jewish question in 1843 was whether and how Jews
were to be 'emancipated' into the political and religious
freedom of post-Enlightenment Europe, while at the same
time retaining their identity. Such was the concrete form
taken by the arch-typical contradiction between particularity
and universality which has been the historical destiny of the
Jewish people (Carlebach, 1978).[1] In Marx's youth the setting
for this was the consolidation of the bourgeoisie in the post-
Napoleonic era, a process accentuated in Germany by the
search for a unified state and culture. As always, Jews were
caught in the middle – scapegoated on the one hand (in
particular because Jewish usurers had caused the foreclosure
of many peasant holdings), swept up by the current of
bourgeois modernization on the other.

Bauer, who appears to have been irked that more attention
was paid to the persecution suffered by the Jews than to his
own (Carlebach, p. 126), entered the lists of this debate
with an ambivalent tract which subordinated the quest for
emancipation to a critique of religion and ended up as an
anti-Semitic tirade. No emancipation could be achieved,
according to Bauer, until men achieved their humanity
and freedom by overcoming religion. Though this stricture
applied to both Christian and Jew, Bauer left no doubt that
it was the latter who had to pay the heavier price. With
theoretical mania and fanaticism, Bauer ransacked Judaic
history to prove that the Jews as a people were unfit for
freedom unless they renounced their identity and became
humanistic. The same goal was offered to Christians; but
since Bauer, following Feuerbach, believed that Christianity
was a much more highly developed religion than Judaism,
he held that the goal of freedom was nearer at hand for
them. Therefore all his critical energies could be reserved
for the benighted Jews.

Bauer's tracts would have undoubtedly disappeared with
scarcely a trace had Marx not found them apt foils for his
early writings on historical materialism. The young Hegelian
Bauer represented an intellectual heritage that had to be

transcended if Marx was to become himself. Bauer's foppery, aridity, academicism, above all the privileged withdrawal from the real life he was purporting to emancipate – all this had to be destroyed and overcome. But as Marx proceeded to do so a curious contradiction of his own was revealed as well.

There are three stages to the reasoning of OJQ. In the first, Marx attacks Bauer's critique of religion. Where the latter would have eliminated religion as a pre-condition for human liberation, Marx recognizes instead a deeper necessity to eliminate the *need* for religion. This can only be accomplished through social revolution. Bauer is fixated on the narrow issue of juridical rights, that is, on political and legalistic emancipation. Marx sees instead the need for *human emancipation*, in which religion, the 'sentiment of a heartless world' (Marx, 1964b) would no longer be needed to console mankind for their unlived lives. Men would discard religion like an unneeded crutch when they achieved mastery over their social being. Note that Marx only recognizes religion as either the reaction to mundane evil and powerlessness, or a social control mechanism. Religion is but the phantom of an oppressed brain, never an authentic response to an existential dilemma. It is as though a rational man never has to face death or deal with metaphysical ultimates. For Marx, the only God worth noting was the one made by man in his prehistorical, and by definition, fallen condition.

The second level of Marx's critique concerns particularity. No issue has been more closely identified with Jewishness, whether elaborated ideologically into the Covenant making them the Chosen people, or enunciated in the endless struggles of ghettoization. Deprived of land and excluded from the means of force and violence, Jews defended themselves over the centuries by tenaciously clinging to their identity. The Jewish sense of a unique destiny by turns haunted and mocked the Christian ideal of a universal faith. And when the ideal of universality took its secular-bourgeois form of emancipated assimilation, Jewish specialness remained like a bone in the throat of Europe. Again, Marx seizes the contradiction to penetrate deeply. Where Bauer would have the Jews abandon who they were, Marx more correctly saw into the hypocritical nature of a society that preached the need for universality while establishing conditions of fragmentation. The self-preoccupation of the Jew as Jew is but the symbol for a ubiquitous self-centredness.

The real villain is not the Jew but the bourgeois order, which dwells on the earth of civil society and creates the heaven of the state over it. It is the bourgeois who makes civil society into the realm of egoism and alienation. When the bourgeois contract dissolved the feudal order it placed each individual against all others in the universal market. But the market cannot achieve universality. It is no more than the rationalized edge of the Hobbesian jungle into which the bourgeois revolution had plunged civilization. Consequently the emancipation of any group can achieve no more than bourgeois partiality allows. This cannot be a true liberty since 'liberty as a right of man is not founded upon the relations between man and man, but rather upon the separation of man from man. It is the right of such separation. The right of the *circumscribed* individual, withdrawn into himself' (Marx, 1964a, pp. 24–5; italics here and elsewhere are Marx's). And 'thus man was not liberated from religion; he received religious liberty. He was not liberated from property; he received the liberty to own property. He was not liberated from the egoism of business; he received the liberty to engage in business' (p. 29).

Until this point there is nothing anti-Semitic about Marx's discourse, and indeed much that can be read as a ringing defence of the rights of the Jewish people. Though Marx offers no comfort to those who would retain their ethnic particularity at all costs, the discourse of the first part of the essay is that of the Enlightenment, and for all its passion, remains under the aegis of reason. Indeed it clearly prefigures the synthesis which is to come, lacking only the economic element which is to assume such a preponderant role in his later thought. The introduction of the economic dimension comprises the third level of the logic of OJQ, where it is clothed in a different kind of discourse – one that has raised the spectre of anti-Semitism in many minds since.

The discourse in question appears in the second part of Marx's review-essay, 'Die Fähigkeit . . .' After summarizing Bauer's excessively abstract and theological position, Marx comes directly to the point. The capacity of the Jew for emancipation may be rephrased as: 'What specific *social* element is it necessary to overcome in order to abolish Judaism?' In other words, what is 'the particular situation of Judaism in the present enslaved world'? The 'real Jew', in Marx's view, is determined by '*Practical* need, *self-interest*. What is the worldly cult of the Jew? *Huckstering*. What is his worldly god? *Money*.' Therefore society must eliminate the conditions that make huckstering possible. And this would 'make the Jew impossible. His religious consciousness would evaporate like some insipid vapour in the real life-giving air of society'. And because Judaism contains the 'universal *antisocial* element of the *present time*', the Jewish question is a much grander matter than might be surmised at first: 'In the final analysis, the *emancipation of* the Jews is the emancipation of mankind from Judaism' (p. 34).

There is more about money – 'the jealous god of Israel, beside which no other god may exist'; and more against the Jews, whose religion is said to contain, 'in abstract [that is, one-sided] form . . . contempt for theory, for art, for history and for man as an end in himself' (p. 37). These essential features of the Jewish creed are realized and come to fruition under civil society, so that Christianity, which 'issued from Judaism . . . has now been reabsorbed into Judaism', which thereby 'could attain universal domination and could turn alienated man and alienated nature into alienable, saleable, objects, in thrall to egoistic need and huckstering' (p. 39). Once, therefore, the egoistic nature of society disappears, 'the Jew becomes *impossible*, because his consciousness no longer has an object'. The subjective basis of Judaism – practical need – assumes a human form, and the conflict between the individual, sensuous existence of man and his species-existence, is abolished.

'The *social* emancipation of the Jew is the *emancipation of society from Judaism*' (p. 40).[2]

So ends 'On the Jewish question' – nine pages too late for the hagiographer of Marx. Yet nine pages not to be discarded, for they contain the first metamorphosis of the critique of political economy. A number of kinds of response to these extraordinary passages are possible. We may dismiss the essay as a whole, like Isaiah Berlin ('a dull and shallow composition' (1963, p. 99)); weigh it in the balance and find it wanting, like Julius Carlebach ('Marx has been proved to be wrong – factually, objectively and historically.' More, he must answer for 'the harm he has done and may yet do through his second essay' (1978, p. 358)); one may find Marx guilty of more or less mitigative degrees of anti-Semitism (Carlebach, p. 358);[3] or one may attempt to demonstrate, as have two recent contributors to the debate, Henry Pachter (1979) and Hal Draper (1977), that when taken in context OJQ is not really very anti-Semitic at all, its crudest features being merely way-stations on the road to the brilliant and liberating synthesis to come, and the rest, an astute analysis of existing economic relations before Marx had really developed the language to do this scientifically. There is yet another position, which combines a number of the above features. It will have to wait, however, until we have examined certain aspects of the essay more closely.

The harshest critic of Marx cannot deny that 'Die Fähigkeit' moves towards an epochal breakthrough. In these concluding pages of OJQ, Marx's insights concerning religion and the state are drawn into the real, practical life blood of society. The economic factor has been flushed. We see it in terms of the monstrous power of money as a fluid and expandable medium. Marx does not yet recognize this form of money as capital, nor is he able clearly to perceive its fantastic power as the fetishization of social relations. Yet many of the elements of the later synthesis have been brought together in these pages. More, the economic domain is developed as the main signifying element of capitalistic society without the economism which is to haunt later Marxian thought. There is no shadow of a base–superstructure dichotomy here, rather a kind of fluid totalizing in which the metonymic identification of the Jew with the satanic power of money locates the economic process concretely in social existence. Yet Marx transcends the concrete even as he touches upon it. These passages may be the first instance in Marx's writings of the inspired mode of abstraction he was later to describe in the *Grundrisse*: 'As a rule, the most general abstractions arise only in the midst of the richest possible concrete development, where one thing appears as common to many, to all. Then it ceases to be thinkable in a particular form alone' (Marx, 1859, p. 104). The discourse of OJQ may lack maturity, but it is replete with genius.

The recognition that Marx was here testing out his wings of abstraction tends to vitiate the line of criticism which dwells on the one-sidedness of his representation of the Jews. The abstraction is not meant to grasp the entire concrete immediacy of a phenomenon, only the historically decisive aspect. This aspect is by its inner nature not 'one-sided' – as would have been the case, according to Marx, with Hegelian idealism, Feuerbachian materialism or, of course, Bauer's 'criticism'. It is rather that which generates all the 'sides', the formative point at which history is lived, and what Marx was soon to call 'sensuous activity' (1968c, p. 28).

But this point in no way disposes of the criticism against Marx's approach to the Jewish question. We are still left with determining the adequacy of his abstraction. After all, to identify an entire people with an economic tendency is not the same thing as deriving the labour theory of value. It is not, so to speak, a very abstract abstraction, and it risks a twofold violation: unfairly to link the Jews with the mainspring of economic activity; and unfairly to link all Jews with what only a small portion of them were doing. If Marx's formulation has the virtue of being outside the rigidities of economism, it does so by standing on a slippery slope where it is vulnerable to a number of charges, not the least of which concerns its truth.

Was Marx being empirically correct when he identified the Jew with the rule of 'Money'? There is of course the infamous association of Jews with usury, a practice which was their main source of wealth in Western Europe from the twelfth to the fifteenth centuries (Baron, 1975). Even though usury became less exclusively a Jewish pursuit afterwards – and indeed was in the process of being transferred entirely to banks and other centres of finance capital by the nineteenth century – Jews were still actively enough engaged in money-lending to hold one-fourth of the liquid assets of the Prussian state (despite comprising less than 2 percent of the population) at the time of the composition of OJQ (Carlebach, 1978, p. 88). Moreover, a great deal of Jewish enterprise was taken up with trading and brokerage of all kinds. Though this is scarcely surprising in view of their systematic exclusion from landedness and other sources of primary production, it does lend a grain of credence to Marx's line of reasoning.

Still, it is hard not to feel some rapport with Carlebach's verdict that 'the more a person knows about Jews and Judaism the less likely is he to take the Marxian analysis of Judaism seriously' (p. 280). To reduce a people, 84 percent of whom were impoverished in 1843, to the bearers of a world-dominating principle of monetary acquisition does not strike one as the most felicitous way to deal with the 'Jewish question'. And the same may be said for the violence done to the tradition of Judaism, with its subtleties and

mystical bent, when it, too, is forced to bear the burden of
the capitalist spirit. Contrary to the impression given by
Marx in OJQ, the 'real Jew' whom he strives to depict with
his materialist method stood for no one principle. On the
contrary, the Jews, then as now, were a heterogeneous
people with a class structure of their own (including a
substantial proletariat) and a complex cultural tradition
(Carlebach, pp. 183, 202). The self-understanding, or
identity, of the Jewish people – which is an essential part of
their historical being – could in no way be represented,
either in 1843 or at any other time, in the terms chosen by
Marx. What he did therefore, was project on to the Jews a
racial stereotype, thereby making them bear the obloquy
associated with it. In sum the logical structure of 'Die
Fähigkeit' contains the germ of historical anti-Semitism.
And it is incumbent upon us to take this concurrence
seriously.

In doing so we should resist the tendency to explain away
the anti-Semitism of OJQ through a facile appeal to historical
context, thereby leaving the germ of historical materialism
intact and pristine. I would hold instead that the true
situation is rather more complex, and that OJQ's anti-
Semitism is not an incidental element in the historical
development of historical materialism itself, indeed that it
gives us some insight into the future difficulties of Marxism.
But first let us consider those who would exonerate Marx.

Both Hal Draper and Henry Pachter make essentially the
same point. Marx should not be judged by the standards of
our day for using the common language of his. In the
early nineteenth century everybody engaged in a kind of
promiscuous racial baiting such that survives nowadays
only in the isolated realm of the ethnic joke. Putting Marx's
remarks in context, then, places a much less malign light
upon them. What hostility Marx felt for his people was more
a matter of class antipathy than genuine racialism, argues
Pachter. It was a type of snootiness the genteel son of a
prosperous and emancipated burgher might instinctively
feel for the shabbily lumpen condition of most of the Jews
of his acquaintance. Indeed, OJQ uses some of the technique
of the joke to make its point. One needs 'a little sense of
humour', according to Pachter (1979, p. 458), to appreciate
this; while Draper adds that 'Die Fähigkeit' should be
considered 'a play on words. Such word-play was indeed a
favourite literary pattern of the young Marx, as it was of

Hegel. In both it was not a humorous but an explicatory
device; a means of developing, out of the different aspects
of meaning packed into one word, various aspects of the
reality which the word reflected' (Draper, 1977, p. 603).

There are two serious errors in this line of reasoning. One
is contained in the suggestion that language is merely a
reflection of reality and not a part of reality; while the other
consists of misreading the passion and intention of OJQ,
and divorcing the essay from Marx's actual condition at the
time. To excise anti-Semitism from Marx's discourse because
everybody else was saying the same thing – as if nobody
therefore could have meant anything – is an argument
which, if pursued to its logical limit, would simply erase all
social science. Imagine making the same judgement on, say,
Goebbels, who after all was only repeating what other Nazis
said about Jews. No, the anti-Semitism of Marx's time was
not the same as that of a century later, specifically being
without racial essentialism and, therefore, genocidal potential and no, Marx was not a bigoted freak, but a fairly
representative man of his day with respect to attitudes
towards Judaism. But once one has cleared these points up,
the anti-Semitism remains; and since Marx is of interest as
the man who transcended the thought of his age, and
provided the project of liberation with its definitive modern
articulation, the extent to which it remains – or is not
itself adequately transcended – becomes of interest in the
understanding of historical materialism.

By anti-Semitism I mean the denial of the right of the Jew
to autonomous existence, that is, freely to determine his/
her own being as Jew. Anti-Semitism therefore entails an
attitude of hostility to the *Jew* as *Jew*. This is an act of violence,
addressed to an essential property of humanity: the assertion
of an *identity*, which may be understood as a socially shared
structuring of subjectivity. To attack the free assumption of
identity is to undermine the social foundation of the self.
Judged by these criteria, OJQ is without any question an
anti-Semitic tract – significantly, only in its second part, 'Die
Fähigkeit'. No attempt to read these pages as a play on
words can conceal the hostility which infuses them, and is
precisely directed against the identity of the Jew.

Anti-Semitism, like all variants of racist thought, involves
a process of abstraction (Kovel, 1970). It is the substitution
of an idea about its object for the sensuous reality of that
object. It is therefore an objectification which reduces the

subjectivity of the other to the level of a thing, and so violates his/her humanity. The kind of substitution by means of which this takes place is the projection of an unacceptable dimension of the anti-Semite's own self on to the Jew. The Jew is then forced to live out, as Other, the bad features of the anti-Semite's existence – and to be punished for them.

The abstraction of 'Die Fähigkeit' is linked to its real object emotionally through hatred and logically through the metonymic substitution of Jew for the power of money. This much is clear from the text, and is manifest at that point where the discourse of the second portion breaks loose from the first. Following this, Marx seems almost eager to put the whole problem behind him. He writes *The Holy Family*, which is much more tempered (and gives credit to Jewish critics of Bauer) (Marx and Engels, 1975, p. 112)[4] and then drops the Jewish question once and for all (although anti-Semitic remarks keep cropping up in his work, and he puts together a very odd piece on the Jews of Jerusalem for the New York *Herald-Tribune* (Carlebach, 1978, pp. 359–64)). The only conclusion that can be reasonably drawn is that 'Die Fähigkeit' was composed under the influence of something very distressing to Marx, and that he responded by repressing everything to do with Jewishness in his later work.

As to the nature of this distress, we have little in the way of reliable evidence. What we do know, however, permits an interesting speculation to be drawn, which may be offered in that spirit and without any claim that it is integral to the argument of this essay. In any case, the following piece of information is too tempting for a psychoanalyst to let pass. It turns out that Marx wrote to Ruge in January 1843, 'I have . . . fallen out with my family and as long as my mother is alive I cannot claim my fortune'.[5] Is it too far-fetched to infer from this (which is consistent with other evidence that Marx's relations with his family, and his mother in particular, were less than sanguine) that he was wrestling with some fairly intolerable hostility towards his mother linked to his *own* desire for money? In this light, the projection of his own greed on to the Jew, and the excoriation of the latter for it, becomes somewhat more intelligible – and the more so when we consider that the Jew was close enough to Marx to warrant an association, yet removed enough (by Marx's own 'emancipation', and indeed by the whole thrust of his revolutionizing thought) to permit the denial of that association. Countless lesser men have fallen victim to such a

reaction, and there is nothing in Marx's genius which rules
out the possibility.

This is as far as we need to go in a psychological direction
where Marx is concerned. For our purposes, the psychological dimension is only of interest in so far as it can be
shown to mediate a historical process. Otherwise it becomes
gossip. The evidence for anti-Semitism is in OJQ itself, and
the repression of interest in the Jewish question thereafter.
Given this fact, one would expect some psychological
dynamism to go along with it. My purpose in presenting
this, however, is not to dissect Marx but to understand better
what became of Marxism. We are led, therefore, not to this
or that peccadillo of Marx's personality, but to what became
of his discourse following the writing of OJQ.

And here our attention is drawn not to the appearance so
much as the repression of anti-Semitism – or to be more
exact, to what became repressed along with anti-Semitism.
Marx did not merely leave behind the Jewish question when
he disposed of Bruno Bauer. He also began to leave behind
the *family* question to which it must have been linked in his
own personal life. More, he began to leave the *personal*
question behind as well. In other words, his work became
sealed off to subjectivity.[6] OJQ manifests a burst of unbridled
energy, an eruption in which – characteristically for intensely
creative activity – hate was spewed forth along with
'sensuous activity' and world-transforming vision. It would
seem that the category of 'money' to which Marx was
transcendently displacing his hatred was incapable of
bearing its theoretical burden without being itself made less
sensuous. Marx could only proceed by splitting his thought –
investing passion in the transfiguration of political economy,
yet at the same time engaging in a divorcing of capitalist
production from its human and cultural underpinnings –
making these underpinnings, which give capital its life, a
matter of 'superstructure', and fetishizing the impersonal
'base' of production. To do otherwise would mean returning
to what had been stirred up by the 'Jewish question'.

Marx's transcendence was therefore partial. There is no
smugness in such a judgement, since in the given world, all
transcendence is partial, and will remain so until the social
conditions for full realization have been achieved. Whatever
the particular psychological mediations, Marx's situation[7]
was defined by an early bourgeois pattern, one in which this
class had not yet achieved full hegemony, but where its

basic relations of domination were in place. During Marx's life this hegemony would occur – and Marx would transform himself into its most devastating antagonist. But he would not be able to rid himself of certain essential bourgeois characteristics, nor should we demand this of him.

Interestingly enough, Marx's anti-Semitism is of an older, even pre-capitalist type. As such it is a kind of vestigial formation, a throwback to a past that was slipping away, yet making a claim as desire. Once capitalist rationalization had taken hold, judgements of the sort bandied about by Marx in OJQ, and which, as Draper points out, were indeed characteristic of his age (Draper, 1977, pp. 592–7), became simply archaic, at least for intellectuals. By the late nineteenth century (Massing, 1967; see also Dawidowicz, 1976, pp. 29–63) anti-Semitism began to take on a new, and far more malignant, form. As Ferenc Feher has pointed out in an important study (1980), the contemporary cast of racism is 'universalistic', while the older version (to which we would assign Marx's behaviour) is 'non-universalistic'. The crucial difference, according to Feher, is provided by the social basis of the two forms, the early one growing out of the 'ritual community' of medieval Europe, the latter out of the universalizing – and de-differentiating – conditions of capitalist society. In the ritual community, 'rigidly separated cultures live side by side between which there is no commerce, not even tacitly tolerated osmosis, but rather, for reasons of principle, a relation of mutual and total exclusion'. Under these conditions each side has a firm, indeed fortress-like identity. Jew and Christian are solidly given entities which react with each other as such. A great deal of domination and cruelty can be thereby exchanged, but this does not penetrate into the essence of personhood, which is never in doubt. In such contexts, the persecution of Jews could be settled – at least from the Christian standpoint – through conversion, that is, by a systematic alteration of ritual. And given such a clear-cut and distinct typology, the kind of racial invective in which Marx engaged, as well as the metonymic identification with money through which he arrived at the critique of political economy, become somewhat more intelligible, if no less stained with racist domination.

With the triumph of exchange value that marked the hegemony of capitalism, this pattern was fundamentally altered. No community could remain rigidly separated from others without compromising the world market. Capital is inherently penetrative; its power necessarily extends to the destruction of autonomous cultural bases and, with these, coherent identities. Under the role of capital the self becomes problematized for the first time in world history: people begin not to know who they are. Contemporary racism must be understood as a reflection of this process – and critically, as a defence against it. Now the racist is not only concerned to mend himself through the expulsion of bad parts of the self on to the victim (for example, Marx's conflict concerning money and his mother, in my speculative example); he is also concerned to exist as such. The threat now is his nothingness, the annihilation of the self; and so, in the new order, racism cannot be appeased through any alteration in the behaviour of its victim (such as conversion), but only through the annihilation of the Other, if necessary through physical extermination. It becomes violent negation of the 'Not-I'. In the modern world, racism tends towards nihilism, and turns to genocide in its more extreme forms, as we know only too well. (And this need not only apply to anti-Semitism, but to another quintessential form of Western racism, that directed against the Black; only recall Kurtz's last scrawled testimony in *Heart of Darkness*: 'Exterminate the brutes!' – an emblem for an entire unspeakable history.)

The nihilistic quality of modern anti-Semitism arises not only from the threat to the self, but also from the deadly rationalization through which its categories are developed. Manifest in the scientific claptrap of the idea of Race, at a deeper level such rationalization is essentially the exchange principle burrowing its way from the point of production into forms of thought. Once installed, it functions to remove all sensuous immediacy from the object, who is thereby deprived of the basic mark of humanity, and prepared for profit or extermination, as just another 'thing' in the world. From a psychological standpoint, the rationalization of exchange denies and so destroys the identity of the other. Identity is to the psychological sphere what use value is to the economic: the assertion of an end-for-itself. Thus capital can generate categories of racism automatically and logically, and quite without any intentionality or malign purpose. Hence, too, the bifurcation of Marxism, one strand of which demolishes the universality of the exchange principle by showing its basis in the domination of one class by another – while another succumbs to this same principle when it

postulates objective primacy of economic production. For if
the economic base linearly determines the cultural superstructure, then it can be 'exchanged' for any element of the
latter, with a corresponding loss of sensuous immediacy,
and a disregard for identity and, indeed, culture. The way
has been opened for Stalinism. More, Marxist economism
cedes the cultural sphere to the bourgeoisie. Nowhere has
this impotence been more historically disastrous than in
questions of racism, which socialism has naïvely thought
soluble through economic justice. When August Bebel casu-
ally proclaimed anti-Semitism the 'socialism of fools' he was
in fact certifying the foolishness of socialists. Blinded by the
categories of economism, socialists consistently underes-
timated the power of racist desire. The bourgeoisie, in the
meantime, had no trouble holding on to the regressive
elements of culture, which they used – and still use – to
secure their domination. It does not take an outright Nazi
to develop the racist strategies of desire. The same process
continues subtly and efficiently throughout the culture
industries of capitalism. Nor would it seem that socialists
have sufficiently absorbed the painful lessons of the past.

For all the embarrassment it has produced, OJQ contains
a stunning insight. For Bebel was in a sense right. Anti-
Semitism was not the socialism of fools, any more than the
Jews discovered capitalism. Yet the folly of anti-Semitism,
particularly in its early, 'ritual community' form, contained
a profound critique of capitalist relations.

The early form of anti-Semitism may be assigned to a pre-
capitalist, or medieval, phase of development. But this does
not of course mean that it was indifferent to capitalist
relations. Quite to the contrary, medieval anti-Semitism
incorporated a premonitory defence against capitalism,
conducted at a level considerably more profound – despite
its irrationality – than that waged by economistic socialists.
For the horror of usury had its rational core, while the
fantastic charges hurled against Jews by virtue of their
enforced participation in the process should be read like a
historical dream, and interpreted as such, instead of being
merely consigned to the scrapheap of unreason.

That only a small number of Jews participated in usury –
and that their actual way of life could by no means be
collapsed into the assumptions of money-lending – is true.
None the less, they were made to represent a practice,
usury, that was in fact the advance patrol of a system of

world domination that would destroy the ritual community
of Jew and Christian alike. This is true in a very material
sense, in that the Jewish usurer became an instrument of
rulers who used him, as a Protestant of the sixteenth century
put it, like a sponge to suck up the wealth of the people,
whence it was squeezed dry into the royal treasury (Baron,
1975, p. 45). And it is also true when seen as a symbolic
innovation. For what the state was promoting through the
practice of usury was the legitimacy of abstraction and
exchange in pure form, manifest as the ability of money to
expand effortlessly. To do so, money has to be released from
the constraints of sensuousness into an abstract numerical
realm that could suddenly grow by 50 percent between
borrowing and repayment. This process does not take place
automatically; it must be secured by destroying the cultural
roots of sensuous immediacy in the ritual community –
which is to say, must destroy that community itself, and
the human associations it sustained. That there would be
passionate resistance to this process is in no way surprising
– nor is it any wonder that the limits of the ritual community
would force that resistance into non-rational channels.
Therefore, when we learn that the medieval Christians
accused Jews of the ritual murder of Christian children, and
of drinking their blood at the Passover feast, we may draw
some method from this madness, as repellent as it may have
been. And we may also achieve some insight into why
the Jewish people so rigidly imposed their own dietary
restrictions. For the real sensuous basis of communal existence was being eroded – its very blood and aliment. Not
until society became an object of reflection, indeed, not until
Freud had deepened that reflection into the subjective
dimension, could this intuition be systematically developed.

However, art had already represented what theory would
take centuries to reach. Shakespeare's usurer, Shylock, is
an authentic prefiguration of Marx's 'real Jew', and the
Merchant of Venice achieves a profound insight into his
predicament. When Shylock avenges himself upon Antonio
(who is the actual merchant of Venice), he is only playing
back upon the Christian master the scorn and obloquy that
he himself had received as Jew. But when he *exacts* the
infamous 'pound of flesh' because of Antonio's forfeiture,
he brings us to the historical heart of the anti-Semitic
complex.

Shylock here moves 'forward' into the furthest reaches of

capitalist calculation – think of the 'cost-effectiveness' that guided the conduct of the Vietnam war; or the money value placed by the Ford motor company on human life when they were trying to decide whether to safeguard the Pinto (Dowie, 1977). But at the same time he moves backwards to archaic talion law, and reveals thereby that the usurious debt and the pound of flesh are *equivalents*: they can be exchanged for each other, as an eye for an eye. Only, however, in the new order, for the insistence with which Shylock pursues his outrageous demand rests upon his confidence that the state will support the inviolability of his contract, lest its own burgeoning economy be brought to a halt. More, Shylock knows that Antonio is obsolete and ready for sacrifice since he represents the *noblesse oblige* of an outmoded ideal. And Antonio knows this too: 'The weakest kind of fruit/Drops earliest to the ground, and so let me' (IV. i. 115).

Yet the Jew is only a tool destined to be discarded, and survived by the principle he represents. For Antonio belongs to the Christian polity. He must be saved, and the merciful Christian morality ('The quality of mercy is not strained') be established as the sweetener of its rapacity. Hence the status of Jew as Other must be preserved. To do so, the exchange principle upon which he would fatten is turned against Shylock: he must cut off *exactly* a pound of flesh, no more and no less; and he must take only flesh, and no blood. Exchange is revealed as beyond human capacity. But it is no less used to stem the ravenous Jew's appetite for Christian blood. (Shylock is continually represented as a ravenous child, despite being a generation older than all the other major characters). In the *Merchant of Venice*, then, the abstracting power of exchange is taken away from the Jew and restored to Christian society, which is thereby prepared for its bourgeois era. The play thus prefigures the rise of the Protestant ethic. And it attempts to do so by reconstructing a new sense of community – and specifically, new families – around the sacrifice of the Jew. These, however, are shadowed by the loss of the old community. The blood Shylock craves, and is not to have, is linked to the mercy he can have only at the price of losing his Jewish identity, that mercy which 'droppeth as the gentle rain from heaven'. Both blood and mercy, then, are symbolic transformations of milk; while the pound of flesh itself is to be taken from Antonio's 'breast', this being in Shylock's words, 'what part

of your body pleaseth me' (I. iii. 147). Thus the old order is
represented as the breast of a lost community torn apart by
the ravening desires of the Jew, and reconstituted by the
multiple marriages with which the play ends – while only
the Jew loses, first his daughter, Jessica, then his identity
itself, when he is forced to convert at pain of his life.

The rationalization for visiting the odium of usury upon
the Jew was the passage from Deuteronomy (23:20): 'Unto
a stranger thou mayest lend upon usury; but unto thy
brother thou shalt not lend upon usury . . .' To secure this
blessing, the Jew, who had known relative freedom from
persecution before the Crusades and in the Muslim world,
had to be made into the universal Stranger, Other to
everyone, in the medieval world order. Once the exchange
function had been wrested away from him by an expanding
capitalism, however, the terms of the Jew's dilemma begin
to undergo a decisive shift (see Nelson, 1969). For now
everybody is to be a stranger to everybody else; and so the
Jew's special experience with estrangement reveals a new
aspect, that of a focus for liberation. But whether this focus
is to be realized depends on a historically new dynamic of
transcendence.

Marx, Engels and, later, Lenin were given to extolling the
progressive moments of capitalism, which they regarded as
a pre-condition for socialist revolution. Considering the
chequered history of socialism, this judgement appears
worse than uncritical, and perhaps at the heart of much of
the mischief which has been carried on under the banner of
Marxism. But there is one element which is indisputable:
that capitalism, by creating a world market, also began
digging its own grave through the emergence of the possibility of world-wide counter-force. In its destructive, predatory path, capital broke through the boundaries of particularity within which feudal and patriarchal domination had
contained human powers. In the bourgeois order, the dream
of a universal goal for humanity condensed from the sphere
of religion and became applied to emancipatory possibilities
no less than those of totalized economic domination. The
Communist Manifesto expressed such a vision – 'Workers of
all countries, unite.' Yet the domination which had created
a universalizing proletariat had to be resisted with powers
drawn from communal life. This however was subject to
different influences from the work-place inasmuch as capital

had split domestic life from production when it dehumanized the latter. Practically speaking, the rise of worker resistance always requires a passage through the cultural dimension. Workers' movements have always recognized this reality – as has the ruling class, which tries to control it through the culture industries. And since culture itself is always organized about a sense of group identity, liberation struggles cannot be divorced from ethnicity or nationhood, usually played out around the theme of dispossession from land. The search for the lost mother- or fatherland is carried forward across the entire annals of liberation, condensing into itself the symbolism of a shattered community and a plundered territorial base.

So much is true of all oppressed peoples. For the Jew, however, who entered the bourgeois era already defined by over a millennium's worth of dispossession, the general predicament found an echo within group identity. Once set loose in the modern world, the wandering, persecuted, marginal Jew becomes identified with liberation itself. This possibility did not erase the former tendency exemplified by Shylock, to be sure; it merely complicated the situation. The heritage of Jewishness entitles one equally to be used as a tool of accumulation or to champion the cause of the oppressed. From the margins, after all, one can move to either side of the basic class dynamic. That Marx only recognized the former direction within Jewishness, is not incidentally related to the fact that he became one of the prime examples of the latter. For to fight for the oppressed requires more than the sense of justice traditionally associated with Jewishness; it also demands a universalizing attitude at odds with the particularity of Jewish tradition. Marx's pathway is not the only possible one towards universalization – although its peculiar violence may have been associated, as I have suggested, with the radicality of his vision as well as with its limits. Zionism also was originally a dissociation from the traditional limits of Judaism within the pale. At first it, too, bore a special liberatory promise[8] – and therefore established an organic rapport with Marxism (Carlebach, 1978). Nor have Marxism or Zionism been the only possibilities of expressing that radicality which has been the modern destiny of Jews, from the time of Spinoza to that of Freud, Schoenberg and Einstein.

This phenomenon, which Isaac Deutscher has aptly called that of the 'non-Jewish Jew' (Deutscher, 1968), can never be

free of ambiguity and contradiction. For either one abandons
the sense of Jewishness altogether, assimilates, and lives
without a past; or one accepts it in one degree of estrangement or another, and lives the fate of an outsider. Within
this range of possibilities, the Jew-as-radical teeters on every
brink. The loss of the past, the complicity in technocratic
domination, the drift into mysticism or nihilism, one degree
or another of anti-Semitism: all such possibilities edge the
path of Jewish radicalism. Indeed, self-hate and anti-
Semitism are as inherent in the Jewish experience as the
Shylock complex, and are particularly embedded in the
dynamic of Jewish radicalism.

The radical begins with hatred of domination, and
proceeds to a level of universality where this hatred can be
transcended. All the great revolutionaries have gone such a
way, and all, being human, have fallen to one degree or
another short of transcendence. Practically speaking, this
means that some degree of unmitigated hate remains to
shadow the radical project. But since this contradicts the
ethos of that project, it must be disposed of, by distortion if
necessary. The situation is compounded in the case of the
radicalized Jew, scion of a people who survived through
the development of extreme particularity, itself a defence
against ages of extreme injustice and oppression. The living
history of injustice provides the matrix for radicalism.
However, the universalization of this response runs afoul
of particularity. The ethos of the 'Chosen People' both
empowers and occludes the impulse towards emancipation.
By being a Jew one is drawn to the cause of justice; and by
being drawn to the cause of justice, one becomes a threat to
the particularity of Judaism. It is not surprising that hatred,
self-hatred and, inexorably, anti-Semitism may develop at
the non-rational edges of this conjuncture. More, Jewish
anti-Semitism may be itself *rationalized* through the fact that
ethnicities are themselves loci of domination. For all that the
ethnic subgroup stands for 'use-value', and is a bulwark
against the atomization and cultural de-differentiation of
bourgeois society, it is more repressive and patriarchal
than that society. Indeed, a good deal of the legitimacy
of bourgeois society is gained by comparison with the
oppressiveness of what it supplants. Behind the walls of the
ethnic fortress are found certain remnants of an ancient
tribal communalism, to be sure. But by and large these have
been reduced to mere gestures, and even chains, as in the

ritualization of Jewish orthodoxy. Within the ethnic enclave,
cultural integrity and respect for tradition can become
excuses for ignorance, obscurantism and the bondage of
women and the young – all fair game for the radical. It
follows that the boundary between an authentically radical
critique of Jewishness and an irrationally hateful attitude of
anti-Semitism is by no means easy to ascertain. Moreover
the two traits may well coexist in the same individual. This
is because they are determined under social conditions
which mandate that levels of the self be split from each other
and be relatively unmediable. It is characteristic of bourgeois
society to impose different terms of development on rationality and desire. Anti-Semitism remains yoked to the latter
realm. Its logic is of desire and the archaic family, attitudes
stemming from which need no more join the plane of
universalized discourse under bourgeois conditions than
the passions of the nuclear family obey the rationalized laws
of the work-place. In this respect, too, the fissures in Marx's
position are an entirely typical feature of the world he
inhabited.

Ultimately, any response to the 'Jewish question' can only
be settled by reference to specific historical circumstances.
Indeed, the same can be said for any religious discourse.
Marx – like Freud – reveals a major limitation in his purely
reductive treatment of religion. His refusal to recognize
that there was an authentically transcendent dimension to
religion – and that this was an emancipatory force – has
exacted a heavy toll from Marxism. Happily, amends have
lately been made, principally from the side of the theologians
of liberation (for one example, see Miranda, 1974).

The emancipatory hope of religion is, however, but the
determinate negation of its real history, which has been, as
Marx, Freud and other radicals observed, that of a buttress
for reaction. This has been perhaps more true for the
rabbinate than for the clergy of any major religion. In any
case, the possibilities for Jewish radicalism seem to exist
in nearly pure negativity with regard to the influence of
organized Judaism, which has always taken for itself either
the defence of the fortress of particularity or, in its more
'advanced' forms in the USA, the most shameless accommodation to bourgeois ways.

The last great formulation of the radical potentialities
inherent in the category of Jewishness as such was that of
Sartre: *Anti-Semite and Jew* (1948) closes a chapter in the self-

definition of Judaism just as the Nazi Holocaust which
inspired it marked the end of a trajectory which began with
the release from the medieval community. Sartre finally
demolished the pretensions of assimilation, and the sterile
rationalizations of liberal humanism with which this was
justified. The authentic Jew was one who accepted Jewishness, and realized his condition in all its awfulness. For what
had happened to the Jews made mere humanism impossible.
'The authentic Jew abandons the myth of the universal man;
he knows himself and wills himself into history as a historic
and damned creature; he ceases to run away from himself
and to be ashamed of his own kind. He understands that
society is bad . . .' (p. 136). A century after the writing of
OJQ, Sartre seems to draw the opposite conclusion from
Marx. Yet the essay closes on the same note: the project is
not to assimilate the Jew but to transform society so that
the domination enclosed in anti-Semitism will not arise, a
solution that can only occur in a classless society. If there is
a difference, then, it lies in Sartre's sensitivity to the politics
of subjectivity and in his recognition that there are times
when the assertion of identity becomes an act in advance of
material considerations.

Sartre's insight, however, is predicated on a historical
vision that analyses each situation concretely. *Anti-Semite
and Jew* is of 1946; it cannot be frozen in history. And the
response to the Jewish question today is built on what was
actually made out of the conjuncture of 1946, with all its
promise and fresh horror. What happened of course was
not the assertion of Sartrean authenticity followed by
working for a classless society, but rather a new set of
contradictions defined by the realities of the state of Israel.

In retrospect, the extremity of the Holocaust exploded the
emancipatory possibilities contained in the identity of the
suffering Jew. Whether or not this would have happened
anyhow outside the instauration of Israel is moot. The reality
is that the inner tendencies of Zionism towards aggressive
expansion became irresistibly reinforced by the need to
ensure that the Nazi nightmare would never again befall the
Jewish people. The possibility that the experience of the
Holocaust could become a spur to universality lost out
to the spurious hope that imperial power would provide
security against its recurrence. And so the Holocaust has
been repressed from history and converted into moral capital
to cover and justify whatever the Jewish people would do

in the way of domination themselves, whether this be the pell-mell immersion in American bourgeois life or the policies of Israel. Needless to add, these two practices became one, and have been used to make each other possible.

In sum, the Jews of the modern world have thrown their lot in with the imperial identity of the West, that is, have chosen to be *Caucasians* after all. Perhaps through the well-known psychoanalytic mechanism of identification with the aggressor (Freud, A., 1946), they have been doing to the Third World what had been for so long done to them within Europe – obviously not with the same bestial abandon, but towards the same end and structure, nevertheless. The Holocaust was no aberration; but viewed from the perspective of four decades, it appears less as that which severed than as that which cemented, the bond of the Jew with Europe. A horrible annealment, it added to the spectrum of Jewish possibilities that of an instrument of direct domination, and in so doing, made Israel into the Shylock of the nations. The nation of Zion has let itself become the broker of Western imperialism in Western Asia, and, indeed, through the whole Third-World.

It should be emphasized that we are describing a tendency inherent to the whole development of Israel, and not simply that of the outrageous Begin–Sharon regime, whose dubious merit it has been to bring it blatantly into the open. A perusal, say, of the diaries of Prime Minister Moshe Sharret – which detail imperial shenanigans of great cynicism and duplicity going back to the heyday of the Labour government in the mid-fifties – should make the point clear (Rokach, 1980). On the other hand, the imperialist tendency of Zionism is only one component, albeit the dominant one, of a complex history that is not yet closed. There are, for example, numerous progressive elements in Israeli society, and even American Jews, long seamlessly assimilated, have been shaken enough by the catastrophic invasion of Lebanon to begin asking questions. Nor are the external relations of Jewishness settled. Anti-Semitism has by no means disappeared within the various nations of the West, nor can we forget its virulence in the Soviet Union (Korey, 1973). And finally, Israel as Shylock, or the cat's-paw of American imperialism in Western Asia, stands on the same slippery ground as his Shakespearian forebear. From day to day one does not know whether it will be cynically sacrificed by its

patron in favour of some more suitable Arab tool in the
overriding global struggle.

If such an event comes to pass, it will once again rewrite
the book on what it means to be a Jew. But until that day,
Jewishness in the modern world is defined in relation to the
Israel of 1982. And it is an identity whose emancipatory
possibility stands in ruins. In a sense the wheel has turned
back to the day of OJQ, with the entire intervening period
being one in which the identity of a Jew would be linked to
a universal liberation because of the possibilities imminent
in Jewish suffering. Since the Holocaust made such suffering
too extreme, and Israel appeared as a means to power, this
prospect has become extinguished.

It may be added that the mode of domination through
which the contemporary Shylock function is played out has
passed from the sphere of usury to that of racism. Racism,
which may be interpreted as the generalization of the
exchange principle – with its reduction of sensuous
immediacy to passive objectification – to the level of peoples
instead of individuals, is automatically generated in the
wake of imperialist penetration, in particular when this takes
the form, as in Israel, South Africa and the USA, of settler-
colonialism. No matter how many countervailing tendencies
may exist within Israel and Judaism, the choice of this path
has made a racist development inevitable. To summarize
with Maxime Rodinson:

*The advancement and the success of the Zionist movement thus
definitely occurred within the framework of European expansion
into the countries belonging to what later came to be called the Third
World. Given the initial aims of the movement, it could not have
been otherwise. Once the premises were laid down, the inexorable
logic of history determined the consequences. Wanting to create a
purely Jewish, or predominantly Jewish, state in an Arab Palestine
in the twentieth century could not help but lead to a colonial-type
situation and to the development (completely normal, sociologically
speaking) of a racist state of mind, and in the final analysis – to a
military confrontation between the two ethnic groups.* (1973,
p. 77)

To excuse this reality because of the suffering borne by the
Jewish people is to step on to the wheel of domination.
Insensibly, such reasoning passes over into racism, for it
can only be sustained by lowering the value of the suffering
and dehumanization visited upon the Palestinian people in

the name of Zionism. Indeed, so long as such a process is carried forward under the name of Jewry, then the terms of what constitutes an 'authentic Jew' take a radically different value from those proposed by Sartre. For now the authentic Jew must be set against what is being done in the name of Jewishness, even at the cost of becoming dissociated from Jewish culture. This is done in the spirit of critique and not of anti-Semitism. It does not deny the Jew the right to an autonomous existence. Rather it insists that what has been done in the name of Jewishness since the Second World War is a profound denial of that autonomy and a betrayal of the heart of Jewish history – its sense of justice. One can no longer, therefore, be an authentic Jew under the given terms of Jewishness. The self-contradicting record of the American Jewish Left[9] is no less an example of this truth than the ever-deepening descent of the emancipatory ideals of Zionism into the quicksand of imperialism. Until such time as Jewry can renounce its hold on domination, the answer to the Jewish question must be a critical one – critical of the foreign policy of Israel and of the domestic arrangements which underlie this policy, critical of the supine accommodation of the Diaspora to these policies, and critical of the lingering mystification in Jewish religion and culture. Perhaps now, in the wake of the Lebanese invasion, a start can finally be made to reshape this question in a manner adequate to what is worth retrieving from the Jewish tradition. Only on this basis can the Jewish people break free of the present tragic phase in their endless migration on the margins of history.

NOTES

1. For a treatment of this theme, see Kahler (1967).

2. There is a terminological distinction here. The term Marx employed, *Judentum*, could refer either to the religion or the people, to 'Judaism' or Jewry. In a letter of March 1843, Marx made the distinction that he found the religious practices 'obnoxious' but would defend the rights of the people. While most of the obloquy of OJQ is directed against the former category, it is not possible completely to separate the vindictiveness from the latter, for the obvious reason that the Jewish people made their religion an integral part of their identity.

3. Carlebach undertakes a comprehensive review of this literature, which is widespread and constitutes the majority opinion on OJQ, particularly from the non-socialist camp.

4. The defence is of Gabriel Riesser.

5. See Carlebach (1978, p. 392, n. 85), which also contains documentation of other evidence supporting this notion.

6. It would take a work of considerably different scope from the present adequately to explore this theme. If one follows not only the infamous Althusserian leap into the mature 'scientific' phase of Marx's work, but attends to shifts within the early work as well, there is an unmistakable tendency to weed out personalistic discourse. Between OJQ, the 'Manuscripts', and *The German Ideology*, for example, one can see this development quite clearly. In my opinion, OJQ is a work marked by genuinely juvenile elements; the 'Manuscripts' represent Marx's most inspired balance between a mediated desire and reason; while *The German Ideology* already shows incipient problems of the sort that are later to surface as economism, and a crypto-acceptance of capitalist relations.

7. The term is meant to call attention to Sartre's (1948) approach.

8. As shown in the path taken by Moses Hess, who began with Marx and conceived of Zionism. Carlebach (1978) has a full treatment of Hess.

9. One small example, noted by Arthur Liebman in his *Jews and the Left* (1979): the New Left journal, *The Jewish Radical*, denied California's Ronald Dellums a re-election endorsement despite admitting that he was one of the most progressive members of Congress (Dellums is perhaps *the* most progressive member of Congress.) The reason – one vote cast in 1969 to deny Israel emergency military appropriations (p. 583).

J ANINE CHASSEGUET-SMIRGEL and Béla Grunberger's
Freud or Reich? (1986) demands that anyone who comments
upon it declare himself in relation to the subject-matter.[1] Let
me say then that I first encountered Reich by reading of his
ignominious death in the *New York Times*. Although my
initial reaction was little more than a vague curiosity, a
number of personal matters led me soon after to seek therapy
with a well-known Reichian, Simeon Tropp. Tropp, who
had been one of Reich's principal lieutenants in the last
phase of his life, made a powerful impression on me, so
much so that I eventually undertook clandestine Reichian
training. I was then a medical student and in those days
Reich's works, with the exception of *Character Analysis*, were
banned in the USA and had to be smuggled in by friends
returning from Europe – a feature that undoubtedly
enhanced their appeal. Indeed, I was for a while rather
inclined to accept the whole package.

After a few years of Reichianism, I began to sour on the
idea, for reasons to be discussed presently, and turned to
Freud and classical psychoanalytic training. Although I
am still deeply involved with psychoanalysis, I have not
remained within the psychoanalytic movement. Instead I
complicated things further by adding a figure 'gone through'
by Reich, namely Marx, not to mention that of a contemporary of Reich's cordially disliked by Chasseguet-Smirgel
and Grunberger: Marcuse (and a few others besides). Worse
yet, I have even made some efforts to do what the authors
claim cannot be done – to try to encounter Freud and Marx
with something of the spirit of a Reich and something of the
spirit of a Marcuse. And since the motive for this, according
to Chasseguet-Smirgel and Grunberger, is fundamentally
one of destroying both founding fathers of modern discourse, it can be seen right away that my vantage point on
Freud or Reich? is scarcely a neutral one.

So be it, for this is a book that demands engagement.

There is nothing neutral about it, and nothing to be gained by passive appreciation. As the authors correctly assert, whether or not Reichianism flourishes as a movement is not the main point. It is rather what Reich stood for, epitomized in his relation to Freud, that counts. Chasseguet-Smirgel and Grunberger care passionately about this, and their combative tract keeps the subject heated until the last page. And for all that Freud wins the contest hands down, their book may be read as a genuine, if backhanded, tribute to Reich.

Here I must express another distinction between my view of Freud and Reich and that of the authors. Chasseguet-Smirgel and Grunberger evidently write from a context – the France of the early seventies – in which the *gauchisme* of the previous decade had spilled over into a number of flirtations with the perennially revolutionizing spirit of Reich. At the same time, they seem to have felt themselves politically marginalized as Freudians.

By contrast, I write from the centre of psychoanalytic culture in a time of general retreat for the Left as a whole. From where I sit, Reichianism is a minuscule and indeed negligible movement in itself,[2] while Freudian psychoanalysis plays a dynamic role in the intellectual life of modern urban society. Despite the fitful yet inexorable decline of clinical psychoanalysis amidst a welter of competing therapies, the prestige and influence of Freud as culture-hero continues to grow. On the surface, then, there would seem to be no contest at all, and scarcely anything to bother writing about. Freud is installed in our pantheon as a kind of Prometheus, while Reich died in prison, mocked and, one might even say, despised. And unlike the Jesus with whom he so palpably identified, no significant move towards resurrection and deification occurs as we come to the end of the third decade after his death. An occasional biography (the latest, by Myron Sharaf (1983), is probably definitive), scattered outcroppings of followers, periodic calls to investigate seriously his innumerable scientific claims – this is all that stands. Reich, in short, remains marginal when he is remembered at all. Why beat, as they say, a dead horse?

Precisely because, as our authors clearly recognize, no matter how low Reich may have fallen he remains the quintessential, complete and perennial revolutionary. Or shall we say, a man of extreme tendencies? Or as the authors insist, a man of illusion, a man who began close to Freud, who traversed the psychoanalytic path and came out facing in the opposite direction from the founding father of psychoanalysis. Reich, the revolutionary, is seen as a threat to Freud, the anti-revolutionary, and since it is Freud who must be apotheosized it is Reich who must be demolished.

As with Edward Glover's *Freud or Jung?* of a half-century ago, Chasseguet-Smirgel and Grunberger are out to show that there is but one legitimate spirit of psychoanalytic discourse, that of its sire. This superiority of Freud extends far beyond the consulting room; to the authors of this book, Freud is nothing less than the peerless philosopher of our time. With respect to Reich, Freud is doubly right – in the sense of being scientifically true and in the sense of being morally as well as politically superior. And if this implies yet a third sense of the term, that of being politically right-wing, so much the better. For in the eyes of our authors, it is the illusionist revolutionary who, given the power, turns bloodthirsty ('Every time an illusion is activated, a bloodbath follows close behind . . .' (p. 17)); while Freud, the quietly heroic dis-illusionist, represents the best, perhaps the sole hope of saving the human race from its destructive tendencies. And of course it must be added – in line with the observation that Reich himself may be less important than the kind of heresy he represents – that all revolutionaries, all people who think they can change the world by radically altering existing institutions, are essentially in the same boat with Wilhelm Reich, even if they may not show his peculiarities.

I shall have more to say about these matters below. First, however, a brief sketch of Chasseguet-Smirgel and Grunberger's main case against Reich – and for Freud – may be helpful here. The theme cuts to the core of psychoanalysis – its reading of desire, and the relation of desire to reality.

Essentially, the difference between Freud and Reich comes down to this: for the former, desire exists in opposition to nature, that is, as fantasy, while for the latter, desire can be realized only in nature. This basic belief of Reich's, which he followed to its catastrophic end, defines his primary illusion for Chasseguet-Smirgel and Grunberger. More, in following his conviction to the breaking point, Reich, who was always paranoid by virtue of his character structure, became frankly psychotic. The customary reading of Reich's relation to psychoanalytic orthodoxy is that he

was all right up until the writing of *Character Analysis* in the
early thirties but fell apart after being expelled from the
psychoanalytic movement in 1934. Chasseguet-Smirgel and
Grunberger argue rather that Reich's paranoia infected his
thinking from the outset, and turned it steadily from illusion
to delusion.

As is well known, Reich took over a branch in the path of
psychoanalysis that Freud had himself turned away from,
and stayed with it until the end. At issue was the significance
of sexuality and the relative roles of the real and imaginary.
At first, Freud had argued for the primacy of the 'actual
neurosis' (*Aktualneurose*) – neurotic formation on the basis
of real, traumatic experience – and for a programme of sexual
reform as necessary for the general health of the population.
His emphasis on the noxious effects of coitus interruptus is
but one example of this tendency, which continued at least
until the writing of 'Civilized sexual morality and modern
nervous illness' in 1908. However such notions may have
hung about somewhere in Freud's thinking throughout his
life, it cannot be doubted that they became increasingly
marginal to psychoanalytic discourse, which became ever
more centred on the dimension of fantasy. The decline of
the seduction theory as an explanation for neurosogenesis,
the supplementation of 'actual neurosis' by psychoneurosis,
the theory of dreaming and its interpretation – all of this
testified to the fact that the locus of psychoanalysis had
shifted to the realm of the imaginary: psychic reality. Above
all, the theory of infantile sexuality established the shift, by
claiming sexuality itself for the sphere of fantasy. Not
altogether – for drives still had to have their source in the
real body – but essentially, for the object of the drive, a
specifically subjective phenomenon became the ultimate
determiner of sexual deployment.

More fundamental still, the fantastic nature of sexuality is
a consequence of existential givens: dependency, prolonged
immaturity, the wishful, that is, illusory character of psychic
activity as such. Thus it inscribes a more basic proposition
than physical sexuality, or, to put the matter slightly differently, fantasy and illusion determine infantile sexuality, and
infantile sexuality determines life in its essentials. We are,
according to Chasseguet-Smirgel and Grunberger's reading
of Freud, primarily determined by the exigencies of infantile
sexuality: by the great facts of the difference between the
generations and between the sexes, by our passionate and

doomed desire for parents, by the inherent state of mental
castration which flows from these foundations – by, ultimately, that which is internal and subjective instead of
external and objective.

The image of human nature which emerges from this
discourse is positively Calvinist in its remorselessness.
Freud was a sceptic and a stoic, but his view was almost
cheerful compared to these Freudians. For them, it is not
enough to have a castration complex: one must also recognize that one is really, inevitably *castrated*. As they freely
admit, this fact implies another which enables them to deal
in advance with all criticism as a manifestation of the
congenital human inability to accept unpleasure and the
lack of narcissistic fulfilment.

For we do not want to believe what the tough-minded
Freudian tells us, because we cannot bear the painful truth
about ourselves. We live by illusion instead, projecting our
dream world outwards, giving it the name of objective
reality, and dreaming that we can save ourselves from the
subjective castration which is our human fate, by changing
the external world. We all become paranoid to some degree
or other, although some are worse paranoids than others,
and cannot abandon their delusory ideas. And of them all,
Reich was the worst paranoid, because he attempted to
subvert this most basic position of Freud's in the name of
psychoanalysis and science.

It is possible to say that Reich's entire course was defined
by his refusal to accept, as Freud had, the limited importance
of real sexual gratification. Despite Reich's early eminence
in the psychoanalytic movement, deep differences with the
mainstream of Freudian thought can be traced to his earliest
writings. These surfaced with the orgasm theory of 1927 and
never ceased widening for the rest of his spectacular career.
The authors provide a more or less accurate account of
the main relevant ideas of Reich and of the points that
distinguish him from Freud. Since Reich was nothing if not
consistent (in thought but not in life), these can be readily
summarized as a rejection of the imaginary basis of infantile
sexuality, or, to be more exact, a rendering of it as epiphen-
omenal. What mattered was not the ineradicable inscription
of a fundamentally tragic situation on the infantile mind,
but how one actually functioned sexually. Sexual stasis
(later, in an entirely logical development, that of the orgone

energy itself) caused the occlusions of neurotic subjectivity,
and not the other way around, as the later Freud held.

Associated with this was a thoroughgoing ontological difference. Subjectivity was to be subordinated to the physical and biological, so much so that it can be said that Reich, for all his contributions to psychoanalysis, was never really a psychologically minded person at all. In this light, his later orgonomic developments seem to be the unfolding of an inner essence. However bizarre they may have been in themselves, the orgone theories were a more authentic expression of Reich than his psychoanalytic phase.

Finally, it should be added that the differences between Reich and Freud were expressed in the remarkable optimism of the former and the pessimism of the latter. Those who put their faith in changing the world, whether of the body or society, can generally look forward to brighter prospects than those who insist that the fault lies in ourselves. Freud's generally bleak prospect for the human species was compounded from a twofold conviction: that we were saddled with ineluctable aggressivity and, perhaps more fundamental, that the pleasure principle prevented us from being truthful about ourselves. As for Reich, even as he was being crushed under the heels of the state, he held out hope for the future triumph of the life force. Indeed, the worse Reich's personal fortunes, the more messianic became his outlook, pulled beyond the mundane on the wings of a cosmic energy.

How is one to decide between these drastically different world-views? Certainly not by Reich's disastrous end and Freud's relative triumph. To die in ignominy does not prove the worthlessness of what one lived for; it only indicates that one did not get along with the world. Neither does Reich's obvious – and obviously worsening – psychosis invalidate what he held. Reich was no more a lunatic than Newton; and nobody disputes Newtonian physics on account of the madness of its progenitor. Moreover, as mad as Reich was towards the end (he believed, for example, that a race of spacemen were involved in changing about the structure of orgone energy, and that the US Air Force was secretly on his side), Sharaf's detailed biography makes it clear that Reich's delusions were of the loculated kind, so that he could be quite capable of not simply normal, but highly rational and indeed brilliant behaviour at the same time as he harboured utterly fantastic beliefs.

There is no reason, therefore, for not assuming that it was 257
the rational Reich who formulated his principal ideas –
almost all of which were presented in the regalia of full-scale
scientific discourse – to a much greater extent, by the way,
than Freud ever bothered to do. Chasseguet-Smirgel and
Grunberger believe that Freud was 'scientific' because he
was not a victim of Reich's illusory tendencies, but this is
slippery ground indeed for deciding on the superiority
of one over the other. Anybody who advances Freudian
psychoanalysis as scientific these days is asking for a lot of
trouble.[3] In fact, one could argue that Freud, who dealt in
the extremely problematic world of intersubjective discourse
as a 'data base', would fare much worse epistemologically
from the standpoint of normal science than Reich, who
ultimately appealed to something 'out there', even if only
the orgonomically healthy could perceive it accurately.

And yet a critical distinction needs to be drawn. Either
one disregards both Freud and Reich as trivial and deluded,
or one gives them both the credit of recognizing that a serious
contradiction exists, which must be carefully assessed. I
think it should be obvious that passive observation of this
matter will not do. One neither can nor should be personally
absent from any judgement drawn. Certainly Chasseguet-
Smirgel and Grunberger's impassioned polemic against
Reich and for Freud is determined in some measure by
concern for the integrity and value of their life's work as
psychoanalysts.

In my case the same basic considerations hold, even if the
trajectory taken is a different one. I shifted from Reich to
Freud, and though I have grown critical of the latter, I have
not swung back to the former. Why? Because, essentially, I
encountered things in my experience with Reichianism
which disappointed me, first with the practice and then the
theory. Indeed, my experience confirmed to some degree
what is said in *Freud or Reich?* I found, in brief, that the
abolition of subjectivity did not suit me; it did not make for
the kind of therapy I wanted, and it presented a foreshort-
ened and, ultimately, repressive view of human life.

For the Reichian, the key thing is 'to get the energy
moving'. Everything else will take care of itself if, and only
if, orgastic potency can be achieved. It matters not what the
orgone therapist *means* to the patient – for example, whether
he behaves in a domineering or repulsive way – so long as
he permits the energy to move. Or rather, there is no way

of connecting these things within the theory. This extreme
naturalism more or less puts any serious reflection upon
either psychological or social relations into a deep shade. It is
not hard to imagine the degree of mischief and incompetence
that can proceed under the cover of this ultimately technocratic approach. If the energy is outside ordinary ken, and
the therapist-expert has special access to it, then the therapist
can more or less get away with anything so long as some
effect is achieved. This is all the more so given the fact that
the therapy clearly taps into powerful and 'moving' feelings,
often in a consciously anti-intellectual, or at least markedly
uncritical, framework.

From another angle, Reich's extreme naturalism made for
repressiveness in the very sexuality he was seeking to
liberate. If 'energy' is all, and energy is contained in orgastic
potency, then a fixed regimen of sexual hygiene is mandated
as a prescription for well-being. Gone was the space for
playfulness and the special madness of sexuality that makes
human existence unique. In its place stood a tyranny of
genitality that could rival that of fundamentalist religious
sects in its subordination of Eros to 'higher' ends, and its
rigid, doctrinaire rejection of homosexuality.

Perhaps the greatest damage wrought by Reich's naturalism was political, both within and outside of the movement he founded. The orgonomy movement exceeded even
that of psychoanalysis in the lack of freedom, its domination
by one powerful man. Nothing is handier than an appeal
to suprahuman influence as a buttress to charisma and
authoritarianism. There was scarcely any dialogue to speak
of, much less a free flow of ideas, within Reich's entourage.
Orgonomy was strictly a one-man operation. Able minds
were now and then drawn to Reichianism, but they either
stayed as passive recipients of the genius's insights, or
withdrew. As a result, the movement showed no real growth
after Reich's death, lapsing instead into a kind of mechanistic
formalism.

As for Reich's external politics, while he remained
attached to a semi-anarchistic vision of 'work democracy' as
a social goal, his lack of interest in, and indeed frank
contempt for, larger-scale social structures rendered the
politics of orgonomy puerile when they were not frankly
reactionary. It was a long descent that led the author of the
Sex-Pol Essays (which seem not to have been available in
their entirety to Chasseguet-Smirgel and Grunberger) to

form a favourable judgement of President Eisenhower
because he seemed to be a 'genital character' (Sharaf, p. 413)
– long and doleful, but not inconsistent with the fundamental inclination of Reich's thought. Note, however, that
the political direction taken by Reich was itself sharply
rightward. Although it does not square with the authors'
linkage of Reichianism and left-wing politics as equivalent
illusions, this is what one might expect from such a pure
naturalism as he developed. By the end Reich was more than
conservative and more than anti-Communist: he actively
believed in plots by 'red fascists' to get him.

Whether Reich's naturalism was cause or effect of his
paranoia is an interesting problem to which the authors
devote considerable attention. I shall not address myself to
the substantive matters of this question, but rather to another
aspect raised by their treatment of it. And here I must sharply
take issue with *Freud or Reich?* For it is hard to avoid
the conclusion that Chasseguet-Smirgel and Grunberger,
despite admitting that mental disturbance does not *per
se* invalidate the work, have in these pages carried the
psychoanalysing of Reich to unseemly proportions.

This is unfortunate, and in more than one sense. To
psychoanalyse someone when you are engaged in an ideological struggle with him strikes me as a bad practice both
clinically and intellectually. It becomes a particularly
unhappy strategy in view of the decision to exempt Freud
from the same treatment. To claim that psychoanalysing
Freud is 'a sterile enterprise' (p. 55), and meanwhile to
declare open season on Reich, down to reducing the orgone
to the paternal phallus, must be one of the least effective
ways imaginable to secure rational assent to an argument.

We may also be reminded here of the injunction against
the throwing of stones by those who reside in glasshouses.
Despite the authors' hagiographic treatment of Freud and
reduction of Reich to a mass of psychopathology, the reader
might recall that the founder of psychoanalysis was himself
prone to serious 'work-related' lapses (the cocaine phase,
the unconscionable ganging up with Fliess against Emma
Eckstein,[4] the peccadilloes concerning the relationship with
Jung, and so on), while the founder of orgonomy was
capable, despite obvious mental disturbance, of great moral
courage and fidelity to principle. If Chasseguet-Smirgel and
Grunberger were to hear somebody reduce Freud's life-
work to various attempts at overcoming his hostility to

women, they would be justifiably outraged. Why do the   260
same sort of thing to Reich?

Matters are only made worse by the authors' efforts at self-justification. At the end of chapter 6 (pp. 196–7), they anticipate criticism for psychoanalysing Reich with such a free hand. Observing quite correctly that they do not, after all, know their subject except through his writings and second-hand accounts, they excuse themselves on the grounds, first, that Reich, being paranoid, wouldn't have tolerated the analytic context anyway; and second, that Freud successfully analysed the paranoiac Schreber strictly through the latter's writings. This assumes that Reich would have had to be 'paranoid' – that is irrational – to refuse an analysis in such a spirit as is evinced here; and it overlooks the fact that Freud studied Schreber to understand him and not to pass judgement. Can one imagine a person who would agree to an 'analysis' for the purpose of being compared with Freud?

At issue here is the spirit of sectarianism – surely as great a contributor to human misery as all other foibles combined. To put the problem at the level of 'illusion' and paranoia seems to me to miss the point by not carrying the analysis far enough. What is destructive is not illusion or paranoia as such, but *socially organized* paranoid illusions, expressed as sectarianism – and backed up, to be sure, by violence against the Other who is deemed to represent evil. Reich was severely subject to the sectarian plague – though the only violence he brought about was to himself. But Freud was no stranger to the bug, either, and I am afraid that Chasseguet-Smirgel and Grunberger have gone one better than him in their attempt to demolish Reich, or, for that matter, as they briskly go about purging the impure from psychoanalysis, namely:

> It is surprising, then, that some analysts are being carried away by fashion and popular consensus, and are trying to explain female sexuality in terms of social and economic conditions. The most basic concern for consistency and integrity would require them to stop practising a profession in which they no longer believe (unless they are victims of an astonishingly split personality). (p. 81)

In sum, we can reframe the question: why must it be Freud *or* Reich? I am not proposing an alternative which flaccidly accepts any and everything. Differences are real, and both Freud and Reich cannot be right. But there is another approach to take, which seems to me to be preferable altogether. Once one abandons the urge to elevate either figure to the ranks of the superhuman, the possibility opens up that it could be neither Freud nor Reich who had the exclusive lock on the truth. This is not to say that they were both wrong, or that it would be impossible to prefer one to the other, at least in limited contexts. It is rather to ask that we not treat great men like gods, but that we take a *critical*, against a sectarian or totalizing approach to the matter of evaluating them.

A critical judgement negates its object without destroying it. Its goal is transcendence, and it recognizes the partiality of all human endeavour – Freud's and Reich's included. Tolerance is not the issue. It is rather to recognize the impossibility of either Freud or Reich solving the dialectical problem before him – that of being human under the conditions of contemporary civilization. To be critical is to recognize this, and to grant each his greatness and his limitation.

Such recognition expresses the whole emancipatory motion of psychoanalytic revolution, viewed as the undoing of repression. Freud discovered that sexuality and infantility were repressed in modern civilization, and since the common term of sexuality and childhood was closeness to nature, that nature was repressed as well. His genius was to raise this dialectic, otherwise blind, into consciousness, whence it could re-enter the history that was transforming subjectivity and the conditions of sexuality and childhood.

But we need to remind ourselves that the real Freud was not necessarily equal to the dialectical power of his own genius. In what I would consider his greatest moments, for example when, in the *New Introductory Lectures*, he expressed *Wo es war, soll ich werden* (literally, 'where it was, there shall I become'), Freud identified the psychoanalytic project with the formation of the conscious subject out of the primordium, not as rejection but as appropriation of desire. For the ego, or 'I', to appropriate the id, or 'it', the subject must dissolve, become open to nature, the unspeakable, and the erotic infantile body. All of this is the domain of the negative, which is both subversive and, to some essential degree, illusory with respect to the socially constructed world. The psychoanalytic recovery of the self requires, therefore, a degree of acceptance of this negative dimension, coupled with an intellectual judgement concerning its unreality. It

is a subtle, dialectical balance, which can in no way be
encompassed in a simple-minded discourse of triumph over
illusion; or rather, psychoanalysis cannot be a gendarme
over illusion and remain true to its emancipatory and transcendent potential.

There is nothing, of course, which says that psychoanalysis must remain emancipatory – a measure requiring
both an affirmation of Eros and a critique of the socially
constructed world. Certainly Freud waffled a good bit on
the point. The same Freud who relentlessly attacked social
repressiveness and hypocrisy could, with an absolute lack
of critical insight, endorse the existing set of repressive social
regulations as if they had been inscribed by Moses in stone.
In the words of Adorno, for Freud, '[t]he fatality was
that, in the teeth of bourgeois ideology, he tracked down
conscious actions materialistically to their unconscious
instinctual basis, but at the same time concurred with the
bourgeois contempt of instinct which is itself a product of
precisely the rationalizations that he dismantled' (Adorno,
1974, p. 60).

The same could be said for *Freud or Reich?* except that in
dealing with Reich, of whom the last thing that could be said
was that he held a contempt for instinct, the authors seem
impelled to press their rejection of nature past the bounds
of Freud, and indeed, what prudent people would deem a
reasonable balance. For example, by more or less consigning
the orgasm theory to a fantasy of bowel evacuation, they are
led actually to reject, or at least minimize, the value of sexual
gratification itself. One does not have to be an ardent
Reichian or a victim of illusion to take exception to a statement such as:

*In reality, orgasm, in itself, has no particular value or merit in our
view. True, it is a discharge of tension, and this is, inherently, a
kind of evacuation (Alexander writes of 'drainage'), but the tension
in question is of a more complex nature than the purely anal.*
(p. 185)

This is, I am sure, cheering news to those who have had
clitoridectomy, not to mention the rest of us who have to
bear up under the common human fate of mental castration.
It is touching to have such consolation.

Chasseguet-Smirgel and Grunberger are good at flailing
away. But they are locked into Manichean dualism and, for
all their pretensions, incapable of critical thought. Critique

requires a dialectical attitude, which demands the holding together of opposites, as well as a view of the whole, and not a fixation on 'inner' or 'outer'. Freud was a great, if lapsed, master at this, while Reich can be said to be less dialectical than Freud. But Reich also set his sights higher and was not afraid to hurl himself into the void. He believed that opposites could be unified, and differentiation abolished. Reich's lapses in his search for a monistic view of the universe were greater than Freud's – worse philosophically, and perhaps the weaker for it; but grander, too, in insisting that human beings were entitled to more gratification than their civilization was affording. We should remember, too, that Reich's views on pleasure could in no way be reduced to any purely sensual calculus. As we have already observed, his views on sexuality had a crypto-Puritanism to them. But beyond this, he so expanded the idea of sexuality as to make it identical with participation in nature and the extrahuman itself.

Reich was, then, a kind of religious visionary. One can take him as such – although not as a way of neglecting his scientific claim, and not as a sign of his psychopathology. His lapse was to absorb the human into an extreme naturalism. Reich's severe naturalism signifies his own abandonment of – or was it an inability to sustain? – the dialectic of being human. Swallowed by nature, negativity vanishes and subjectivity returns as epiphenomenon. The results become mechanistic, even disastrous; we have seen their deleterious effects, and would share to this extent in the critique of Reich.

But let us affirm as well the magnificence of his tragic and doomed life. And let us take Reich seriously enough to wonder whether the savage fate handed to him by the authorities – psychoanalytic, Communist and of the US state apparatus – was more than a reaction to his difficult personality. Instead, could the repression of Reich have been also a sign of the seriousness of the forces his insights unleashed? If it can be said that Freud and Reich each slid off the perhaps impossible point of the dialectic, it can also be said that Freud slid in the safer direction, that of 'bourgeois contempt for instinct', leaving for Reich the direction of hell.

Why should we give any credence to Reich, considering all that is manifestly unreliable in his life's work? Because there is much more than a philosophical interest in what he achieved. Set aside the haste, the grandiosity, the gross

overreach, and what remains is remarkable. Or better, do
not set aside the derelictions, but consider their effects upon
Reich's discourse, and see what lies there nevertheless. A
major problem with Reich was that he so personalized his
thought as to lose track of the dialogue which forms the
fabric of normal scientific activity. He spoke *at* science, not
to scientists, who understandably turned away. It thus
becomes exceedingly difficult to engage the truth-value of
what he is saying. The mode of his presentation was so self-
referential, so sealed away in a cocoon of internal logic, so
alien to everyday discourse and, above all, so repudiative of
everything else that anybody had done in the way of science,
that out-of-hand rejection was virtually automatic.

It is true, then, that Reich's work has never been put to
an adequate test, having been subjected instead to the
partisanship of either true believers or true unbelievers,
and essentially remaining outside of rational inquiry for
methodological reasons. Whether this limit can ever be
overcome is arguable. One would have thought so – but one
has thought so for decades now, with little change in the
situation.

If, however, we bracket the science and concentrate
instead on the *prescience*, then a different picture emerges.
Reich's vision led him to the edge of the known, where he
touched upon many things that suggest an emergent truth.
Nor should we overlook the fact that he seems to have
anticipated much which has by now become routine. I would
share the authors' opinion that Reich's views on the sexual
liberties to be offered to children were deeply flawed. I
would also claim, however, that his role in promoting an
atmosphere of spontaneity in early childhood education
(principally through his lifelong friendship with A. S. Neill)
should be appreciated. To do less than this is to admit the
wish to turn back the clock to the days of the authoritarian
classroom. When we examine the sphere of more immediate
interest to him, a case could be made for Reich having
contributed to more movements in contemporary psychotherapy than anyone with the exception of Freud. Family
therapy, sex therapy, Gestalt therapy, aside from the more
obviously 'Reichian' body treatments – all these owe more
to Reich than is generally admitted. In addition, the powerful
'holistic' tendencies in contemporary health care derive as
much, if not more, from Reich as from any other individual.

I am not interested here in delineating Reich's precise

relationship to these movements, or in weighing their entire value, about much of which I would have reservations. The point is only that Reich seems to have been able to sense some basic things about the organism. What yielded to a repressive naturalism or floated off into grandiose speculation could also recapture a primitive, even Taoist respect for the integrity of life.

Given the fact that Reich operated – as we still do today – in the context of rampant technological domination, we should not be surprised that this most eccentric of geniuses could also enunciate some good, plain – and protective – sense. It should not be forgotten that, with the aid of his much-maligned and indeed ridiculed theory of the orgone, Reich was able courageously to call attention to the severe biological dangers posed by even very low doses of ionizing radiation many years before the mainstream of scientific medicine woke up to the threat. A lucky stroke induced by paranoia, or a prescient insight into the life process? In any case, not a simple matter of illusion.

If Reich was driven by paranoia, then we should develop more respect for paranoia. Kirilian auras, the recent reopening of the problem of biogenesis, the expansion of our conception of viruses and other intermediate forms of life . . . these and other lines of contemporary scientific investigation, anticipated in one way or another by Reich, tell us that the man is neither to be ignored nor to be reduced to the sum of his psychopathology. Perhaps we can say that, within the social context of modern science, it took a certain madness to achieve certain fundamental insights. The same madness could distort the insight and pull it outside of constructive dialogue. This is, however, no reason to despise the madness. It rather demands that we criticize the social context in greater measure than its victim.

And so Wilhelm Reich cannot be critically appreciated unless his society is critically measured as well. Much as he attempted to deny the social – a denial that led to his tragic downfall when he refused the US government's jurisdiction over his case – Reich's whole life and work remains defined by social forces. The dualism he rejected with his radical monism was a historical product. Who is Reich, after all, but the most extreme anti-Cartesian of our time? And since the Cartesian split between psyche and nature defines the rationality of the modern age, Reich was necessarily mad. His madness cannot be reduced, however, to the psycho-

pathological because he poses for us in the sharpest terms
imaginable the unbearable price extracted by society for its
domination of nature. It is ironic, then, that a man who so
violently rejected the significance of the social needs to be
judged ultimately according to one's assessment of
civilization.

All this is of no matter to Chasseguet-Smirgel and Grunberger, who have no difficulty in consigning Reich to the
trashcan of history precisely because they have no interest
in, or to be more exact, they have a fear of and active hostility
towards, any assessment of civilization which calls into
question the existing order of things. Hence their warning
against the 'bloodbath' which is sure to ensue after any
fulfilment of revolutionary ideals. Hence, too, their hatred
for Marcuse along with Reich, their blanket condemnation
of the Freudo-Marxist project, and their dismissal of Marx,
or indeed, all political radicalism. And they bend psychoanalysis to this purpose. No paraphrase or summary could
convey the spirit in which this is undertaken better than a
sampling of their remarks on the subject (some of these are
meant as a gloss on *Civilization and its Discontents*, but they
express also what might be called the authors' enhancement
of Freud's attitude, their Calvinist rendition of his
scepticism):

*Freud's work is a repudiation of Illusion, especially the illusion of
alternative societies, and the illusion of the overthrow of the process
of civilization . . . We have no choice. The alternative to civilization
is not the pastoral idyll, but barbarism . . . (p. 68)*

*Psychoanalytic theory . . . considers that primary drives – aggres-
sivity and the hunger for love – determine the economic conditions
themselves. This theory tends to see social institutions as the
exosmosis of the unconscious, a projection of the drives and the
defences against the drives . . . [This] accounts for the resistances
which this kind of work inevitably encounters. (p. 205)*

*The aim of political ideologies seems to be to ascribe the source of
human suffering to external factors. This usually entails blaming
a system (private property, capitalism, patriarchy, the 'consumer
society'), or a group of people (Jews, the bourgeoisie, 'armoured
characters',* homo normalis, *or Oedipalists), or even society in
general, for human suffering. Ideologies never seek to explain these
miseries as the effect of the drives, or of the human condition itself,
but they try, instead, to escape this suffering. And this, no doubt,*

is their main function. Furthermore, they extend the promise of a reconciliation between man and his lost unity; be it Marx's 'complete man', or the purified Aryan race, the non-armoured genital character enjoying his full orgasmic capacity, or the neo-Rousseauist return to nature. All these ideologies are based on a denial of castration: a castration which psychoanalysis stresses and which religions deny. (p. 208)

These explanatory models of political ideologies are very much like the 'influencing machine' fantasy that is so characteristic of paranoid-schizophrenics, which has been brilliantly described and analysed by Tausk (1919). (p. 211)

Human beings can only act and create on the basis of their internal psychosexual model. We project this model out on to the world when creating political systems, institutions and economic structures, thus making them in our own image . . . political ideologies . . . foster the illusion of the possibility of escaping from castration . . . At the heart of all ideologies lies the romantic and fashionable idea of 'changing the world'. Psychoanalytic understanding tends to act against the idea. (pp. 212–13)

This is miserable, mean-spirited stuff. It makes me ashamed as an analyst to see it so used. It is not that there is no truth to what they say. There is actually an important truth embedded here, a truth of the critique of messianic and objectivizing doctrines. However, this truth, which is specifically psychoanalytic, is perverted by the mean-spirited and, yes, grossly *ideological* temper in which it is expressed. I have referred already to the hopelessly undialectical character of the authors' thought. If there were any questions on this score, these quotes, lost in blinkered single vision, should settle them.

Interestingly, the authors themselves give the lie to their uncritical dichotomization when they admit, as if unaware of the implications, that 'every psychic manifestation, all human behaviour . . . is related, *although sometimes at great distance*, to the primary drives' (p. 211; my italics). Who could disagree with this sensible statement, which substitutes 'related to' for 'caused by', and admits that there may be something else, some mediation, just possibly having to do with the real practical world, substantially between the drives and at least some behaviour? Evidently Janine Chasseguet-Smirgel and Béla Grunberger, for it flies in the face of

their subjectivization of reality and their inability to deal
with multiple causation.

But these flaws are perhaps the less interesting side of our authors' defence of psychoanalytic hegemony. I am more taken with its ideological basis. To be blunt, which side are the authors on? For whom are these reflections into the human condition written? Ostensibly, everyone; that is, there is a clear universalizing attempt, evinced, if by nothing else, in the ubiquitous reference to 'Man'. Yet (setting aside the sexism) consider how ethnocentric, how utterly parochial, are the thoughts expressed here. Who else but a late-capitalist professional élite would be the least interested in these notions, and who other than the bourgeoisie can be served by them? From where else could they have come but Europe – a Europe, now North America as well, preaching of civilization to the barbarians, baffled by the barbarous turn of its own civilization.

Imagine our analysts attempting to convince, say, Black Africans in Soweto of the need to accept their 'castration', or to give up on the hope of changing the world because the *real* problems are within. Or the Filipinos who are waiting to overthrow the US-imposed Marcos dictatorship. Or lecturing Nicaragua's Sandinistas on the inevitable bloodbath to which their search for the ideal – that is, a free and self-determining society – must lead. The latter would tell them, by the way, that there were no executions of the hated dictator Somoza's bloodthirsty National Guard after the triumph in 1979 – perhaps because none of the Sandinistas read this book – but that there has been quite a bloodbath since, 8,000–9,000 lives more or less, instigated by a bourgeois counter-revolution bent on revenge. Or they might point out that Salvador Allende in Chile tried to change the world, refused to kill anyone or even to arm the people, and for his pains got butchered, along with more than 20,000 of his people, by another bourgeoisie bent on revenge. So if there is a psychohistorical problem worth investigating, it is that of the boundless savagery of the bourgeoisie (or any ruling group threatened from below) – a phenomenon that takes us, once again, into the domain of the repression of desire.

It may of course well be that there is no way radically to improve this civilization, although I must add that the prospect makes me shudder. But if so, it is because the forces on the ruling side are, taken all in all, the stronger. Never let it be said, however, that this makes what they are saying true. And so long as this is the case, we will need divinely inspired paranoids, who will not be thanked for their services, to point a way out. I happen to think, though, that there will be a better day. I know it may be an illusion to think so, but it is not entirely an illusion, and in the difference, everything may reside. The paranoid visionary Rousseau helped point the way to a French Revolution that gave us a bourgeois society for the likes of Janine Chasseguet-Smirgel and Béla Grunberger to defend. Can we say what the visionary paranoid Reich was prefiguring?

NOTES

1. This essay was originally written as an introduction or afterword to *Freud or Reich? Psychoanalysis and Illusion* (1986). The authors, however, refused to have it appear in the volume. It is reprinted here with some modifications.

2. It is worth noting that where Reichianism today hangs on in the USA, it is most often, but by no means always, a distinctly right-wing phenomenon; this being associated with Reich's own markedly anti-Communist swing in his last years; see below.

3. See, for example, Grunbaum (1984).

4. Jeffrey Masson's *The Assault on Truth* (1985), despite its gross defects, has an illuminating account of this shameful chapter in the history of psychoanalysis.

PART FIVE

THE CRISIS
OF MATERIALISM

IN 1981 I became deeply affected by the nuclear crisis; and in 1983 I became drawn into the defence of Nicaragua's Sandinista revolution against the Reagan administration. These causes – the first of which led me towards non-violent civil disobedience and anti-militarism (as well as *Against the State of Nuclear Terror* (1984a)), while the second eventuated in four trips to Nicaragua in as many years – deeply affected my work. On a political level, they led to new affiliations, along with confrontation and conflict with a number of previously held positions. I fell out with the *Telos* group, many of whom were so suspicious of the Soviet Union as to edge towards the Nato position in the nuclear arms race, and who could not share my enthusiasm for Nicaragua. In the course of this, I began to re-examine my 'Western Marxism'. On the one hand, I found myself much more struck by the pervasiveness of anti-Communism among people who defined themselves as radicals and Marxists; while on the other, my experiences in Nicaragua, as my first direct exposure to a revolution in the flesh, made me considerably more open to political formations which engaged Leninism. As a result, I came to feel that my former position was based on a mechanical, abstract and derivative notion of what actually went on in a revolution. It is not that I became any more disposed to authoritarianism than I had been a decade ago – only that the world looks different at close range than it does from the perspective of a philosophy journal. Faced with the reality, I was led to see new possibilities. It should be added that the reality was one of the Third World, and the possibilities included those forms taken by revolutionary experience in the Third World.

A particularly stunning confrontation was with the encounter of liberation theology with Marxism-Leninism in Nicaragua. Anyone who visits Nicaragua can see that something quite unique in history is taking place there between the liberation church and the revolutionary government. Whatever the long-range possibilities for Nicaragua, the effect of this on my sensibilities has been comparable to my encounters with Freud and then Marx. And of course it could not help but radically affect my identity as a psychoanalyst and a Marxist.

I thus began to explore the dimension of spirituality, both in itself and within psychoanalysis and politics. Obviously, a project of this sort does not come out of the blue; and a reflection back over my life and work can reveal many antecedents. The first of the essays in this section, for example, 'Some lines from Blake', an unpublished piece written in 1977, testifies to an affinity with the *visionary* which extends from the beginnings of my intellectual identity. I discovered Blake at Yale in the mid-fifties, and the Geoffrey Keynes edition of the complete works has been one of the most thumbed books in my personal library. I took it with me to Nicaragua, and would take it to the proverbial desert island. I have also made it a practice to weave a set of allusions to Blake throughout my writing. The essay tries to say something of what I hear in Blake, beginning with the tension between visionary and psychoanalytic experience.

'Human nature, freedom and spirit' was written in 1985 at the invitation of John Clark, for a Festschrift honouring Murray Bookchin, the anarchist philosopher and principal expositor of the discourse of *social ecology*. I have had substantial political differences with Bookchin (who rejects Marxism and is hostile to the Nicaraguan revolution), but remain convinced of the importance of many of his insights. A rethinking of our relationship to nature strikes me as indispensable for any project of survival, much less emancipation, and social ecology is a basic way of rephrasing this relationship. The main theses of the essay are not limited to social ecology, however, but integral to any progressive philosophy. The most radical and important of these – that spirit is a material category – is one I am currently developing. As part of this approach, I argue here that a reappropriation of the concept of *human nature* is indispensable, even if it goes against the inclinations of many progressives who sense the reactionary implications of the term. The questions are: Does human nature contain *spiritual* capacities? Do these play a role in our larger relations to nature? Is this role necessary for social transformation?

'Marx, Freud and the problem of materialism' was read at a SUNY-Buffalo conference on Marxism in 1984, and published in *Dialectical Anthropology*. It represents a growing feeling on my part that the Marx–Freud dialogue points in the direction of the spirit, despite the fact that this dimension was relentlessly criticized by both Marx and Freud. It is one thing to demystify, that is, lay bare the historical and subjective distortions of the spirit, and another to lay claim to having abolished the category altogether. Not only did Marx and Freud fail in the latter project; it can be argued that a kind of spirituality lies embedded in their discourses, and, more significantly, that Marxism and psychoanalysis alike suffer from the failure to recognize this fact. I am currently trying to work my way through this problem. The essay represents a theoretical jumping-off point for the endeavour.

'Cryptic notes on revolution and the spirit: times change' represents another venture into the same area, now from a more political angle. Originally published in London, then reprinted in the USA, the essay was inspired by my exposure to liberation theology in Nicaragua. 'Cryptic notes' is animated by the impact of this encounter: by the realization that there is something in liberation theology – and Nicaragua – which my previous experience could not encompass. There remains an obdurate tension between this experience and my critical faculties, which have included a goodly store of anticlericalism and a feeling for the historically repressive role played by religion. Thus there are as many questions at the current point in my trajectory as there were at the beginning – including, to be sure, the question of what will be left of my psychoanalytic identity after I pass through it.

1. Man has no Body distinct from his Soul; for that call'd Body is a portion of Soul discern'd by the five Senses, the chief inlets of Soul in this age.
2. Energy is the only life, and is from the Body; and Reason is the bound or outward circumference of Energy.
3. Energy is Eternal Delight.
William Blake, *The Marriage of Heaven and Hell*[1]

Let us bear this firmly in mind, for it is the key to the whole theory of repression: *The second system can only cathect an idea if it is in a position to inhibit any development of unpleasure that may proceed from it.*
Sigmund Freud, *The Interpretation of Dreams*; Freud's italics

We have decided to relate pleasure and unpleasure to the quantity of excitation that is present in the mind but is not in any way 'bound' . . . The impulses arising from the instincts do not belong to the type of *bound* nervous processes but of *freely mobile* processes which press towards discharge.
Sigmund Freud, *Beyond the Pleasure Principle*

WHILE it is generally all too facile to draw parallels between earlier thinkers and Freud, the case of William Blake is an exceptionally intriguing one. For one thing, there is just too much explicit 'metapsychology' in the lines from Blake to be passed by. These are not pre-Freudian intuitions, in the manner of a Pascal or St Augustine, but almost exact enunciations of what Freud held to be most essential about the psyche. Even more remarkable is the attitude in which the lines are set. The Voice of the Devil speaks here in hellish Contraries to the official opinion encoded in bibles, school-books and the law. Was Freud then, like Milton, 'a true poet and of the Devil's party without knowing it'?

To judge by the whole body of psychoanalysis: scarcely. Freud himself may have been secretly – with or without knowing it – of the Devil's party; but what he created has remained firmly within established boundaries. And this is because of Freud's ultimate loyalty to these boundaries, to

his firm delineation between reality and pleasure principle,
and his adherence to the former as a source of value despite
the fact that he had unmasked it as illusion. In the words of
Theodor Adorno, Freud 'concurred with the bourgeois
contempt of instinct which is itself a product of precisely the
rationalizations that he dismantled' (1974, p. 60). It is not
enough to say that Freud created a fundamentally radical
doctrine that was somehow captured by bourgeois interests
– it is necessary to recognize and spell out the points within
Freud's psychoanalysis which already represented those
interests and sought their embrace. Freud was ambivalent,
but ultimately believed in reason, knowing it to be but the
'bound or outward circumference' of desire – yet he had no
faith in the desire which gave reason life. He wanted men
and women to be more reasonable, and foresaw the 'still
small voice' of the scientific attitude overtaking the blindness
of instinctual and infantile passion. But his ambivalence
towards desire forced him to take reason for granted. It was
something that came from beyond history to be laid on top
of history. Reason – and the reality principle – were somehow
just there, to be acquired; and men and women became
therefore for Freud children who had not yet used all their
faculties and needed growing up. From such a position it is
only a short step to psychoanalysis as a branch of mental
hygiene – an apostle of sanity and maturity, that is, bourgeois
normality.

In this matter, Blake diverged, and paid for it. As T. S.
Eliot wrote, in an amazing burst of fatuity, had Blake's
genius 'been controlled by a respect for impersonal reason,
for common sense, for the objectivity of science, it would
have been better for him' (*The Sacred Wood*, 1920, quoted
in Bottrall, 1970, p. 97). It depends. Blake suffered but
shouldered the load cheerfully, felt it worth the hardship,
could even poke fun at himself.

*I then asked Ezekiel why he eat dung, & lay so long on his right &
left side? he answer'd, 'the desire of raising other men into a
perception of the infinite: this the North American tribes practise, &
is he honest who resists his genius or conscience only for the sake
of present ease or gratification?' (The Marriage of Heaven and Hell,
p. 186)*

The secret of Blake's divergence lies in his calling as visionary
and prophet. Unlike Freud, for whom the past held the key
to being, Blake kept his eye ahead, letting the past go

through to beam upon the future. Yeats said it beautifully
of him: 'There have been men who loved the future like a
mistress, and the future mixed her breath into their breath
and shook her hair about them, and hid them from the
understanding of their times. William Blake was one of these
men, and if he spoke confusedly and obscurely it was
because he spoke of things for whose speaking he could
find no models in the world he knew' (W. B. Yeats, *Essays*,
1924, quoted in Bottrall, 1970).

And this is still so. The world has not yet provided models.
The fault is not Blake's, who was a seer but no obscurantist
mystic, but history's, which has served up a certain version
of reality, and created a science whose pretensions have
been to establish this version of reality as 'nature'. Blake was
not against science, but one of the first, and deepest, critics
of *established* science. At the end of his *Vala*, after the Last
Judgement of the Ninth Night, when the Earth rises again,
so does a rejuvenated science:

> The Sun arises from his dewy bed, & the fresh airs
> Play in his smiling beams giving the seeds of life to grow,
> And the fresh Earth beams forth ten thousand thousand springs
>   of life.
> Urthona is arisen in his strength, no longer now
> Divided from Enitharmon, no longer the Spectre Los.
> Where is the Spectre of Prophecy? Where is the delusive
>   Phantom?
> Departed: & Urthona rises from the ruinous Walls
> In all his ancient strength to form the golden armour of science
> For intellectual War. The war of swords departed now,
> The dark Religions are departed & Sweet Science reigns.
>
> (*Vala*, p. 371)

Science can be sweet for Blake because he recognizes that
for us the world is the *known*, apprehended world, and that
our knowledge begins with the senses and never really
leaves them, except through the falsifying lens of repression.

> We are led to Believe a Lie
> When we see not Thro' the Eye
>
> ('Auguries of Innocence', p. 121)

The science that he cudgelled, and which still persists, is
one with the dark religion that is to be overcome: each forces
a forgetting of the truth that our knowledge is not 'out there'
but a sensuous and social product:

*. . . a system was formed, which some took advantage of, & enslav'd
the vulgar by attempting to realize or abstract the mental deities
from their objects: thus began Priesthood . . .*

*And at length they pronounc'd that the Gods had order'd such
things.*

Thus men forgot that All deities reside in the human breast.
(*The Marriage of Heaven and Hell*, p. 185)

Knowledge can not be severed from either its subject or
object. There is an imaginary, and a real, but the *imagination*
invests both and is with knowledge from the beginning.

*You certainly Mistake, when you say that the Visions of Fancy are
not to be found in This World. To Me This World is all One
Continued Vision of Fancy or Imagination, & I feel Flatter'd when
I am told so.* (Letter to Dr Trusler, 23 August, 1799, p. 835)

For Blake, the means of true science was to let the sensuous
imagination play on reality to reveal forms nascent within
the established system of order. The imagination is not only
the midwife of such forms – it is their progenitor as well. His
vision of the future is one of the transformation of reality by
the liberated imagination – a process which excludes neither
science nor technology:

*. . . the whole creation will be consumed and appear infinite and
holy, whereas it now appears finite & corrupt.*

*This will come to pass by an improvement of sensual enjoyment.
But first the notion that man has a body distinct from his soul is to
be expunged; this I shall do by printing in the infernal method, by
corrosives, which in Hell are salutary and medicinal, melting
apparent surfaces away, and displaying the infinite which was hid.*

*If the doors of perception were cleansed every thing would appear
to man as it is, infinite.*

*For man has closed himself up, till he sees all things thro' narrow
chinks of his cavern.* (*The Marriage of Heaven and Hell*, p. 187)

It is doubtful that Blake would have proposed cleansing
the doors of perception with drugs or mantras. Instead it
involved *praxis* – self-reflective and imaginative work on
reality. He refers here to his craft as printer and engraver (in
which this supposedly mad visionary made certain practical
and technical advances which still elude his successors), but
the notion applies to the entire socially organized sphere of
work, including the making of language and poetry, and,
to be sure, science itself.

Blake represents the spirit of the Enlightenment unbridled, whereas Freud pursues it in bound form, as the still, small voice of reason. It is not enough to regard the difference as one between a Utopian and a sceptical temperament: it is ontological as well. For Freud came to metapsychology through the positivism of Helmholtz and Brücke; he was the heir to generations of a bourgeois hegemony in science that had sedimented out into a crude materialism. He made his break with his discovery of the laws of 'psychic reality' – but in doing so had to pass through the materialist crust and carried much of it along with him. Thus the 'qualities' of the mind were subordinated to, and ultimately described in terms of, the 'quantities' of a material world: 'We have decided to relate pleasure and unpleasure to the quantity of excitation . . .' And as he had written in the 'Project', 'In the external world . . . according to the view of our natural science, to which psychology too must be subjected here, there are only masses in motion and nothing else' and since 'science recognizes only quantities . . . it is to be expected from the structure of the nervous system that it consists of contrivances for transforming external quantity into quality' (1895, pp. 308f). The gap between body and soul was closed from the side of the body, and something of soul obscured thereby.

The bourgeois tide scarcely lapped at Blake's feet. Never having been separated by the exchange principle, the unity of body and soul was already given, and came from the soul, the centre of knowledge and desire. The ego was eternally a body-ego, and the body, an ego-body: the portion of soul discerned by the five senses. And what of quantity, and the Kantian categories of space and time?

As to that false appearance which appears to the reasoner
As of a Globe rolling thro' Voidness, it is a delusion of Ulro.
The Microscope knows not of this nor the Telescope: they alter
The ratio of the Spectator's Organs, but leave Objects
  untouch'd.
For every Space larger than a red Globule of Man's blood
Is visionary, and is created by the Hammer of Los:
And every Space smaller than a Globule of Man's blood opens
Into Eternity of which this vegetable Earth is but a shadow.
The red Globule is the unwearied Sun by Los created
To measure Time and Space to mortal Men every morning.
                                                      (Milton, p. 413)

One neither dissects such thoughts with the logos of
traditional science and philosophy nor relegates them to a
poetics which is merely beautiful and hence unanalysable.
Instead they require a mode of discourse equal to their
reality.

To recapture the imagination language must be up-ended.
This is why Freud, however much he was trapped by a
reason he could not scrutinize, stands at that juncture where
modern thought gives itself the opportunity to catch up with
Blake. To provide models for what Blake saw, thought has
to reflect on itself until the unthinkable is drawn from behind
its shroud of symbolic potentiality. More than a job of
linguistic self-reflection, this requires reappropriating what
civilization has pushed aside, including its filth, what Freud
called, 'matter in the wrong place'.

> *Does the Eagle know what is in the pit?*
> *Or wilt thou go ask the Mole?*
> *Can Wisdom be put in a silver rod?*
> *Or Love in a golden bowl?*
>
> (*The Book of Thel*, p. 162)

For the senses to rise again, that which has been defiled must
be traversed. Here is the recovery of the body, signalling the
end of Blake's master-work, *Jerusalem*:

> *. . . Circumscribing & Circumcising the excrementitious*
> *Husk & Covering, into Vacuum evaporating, revealing the*
> *lineaments of Man,*
> *Driving outward the Body of Death in an Eternal Death &*
> *Resurrection,*
> *Awaking it to Life among the Flowers of Beulah, rejoicing in*
> *Unity*
> *In the Four Senses, in the Outline, the Circumference & Form,*
> *for ever*
> *In Forgiveness of Sins which is Self Annihilation; it is the*
> *Covenant of Jehovah.*
>
> (*Jerusalem*, p. 566)

Reason, the 'outward circumference of energy' is here
revealed not as disembodied scientific thinking, but as
part of a reconciliation with concrete aspects of evil. The
imagination can only be won by plumbing the depths.
Blake, like Freud, realizes that evil exists there, that reason
circumscribes terror, that the wound begins in childhood.

And if the Babe is born a Boy
He's given to a Woman Old
Who nails him down upon a rock
Catches his shrieks in cups of gold.

('The Mental Traveller', p. 111)

And that it remains in sexuality, and must be transcended through sexuality.

Therefore the Male severe and cruel, fill'd with stern Revenge,
Mutual Hate returns & mutual Deceit & mutual Fear.

Hence the Infernal Veil grows in the disobedient Female,
Which Jesus rends & the whole Druid Law removes away
From the Inner Sanctuary, a False Holiness hid within the
*   Centre.*
For the Sanctuary of Eden is in the Camp, in the Outline,
In the Circumference & every Minute Particular is Holy:
Embraces are Cominglings from the Head even to the Feet,
And not a pompous High Priest entering by a Secret Place.

(*Jerusalem* III, p. 526)

More: as one for whom imagination grasps the real, and for whom the real is a prefiguration of the future, Blake, despite all his extravagant excursions into myth and fancy, remained continually in touch with actual history. In this he is greatly the superior of Freud, whose deep insights into history, beclouded by *his* myth of the Primal Crime, ended up as rationalizations for the bourgeois order. Blake's Last Judgement is no religious accounting, but political revolution.

And every one of the dead appears as he had liv'd before
And all the marks remain of the slave's scourge & tyrant's
*   Crown,*
And of the Priest's o'ergorged Abdomen, & the merchant's thin
Sinewy deception, & of the warrior's outbraving &
*   thoughtlessness*
In lineaments too extended & in bones too strait & long.
They show their wounds: they accuse: they sieze the opressor;
*   howlings began*
On the golden palace, songs & joy on the desart, the Cold babe
Stands in the furious air, he cries: 'the children of six thousand
*   years*
Who died in infancy rage furious: a mighty multitude rage
*   furious,*

Naked & pale standing in the expecting air, to be deliver'd.
Rend limb from limb the warrior & the tyrant, reuniting in
pain.'

(*Vala*, 'Night the Ninth', p. 354)

Here the visionary poet comes up against that perennial demon of the Left – the violence that is both implicit in its doctrine and repugnant to it. Many have recoiled from the contradiction, or submerged it beneath moral expediency. Freud's own conservatism may have stemmed from it. Blake, true to form, meets the monster head on.

Not without pause: indeed the immense and gorgeous work from which these lines are drawn, *Vala*, was never set by Blake in a completed engraved form. We know also that his spectacular lyric, 'The Tyger', was held up some months – and went through some relatively darker earlier drafts – while Blake anxiously followed a particularly bloody turn the French Revolution was taking in the autumn of 1792 (Nurmi, 1970). For the Tyger is not merely the spirit of imaginative energy – Blake would never have rested with such an idealistic and purely romantic notion – he is this spirit as embodied in the French Revolution itself. Human powers are held back by real oppression, whether in the form of classes, the state, the very 'dark Satanic Mills', or the patriarchal family. Hence the imagination is not to be restored 'in the head', but by a grappling with evil as it has been embedded in reality. Whether or not the struggle results in a blood-bath depends on how desire is realized. If it is perverted, then the imagination fails and mayhem ensues. The surfeit of violence which dogs history is not the consequence of desire but of its thwarting. Since desire has to be as fully realized as the evil it opposes, we can see why Blake insists that political struggle has to include the means of the body: sensuousness. To deprive us of bodily desire – or vitiate it by moralization – is to deprive us of the weapons to combat evil and realize the imagination. It is the criterion of true sin.

Holiness is not The Price of Enterance into Heaven. Those who are
cast out are All Those who, having no Passions of their own because
No Intellect, Have spent their lives in Curbing & Governing other
People's by the Various arts of Poverty & Cruelty of all kinds. Wo,
Wo, Wo to you Hypocrites. Even Murder, the Courts of Justice,
more merciful than the Church, are compell'd to allow is not done

in Passion, but in Cool Blooded design & intention. ('Vision of
the Last Judgement', p. 650)

And,

*You cannot have Moral Virtue without the Slavery of that half of
the Human Race who hate what you call Moral Virtue.* (p. 650)

Desire, the path to heaven, joins heaven with hell and
accepts the risk of breaking with the morality that floats on
domination. Already, in *The Marriage of Heaven and Hell*,
Blake had set out the way to liberation as the Contraries of
Hell, embodied in fiendish Proverbs:

The road of excess leads to the palace of wisdom.

Prudence is a rich, ugly old maid courted by Incapacity.

He who desires, but acts not, breeds pestilence.

The tygers of wrath are wiser than the horses of instruction.

*Sooner murder an infant in its cradle than nurse unacted
    desires.*
(The Marriage of Heaven and Hell, pp. 183–5)

The proverbs are seemingly antithetical to the psychoanalytic canon which postulates that the reality of desire can
only be confronted in the abstinence of the analytic setting.
In fact they have precisely the same intent. For Blake is not
advancing a philosophy of 'acting out', which is blind and
impulsive, hence the truncation of desire, but, again, one of
praxis: conscious and self-reflective activity. Unless desire is
realized through a praxis of the imagination, he is telling us,
we are in fact more likely to murder infants in their cradles,
or at least to destroy their human capacity before it can grow.

By the same token, the abstinence of the analytic setting,
and its proscription against acting out, are subsidiaries
within psychoanalytic praxis designed to secure its central
and characteristic mode of activity, *speech* between analysand and analyst. Properly done, then, analysis works
towards cleansing the doors of perception. That it stops
short of the goal and fails to reveal all things as 'infinite' in
the Blakean sense, is a limit of its praxis, but no fault. The
fault is rather that our world turns out so few Blakes – in
other words, that it sees to it that the visionary potentiality
is in fact murdered in its cradle. The past that analysis
reconciles us to is an already damaged one; and the present

to which it leaves us, reconciled and restored, is no less warping.

That Blake asked too much of men, given our institutions, is indisputable. But what is a prophet for except to affirm the non-necessity of what is? Yet Blake's vision is so awful, so little realized by what followed – even by visionaries – as practically to mock us with its radical transcendence. It requires of us a kind of absolute faith in the unity of existence that seems a guarantee of despair to sensibilities disillusioned by history:

> *If the Sun & Moon should doubt,*
> *They'd immediately Go out.*
>
> ('Auguries of Innocence', p. 121)

But Blake will not relent. The transcendent is not in the stars, nor the abstraction of history, but always immediate, renewed in each person and present in the humblest details.

> *The bat that flits at close of Eve*
> *Has left the Brain that won't Believe.*
>
> ('Auguries of Innocence', p. 118)

The objective bat and the objective brain may seem to be two disjoined lumps of protoplasmic matter. And ordinary flattened thought would dismiss the proposition of their unity as nonsensical. But the bat as apprehended flitting through dusk, the perceived bat, exists as represented to the brain's mind by the oscillations of the wings and the play back and forth between the dark bat and the darkening sky. To have watched a bat appear, disappear and reappear at close of eve is to sense the tenuousness of our experience. When the bat is gone does it cease to exist? Are those vacuoles in space-time where it existed an instant ago? We believe in the constancy of an object – that the bat has been there all the time – through a mental construction of it that endures when it is beyond sense-presentation. But the bat? Will we ever know whether *this* bat was there? Or was it a figment – the bat of night: nasty creature standing for all the horrors that emerge in the dark? We wish them to disappear into the holes left behind when the bat vanishes. The full bat will not exist for us unless we are willing to fill those holes. The repressed self is severed from its objects: it becomes dead matter, a disembodied brain in an impoverished half-world. Reason ceases to be the circumference of energy and turns into its spectral antagonist.

To appropriate the bat-object means more than passive acceptance. It means praxis as well; here poetry, which creates in its significations a transformation of what it signifies. The bat seen is the first step; it can only become ours when it is the bat transformed into words under the sway of the unifying imagination. Now it is not enough that the bat in general should symbolize this or that at a distance. The symbolic transformation has to be anchored in immediacy, as by the dream-work. Here the poet draws upon the primitive sense modalities of rhythm as mediated through the concrete memory of spoken words. Word-presentations become thing-presentations again. The iambic metre serves as a rocking, lulling backdrop to the activity of the couplet. The soothing rhythm evokes the infant's sleep in the mother's arms – or in the womb, for the basic iambic beat is tuned to the sound of a heartbeat: *lub-dub*. Against its reassurance and promise of fusion enters a staccato burst of harsh, bitten-off monosyllables – *bat-that-flits-at* – followed by a transitional sound – *close of* – and then a long open one – *Eve*. The sounds flutter as mysteriously as their object. The line fairly swoops towards its conclusion. Is Eve the devouring maw of night or its protecting mother? The next one repeats the pattern, although in more scattered form: the bat has already flitted away, gone from the objectified brain who won't believe but captured for eternity in its whole circumference by the poetic imagination.

NOTE
1. All page references are to Keynes (1956).

15 HUMAN NATURE,
FREEDOM AND SPIRIT

THE self-regulating character of natural process is an
axiom for social ecology, indeed, for all progressives
who seek to redefine our relationship to nature. The order,
harmony and symmetry of the natural world stand in sharp
contrast to the disequilibrium and chaos of human society,
manifest as ruthless exploitation of the ecosphere and social
domination, with its inevitable train of isms: imperialism,
militarism, racism, sexism and so forth. Non-human life, by
contrast, exists within an immense matrix of checks and
balances. Its ecological lawfulness stems not from any
conscious decision on the part of one creature or another,
but from the collective inability of all creatures to step out of
line. Each living non-human being pursues its survival
interest (as individual or species), at times at the expense of
other beings, at times in co-operation with them, but never
outside the mutually interrelated framework of all beings.
Those creatures who behave with reckless abandon are
quickly snuffed out, no matter where they may be situated
in the chain of being. And the survivors survive with each
other. The most predatory relations between particular
living creatures are, from the standpoint of the whole of life,
manifestations of utter dependency. Thus all beings contain
each other. The colossal blue whale lives within the being
of the tiny krill it consumes by the billion, and vice versa.
And so on, upwards, downwards, inwards or outwards, to
the edge of the universe.

Except for humans, or as we can say here with gender
accuracy, 'Man'. Man is the only creature who has been
able, until now, to step out of line and get away with it. As
the only being with the gall to consider himself the Lord of
Creation, Man is only too capable of not recognizing himself
in the beings subject to his dominion. For Man, reckless
abandon is the hallmark of his tenure on earth; and if he has
not been snuffed out so far, it is due only to the fiendish
ingenuity of the technological means he has developed to

squeeze the ecosphere out of ever more 'raw materials' and
energy, and to perfect the domination of his fellow creatures.

The ecological impulses grow out of the crisis induced by
human recklessness. Social ecology in particular is a call for
people to rethink their domination of nature – and to change
this relationship in practice. The principal insight of social
ecology is to identify domination – and the resulting chaos
– as a function of estrangement from nature. And its principal
practice is that of a reconciliation with nature – a reclamation
of our natural tendencies, whether through direct trans-
actions with the material world (food production, nutrition,
etc.) or within social relationships (feminism, building
community, etc.). But these laudable projects are predicated
on something which is assumed rather than demonstrated,
namely, that we have, within our own being, such 'natural
tendencies' as should be reclaimed. They are, in other
words, statements grounded in a notion of 'human nature'.
And this raises a problem, particularly for a movement on
the Left such as social ecology. For the Left has something
of a taboo towards ideas concerning human nature. The
Right, on the other hand, seizes avidly upon the theme. To
practise a reconciliation with nature we have to appeal to
human nature; but in so doing we draw on something
that has been by and large appropriated by conservative
discourse.

It is not hard to see why. For 'nature' connotes what is
merely animal, unchanging and prior to human effort.
Nothing is better suited than an appeal to nature to deny
the possibility of historical change, much less amelioration.
If black slaves, 'by nature' are simple creatures, and close to
the land, then why bother to free them? This kind of
argument was regularly made in defence of slavery (and
now of apartheid); and a similar line of reasoning has
classically been adopted to prove, for example, that women,
being closer to nature, are suited by divine plan for reproduction rather than the demands of 'civilization'. It is hard
to find a pernicious tendency that has not been justified by
an appeal to human nature. By contrast, people interested
in progressive social change insist that we are not locked,
'by nature', into any pattern of behaviour. This line of
reasoning tends to maintain a more or less absolute division
between the human and natural world. Animals and other
'lower' creatures have fixed instinctual natures; whereas
human nature, if it exists at all, is defined by plasticity and the

capacity to transcend instinct. In the classical nature–nurture
debate, the Left, with good reason, comes down solidly on
the side of the latter term.

There is another aspect to the meaning of human nature
which gives the progressive cause even more grief. This is
the exceedingly widespread notion that human beings are
'by nature' wicked, sinful, egotistic and foolish creatures. It
is remarkable how many progressive people share in this
conviction, which is typically associated with the conservative political philosophy of Thomas Hobbes, but was also
articulated by Shakespeare and many of the greatest
observers of the human scene, Freud included. Unlike the
fallacy alluded to above, this sceptical judgement on human
nature does not rely on any pseudo-scientific claims about
some oppressed group. It is rather a claim about the general
essence of human being, something which holds true for all
people in so far as they are human. This is a valid use of the
term, nature. We say without difficulty, for example, that it
is in the nature of dogs to relate primarily to the person of
their master, and cats to the master's dwelling. Moreover it
is much more difficult to dismiss this kind of view about
human nature, for however ideologically contaminated it
may be (as, for example, in the case of Freud), it also has the
weight of truth we associate with high tragic art. Scepticism
about human nature may be peevish and misanthropic; but
to dismiss it out of hand means turning away from what we
generally recognize to be among the greatest products of the
human mind. It is not, after all, a very persuasive argument
to reject the view of human nature as expressed, say, in *King
Lear* or *The Brothers Karamazov* as an ideological distortion
imposed by the patriarchal family. One might well say that
Shakespeare and Dostoevsky are representing the awful
truth of the patriarchal family, and that their art, like all great
art, has a subversive and critical function because of its utter
truthfulness. We might want, because of our experience of
this truth, to be rid of patriarchy, as in my opinion we
should. But it is impossible to avoid the impression that
what they are representing has a deeply 'nature-al'
character. They are speaking of a kind of inherent
compliance with domination.

Tragedy indicates properties of the self which in some way
'come before' institutional formations such as patriarchy and
capitalism, and are drawn into these as well as other kinds
of domination. In any case, I think it fair to say that the

claims of a sceptical view of human nature are exactly those
of tragedy. If tragedy has any truthfulness for us, if, that
is, we think that the representation of human beings as
creatures capable of tragic flaws is a deeply true statement,
then we are not entitled to make any simple identity between
emancipation and human nature.

And this leaves the social-ecology movement in something of a quandary. For social ecology is nothing if not
emancipatory in intent; and its principal thesis, as noted
above, is the reconciliation with nature, which must include
our tragic capacity. On what rational basis can we claim that
putting ourselves in touch with our 'natural' feelings and
impulses will fulfil the project of social ecology? Given the
real behaviour of people – the copious evidence of egotism,
power-hunger, hostility and plain cantankerousness, to
mention only a few of the better-known vices – what entitles
us to believe that it is not better, in the long run, actually to
suppress rather than express our inner nature? Perhaps the
truth about human nature is that it indeed breaks with the
rest of nature – that we are a sport, a genetic freak that has
lost the internal capacity to stay in line with the universe.

I am not going to put these doubts to rest. I am not sure I
can do so in any case, but certainly not within these brief
confines. I can only offer here some ruminations that might
enable us to frame some useful questions with which to
address human nature.

I think we should begin by recognizing that, whatever the
cause, we remain defined as creatures with a problematic
relation to nature. In other words, there is something *essential*
about human beings which sits uneasily with the rest of
nature, and cannot be collapsed into the kind of mutual
interrelatedness that marks the remainder of living creatures. It is no verbal trick to claim that 'human nature'
consists of actively establishing some distinction, or separateness, between ourselves and the remainder of the
universe. The simple fact that we regard our nature, and the
relation with nature, as a problem bears witness to this
overriding truth about human beings.

Now there is a great deal to be said about this conjuncture,
and I can do no more than suggest a few of the themes which
arise from it before passing on to the main portion of my
argument. In the first place, the terms, 'some distinction' and
'separateness' are very abstract categories, encompassing
within their conceptual boundaries a veritable bestiary of

implication. We might say, roughly, that the possibilities range continuously between a kind of distinction called 'splitting', and another called 'differentiation'. It will be helpful to bear in mind that when two entities *split* one from another they separate completely, neither being mirrored in one another nor maintaining any connection thereafter. On the other hand, when they *differentiate* from each other, they remain associated, connected, and indeed, mirrored, so that each could recognize itself in the other. The point of this conceptual by-play is to give us room within the basic framework of human nature for outcomes that we consider bad and those we consider good, and to do so within an ecological perspective. Splitting, in this sense, reflects what we don't want – even if we have to recognize its reality and power over human life: it is the basic property of domination, whether of class, sex, race or, more generally, of nature itself. The dominator, in other words, must dissociate from and not recognize himself in, the dominated. Differentiation, on the other hand, represents what we strive for: it is that outcome of human nature in the direction of ecological interrelatedness and the essential unity of all beings. It is important to keep in mind, however, that neither of these ends of the spectrum represents an absolute (except in death). No splitting ever denies the essential interdependence of all creatures (the master needs his slave, the capitalist his proletarian, the ascetic his body); and no degree of differentiation is ever so finely drawn as to obliterate the essential 'differentness' between human beings and other forms of life – and the tragic implications this holds.

It should also be pointed out that although classical Marxism and social ecology are not on the best of terms, the view of human nature expressed here is Marxist as well as social-ecological. To be more exact, it is a view compatible with a reading of Marxism, although by no means the only compatible view – nor necessarily the predominant view among actual Marxists, including Marx, who is open to much challenge on this point. Nevertheless, there is an approach to historical materialism that is, in my opinion, consistent with a differentiated approach towards nature. We cannot address this theme adequately here, except to say that it builds upon Marx's claim, in his 1844 'Manuscripts', and again in *Capital*, that we are part of nature as well as the transformer of nature. Indeed, there is probably no more fundamental or concise statement of Marx's

ontology than this. The labour process is the conscious 293
transformation of nature, by means of which we create
objects in the world and, in so doing, create ourselves
as transformed beings. Marx's key notion of alienation
expresses more or less exactly the idea of splitting as applied
to labour and the class struggle. And the revolutionary goal
of a classless society is in all fundamental respects the
overcoming of splitting and the rise of a truly differentiated
– that is, fully human – being.

But neither Marxism nor classical anarchism has ever
bothered much with the actual 'nature' of such a fully
realized, differentiated human being. Preoccupied with the
external, object world, they fail to investigate the subjective
conditions of emancipation and domination. Whether social
ecology can go further depends upon the degree to which
it can appropriate what has been left till now to frank
mysticism or bourgeois disciplines such as psychoanalysis:
the domain of the self. The track record of radicals in this
respect has not been encouraging so far. In the face of all
evidence to the contrary, they have continued to assume
that rearranging the world will in itself bring about the free
realization of human beings. To use the terms we are
developing here, in conventional radical practice subjectivity is *split away* from the external object world instead of
differentiated from it. And this – as we used to say in the
sixties – is part of the problem instead of the solution.

TOWARDS AN ECOLOGY OF THE SELF
But can there be an 'ecology' of the self? The term certainly
sounds virtuous. It would make a good slogan, neat and
appealing enough to deflect critical inquiry. Once we take a
closer look, however, the fit is not so neat. In fact, we have
to ask whether there is a fundamental contradiction between
the *logos* of the self and ecological fitness.

Subjectivity, or inwardness, appears to be a property –
potential, at any rate – of living matter. We know it more
commonly by the name of consciousness. Its presence seems
to depend on life becoming complex to the point where
nervous tissue appears. We should be open to the possibility
that all life possesses some degree of consciousness, as is
suggested, for example, by studies of plants. Indeed, given
a process view of physical reality, such as was developed by
Whitehead (1960), we should even be open to the presence
of some kind of rudimentary consciousness in all matter.

However, consciousness necessarily depends also on an
organism's activity in the world, which is to say its ecological
interrelatedness. In this respect, all beings are differentiated
from each other through their ecological activity; and their
consciousness is the mark of their differentiation. One
cannot become conscious of a thing if one is identical to that
thing. Some separateness must occur, some distancing, if
consciousness is to take place – and this requires a being's
activity in the world, and its alteration of other beings as a
result of that activity. Because being is not passive but gained
through an organism's activity, consciousness is of what
one is not. Consciousness registers the alteration made in
reality as a result of the activity through which being has
been asserted. This is consistent with the Hegelian insight
that consciousness arises through negating other beings.
Consciousness is of lack; it registers non-being within being.

Differentiation is therefore not simply a property of
humanity, but characterizes all life. What does it mean,
then, for a being to become human? Only this: that we are
self-conscious and not simply conscious – and that for this
to be, a twofold motion of *hyper*-differentiation is required.
This double transformation consists of the emergence of a
particular gradation within subjectivity, the *self*, and in the
same moment, indeed, as the condition for the emergence
of the self, the *projection* of the self into the world and the
alteration of the world to form *objects*. This latter process we
recognize as Marx's labour process; but we now see (as Marx
suggested but never pursued) that the object is subjectified
from the moment of its creation. The world is not simply
altered to make way for an organism; it is not simply negated,
in other words. It is transformed as well to contain the being
– now the self – of its human inhabitant. Indeed, this self-
transformed-world is nothing other than 'nature' itself. For
infra-human beings, nature as such does not exist: they are
already in nature. For us, nature exists because we have lost
it. But it never exists 'out there', a passively contemplated
object: for us, outside of nature, nature is constructed; it is,
and must always be, *Other*. And it follows that nature-as-
Other is also inside, as 'human nature'. I do not here mean
that the Otherness of nature has to be absolute, as it has
been constructed by the modern West. In other words,
nature can be differentiated as well as split, an ideal that
corresponds to the practice of numerous primitive groups.
However, even in this ideal case, nature remains Other, as

well as constructed. Thus, it makes sense to talk of an
unalienated relation to nature, and to insist that people can
achieve this, or at least approximate to it very closely.
However, lack of alienation means lack of estrangement,
and not identity. Nature can be Other, therefore, and still
be *recognized*, the way we can love another human being,
recognize one's self in him/her, and yet not collapse our
beings together (as would happen, for example, in the case
of psychosis).

In any case, as soon as humans became such, they insisted
upon defining themselves as distinct from nature, even
as they recognized themselves in nature. Consider, for
example, burial rites, the signs of which tell archaeologists
that human groups have appeared. To bury its dead with a
certain degree of ritual tells us that a creature refuses
to accept the factualness of death, with its ultimate de-
differentiation. Only a 'self', a subjectivity with inwardness
and self-consciousness, would bother to rearrange and
adorn a corpse of its own kind. So it is with the rest of
primitive society. The gulf between palaeolithic peoples –
or any aboriginal group – and modern, Cartesian, atomized
'Man' is enormous. Yet it is not even on the same scale as
that between any of these groups and any other living
creature, so far as the relation to nature goes.

The same relationship can be drawn from the other end.
The self does not arise prior to the transformation of the
world, but in the transformation of the world. As the object
is made, so is the human subject. As the object is subjectified,
so is the subject objectified. The self only comes into being
as its being is projected into the world. But this can only
mean that human being is divided from the very inception
of human subjectivity. We are not merely conscious, but
self-conscious. A reflection has entered subjectivity and,
with it, the world is transformed in human terms.

We know this from common introspection. For the self,
the most quintessentially human of developments in the
universe, is never (except, perhaps, as the end-point of
extreme mystical practice) homogeneous. Consciousness,
the indication of a being's differentiation, is itself differentiated (this is the hyper-differentiation referred to above)
into a centre, the 'I', and a periphery containing the object
world. Both the I-centre and the object-periphery are capable
of crucially different variations according to social
conditions. But they do not collapse into one another. Setting

aside the possibility of mystical experience, to which we
will return briefly below, the 'I' remains distinct from its
representations even though it has created them and
invested them with its own being. This reflects the fact that
for human being to come into existence, the self projects
itself into objects as it is created. And these objects, however
subjectified, belong to the material universe; they are phys-
ically other than the self's body. The boundaries of the self
always exceed the material limits of its substratum. This is
so whether we are talking of the elementary social relation
to other body-selves, or of the projection of the self into the
natural universe as such. We may express this situation
phenomenologically by saying that within the self the object-
periphery contains a degree (depending on many
conditions, including, foremost, social arrangements) of
Otherness. Nature, as we have noted, is the universal Other
– and God may be described as the absolute Other. But there
are many particular Others as well, depending upon history.
We cannot of course take them up here, but it is remarkable
to what extent history itself is a record of Otherness.

Because the self contains the topology of the I and the
Other, any facile identification between the human and
natural worlds is cast into a deep shade. The very notion
of self means, irrespective of any pathological distortions
forced upon it by capitalism, patriarchy or historical condition whatever, a degree of radical separateness from
the universe. 'Self' entails an internally coherent point of
distinction: an 'I' that posits itself outside the flux of
universal being. Whether the self exists 'in-itself' or 'for-
itself', it is still itself, standing apart from the universe, non-
identical to any other being. There is, in other words, a
certain primary alienation to human being, an aloneness
outside the living web of interconnectedness which forms
the ground of ecology.

I am not lamenting this fact, though it surely underlies
the tragic qualities of human existence – and this is at least
as true for primitives, who have a sense of tragic and
existential givens that is highly developed, as it is for us (see
Diamond, 1974a). There is no point at all in lamenting the
fact, since the 'I' who may bother to lament is a being who
owes the capacity to lament to his/her being human. And
we may just as well be proud as ashamed of this humanness
(though there is no point in this, either), since everything
we value is a product of our aloneness, or to be more exact,

of our efforts to overcome it. The making of objects in the world – to return to Marx's notion of labour – is never reducible to utilitarian principles. When labour is not alienated – consider the play of a healthy child, or aesthetic production – it is responsive to the need of overcoming the self's aloneness. And because no objective transformation can overcome an ontological condition, labour has continually to rework the object-world – this being another way of saying that we are a creative species. Language itself is a product of the self's hyper-differentiation, for if consciousness were undivided there would be no need to exceed the level of the sign. And if the Other could be named, there would be no poetry. Finally, without the self's ontological isolation, desire would never arise. Human sexuality would be reduced to procreation, and love, as maddening as it may be, would not exist.

Obviously, we cannot pursue these matters here. But perhaps it can be seen how ill they fit into ecological garments. For each human quality, whether valued like language or cursed like domination, occurs because of a refusal to accept the given – a stepping out of line, we might say. If we were not skewed from the universe, nothing we deem desirable, indeed, the very existence of desire and value itself, would ever come to be. Taken all in all, it seems that the primary ecological relation of the self is that of negation. This does not mean that the self does not also incorporate nature. It does, for the simple reason that we are flesh. But it *defines itself*, that is, comes into being as a self, through an act of refusal; and nature becomes that which is refused, even as it is reincorporated. How else are we to understand – to take but one, albeit very important, fact – the necessity for preparing, that is, transforming, food, and eating it in a certain 'anti-natural' way? All the 'natural living' in the world will not eradicate this essential human tendency.

Because of this basic negativity, the relationship between the self and nature cannot be comprehended through any simple extrapolation of an ecological model grounded in unity-in-diversity. We are too cantankerous a creature for that. It must be stressed, however, that this by no means dooms social ecology to irrelevance: the fundamental, life-threatening imbalance with nature remains in any case, and defines the ecological project. Put another way, being skewed from the universe is one thing, but being berserk is

another, and it is the job of social ecology to deal with the
distinction. If the relation of the self to ecology is negative,
then the term, 'social ecology', comprises a dialectical practice defined by the play of opposites and a certain irreducible
existential tension. For this very reason, freedom becomes
its primary category. And so we have to define the self and
its relation to nature in such a way that the category of
freedom can be developed.

EGO AND SPIRIT

We have seen that the general notion of human being is
expressed in the form of the self. But it is not yet clear as to
how the critical qualities of splitting and differentiation can
be deployed within varying configurations of selfhood. A
moment's reflection tells us, however, that the answer to
this problem should be close at hand. As theoretical and
abstruse as some of the issues may be, their ultimate point
of reference is in lived human life, and must be expressible
in ordinary language. Or rather, at least one pole, that of
differentiation, should be expressible in ordinary language.
The other pole, that of splitting, requires an expression
standing apart from everyday life, for the obvious reason
that its point of reference is in the élite rather than the
masses. And for this purpose we have a handy term, recently
appropriated by psychoanalysis, but of an ancient lineage
and in the public domain: the 'ego'.

As the Greek term for 'I', Ego refers to self-experience;
and as the Freudian term for the effectual, reality-orientated
portion of the 'mental apparatus', Ego becomes a good way
of describing the self-experience of domination, and the
mental organ of splitting. Of course, this is not how the
Freudians and the mental-health establishment regard the
term. For them, Ego has a value-free connotation as a
coherent ensemble of functional mental relationships. It is
what gets us to work on time, represses the unrealistic and
threatening mental contents of the 'id', and in general
handles what the eminent ego psychologist Heinz Hartmann (1964) termed (in a deliberate appropriation of
biological discourse) the 'adaptation to reality'. In the most
widely adopted psychoanalytic perspective, Ego is reified
into an organ of the psyche, as though it were a mental
mapping of the central nervous system which is presumed
to be its 'seat'. In the harmonious domain of the ego, the self

is considered one of the ego's subfunctions – along with reality-testing, motility, repression and so forth.

This is not the place to take up the poverty of psychoanalytic theory. But a glance at what has been said so far will tell us that once the notion of the ego has been stripped of its scientistic gloss, it emerges as a pretty fair specimen of what we mean by the form of self-experience called splitting. And we can also see why this should be identified with domination. If we regard Ego not as an organ in the natural world but a lived form of historical experience (that is, if we reverse the reification of psychoanalysis and place Ego within Self instead of the other way around), we see that egoic being is self-experience in which the rationalistic, all-knowing 'I' crowds out every other self-phenomenon. In the egoic topology of the self, ontological space is occluded by the I-centre. There is no recognition therefore of Self in Other, and the sharpest of boundaries is drawn between Ego and Id. Three interconnected kinds of practical consequence, each of great importance, result:

– The object-world is regarded as immediately without value, and is treated in a dehumanized way. If the egoic self is white (which turns out historically to have been the case), it regards any non-white human being as less than human, that is, in a racist way; if the egoic self is male (which turns out historically to have been the case), it regards any female being as less than human, that is, in a sexist way; if the egoic self is bourgeois (which turns out historically to have been the case), it regards any proletarian as less than human, that is, freely engages in capitalist relations. Generally speaking, the egoic position is one that regards all of nature as without value: as inert matter, 'stuff', raw materials. The ego is therefore the commodifier as such, the pure culturer of exchange-value, the technocrat.

– The ego inhabits a purified zone of rationalization. This is masculine, and the forms of Otherness created in the egoic mode are also configured by maleness. In fact, the egoic mode is that species of self-experience whose dynamic of desire is, precisely, the Oedipus complex. The Freudian hypostatization of the Oedipus complex to the status of a universal demands that the ego be hypostatized too; each concept demands the other. Together, Ego and Oedipus define the subjective relations of domination.

– Because of the radical distinction betwen the ego and its Oedipal desire, a heightened sense of Otherness ensues, continually repelled by bourgeois rationalization, and just as continually returning. Egoic experience gravitates towards paranoia, and does so precisely because of the splitting and domination conjugated into it. The psychoanalytic division between Ego and Id is puffed up technocratically into a paradigm of rational function. The concrete effects, however, are the repression of the body and the inevitable return of the repressed. Ecologically, nature turns into wilderness which must be 'tamed', that is, paved, converted into Disneyworlds or simple raw materials. Thus the splitting of the subject results in the de-differentiation of the Object. From another angle, the sacred is lost, madness appears as radical alienation, and the stage is set for the spectacular persecutions which have graced the twentieth century, age of the Holocaust, anti-Communist crusades and nuclear terror.

Egoic experience reflects one pole of the possibilities afforded to the self – that of non-recognition and splitting with nature. This is manifest subjectively as the split between Ego and Id; organismically as the (Cartesian) split between the all-active, knowing, dematerialized Mind and the brutally material body; and historically in the domination of nature. Ego is thus the specific antagonist of any emancipatory project. It is what an ecologically sensitive practice must overcome.

But what possibilities for the self exist on the other side? What is the emancipatory potential within self-experience? Here, in contrast to the notion of the ego, we must break with established 'psy' discourse[1] and find our bearings in primitive and elemental existential givens. The reason is self-evident: psy discourse, being technocratic, is established to exclude emancipatory possibilities. By its own 'nature', it is the work of the ego, and serves to contain the self within egoic bounds, as we have seen in the case of psychoanalysis. Thus the term, 'self-actualization', which expresses one way psy discourse tries to encompass emancipation, immediately reveals its egoic limitation. The self, actualized, remains Self: more supple and tuned-up, perhaps, but still within itself, still bound away from its own projections in the universe (what Blake would have called its emanations).

On the other hand, we find an immediate recognition of

what we are trying to say in the oldest, commonest and least scientific of terms concerning human existence. For what is the clumsy expression, 'differentiated self-experience', if not another term for the *spirit*? And what is such a kind of Self, if not the *soul*? And is it not a sign of our estrangement and our splitting to have so much difficulty in recognizing these terms, and integrating them into theory and practice? Perhaps this is, in part, because we mistake them so. Spirit and soul are usually regarded as immaterial, belonging to sublime and transcendent realms and not of the mundane world. This reading, however, is itself confined within the domain of the Cartesian ego, where consciousness and matter are severed from each other. From the perspective of a being trapped within himself, the world is devoid of being. Any access of vital force refluxes back into the self, pushing it 'higher', into the spirit realm, where it can then be rejected by the ego as irrational, infantile, syncretic and savage.

In reality, however, we talk of Spirit in order to represent the closest attainment possible, within the confines of the human situation, to an unmediated relation with nature. Spirit occupies the differentiated pole of self-experience: the self recognizing itself in nature, Ego in Id, male in female (and vice versa), psyche in soma.[2] Spirit is directly sensuous; the word itself comes from a direct drawing in of the breath, and the relation to breathing is preserved in all true senses of the term. Although mystical practice pertains to the spirit, Spirit is not in itself mysterious or obscure; it only becomes obscure through the agency of the ego. Rather is Spirit a state of direct, vivid experience, felt throughout the widest reaches of being. Indeed, because of the ontological tension between the self and nature, Spirit can take the form of a violent eruption with respect to the pre-existent state of being. More, this involves an overcoming of the mind–body split. In a recent important contribution (which explores the ramification of the theme through Merleau-Ponty, Heidegger, Kierkegaard, Buddhism and pre-Socratic Greek thought, among others) David Levin (1984) notes that a great variety of world traditions respect the identity epitomized in the Greek word *psyche*, which can interchangeably mean 'breath', 'soul', 'Spirit' and 'Self'. We could add to this the insights of Reich into the centrality of respiration, as well as those of virtually any 'holistic' – that is, differentiated – medical tradition. Indeed, wherever the ego is undone or deconstructed, or wherever we can point to a mode of being

prior to the egoic, the unity of Spirit and breath is disclosed.
This may be mediated by changing oxygen tension in the
brain stem; but the phenomenon cannot be reduced to
physiology. Spirit is, in the first place, the point at which
consciousness and nature come together. Or, since Spirit
should not be described in dimensional terms, we could say
it is the occasion of experiencing the self as united with the
natural world.

But Spirit is much more than this. 'To inspire' means to
draw in the breath, but also, and more frequently (in the
words of the *American Heritage Dictionary*), 'to animate the
mind or emotions of; to stimulate to an indicated feeling or
action; to elicit or create; and to affect, guide, arouse or
communicate with by divine influence'. In sum, Spirit
represents the subjective condition for actions of great
magnitude to be done; and the problem of Spirit is also the
problem of radical will.

It is amazing how little exploration has taken place of this
dimension, which one would think decisive for the future
of any social transformation. Made invisible by dematerializ-
ation, or reduced to some vicissitude of Oedipal libido by
psychoanalysis, the notion of Spirit as animating force
survives only as a colloquialism. And yet the 'spirit', or lack
thereof, of historical agents is rightly invoked as a decisive
determinant wherever politics takes place. It is obvious that
material circumstances can only lead to social transformation
if they are either translated into or combined with spiritual
arousal. But it is far from obvious just what the connection
is between these phenomena, nor can this be grasped until
Spirit is understood as a real material force of its own.
Indeed, given the redifferentiation with nature implied in
the relations of Spirit, we must insist that Spirit be regarded
as a material category, no less than that matter be regarded
as itself infused with a degree of Spirit.

These concepts are historically decisive, and frame what
can be called (at the risk of standing against the tradition
which bears this name) a historical materialism of the spirit.

What happens when a hitherto torpid and oppressed
mass of people takes control of its destiny? Under what
conditions does a people become – and stay – 'inspired'; and
how does this state of being lift them out of their old selves
and give them what appears to be superhuman strength,
courage and intelligence? How do we understand the fact
that capitalist production in the immediate wake of the

industrial revolution was compatible with a militant, often 'inspired' proletariat – while today's work-force has all but disappeared as a conscious political agent? What is the role of liberation theology in contemporary politics? And how can ecological politics mobilize the spirit?

As what? As the living, indwelling force of emancipation. If the ego encompasses domination and Oedipal desire, the spirit contains within its own relations a desire turned against the ego and towards emancipation. The prevailing psy rationalization places Self within Ego and relegates Spirit to the id, or non-rational, zone of the psyche. Under these conditions, emancipation can have no rationality. But if Spirit is a form of being – as people have always regarded it to be – then it is the negative of the ego, and the emancipatory negative of the ego's domination. It places emancipation within the possible relations of being.

This was the insight of Gandhi, of Jesus, of the *Tao te ching* (Clark, 1983). It may be the oldest insight in the world, and it is, I would submit, the basis in 'natural law' for the ontological legitimacy of revolution.

And it is not that simple. Or rather, 'natural law' and the insights of prophets are one thing, the 'fallen' human condition, another. Spirit is the possible, perhaps the necessary ontological ground of emancipation, but it is not yet emancipation, or even something good in and of itself. In the actual world of human beings, the psyche has become so deformed by domination as to be capable of negating the spirit and turning it to evil. Domination, sedimented inward, turns our original nature to 'second nature'. The ego is a reaction to this cauldron of repressed desire, and turns a polite and reasonable face to the world. Whatever overcomes the ego and moves towards Spirit also removes the inhibitions placed by egoic repression upon the destructiveness of second nature. Spirit can become commingled, therefore, with desire of a highly malignant kind. It can animate, in short, what is worst within human beings no less than what is best. No appreciation of Spirit should forget, for example, that Fascism has an undoubted spiritual appeal, that Hitler valorized the mystical union of the Germanic peoples, through their 'blood', with nature, that Ronald Reagan appeals quite successfully to the 'American spirit' (the spirit of small-town life but also of Rambo), that hundreds of thousands of sophisticated people have thrown themselves after the spiritual guru, Bhagwan Shree Rajneesh, and that

the great mass of religious experience has tended, in the real
world of Church and State, to impose an ethos of suffering,
blighting of intelligence, and passive submission to
domination.

In the historical world nature turns inwardly into 'second
nature' because of the radical separateness which makes us
human. Nature is always Other, always shadowed by loss.
Our subjectivity contains the representation of nature, not
nature itself; and this very representation is shaped by a
desire which always remains ambivalent. Spiritual being –
the 'highest' we can attain – activates that desire in all its
love and hate, its humility and grandiosity. Hence the tragic
nature of the human condition, which an ontology must
represent if it is not to become banal, a fairy-tale of instant
reunification. The great mystics may have been able to
approximate unification with nature – but not without
passage through 'the dark night of the soul', and not, it must
be added, without an eventual return to the mundane,
fallen world, which is rejoined in all its concreteness and
unfreedom.

It follows that the mark of a genuine spiritual quest (which
need not, it seems to me, be along mystical lines) – as against
the perverted specimens alluded to above – is, to use the
phrase of liberation theology, an option for the poor and
oppressed. If Spirit is to be freed from second nature, then
the domination embedded in second nature needs to be
overcome. And this cannot be begun except through
concrete practice. Indeed, one of the few certainties of the
human predicament is that personal fulfilment cannot take
place without general emancipation. This may mean that it
cannot take place at all, which would be another tragic fact
about our species. Such is idle speculation, however. As a
practical matter, what we mean is that for a spiritual practice
to be authentic, it must be on the side of emancipation, and
actively so. The tragic character of human experience means
at bottom that we are thrown into being and given the
chance to be free. And since no one can be free until
everyone is free, the realization of our 'nature', and the
redifferentiation with nature implied in the relation of Spirit,
draws us back once again to society and its transformation.

NOTES
1. Psy discourse refers to the language of the technologies of mind
and behaviour, that is, the mental-health industries and the whole

massive apparatus established to fit subjectivity into late capitalist
society. The term was coined by Robert and Françoise Castel
and Anne Lovell in their excellent book, *The Psychiatric Society*
(1982).

2. We should observe, although we cannot take up, the marked
ambivalence of psychoanalysis here. However its theory and
ideology may tend to enshrine the ego, the original impulse of
psychoanalysis as a praxis remains the dismantling of the ego,
its redifferentiation with Id. Of course, given the association of
the ego with domination, this ambivalence is entirely
understandable.

16 MARX, FREUD AND THE PROBLEM OF MATERIALISM

THERE ARE a number of senses in which the term materialism can be used:

1. What might be called *classical materialism* is a position of great antiquity and prestige in the West, its influence growing according to the successes of modern science. Classical materialism itself has two aspects:

– a doctrine about the nature of reality, in which it is claimed that in its essential properties, the world is made up of matter alone, that is, entities defined by physical properties – fundamentally, extension and duration;

– an epistemology in which the secondary qualities of mind, consciousness, will, intention and desire, are accounted for in¯purely materialistic terms. In the modern world, this project has largely befallen certain schools of psychology, for example, behaviourism. Its relation to psychoanalysis will be discussed below.

2. A commonly held value-position, according to which those things in life are desired which money can buy. This view is as disparaged as it is popular; hence its association with classical materialism is often hotly denied. However, it may be argued that a world-view which relegates all spiritual entities to a second-class existence has enabled crass materialism to flourish, even if it has not directly encouraged it.

3. Marx's historical, or dialectical materialism, which may be itself directly opposed to the crass sense of the term and attempts a revolutionary transformation of classical materialism. Before we proceed, a word or two about definition. Marx himself eschewed labels and never called himself either a historical or dialectical materialist. He was, however, a profoundly dialectical thinker who engaged the

problem of materialism and made history into a central category. Hence the term has heuristic value in discussing the Marxist tradition. Within the present scope, I cannot go into many aspects of Marxian materialism, such as its evolution from the doctrines of Hegel and Feuerbach, or the subsequent variations of Engels, Lenin, the Soviet tradition and the whole range of Marxisms that go under the rubric of 'Western'. My aim is more modest and perhaps more problematic as well. It is to draw together the Marxist positions on materialism into a form representative of the tradition, which also shows the limits of Marx's approach and allows it to be usefully compared with that of Sigmund Freud. In doing this, I shall simply designate the whole tradition as 'historical materialism', and so set aside the interesting distinction between historical and dialectical materialism, the latter term of which has variously been used (a) synonymously with historical materialism, or (b) to designate the extension of historical materialism into the realm of nature, or (c) to designate the Soviet tradition as such. I am using the single term of historical materialism in order to confront more directly the central problem contained within it, namely, the relation between history and nature. It should be added that to do fuller justice to the topic would require an excursion into the question of the 'dialectics of nature'. This, however, exceeds my present scope.

Marx's historical materialism is at the same time an affirmation of classical materialism and a radical break with it. Marx participates in the Western tradition of materialism by consistently indicating the obdurate external nature which enters into every human act. Further, he insists upon the immediate production of the material means of life as the determining nexus of human existence – a process that requires acting upon and transforming nature. Labour, which as we shall see is Marx's central category, is fundamentally the metabolism between humanity and nature. In every instance it includes something of the real material world which is to be transformed; while the transforming agent, 'man', is also part of nature. And so 'man' is the self-transformation of nature. As nature is that which exists outside our perception and has an objective lawfulness irrespective of our subjectivity,[1] it is clear that historical materialism belongs to the tradition of classical materialism. Without this root, the Marxist critique of bourgeois ideology

as 'idealist' would have no launching point. It is by calling
attention to the missing material term that Marx exposes the
apparently self-subsisting framework of ideas by means
of which the class-bound domination by one portion of
humanity – males, whites, the bourgeoisie – is sustained
over others.

However one cannot take an examination of Marx's
materialism very far without recognizing its radical distinction from the classical tradition. This is claimed in the
first thesis on Feuerbach: the primary datum of Marx's
materialism is not matter as such, but 'sensuous human
activity'.[2] And although labour engages nature in all its
manifestations, it is not simply the transformation of nature,
but the *self*-transformation, that is, nature transformed
subjectively. Consciousness does not only arise from the
labour-process ('the being of men determines their
consciousness'); more profoundly, consciousness is *constitutive* of the labour process. The famous passage in *Capital*
about the architect and the bee is only the most colourful
example of this theme. From the beginning of his so-called
philosophical period to the end of his life, Marx embeds
consciousness in all propositions about the world. A nature
that is 'out there' is for Marx an empty abstraction; reality is
human reality, and matter therefore is humanized matter,
matter grasped consciously.

Thus Marx is a classical materialist because he asserts that
consciousness arises outside itself, that is, from nature;
but he is a historical materialist because he asserts that
consciousness is essential to the labour process, and that
labour creates nature as an object for humanity. Without
labour, nature becomes a meaningless aggregation of
'things', entities that exist wholly within themselves and
are therefore wholly indeterminate. With labour, nature
becomes a determinate set of objects: entities-for-us. And as
the object is created through labour, so is the subject, as a
determinate ensemble of consciousness. This interpretation
of matter and consciousness in Marx's work comprises the
great post-Cartesian break in Western thought. More than
any other, it defines the modern project.

The critical notion of historical materialism is labour,
which for Marx becomes a transhistorical category. By
'transhistorical', here, I am referring to that which is always
present in every human, or historical situation. The idea of
the transhistorical is itself shaped by Marxism, for it refers

to those entities which might go under the heading of 'human nature' under classical discourse. To say that something is transhistorical means that it has the quality of nature in so far as it is always there in every human instance. However, to say something is transhistorical within the framework of historical materialism does no more than assert its brute existence; the definition and quality of the thing – that is, its emergence as a truly human object – has to be given concretely within history. Thus the notion of human nature is an empty and meaningless abstraction outside of its historical specification. Because history defines what is human, labour, as the history-making process, is quintessentially transhistorical. It follows that the concrete reality of labour exists only according to its actual historical elaboration. The historical reality of labour is a function of the form of domination with which it articulates, the degree of domination at a given time being manifest as alienation of the labour in question. Alienation means estrangement, and implies the existence of a condition from which one is alienated. This for Marx would be the exercise of full human capacity as it has evolved for a given stage of historical development. The kind of labour in this state would be known as *praxis*. It would be inconsistent for Marx to postulate praxis as an absolute form of pure labour standing outside history. However, this need not be done, since praxis can be defined concretely as those forms of labour which emerge once domination is removed. In other words, praxis is labour freely and self-determinatively done.

The realization of the role played by domination – whether of class, gender, race or age – enables us to lift a terminological burden from the category of labour. We are used to thinking of labour as toil, or compulsory work. But this is specifically the form taken by labour under the conditions of capitalist development, as the nature-transformation which generates commodities. Obviously, capitalism did not invent labour in the form of painful toil. That honour goes to earlier forms of domination. But it has pioneered in a conception of work as radically differentiated – or split – from play, or pleasurable, spontaneous activity (for example, Diamond, 1974a, pp. 138ff, esp. p. 142). The distinction is not the degree of pain, or effort involved, but the fact that one activity generates exchange-value and the other doesn't. The absolute hold of exchange-value over capitalist culture has excluded any non-economic sense of the term labour.

Thus we must add that, in this split, the work-term steadily
overpowers the play-term. Take, for example, the realm of
sport. Not only do professional sports become ever more
corporatized; but so-called amateur sports become ever more
professionalized; while the spontaneous and the playful
exercise of muscular faculties becomes increasingly subjug-
ated to work discipline. Yet, however bourgeois thought
may distort it, the category of labour includes both work and
play. For labour is whatever purposively and consciously
transforms the object-world (that is, the form according to
which nature is presented to us). And this condition is as
much met by a child putting one block on top of another as
it is by extracting coal from a mine. Indeed we are obliged
to go further: the category of labour extends to speech-acts
as well as to work and play, as speech clearly involves the
purposive displacement of elements: molecules of air, the
vocal cords, even the physiology of the brain during the act
of speaking. More, speech creates new material entities as
well as new configurations of subjectivity. Having recognized this, we can go on to include thought itself within
the Marxist category of labour – both because it is the
internalization of trial actions, as virtually every school of
psychology has held; and because it necessarily involves
material transformation of the brain. Even dreaming may be
seen as a species of labour once we relinquish the workhouse
logic which refuses to recognize purposiveness in anything
but the generation of wealth.

What distinguishes different kinds of labour are the
radically distinct social purposes to which they are put and
by which they are valued. This is the most immediately
evident signature of any historical formation. No doubt, all
societies greatly value those forms of labour which transform
nature so as to provide the immediate material necessities
of life – food, shelter and clothing. But such labour, no more
than any other, cannot be reduced to its merely material
elements. The full range of consciousness is implicated in
all production, and all forms of labour are related one to the
other, even if the relation be only a negative one, as in the
scission between work and play under capitalism. Thus in
capitalist production labour is rendered *abstract*, through
a devaluation of sensuousness. It is the 'materialism' of
coldness; hence, the burgeoning of crass materialism in
capitalist society. By contrast, in functioning primitive
societies – as well as, to a lesser extent, their pre-capitalist

remnants – play, fantasy and the dream figure very prominently in all aspects of social production.

We may summarize the historically materialist view of the labour process in the following rough schema:

$$[S_1, O_1]^{t_1} \rightarrow [S_2, O_2]^{t_2}$$

where S and O are configurations of subject (consciousness) and object (matter) existing before (t_1) and after (t_2) the transformation effected by labour. Note that the labour process is inherently temporalizing. The notion it generates from t_1 to t_2 is the human time-scale of history. Note, too, that both subject and object are present in each of its moments.

Since human beings are part of nature, so also is their labour. And since labour contains consciousness at every point, so therefore must it be held that nature contains consciousness, that is, that consciousness or subjectivity is immanently part of nature. Labour, then, may be said to be the means by which nature brings forth the consciousness that is immanent in it. Labour is nature made conscious, which consciousness is then reflected back further to transform nature and bring about yet more consciousness. We can do no more here than suggest the outlines of this dialectic, which undoubtedly involves the historical emergence of language and is in any case still largely obscure. We should also distinguish between consciousness that emerges under unalienated conditions of praxis and that stemming from the alienated labour of domination.

This distinction is highly important. For if it were labour in general, and not praxis, that caused consciousness to evolve, we would be forced to conclude that the mere passage of historical time would bring about every higher degree of consciousness. This subscription to the myth of historical progress was done most famously by Hegel, and has been repeated endlessly since by those who confuse the self-evident historical increase in our technical mastery over nature – that is, the development of the object-term in labour – with that of consciousness, which has by no means shown a corresponding development over historical time. It is for this reason that a comma alone links the subject and object terms in the formula for labour – a comma showing association but no intrinsic or necessary connection.

At this point we reach an impasse within the terms of the Marxist tradition. We have seen that Marx introduces the

subject into materialism, and by so doing breaks with the
classical philosophical tradition, and with the materialistic
value position as well – for a subjectified materialism is
necessarily a moral doctrine. Human nature cannot be
realized until its subjectivity is realized in history, which is
to say, until humankind becomes free. Yet we may see by
studying Marx closely that this very same subjective term,
which represents the most original and fundamental dimension of his philosophy, is both sketchily and imperfectly
drawn. Marx, and the Marxist tradition as a whole, are
poorer in conceptions of consciousness and subjectivity than
the logic of historical materialism demands. According to
historical materialism, consciousness is the conceptual equal
of matter. Moreover, it is immanently in nature, from which
it is drawn forth by the labour process. However, we must
also recognize nature as that realm which exists independently of our perceptions, and whose laws are not a function
of our thought but of their own self-subsisting reality. Not
to do so would be to deny all objective knowledge. To square
these two kinds of propositions about the relation between
consciousness and nature requires a subtle and differentiated notion of subjectivity.

I would submit that such a notion is defective, if not
entirely lacking, in Marxism, both through inattention and
a certain core attitude towards subjectivity. This attitude is
characteristic of the Western tradition as a whole, and Marx's
uncritical adoption of it led him to take a two-dimensional
view of subjectivity – and, more basically, made his transcendence of classical materialism imperfect. For Marx saw
consciousness entering into nature; he did not see nature
entering into consciousness. And this was because he stood
in that Western line that assumed a more or less radical split
between the human and natural world. The quality of the
barrier between humanity and nature is suggested by the
following quote from Alfred Schmidt's *The Concept of Nature
in Marx*: 'Marx saw this as yet unmediated part of nature as
only relevant from the point of view of its possible future
modification' (1971, p. 200). Thus nature-in-itself was
merely inert: a mass of 'raw material'. This is consistent
with the image of Marx as the thoroughgoing champion of
humanity, a description that is otherwise justly celebrated
but here shows its more problematic side. According to this
conception, 'man', although part of nature, is also 'the
measure of all things' – and nature is correspondingly

stripped of intrinsic value, becoming only the projection of   313
human imagery and need. From another angle, it may be
said that for Marx the labour process has a unique, or at least
a privileged, degree of transhistoricity. Nature only takes
on full reality by means of historically developed categories
of appropriation. Consciousness transforms nature through
the labour process; but nature does not otherwise transform
consciousness.

Such is the Promethean self-image of Marxism. As we
know, Marx himself was fond of this image, which is indeed
of an appealing grandeur. But we should also recall that
Prometheus paid dearly for his hubris. In the image of the
eagle pecking away at his liver for all eternity we have a
representation of the revenge of nature that the Greek legend
was wise enough to include, but of which contemporary
Marxism seems nearly oblivious.

For there are a number of serious problems with the
Promethean image of a consciousness that is purely active
in its transformation of nature, and is not itself transformed
by nature. At the level of philosophy, it leads to an imperfect
transcendence of the subject–object dualism. By proclaiming
'man' as the self-transformative principle of nature, Marx
undoes the Cartesian split: for Marxism, there can be no
pure, de-naturalized consciousness; there is only practically
formed consciousness arising from historical 'sensuous
activity'. Thus nature is in humankind. As Schmidt puts it:
'Nature became dialectical by producing men as transforming, consciously acting Subjects confronting nature itself
as forces of nature' (1971, p. 58). But the dialectic is attenuated here. Once nature somehow 'produces' men, it
confronts man as an external and inert agglomeration of
things that can only be secondarily reappropriated through
praxis. Thus dualism sneaks back into Marxist discourse; it
has been dismantled in one direction only: through the
transformation effected by consciousness on nature through
the labour process. This produces history – and it is history
alone that alters consciousness. Nature in-itself is inert in
this respect. Only the historical transformations of nature
– 'second nature' – react back on to consciousness and
transform it.

At a more practical level, Marx's crypto-dualism fails to
resolve the problem of gender and sexuality within historical
materialism. If 'sensuous activity' is historical materialism's
starting-point, then it would stand to reason that sexuality

would be one of its leading categories, there being no more
intense location of sensuousness. Yet as we know, although
Marxism in general takes a morally virtuous position where
sexuality is concerned, its actual treatment of the question
is almost wholly reductive and derivative. For Marxism, the
undoubtedly essential connection between sexuality and
class struggle becomes inflated to become the principal if
not the sole determinant of all matters having to do with sex
and gender. In my opinion – although it would take us far
beyond the present scope to develop this point adequately
– the reason for this is no simple intellectual or moral error.
It rather lies deeply embedded in the *historical* nexus of
which Marx is but an exceptionally illustrious representative, namely, that habit of mind (or to be more exact, and
Marxist, that species of alienated mental labour) which splits
'Man' from nature, and sees the former active, the latter,
passive. For reasons I cannot go into here, this position does
not generate the masculinist way of speech ('man', etc.) idly.
It rather creates a realm of discourse in which humanity,
consciousness, activity and maleness become different
facets of the same term. Meanwhile, at the other – and
degraded – pole reside nature, passivity and the female.
And this pole is not merely there: it is fled by the masculinist
position. The vaunted activity of masculinity is compounded
out of fear. Thus Promethean Marxism cannot begin to
resolve the question of sexuality within its own terms;
indeed, it can only perpetuate it.

The final problem with Marxism's one-sided dialectic of
consciousness and nature is one which Marx was in little
position to observe, but which oppresses us daily and in an
ever more frightening spiral. And this has to do with the
historical consequences of an attitude that regards nature as
neither active with respect to consciousness nor as
possessing any end in itself, but merely as the passive and
inert repository of resources for 'man' (again the masculinist
pronoun applies). As with the sexual question, with which
it bears a striking inner homology, this *ecological* question is
denied resolution within the terms of Promethean Marxism.
Again, despite virtuous intentions, there is little actual
resistance within the Marxist tradition to the inexorable logic
of technological development, up – or down – to the level
of the thermonuclear warhead as a means of projecting
violence. Nor, correspondingly, can there be adequate
resistance to the political gigantism, or statism, that ac-

companies the wholesale domination of nature. Again, the root of the problem lies in the alienated mental labour which weakens the subject-term in the concept of labour by denying to nature any power over consciousness. The best that can be hoped for within the traditional perimeter of Marxism is expressed somewhat plaintively by Schmidt, who projects the Marxist goal as one in which the 'encroachments [of man over nature] will be rationalized; so that the remote consequences will remain capable of control. In this way, nature will be robbed step by step of the possibility of revenging itself on men for their victories over it . . .' (p. 152). A feeble hope, whose rationality sees itself as entirely outside, and hence alien to, the entity – nature – it bids to control.

The response to these various dilemmas does not reside in importing a feminist or ecological awareness and tacking it on to Marxism. It is, rather, necessary for awareness of this kind to grow organically out of a Marxism whose dialectic between consciousness and nature is complete instead of one-sided. The answer therefore does not lie in more parks and nature-preserves, or in the more rational husbanding and recycling of resources (all of which would of course be highly welcome), but in a historical materialism as open to the direct mediation of nature into consciousness as it is to the mediation of consciousness into nature. What is needed is a consciousness that can assume a passive as well as an active relation to nature, and not fear annihilation as a result. This requires, among other steps, an opening up of the notion of human nature, and for this project, the insights of Marxism's great contemporary antagonist, Sigmund Freud, provide a powerful guide.

That Freud was consciously hostile to Marxism is a matter of record. Nor should there be any doubt that the psychoanalytic movement as a whole is deeply antipathetic to Marx, and that it has good reason to be so. Between Marxism and psychoanalysis lies a profound ideological gap defined by irreconcilable class and professional interests. At the level of concrete practice there can be no synthesis, since one cannot espouse the value position and dominant identity of one without rejecting the other. To have made the choice, however, does not close the books on the matter. It only opens the possibility for the critical appropriation of one discourse to the other. The fact that psychoanalysis and Marxism are each dialectical exposures along different planes of human reality – and that they are each contingent and partial for all their grandeur – provides the incentive for such an appropriation. The radical opening on to subjectivity offered by historical materialism means that Marx is accessible to such an appropriation, however crudely materialistic much of the Marxist tradition itself may have been. And as for Freud, the fact that he seems to have been almost perversely ignorant of Marxism raises the possibility that he might have been, as Blake said of Milton, 'of the devil's party without knowing it'.

I believe that one should consider Marxism the dominant discourse – not because of any superiority in explanatory power, which is an entirely moot point given the different domains of discourse – but for Marx's greater sense of justice. This means that critical appropriation between Freud and Marx should work towards using each to develop the other within the greater project of developing historical materialism. In other words, Marx should be used to make Freud more historically materialist, and Freud should be used to develop Marxism further towards the same goal.

That Freud was of the materialist camp can scarcely be doubted, even if later generations of psychoanalysts have done much to erase the stain of this association. Throughout his life, Freud never abandoned the goal of locating subjectivity within physical process; and the early Freudo-Marxists, Wilhelm Reich and Otto Fenichel, were quick to recognize (however much they divided paths later on) the logical compatibility between historical materialism and Freud's discourse.[3] The key bridging concept was that of the 'instinctual drive', which Freud located at 'the frontier between the mental and the somatic . . . [the] measure of the demand made upon the mind for work in consequence of its connection with the body' (1915a, p. 122). And since the drive, whether as sexuality or aggression, provides the impetus and motivating force behind consciousness, it can readily be seen how Freud provides a possibility for rounding out the materialist dialectic. For where Marx had shown consciousness acting upon nature, Freud now opened a way to see consciousness in a passive relation to nature, acted upon instead of acting.

It is not hard to imagine why psychoanalysis would try to eliminate Freud's instinct theory. As a materialist, Freud had postulated a cause for behaviour that stood outside of established relations, and so became an affront to the practice of psychotherapy which provided the livelihood and class position of analysts. Freud's views were rightly considered subversive; by denying the transparency of consciousness he had continued the unseating of 'man' from his throne at the centre of the universe (however much he may have tried to re-establish this at other levels). Although the concept of instinctual drive itself became reified in the practice of later analysts (thereby allowing the neo-Freudian revisionists to look relatively progressive), properly understood, it, too, abolishes Cartesianism. But where Marx had healed the split by showing us nature (and human nature) humanized, Freud asserts the actual materiality of humanity and the continuity between consciousness and physical nature.

The revisions of Freud have generally tended to redress his affront to human dignity by retaining the notion of the unconscious in a weakened form. For neo-Freudians, the unconscious consists purely of 'hidden meanings' – that is, transcriptions of what is manifestly stated, of different content, but of the same, ordinary-language form. Freud, however, was unmistakably clear on this point. The unconscious was not at all structured like ordinary language. It consisted of 'word-presentations' only in its uppermost, pre-conscious reaches; the true unconscious was composed of 'thing-presentations' (1915b). Thus, as one descends into the unconscious world, recognizable social relations fade away and dissolve into primordial elements until they take upon themselves the thing-like form of unmediated nature. How far back this edge of mediation can be pushed is an unanswered and perhaps unanswerable question. We must hold that some remnant of mediation remains if the unconscious is to be at all apprehensible. Human nature, as an object in nature, always shows some mark of second nature. But the essence of Freud's position is not that mediation disappears entirely, but that it occurs further back than the socially transcribed order can reach. Neo-Freudian revisionism attempts, by contrast, to place the edge of mediation forward, so that the unconscious becomes relatively intelligible and modifiable within the terms of psychotherapeutic practice. Freud's more radical position, by contrast, is therapeutically pessimistic; its breakthrough consists not in showing us how technically to adjust our nature, but in giving us a way of regarding the immanence of consciousness in nature. For the *un*conscious is just that: the being-

in-nature of our subjectivity, awaiting its drawing forth by
praxis.

The realm explored by Freud as the empirical ground of his doctrine was that of childhood, the ontogeny of the individual. Once this is brought into focus, the distinctions between Freudian and Marxist discourse can be made more intelligible. Marx simply did not recognize the praxes of childhood, and of intimate, domestic life in general, as having any decisive influence on consciousness. Consciousness simply appears for Marx, without ontogeny, in its adultomorphic form, and then begins acting upon nature in the labour process. Now, whatever the reasons behind Marx's strategy, it must be stated that in this respect it is simply mistaken, albeit it is a characteristic illusion of the West (to be more specific, of males in the West), which regards consciousness as emergent fully grown from the nature which is its source. In reality, subjectivity emerges point-by-point in the course of childhood, according to the labour/praxis (the distinction obtains here as well, as a function of the degree of alienation and domination inherent in infantile relations) of childhood. There are tremendous fluctuations and variations in the process, but no quantum leaps; the growth of subjectivity is as continuous as any other organic process.

There is a decisive turn in the growth of subjectivity which deserves emphasis here. With the appearance of language, roughly in the second year of life, consciousness begins to take on a roughly adultomorphic shape. Now the child becomes able to append word-presentations to experience, and so can begin to objectify subjectivity. The 'me' appears alongside the 'I'; and with this step, the self can become drawn into objective social labour. In pre-language children, by contrast (and here we must continually recall that the protolinguistic, psychically archaic layer remains active throughout life, albeit in continually changing ways), consciousness and subjectivity exist along an entirely different gradient: drawn not into objective social labour but on a vector pointing towards fusion with an organic primordium. We are led logically to assume that a differentiated consciousness originates in the intra-uterine environment, since the nervous system of a seven- or eight-month-old foetus is developed enough to begin responding to stimuli – and the functioning of nervous tissue as a whole must be regarded as a means for gathering and concentrating those events called consciousness.

To be in a passive relation to nature means opening the self towards this primordial continuity and restoring, through an ablation of the ego and its discriminative language, attachment to the organic universe. This can only come about, as Blake recognized, through sensuous enjoyment, hence the privileged role of sexuality, which derives from the fact that it is here nature makes its most direct sensuous claim through the capacities of the nervous system and the sense organs, which are portions of protoplasm modified to respond to the flux of the physical world.

It is not, however, the nervous system which becomes conscious; it is the organism, using its 'naturally' given nervous system for labour, or praxis, to create the self. And since the labour of the infant is upon the other person as object, the self is, as Marx held, the 'ensemble of social relationships' (1844b, p. 402), albeit social relations of infantile as well as adult labour. Before, however, the self is drawn into objective social labour of the kind mediated by language and described by Marx, it engages in an infantile labour whose product, or object, is subjectivity itself. Therefore the actual object of infantile labour is subjectivity: the imaginary realm. At the ontogenetic foundations of the subject, the material thing made in the world (whether the pile of blocks or the nuclear submarine) is only the perceptual underpinning of the object; its real content is the configuration of the Other, elaborated from the person or body of the caretaking individual(s) or of the self.

The mode of relationship between the emergent subject and its Other is desire, the configuration of primary consciousness as it practically develops in the world. Desire provides the matrix along which infantile labour directs itself; and it reflects as well the magnetic pull exercised upon subjectivity by virtue of its origin in nature and its passive relation to nature. Desire is before language, although it uses the fragmentary nature of early language to make itself known. Its object cannot therefore be named. At the same time, it is the province of an uncompleted subject, open to fusion with that which it sees as beyond itself. Desire embraces that which we call love, which is obliged to take into account the real external nature of an object. Desire disregards this entirely. Moreover, it is as closely linked to hatred as it is to love. For when the terms of the primordial

self are not met – and they can never be fully met considering
the formation of the self in the process of separation from
others – then hatred shapes the contours of desire as much
as does love. What determines the balance between love
and hate in desire is specific to each individual – and is a
historical question dependent upon the actual labour or
praxis of the family and childhood.

By placing Freud within the framework of historical
materialism, we remove the iron hand of biological deter-
minism from psychoanalysis while retaining a radical
relation to nature. For desire both defines the pathways of
infantile labour and is created through that labour. The point
of potential mediation may be placed further back than
allowed within the confines of bourgeois psychotherapy,
but this does not mean that praxis is unable to modify or
even partially gratify desire, whether in the infantile or adult
period. Rather does it demand of praxis that it take upon
itself a sufficiently radical form to be adequate to desire. A
historically materialist psychoanalysis requires a revolutionary as against a psychotherapeutic praxis. Between
the facile optimism of neo-Freudianism and the deeply
pessimistic assumption of Freud that nature and civilization
were unalterably opposed, it poses the possibility of a hope
that cannot be put to the test except by transforming reality.

As Marx said in another context: we do not only make our
own history; we make our own nature – but we make neither
as we please. First and second nature alike weigh on the
brains of the living. A psychoanalytic historical materialism
strengthens praxis by allowing it to listen to nature instead
of only opposing itself to nature. Thus praxis becomes more
fully itself. By opening itself to nature, it achieves the fuller
realization of consciousness which is its defining feature.

Strangely enough, such a 'fuller realization of consciousness' can only be conceived as a spiritualization of Marxist
praxis. Once freed of its bourgeois lineaments, Freud's
unconscious becomes that 'it' (that is, 'id') comprised by
nature's indwelling in us. The radically enhanced role of
labour arising from the Marxist perspective can only be
interpreted as allowing that 'it-ness' to rise to its full spiritual
height. This does not mean bypassing the body, sexuality
and desire – any more than it means bypassing the imperative of overcoming historical domination. Both tasks were
prescribed by the two great realists of the modern age,
whose ultimate legacy was to locate the spiritual dimension

of nature in corporeal and historical concreteness, and to set
the practical goals by which freedom could be realized.

NOTES

1. The definition of A. N. Whitehead, scarcely either a Marxist or
a classical materialist. Nature is 'a complex of entities whose
mutual relations are expressible in thought without reference to
mind, that is, without reference either to sense-awareness or to
thought' ('The concept of nature', in Northrop and Gross, 1961,
p. 201). It should be noted that Whitehead goes on to insist that
by this, 'no metaphysical pronouncement is intended'.

2. 'The chief defect of all previous materialism (including
Feuerbach's) is that the object, actuality, sensuousness is
conceived only in the form of the *object or perception*, but not as
sensuous human activity practice, not subjectivity' (Easton and
Guddat, eds, 1967, p. 400).

3. See the *Sex-Pol* essays (Reich, 1972b) and Fenichel (1967); also,
the important study by Jacoby (1983).

17 CRYPTIC NOTES ON REVOLUTION AND THE SPIRIT

Times change

A SPECTRE haunts the left: the spirit. This was not always so. Fifteen years ago, revolution was considered the province of atheists or agnostics, and religion was for and of the establishment. There were exceptions, but there have always been exceptions. The Buddhists who immolated themselves in Saigon, A. J. Muste, Dorothy Day, Thomas Merton in the USA, Niemöller and Bonhoeffer in Germany – these were people of the spirit who bore witness against the state. Yet they had little sustained appeal to the Left in North America and Western Europe. Even Martin Luther King, perhaps the most consequential figure in this series, was considered more a black than a religious phenomenon. Then a change occurred, a fall and rise, and now everything looks different.

The fall. Marx had been relatively tolerant of religion, but Marx did not have to build a Communist society on top of one with many feudal, even theocratic features. Lenin and Stalin did; and in fighting with an implacably hostile Eastern European Church, they created an aura of extreme opposition to religion which was to shadow the radical project so long as it remained yoked to Bolshevism. Thus, the basis of the Left's rejection of religion would last only as long as the legitimacy of Soviet Communism itself. *Sic transit . . .* For a while, Mao picked up the slack. With the demise of the Great Helmsman, the journey of China down the capitalist road, and the sixties generally in full retreat, a chasm appeared on the Left. It is one thing to fight the system, its brutality, rapacity and violence, but in the name of what alternative? It was rediscovered that one has to believe in something if any real change is to be sought. A negative reaction, alone, leads to nihilism or an accommodation with the system. The alternative of social democracy consumes social space and comes to rest, for example, in Mitterandism: a 'socialism' whose god is technocracy and the bomb. To hold up the existing Western form of parliamentary

democracy as a standard of civilization is a favourite stratagem of those who wish to defend us against the perils of
Soviet power. Yet it is doing nothing more, ultimately,
than justifying bourgeois privilege, and no more merits a
transcendent faith than any other feature of the capitalist
world.

The rise. Religion had been seeping back into modern life
for some time. The globalization of capitalism in the post-
war era brought the Catholic Church into the twentieth
century (ratified in the Vatican II Council of 1962–5), and it
brought the East to the West. At the same time, Soviet
Communism, unable to capture the ground of everyday life,
made a deal with the Church, which gave the latter a
new lease and weakened the Left critique of Catholicism.
Meanwhile, the spiritual vacuity of advanced capitalism
provided a broad opening for religious movements in the
West. The catastrophic consequences of modern technology, bringing environmental collapse and the spectre of
omnicide through the nuclear state, widened the possibilities for religious revival. Thus modernity, instead of
dispelling religion, was itself being overtaken by religion.
New sects, mostly drawing on the East or archaic traditions
(witchcraft and so on), began to appear and enlisted many
young people; fundamentalist Christianity surged; and the
traditional Christian churches themselves showed renewed
vigour. Some of the new religious movements have been
frankly right-wing (for example Moon, Falwell); others have
served as quietistic, inward-turning substitutions for
political radicalism. But religion's other-worldliness is
always available as a critique of this world. The post-modern
stream of religious activity was bound, therefore, to include
among its tendencies a leftward flow.

One of the most enduring monuments of the explosive
year of 1968 was the conference of Catholic bishops in
Medellín, Colombia. It was here that an explicitly radical
interpretation of the gospel was formally introduced to the
world. The theology of liberation had arrived. Although
more or less confined to South America, where it was a
response to the breakdown of normal capitalist relations of
dependency and the rise of local Fascism, liberation theology
established the Church as a main conduit through which Left
opposition could take shape. Moreover, the omnipresence of
transnational capital as well as the steering role played by
the US state-security apparatus on the South American

continent brought liberation theology on to an international
plane. In Allende's Chile, and now more tellingly in
Sandinist Nicaragua (where major sectors of the state, for
example, foreign relations and culture, are now headed by
individuals representing religious radicalism), the emancipatory motion of religion has achieved world-historical
significance.

Of comparable importance is the widespread religious
rejection of the nuclear state. Significantly, religion has
been the objective vanguard of the anti-nuclear movement,
leaving Marxism and other radical groups to catch up. This
has to do with the uniquely 'cosmological' nature of the
nuclear threat and the crisis it poses to rationality. Only
those positions which were already in rejection of the
dominant rationalization (including feminism along with
religion) have been in a position to respond with sufficient
decision to the nuclear alarm. By contrast, the traditional
Left has been revealed as stuck to the logic of the system.
Over the bomb, 'backward' religion has been more radical
than 'scientific' socialism.

A HISTORICAL MATERIALISM OF THE SPIRIT?
The re-emergence of an emancipatory potential for religion
is systematic, and can only be sharpened in the future. But
it is only a potential – and for many things, evil as well as
good. Proclaiming a 'new age of spirit' is not necessarily
good news for those who would rid society of injustice,
violence and scarcity. It does little good to say of, for
example, Khomeini, that his is not a 'true' kind of spirituality.
Aside from begging the question of just what true spirituality
is, this fails to appreciate that Khomeini is in fact closer
to the spirit than liberal, technocratic modern capitalism.
Islamic fundamentalism – or right-wing Christian evan-
gelism, or the Moonies – are vicious, repressive assaults on
human beings. But they are also in some way truly spiritual
– unless one wants to deny that spirituality has anything to
do with fervid belief, rejection of this world, and a relative
abandonment of ordinary practical reason.

To the modern secular radical, an acceptance of spirit
means a rejection of the Enlightenment and modernity, the
very traditions from which political radicalism springs. Marx
sounded the theme first: the idea was not to destroy religion;
it was to create a world in which religious questions would
no longer arise, a world brought under full human control;

an enlightened, fully modern world. Marx was not atheistic,
but post-atheistic (Parinetto, 1983–4). To smuggle faith back
into radical politics smacks of regression, of making an
accommodation with obscurantism. There is something
shameful about it. One senses the elders saying, 'I told you
so . . . they all return.'

So much the worse, then; for without faith, radical change
is doomed. It doesn't even exist. How does one get from
here to *there*, if *there* is by definition radically different
from *here*? Here is domination which survives through
reproducing itself. The ruling ideas are the ideas of the
ruling class; one is not supposed even to imagine the
alternative. There is emancipation, which has to be made,
but first envisioned. The object of labour exists in the mind
before it exists in reality. If it can't exist in the mind, then it
can't exist in reality – and that is the way things are set up
to work so far as radical change goes. It has to be unthinkable,
and so impossible – unless there is some vision of the non-
existent, something to leap towards: some faith.

Has there been a revolutionary transformation that wasn't
made by a crazy, visionary affirmation of what was not
there? The bigger the change, the crazier the vision, the
more reckless the faith. Consider the abolition of slavery.
Now we know that slavery went because it had become a
fetter on capitalist production; and it only went, in the USA
at any rate, through a horrid war which was settled in favour
of the materially more powerful side (and where the weaker
South had the greater *élan*). But it also went when the
'material' forces were translated into a practical vision by
faith. Could slavery have been defeated without a John
Brown to ignite the material mass of its contradictions?
Perhaps – but it would have taken someone else doing the
same thing. Or could the Nicaraguan revolution have been
made except by people who believed so strongly that they
were willing to suffer enormously against extraordinary
odds for many years in order to get their goal? Yes, Somoza
had weakened his position fatally by shutting out most
of the bourgeoisie along with everyone else through his
incredible corruption and greed. In this sense the revolution
could never have triumphed were not the way prepared for
it by the material crumbling of the autocracy: the 'objective
conditions' had to be met. But this was only known after the
fact, while the FSLN began its operation in 1962, seventeen
long and harrowing years before the triumph. And the same

was true for Ho, for Mao, for Lenin. No revolution, no matter how ripe the opportunity, can ever be made unless people are animated by faith, unless they are grasped by the spirit. This is exactly what the Left today in the West has been unable to inspire. Apathy, inertia, despair, cynicism – these are the accurate descriptions of the present state of radical possibilities, and not *élan*, zeal, a willingness to sacrifice, or a fervid belief in something beyond the self which can be realized through historical action.

And so one turns to the religious revival for a lesson or two. But this cannot be enough for the radical. At the most, a tactical alliance with one or another progressive religious movement can arise if one cedes to religion the province of faith, and then tags along, hoping to pick up some magic through contagion. The radical – whether Marxist, feminist, anti-nuclear activist, anti-imperialist or ecologist – who takes a passive attitude towards the question of faith and the spirit becomes a parasite of religion, absorbing religion's contradictions and partiality. The record of religious misery, the Fascist accommodation of which every denomination has shown itself capable, the stunting of spirit imposed by every institutional arrangement – all this reminds us to appreciate religion, and not deify it. To *appropriate* faith and not just tag along, radicalism cannot surrender its legacy of critical rationality. It must still emancipate religion. But sociological critique of the Church is not enough for this. We must develop rather a historical materialism of the spirit, no less than spiritual insight into historical materialism.

THE METAHISTORICAL

Spirituality is the opening towards the spirit, faith, the grasping towards it. Spirituality is consciousness of an Other, beyond the edge of the self and the given. This Other is the spirit – a presence *within* the world. The spiritual attitude oscillates back and forth, now locating spirit beyond the given world (that is, transcendently), now recognizing spirit in objects at hand (that is, immanently). In truth spirit is neither and both: in and out of what is given to us at the same time. The problem for spirituality is to comprehend this difficult truth without going mad or yielding to domination.

Since the given includes language, spirit resists language and one properly feels foolish writing about it. Outside the ordinary boundaries of experience, spirit may become located either deeper within the self and/or projected

outward on to the objects of nature, eventually the universe.
One prefers the 'and', but the logic of writing – one word at
a time – forces the 'or' upon the page. The spirit is a special
kind of self-experience . . . and/or the spirit is a universal
principle, a deity whether dwelling beyond or in phenom-
enal nature. One meditates and reveals the spirit-self; and
one prays, and addresses the deity.

Mystical experience is self-reflection on the spirit; it is to
make the spirit densely present, the spirit-self as deity: God
is within you; you are God; for the Buddhist it is the insight
that all beings are already Buddhas, except they don't know
it. The more theistic a religion, the more a discrete deity
occupies spiritual space and the less inclined to mysticism.
Or, the spirit may be directly deployed into historical action,
whether by mystics, ordinary religious people or non-
religious people who just happen to 'have' the spirit without
dressing it up in religious clothes. After all, if the spirit resists
language, it can resist religion, which is a particular form
taken by language. Religion is an attempt to make the spirit
intelligible, and to live it according to a shared tradition,
embedded, it goes without saying, in a particular history.
Religion is historical; spirituality, transhistorical; it occurs
everywhere, in every historical situation, shaped and given
religious word-forms by that historical situation. Religion is
the historical systematization of spirituality. It is the way
people in different contexts frame their life-experience spir-
itually. The spirit, however, which is spirituality's object,
pertains to our relation to nature. It takes place because we
are natural beings, whether we concentrate spirit mystically,
or elaborate it religiously, and however we name it. This
doesn't make the spirit somehow 'greater' than religion, or
even prior to religion. It simply establishes us as creatures
fated to define ourselves historically, forever groping
towards our nature. And it gives a basis to criticize religion,
or any other historical process, according to its realization
of spirit. The modern era has witnessed a breakup of stable
religious configurations and the emergence of other modes
of spiritual realization, including, most important, revolution itself. And it includes, necessarily, the encounter
between religion and revolution as the prelude to an as yet
unrealizable degree of spiritual attainment.

As a relation to nature, the spirit becomes a member of
the class of transhistorical existents, among which may
be included sexuality, dependency, language, selfhood,

consciousness and desire. The transhistorical is a way of taking a materialist attitude towards 'human nature' without relapsing into reactionary biologisms such as socio-biology, or Freud's theory of instinctual aggression. Biologism is a variant of the orthodox materialism that has dogged Western science. *Only* matter exists. Mind, spirit, desire, consciousness – these are at best epiphenomena, shadows on the wall of the cave.

Marx overthrew this – whatever Marxists may have done to the contrary. Marx insisted that we are real, material, naturally conditioned beings, who also have consciousness as an essential element of our nature. Consciousness is expressed through labour, which transforms nature to create history. Hence, *historical* materialism. Whatever Marxism has subsequently done with this idea, the radical position it affords consciousness prevents a foreclosure of spirituality within the terms of historical materialism. For if consciousness is no epiphenomenon, as classical materialism had held, but a real part of the transformation of the world, then its limits cannot be drawn in advance. Because historical materialism does not reduce spirit to matter it leaves open the possibility for spiritual transformation through revolution. Hence its truly radical quality.

This is not to deny a profound tension between spirituality and historical materialism. For spirituality the search had to be distinguished from the spirit – the object of that search. Both are transhistorical, and like other transhistorical things, are natural to us: rooted in our relation to the physical universe, as this universe presents itself in our body and brain; present in our innate sociability, that is, the natural need to live collectively; and subject, as history is entered, to various degrees of repression and distortion. In all these ways the spirit behaves like a proper kind of transhistorical entity. But there is a reason why spirituality as well as spirit must be invoked, one crucial aspect in which the spirit is totally unlike everything else transhistorical – indeed, it is defined by this distinction.

The spirit is transhistorical and also metahistorical. It not only appears across all historical situations: it is essentially beyond history. Spirituality, which never leaves the historical bounds of the self (even the most ardent mystic must eat, and speak in language to do so), reaches from the self towards the spirit, yet never completely attains it. History is the domain of language and the Word. Nothing

– whether imaginary or objectively real – enters the historical until it can be said, and later written (by the emperor's scribe). All dimensions of the transhistorical, including spirituality, can be attached to words, and described in language – whence they become shaped in one way or another according to prevailing social relations. This is true for the most primordial and imaginary state of the psyche. We have consciousness *of* something that can be named; desire *for* some object (the breast, the phallus); *this kind* of sexual identity . . . Each signification by language brings the transhistorical into history. It makes the imaginary into something around which collective life is organized. Our labour (and language is a form of labour) creates an object distinct from, set against all other objects: I am (or want) this and not that. Labour differentiates the world, and the self is built out of this. The self, then, is the integral of the transhistorical as it enters history through language and consciousness. It is Marx's ensemble of social relations – an internal representation of the class and gender system, history writ subjectively. Historical consciousness is *self*-consciousness, formed out of reflection on the historical self.

The transhistorical is the raw material of history, but the spirit is outside of history. Being named, it is lost. The Tao that can be spoken is not the Tao. The deity eludes all significations. The spirit is the registration on the self of the self's primary, original relation to the universe, and spirituality is the transhistorical wish to restore that relationship and name the spirit. No doubt this is related to the apprehension of death. Yet spirit and spirituality are not explained away by this fact. We cannot face non-existence because we are made of word-consciousness, the consciousness of history. The spirit remains outside this, not self-consciousness but consciousness beyond self, beyond the word. We fear the non-existence of the historical self and the union with nature. Fear of death is fear of the spirit; the one is not to be reduced to the other.

Because the spirit is located beyond history, beyond the state, beyond patriarchy and the capitalist relations of production, it is the source of all that is irreducibly critical of the existing order. The *Tao te ching*, as John Clark (1983; see also Needham, 1956) has recently pointed out is perhaps the most advanced and systematic critique of domination ever written. It is the first, and greatest, of anarchist classics. The spirit is the ontological basis of all 'higher law'. It cannot be subsumed into any existing system of domination, whether by ruler over ruled, capitalist over worker, male over female, white over black. It will have nothing of domination. Thus domination is to be overcome by a spiritual transcendence, a leap outside history.

HOW DOES SPIRIT ENTER INTO HISTORY?

The spirit is transhistorical because people at all times and places, in whatever culture and class, have moved towards its realization and attainment. But if it is beyond history, and naming, how does it enter history? Not by direct mystical apprehension, which is for the few and requires worldly withdrawal. The mystic and seer concentrate spirit; they do not, however, determine its deployment. Spirituality reaches towards spirit. Is the process only a one-way street? Does not spirit reach towards the historical self?

Spirit is absolute; it can never be attained by a relative being. In Zen one has not even to hold on to the ideal of enlightenment; to think that one has attained emptiness is not to attain emptiness. Similarly, the more advanced notions of God stress the quality of unattainability: even as God dwells within, He (or better, It) is experienced only by a complete emptying of the self, an utter surrender of all possessions, including that of cognition. Spirit is only known by the traces made in consciousness by the transhistorical motion known as spirituality. But spirituality must use what is there in the historically determined self as the means to achieve its impression upon consciousness.

The notion of spirituality is the emptying and dissolution of the self, which, as it empties and dissolves, spills forth desire. Desire is the instrument through which spirit makes itself known in history. Perhaps it would be better to say that, in these moments when we cannot express our spirituality directly, we choose desire, which of all the transhistorical existents follows the track of the spirit most closely. Desire shares with the spirit an antipathy for discursive language and historically installed distinctions. And desire is on close terms with nature, which it knows through sensuality. The five senses are the chief inlets of Soul in this age, wrote Blake. In recognition, religion teaches that the path to spirit traverses the humid lowlands of desire. Desires are inexhaustible, the Buddhist vows: I will put an end to them. Desire derives from infancy and is of the infantile body, which is the family, and through it, history, transcribed on to flesh. Desire is for the breast of the mother and the phallus of the father, mediated sensuously on the body. Through desire, domination as well as emancipation is reproduced in the nascent self according to the deployment of love and hate. Dissolved in the flux of desire, capacities for good and evil mingle in the psyche. Connectedness may become selfish possession or living solidarity: the positing of the self may become freedom or the destruction of the other. Desire, configured at the boundary between history and nature, presents itself as a multivalent field of impulsion, to be employed in historical action. What role then is given to the spirit? Only this: that desire, because it reaches into nature, reaches also for spirit, and by being up against nature, may be touched by it. The moment of spiritual contact is therefore that in which desire, and through it, history can be transformed. The peculiar relation between desire and spirit is such that desire is the necessary conduit for spirit, yet one which must be transcended if spirit is to be realized. Nevertheless this does not abolish desire. Spiritual transcendence (which, it may be repeated, need not be confined to the domain of religion) also frees desire to take on new objects. Although it cannot dictate the precise shape of these objects, spirit allows desire to reshape history – that is, it affords the possibility for a revolutionary deployment of desire. In any case, without spiritual transformation, desire remains trapped in archaic patterns; with it, new possibilities unfold. But whether these possibilities lead to emancipation is given neither in the spirit, which remains beyond human grasp, nor in desire, which can be linked to submission to a Khomeini or Hitler, as well as to sacrifice and dedication for the goal of emancipation.

The spirit provides the opening, the necessary condition; and for this, the spiritual revival is a great blessing to the world. But the actual prospect for emancipation depends on the synthesis forged between spirit, desire and a critical rationality that can grasp the objective moment.

PRACTICAL CONSEQUENCES OR
WHAT IS TO BE DONE?

Spiritualized desire = soul force, and soul force when it intersects with objective possibilities is the animator of history. Among the objective possibilities: the subjective state of a people, or class, as it has been objectively determined. It is for conscious revolutionaries to appreciate emancipatory possibilities and make them happen, through alliances with the progressive Church or indigenous cultural movements . . . wherever soul force is immanent.

Such alliances must be organic rather than tactical. A tactical alliance is one in which the parties pool forces but remain essentially unchanged throughout and part ways once the goal is achieved. An organic alliance implies mutual transformation. The Church must be revolutionized and the revolution spiritualized. Transformation does not imply loss of identity, or dissolution of differences. Because spirit and matter – at least in this fallen age – remain distinct, because spirit cannot be spoken in the words of history while the revolution must achieve real power, an essential distinction remains between spiritual and worldly praxis. But every religion has been stained and clotted by historical domination even as it has borne the spirit. Every Church has sooner or later become an instrument of the ruling class, from whose bondage it must be perpetually liberated. To the extent that a given Church is integrated into the ruling class, or incorporates domination in whatever form, it becomes unable to realize a spiritual attitude. State religion contradicts itself. For spirit inheres in the dissolution of self and the recognition of unity with all beings. So long as the partiality of one part of humanity over another is maintained, that realization, the pre-condition for spiritual development, cannot be met. Sentient beings are numberless. The Buddhist prayer also proclaims: I vow to save them. And until I save them, I cannot save myself. This condition may have been obscured in ages when a settled feudalism provided some basis, however illusory, for a notion of universal inter-connectedness. In the modern world, irreversibly stamped with the breakup of empire and the revolutionizing of all social relations, it can no longer be sustained. Hence religion either revolutionizes itself or it becomes irrelevant, or regresses into theocracy, Fascism and the pack of ridiculous guru-doms that litter the Western world. Only a realized self can be let go into a full spiritual development. Practically speaking, this means a self that has accepted the necessity of radical social transformation. In fact this is what has underlain the emergence of the theology of liberation, which is the struggle for justice within the terms of religion. Hence the encounter with Marxism. Without an internal spiritual transformation the course of revolution is equally disastrous. To deny the possibilities for spiritual develop-

ment is to deny the possibilities for self-development, or
individuation. Denial does not extinguish spirituality; rather
it forces it into a backward path, where it becomes attached
to regressive positions of desire; on to the Führer, the
Maximum Leader, or the Party as deity, infallible, mystically
above society, the unmoved mover. The failure of revolution
has been to oscillate between a spiritless social democracy
(itself a seedbed of Fascism and jingoism) or a false spiritual
totalization of the revolutionary state apparatus, at times
with pseudo-spiritual overtones, as in Nazism. One of the
remarkable – albeit fragile – features of the Nicaraguan
revolution to date has been its conscious effort to reach
towards such a spiritual transformation as would forestall
totalization. Thus 'hard-liner' Tomás Borge called, towards
the time of the Sandinista triumph, for incorporation of
liberation theology into the Revolution, precisely to
humanize the latter and prevent the customary spectacle of
retribution (Randall, 1983).

Revolution is the desire for transcendence as manifested
in history. An age of endless revolution, now thrown back,
now pressing forward, is also the age of a potential spiritual
transformation of humanity. The very absurdity of such a
proposition, as observed within the field of view provided
by late capitalism, forces us towards radical faith. I believe,
because it is absurd. Such a faith can only be realized if
capitalism, late or otherwise, is overthrown. If, when, or as
this happens, will be the occasion to reach beyond the self
and towards the realm of the spirit. Marx's notice that the
revolution would remove the very need for religion is
revealed as one of his gravest misconceptions. Where else
is the soul force which gains revolutionary triumph to go?
The revolution will signal the beginning not only of true
human history, but of true spirituality as well.

Adorno, Theodor W. (1967) 'Sociology and psychology', *New Left Review* 46: 67–97.

—— (1974) *Minima Moralia*. London: New Left Books.

Ariès, Philippe (1962) *Centuries of Childhood*. New York: Random.

Aronowitz, Stanley (n.d.) 'The end of political economy', unpublished MS.

Avineri, S. (1968) *The Social and Political Thought of Karl Marx*. Cambridge: Cambridge University Press.

Baron, Salo (1975) *Economic History of the Jews*. New York: Schocken.

Basch, M. (1976) 'Theory formation in Chapter VII: a critique', *J. Amer. Psychoanal. Assn* 24: 61–100.

Berlin, Isaiah (1953) *The Hedgehog and the Fox: An Essay on Tolstoy's View of History*. New York: Simon & Schuster.

—— (1963) *Karl Marx: His Life and Environment*. London: Oxford University Press.

Bookchin, Murray (1973) 'The myth of city planning', *Liberation* 18.

—— (1978) 'Beyond neo-Marxism', *Telos* 36: 5–29.

Bottomore, T. B., ed. and trans. (1964) *Karl Marx: Early Writings*. New York: McGraw-Hill.

Bottrall, Margaret, ed. (1970) *William Blake: Songs of Innocence and Experience, a Casebook*. Nashville: TN/London: Aurora.

Braverman, Harry (1974) *Labor and Monopoly Capital*. New York: Monthly Review.

Carlebach, Julius (1978) *Karl Marx and the Radical Critique of Judaism*. London: Routledge & Kegan Paul.

Castel, Robert, Castel, Françoise and Lovell, Anne (1982) *The Psychiatric Society*. New York: Columbia University Press.

Chasseguet-Smirgel, Janine and Grunberger, Béla (1986) *Freud or Reich? Psychoanalysis and Illusion*. London: Free Association.

Chomsky, Noam (1967) 'On the responsibility of intellectuals', *New York Review of Books* 8: 16–26.

Clark, John (1983) 'On Taoism and politics', *J. Chinese Philosophy* 10: 65–8.

Dawidowicz, Lucy (1976) *The War against the Jews 1933–45*. New York: Bantam.

De Mause, Lloyd (1974) *The History of Childhood*. New York: Harper & Row.

Deutscher, Isaac (1968) 'The non-Jewish Jew', in *The Non-Jewish Jew and Other Essays*. London: Oxford University Press, pp. 25–41.

Diamond, Stanley (1951) 'Dahomey: a proto-state in West Africa', Columbia University, Ph.D. dissertation.

—— (1974a) *In Search of the Primitive*. New Brunswick, NJ: Transaction.

—— (1974b) 'The rule of law versus the order of custom', in Diamond (1974a), pp. 255–80.

—— (1974c) 'Plato and the definition of the primitive', in Diamond (1974a), pp. 176–202.

—— (1980) 'Theory, practice, and poetry in Vico', in Stanley Diamond, ed. *Theory and Practice: Essays Presented to Gene Weltfish*. The Hague: Mouton, pp. 309–30.

Dodds, E. R. (1951) *The Greeks and the Irrational*. Berkeley, CA: University of California Press.

Donzelot, Jacques (1979) *The Policing of Families*. New York: Pantheon.

Dowie, Mark (1977) 'Pinto madness', *Mother Jones* 2: 18–32.

Draper, Hal (1977) *Karl Marx's Theory of Revolution*, vol. 1, *State and Bureaucracy*. New York: Monthly Review.

Easton, Lloyd D. and Guddat, Kurt H., eds and trans. (1967) *Writings of the Young Marx on Philosophy and Society*. Garden City, NJ: Doubleday (Anchor).

Ehrenberg, V. (1960) *The Greek State*. New York: Barnes & Noble.

Eliot, George (1860) *The Mill on the Floss*. Harmondsworth: Penguin, 1979.

Engels, Frederick (1972) *The Origin of the Family, Private Property and the State*. New York: International.

Erikson, Erik (1958) *Young Man Luther*. New York: Norton.

—— (1959) *Identity and the Life Cycle*. New York: International Universities Press (*Psychol. Issues*, Monogr. 1).

—— (1968) *Identity, Youth and Crisis*. New York: Norton.

—— (1969) *Gandhi's Truth*. New York: Norton.

Ewen, Stuart (1976) *Captains of Consciousness*. New York: McGraw-Hill.

Feher, Ferenc (1980) 'István Bibó and the Jewish question in Hungary', *New German Critique* 21: 3–47.

Fenichel, O. (1938) 'The drive to amass wealth', in *Collected Papers* (2nd ser.). New York: Norton, pp. 89–108.

—— (1967) 'Psychoanalysis as the nucleus of a future dialectical-
materialistic psychology', *Am. Imago* 24: 290–311.

Ferenczi, Sandor (1909) 'Stages in the development of the sense
of reality', in Ferenczi (1952), pp. 213–39.

—— (1952) *First Contributions to Psycho-Analysis*. London:
Hogarth.

Feyerabend, Paul (1975) *Against Method*. London: New Left Books.

Flaubert, G. (1857) *Madame Bovary*, M. Marmer, trans. New York:
New American Library (Signet), 1964.

—— (n.d.) 'The trial of *Madame Bovary*', in Flaubert (1857),
pp. 325–403.

Foucault, Michel (1965) *Madness and Civilization*. New York:
Random.

Frankel, Hermann (1978) *Early Greek Poetry and Philosophy*, Moses
Hadas and James Willis, trans. Oxford: Blackwell.

Freud, Anna (1946) *The Ego and the Mechanisms of Defense*. New
York: International Universities Press.

Freud, S. (1891) *On Aphasia*. New York: International Universities
Press, 1953.

—— (1895) 'Project for a scientific psychology', in James Strachey,
ed. *The Standard Edition of the Complete Psychological Works of
Sigmund Freud*, 24 vols. London: Hogarth, 1953–73. vol. 1,
pp. 295–397.

—— (1900) *The Interpretation of Dreams*. *S.E.* 4–5.

—— (1905) 'Fragment of an analysis of a case of hysteria', in *Three
Essays on the Theory of Sexuality*. *S.E.* 7, pp. 1–123.

—— (1913) *Totem and Taboo*. *S.E.* 13.

—— (1914) 'On narcissism'. *S.E.* 14, pp. 67–102.

—— (1915a) 'Instincts and their vicissitudes'. *S.E.* 14, pp. 117–40.

—— (1915b) 'The unconscious'. *S.E.* 14, pp. 159–216.

—— (1920) *Beyond the Pleasure Principle*. *S.E.* 18.

—— (1927) *The Future of an Illusion*. *S.E.* 21.

—— (1930) *Civilization and its Discontents*. *S.E.* 21.

Fried, Morton (1967) *The Evolution of Political Society*. New York:
Random.

Friedlander, S. (1970) 'Receptive language development in
infants', *Merrill-Palmer Quart.* 16: 7–15.

Fromm, Erich (1966) 'The application of humanist psychoanalysis
to Marx's theory', in Erich Fromm, ed. *Socialist Humanism*.
Garden City, NJ: Anchor, pp. 228–45.

Giedion, Siegfried (1962) *Space, Time and Architecture*. Cambridge,
MA: Harvard University Press.

—— (1964) *The Eternal Present*. New York: Pantheon.

—— (1971) *Architecture and the Phenomena of Transition*. Cambridge,
MA: Harvard University Press.

Gill, M. M. (1976) 'Metapsychology is not psychology', in Gill
and Holzman (1976), pp. 71–105.

Gill, M. M. and Holzman, P. S., eds (1976) *Psychology versus
Metapsychology: Psychoanalytic Essays in Memory of George S. Klein*.
New York: International Universities Press (*Psychol. Issues*,
Monogr. 36).

Glotz, Gustave (1929) *The Greek City and its Institutions*. New York:
Knopf.

Grunbaum, Adolf (1984) *The Foundations of Psychoanalysis*.
Berkeley, CA: University of California Press.

Habermas, Jürgen (1971) *Knowledge and Human Interests*. Boston,
MA: Beacon.

Hartmann, Heinz (1939) *Ego-Psychology and the Problem of
Adaptation*. New York: International Universities Press, 1958.

—— (1959) 'Psychoanalysis as a scientific theory', in Hartmann
(1964), pp. 318–49.

—— (1960) *Psychoanalysis and Moral Values*. New York:
International Universities Press.

—— (1964) *Essays on Ego Psychology*. New York: International
Universities Press.

Heilbroner, Robert (1975) 'Marxism, psychoanalysis, and the
problem of a unified theory of behavior', *Social Research* 42:
414–32.

Hesiod (1959) Richard Lattimore, trans. Ann Arbor, MI: University
of Michigan Press.

Holt, R. R. (1965) 'Ego-autonomy re-evaluated', *Int. J. Psycho-
Anal.* 46: 151–67.

—— (1976) 'Drive or wish? A reconsideration of the
psychoanalytic theory of motivation', in Gill and Holzman
(1976), pp. 158–97.

Hook, S., ed. (1959) *Psychoanalysis, Scientific Method, and
Philosophy: A Symposium*. New York: New York University
Press.

Horkheimer, Max (1974) *Eclipse of Reason*. New York: Seabury.

Jacoby, Russell (1971) 'The politics of subjectivity', *Telos* 9:
116–126.

—— (1975) *Social Amnesia: A Critique of Conformist Psychology from
Adler to Laing*. Boston, MA: Beacon.

—— (1983) *The Repression of Psychoanalysis*. New York: Basic.

Jay, Martin (1973) *The Dialectical Imagination*. Boston, MA: Little,
Brown.

Kafka, Franz (1946) *The Great Wall of China*, Willa and Edwin Muir,
trans. New York: Schocken.

Kahler, Erich (1967) *The Jews among the Nations*. New York:
Frederick Ungar.

Kernberg, Otto (1975) *Borderline Conditions and Pathological*
Narcissism. New York: Aronson.

Keynes, Geoffrey, ed. (1956) *Poetry and Prose of William Blake*.
London: Nonesuch.

Klein, G. S. (1967) 'Peremptory ideation: structure and force in
motivated ideas', in R. Holt, ed. *Motives and Thought:*
Psychoanalytic Essays in Honor of David Rapaport. New York:
International Universities Press, pp. 80–128 (*Psychol. Issues*,
Monogr. 18/19).

—— (1969) 'Freud's two theories of sexuality', in Gill and Holzman
(1976), pp. 14–70.

Kohut, Heinz (1971) *The Analysis of the Self*. New York:
International Universities Press.

Korey, William (1973) *The Soviet Cage*. New York: Viking.

Korsch, Karl (1970) *Marxism and Philosophy*, Fred Halliday, trans.
New York: Monthly Review.

Kovel, Joel (1970) *White Racism: A Psychohistory*. New York:
Pantheon.

—— (1971) 'Interpreting the literary unconscious', *Psychiat. Soc.*
Sci. Rev. 5: 20–7.

—— (1974) 'Erik Erikson's psychohistory', *Soc. Policy* 4: 60–4.

—— (1976) 'The Marxist view of man and psychoanalysis', *Social*
Research 43: 220–45.

—— (1977) *A Complete Guide to Therapy: From Psychoanalysis to*
Behavior Modification. Sussex: Harvester.

—— (1978) 'Rationalization and the family', *Telos* 37: 5–21.

—— (1980) 'The American mental health industry', in David
Ingleby, ed. *Critical Psychiatry*. New York: Pantheon,
pp. 72–101.

—— (1982) *The Age of Desire*. New York: Pantheon.

—— (1984a) *Against the State of Nuclear Terror*. Boston, MA: South
End.

—— (1984b) 'From Reich to Marcuse', in Sonya Sayres *et al.*, eds
The Sixties without Apology. Minneapolis, MN: University of
Minnesota Press, Social Text, pp. 258–61.

Krader, Lawrence (1968) *Formation of the State*. Englewood Cliffs,
NJ: Prentice-Hall.

Kuhn, T. S. (1962) *The Structure of Scientific Revolution*. Chicago:
University of Chicago Press.

Lasch, Christopher (1977) *Haven in a Heartless World: The Family*
Besieged. New York: Basic.

—— (1978) *The Culture of Narcissism*. New York: Norton.

Letelier, O. (1976) 'Economic freedom's awful toll', *The Nation* 28
August, pp. 137–42.

Levin, David Michael (1984) 'Logos and psyche: a hermeneutics of breathing', *Research in Phenomenology* 14: 121–47.

Liebman, Arthur (1979) *Jews and the Left*. New York: Wiley.

Lukács, G. (1923) *History and Class Consciousness*, Rodney Livingston, trans. Cambridge, MA: MIT Press, 1971.

Luxemburg, Rosa (1971) 'Organizational problems of Russian social democracy', in Dick Howard, ed. *Rosa Luxemburg, Selected Political Writings*. New York: Monthly Review, pp. 283–306.

McCarthy, Mary (1964) 'Foreword', in Flaubert (1857), pp. vii–xxiii.

Marcuse, Herbert (1955) *Eros and Civilization*. New York: Vintage.

—— (1964) *One-Dimensional Man*. London: Routledge, 1968.

—— (1970) 'The obsolescence of the Freudian concept of man', in *Five Lectures*. Boston, MA: Beacon.

Marx, K. (1844a) 'Economic and philosophical manuscripts', in Easton and Guddat (1967).

—— (1844b) 'The sixth thesis on Feuerbach', in Easton and Guddat (1967).

—— (1859) *Grundrisse*, Martin Nicolaus, trans. Harmondsworth: Pelican, 1973.

—— (1867) *Capital*, 3 vols. New York: International Publishers, 1967.

—— (1963) *Early Writings*. New York: McGraw-Hill.

—— (1964a) 'On the Jewish question', in Bottomore (1964), pp. 1–40.

—— (1964b) 'Contribution to the critique of Hegel's philosophy of right', in Bottomore (1964).

—— (1967) 'Theses on Feuerbach', in Easton and Guddat (1967).

—— (1968a) 'Theses on Feuerbach', in Marx and Engels (1968).

—— (1968b) 'The Eighteenth Brumaire of Louis Bonaparte', in Marx and Engels (1968).

—— (1968c) 'First thesis on Feuerbach', in Marx and Engels (1968).

Marx, Karl, and Engels, Frederick (1968) *Selected Works*. New York: International Publishers.

—— (1975) *The Holy Family*. Moscow: Progress.

Massing, Paul (1967) *Rehearsal for Destruction*. New York: Fertig.

Masson, Jeffrey (1985) *The Assault on Truth*. Harmondsworth: Penguin.

Meissner, W. W. (1976) 'New horizons in metapsychology: view and review', *J. Amer. Psychoanal. Assn* 24: 161–81.

Melville, Herman (1952) 'Bartleby', in Jay Leyda, ed. *The Portable Melville*. New York: Viking, pp. 465–511.

Merleau-Ponty, M. (1964) 'The child's relations with others', in J.

Edie, ed. *The Primacy of Perception*. Chicago: Northwestern
University Press, pp. 95–159.
Miranda, José (1974) *Marx and the Bible*, John Eagleson, trans.
Maryknoll, NY: Orbis.
Moore, Barrington, Jr (1966) *Social Origins of Dictatorship and
Democracy*. Boston, MA: Beacon.
Morgan, Lewis Henry (1877) *Ancient Society*. New York: Holt.
Mumford, Lewis (1961) *The City in History*. New York: Harcourt
Brace.
Murray, H. A. (1938) *Explorations in Personality*. New York: Oxford
University Press.
Nash, Roderick (1967) *Wilderness and the American Mind*. New
Haven, CT: Yale University Press.
Needham, Joseph (1956) *Science and Civilization in China*, vol. 2.
Cambridge: Cambridge University Press.
Nelson, Benjamin (1969) *The Idea of Usury: From Tribal Brotherhood
to Universal Otherhood*, 2nd edn. Chicago: University of Chicago
Press.
Norberg-Shulz, Christian (1971) *Existence, Space and Architecture*.
New York: Praeger.
Northrop, F. S. C. and Gross, Mason W. (1961) *Alfred North
Whitehead: An Anthology*. New York: Macmillan.
Nurmi, Martin K. (1970) 'Blake's revisions of "The Tyger"', in
Bottrall (1970), pp. 198–218.
Ollman, B. (1971) *Alienation: Marx's Conception of Man in Capitalist
Society*. Cambridge: Cambridge University Press.
Pachter, Henry (1979) 'Marx and the Jews', *Dissent* 26: 450–67.
Parinetto, Luciano (1983–4) 'The legend of Marx's atheism', *Telos*
58: 7–19.
Peterfreund, E. (1971) *Information, Systems, and Psychoanalysis*.
New York: International Universities Press (*Psychol. Issues*,
Monogr. 25/26).
Petremente, Simone (1977) *Simone Weil: A Life*, Raymond
Rosenthal, trans. New York: Pantheon.
Plato (1956) *The Republic*, Rouse, trans. New York: Mentor,
414–15E.
Poster, Mark (1978) *Critical Theory of the Family*. New York:
Seabury.
Randall, Margaret (1983) *Christians in the Nicaraguan Revolution*.
Vancouver: New Star.
Rapaport, D. (1959) *The Structure of Psychoanalytic Theory: A
Systematizing Attempt*. New York: International Universities
Press, 1960 (*Psychol. Issues*, Monogr. 6).
Rapaport, D. and Gill, M. M. (1959) 'The points of view and

assumptions of metapsychology', *Collected Papers*. New York: Basic, 1967, pp. 795–811.

—— (1967) 'The points of view and assumptions of metapsychology', in David Rapaport, ed. *Collected Papers*. New York: Basic, pp. 795–811.

Rapp, Rayna (1977) 'Gender and class: an archaeology of knowledge concerning the state', *Dialectical Anthropology* 2, 4: 309–16.

Reich, W. (1927) *The Function of the Orgasm*. London: Condor.

—— (1929) 'Dialectical materialism and psychoanalysis', in Reich (1972b), pp. 1–74.

—— (1972a) 'What is class-consciousness?', in Reich (1972b), pp. 275–359.

—— (1972b) *Sex-Pol Essays: 1929–1934*, Lee Baxandall, ed. New York: Random.

Ricoeur, P. (1970) *Freud and Philosophy: An Essay on Interpretation*, Denis Savage, trans. New Haven, CT: Yale University Press.

Rodinson, Maxime (1973) *Israel – A Colonial-Settler State?* New York: Monad.

Rokach, Livia (1980) *Israel's Sacred Terrorism*. Belmont, MA: Association of Arab-American Graduates.

Rubinstein, B. B. (1976) 'On the possibility of strictly clinical psychoanalytic theory: an essay in the philosophy of psychoanalysis', in Gill and Holzman (1976), pp. 229–64.

Sappho (1951) Mary Bernard, trans. Berkeley, CA: University of California Press.

Sartre, Jean-Paul (1948) *Anti-Semite and Jew*, George Becker, trans. New York: Schocken.

—— (1976) *Critique of Dialectical Reason*. London: New Left Books.

Schafer, R. (1973) 'The idea of resistance', *Int. J. Psycho-Anal.* 54: 259–86.

—— (1976a) *A New Language for Psychoanalysis*. New Haven, CT: Yale University Press.

—— (1976b) 'Emotion in the language of action', in Gill and Holzman (1976), pp. 106–33.

Schmidt, Alfred (1971) *The Concept of Nature in Marx*, Ben Fowkes, trans. London: New Left Books.

Service, Elman (1971) *Primitive Social Organization*. New York: Random.

Sharaf, Myron (1983) *Fury on Earth: A Biography of Wilhelm Reich*. London: Deutsch.

Shorter, Edward (1975) *The Making of the Modern Family*. New York: Basic.

Simon, Bennett (1978) *Mind and Madness in Ancient Greece*. Ithaca, NY: Cornell University Press.

Snell, Bruno (1953) *The Discovery of the Mind*. Cambridge, MA: Harvard University Press.

Speer, Albert (1970) *Inside the Third Reich*. New York: Avon.

Spitz, R. (1965) *The First Year of Life*. New York: International Universities Press.

Stewart, W. A. (1967) *Psychoanalysis: The First Ten Years, 1888–1898*. New York: Macmillan.

Stoller, R. J. (1968) *Sex and Gender*, vol. 1. New York: Science House.

—— (1976) *Sex and Gender*, vol. 2. New York: Aronson.

Summerson, John (1963) *The Classical Language of Architecture*. London: BBC.

Thass-Thienemann, Theodore (1973) *The Interpretation of Language*, vol. 2, *Understanding the Unconscious Meaning of Language*. New York: Aronson.

Thomson, G. (1965) *Studies in Ancient Greek Society*. New York: Citadel Press.

—— (1967) *Aeschylus and Athens*. New York: Haskell.

Weber, Max (1946) 'Religious rejections of the world and their directions', in Hans H. Gerth and C. Wright Mills, eds *From Max Weber*. New York: Oxford University Press.

Whitehead, A. N. (1960) *Process and Reality*. New York: Harper & Row.

Winnicott, D. W. (1953) 'Transitional objects and transitional phenomena', *Int. J. Psycho-Anal.* 34: 89–98.

Winsperar, A. (1956) *The Genesis of Plato's Thought*. New York: S. A. Russell.

Zaretsky, Eli (1973) 'Capitalism, the family and personal life', *Socialist Revolution* 22: 13–14, 15.

—— (1975) 'Male supremacy and the unconscious', *Socialist Revolution* 24: 7–57.

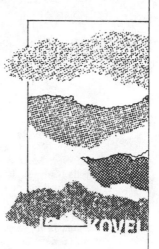

This first edition of
THE RADICAL SPIRIT
Essays on Psychoanalysis and Society
was finished in July 1988.

It was set in 10/13 pt Palatino
on a Linotron 202
and printed by a Crabtree Sovereign SP56
on 80 g/m² vol. 18 book wove.

The book was commissioned by Robert M. Young,
edited by Barry Richards,
copy-edited by Peter Phillips,
indexed by Sue Ramsey,
designed by Carlos Sapochnik,
and produced by David Williams and Selina O'Grady
for Free Association Books.